New Directions in Police Training

Edited by Peter Southgate
Home Office Research and Planning Unit

London: Her Majesty's Stationery Office

ISBN 0 11 340889 7

Contents

III   The Impact of Training

IV   Conclusions

Contributors

Ray Bull is Professor and Head of the Department of Psychology at Glasgow College of Technology. From 1973 to 1986 he was Lecturer, Senior Lecturer, then Principal Lecturer in the Department of Psychology at North East London Polytechnic. His main professional interests lie in the applications of psychological knowledge.

Anthony Butler is an Assistant Chief Constable in the Leicestershire Constabulary. At the time of writing his contribution to this book he was a Divisional Chief Superintendent in the West Midlands Police. He holds a PhD degree in Psychology and is the author of a number of publications on police management.

Raymond Cochrane is Professor and Head of the Department of Psychology at the University of Birmingham where he has been teaching and researching since 1973. He has a range of police-related research interests, including training, community relations, crime prevention and tension monitoring.

John Elliott is Professor of Education at the University of East Anglia. He is a member of the team which was commissioned by the Home Office in 1983 to carry out the Stage II Review of Police Probationer Training; this Review was published in 1987. Since the beginning of 1986 he has been leading a team from East Anglia who are assisting the Central Planning and Training Unit with the development of a new system of probationer training.

Nigel Fielding is a Lecturer in Sociology at the University of Surrey and Editor of the Howard Journal of Criminal Justice. He is currently completing a book on police training and analysing the results of a comparative study of permanent beat and relief policing.

Trevor Hall is Race Relations Consultant to the Home Office where his responsibilities include giving advice on race relations training and policy, especially for services within the Home Office sphere of responsibility such as police, prisons and probation.

Keith Harper is an Inspector in the Greater Manchester Police. A Law graduate, he has collaborated since 1984 with Stephen Stradling on research into various aspects of police training, and is currently completing research for a higher degree on police probationers and the Tutor Constable attachment.

Peter Horncastle worked with Ray Bull on studies of police training at North East London Polytechnic from 1982 to 1987 as Research Assistant then Research Fellow. His qualifications and special interests are in the field of occupational psychology, and he is now with British Telecom as a Selection Methods Adviser.

Martin Lightfoot is Director of the Centre for the Study of Community and Race Relations at Brunel University. He has taught in schools and universities, and has been a Director of Penguin Books Ltd, Managing Director of Penguin Education, Deputy Education Officer (Services) with the Inner London Education Authority, Director of the Schools Council Industry Project, and a Specialist Adviser to the House of Commons Select Committee on Education, Science and Arts.

Mary Manolias is a Principal Scientific Officer in the Home Office Scientific Research and Development Branch, where her work has involved a special interest in problems of police stress. She was responsible for co-ordinating a series of workshops for the ACPO Working Party on this subject, and is now a member of the Police Joint Working Group on Organisational Health and Welfare.

Florence Marden qualified in Psychology and Public Administration and has particular interests in the behavioural aspects of human resources in organisations. Before coming to the United Kingdom she was responsible, for a number of years, for organising experiential learning programmes at John Jay College of Criminal Justice in New York. She is currently involved in work on counselling and interpersonal skills at the Central Planning and Training Unit, Harrogate.

Paul Mathias was formerly Chief Instructor, Policing Skills Training, at the Metropolitan Police Training Centre, Hendon, and holds an MSc in Organisational Psychology. He was responsible for providing staff training, assessing Policing Skills, introducing a staff selection programme and enhancing training materials and techniques. He is currently a Superintendent with Divisional managerial responsibilities at Chingford in north east London.

Susan Phillips is a Research Fellow in the Psychology Department at the University of Birmingham. She has a special interest in applied research in training, police-community relations and civil disorder.

Michael Plumridge went to the Police Staff College at Bramshill in 1971 as the college's first specialist in Management Studies. He was Director of Carousel Courses and Adviser on Management and Organisation Development until 1988, when he moved to Roffey Park Management College as a Senior Consultant. From 1979 to 1985 he served on the Executive Committee of the Association for Management Education and Development.

Leslie Poole is the Director of the Central Planning and Training Unit at Harrogate where his responsibilities include the training of police trainers, research and planning for training and curriculum design. He holds the rank of Commander in the Metropolitan Police.

John Shaw is a Senior Lecturer at Manchester University and an Associate Fellow of the British Psychological Society, and has spent his whole career in continuing education and training. He has had a long association with the Home Office, in particular as a consultant and director of seminars in community and race relations training, and is currently involved in a programme of seminars aimed at training Race Relations teams for all penal institutions in England and Wales. He has co-edited a comparative study of organisational change programmes in equal opportunity and race relations in Britain and the United States.

Eric Shepherd is Director of the Applied Psychology Unit and Centre for Interview Research and Development at the City of London Polytechnic. His work has concentrated upon the development of interviewing skills across a wide range of contexts, including forensic, clinical, counselling and managerial. Together with Dr Angela Summerfield he designed the Metropolitan Police's Human Awareness/ Policing Skills training and trained their first generation of instructors. He has subsequently been involved in designing and developing the Merseyside Police Interview Development Unit.

Peter Southgate is a Principal Research Officer in the Home Office Research and Planning Unit. He has been responsible there for a number of studies of policing, focusing particularly upon issues of police-public relationships and training.

Stephen Stradling is a psychologist with long-standing interests in training, development and evaluation. After a number of years at the University of Salford he is now in the Department of Psychology at the University of Manchester where he maintains close links with Greater Manchester Police.

Foreword

The Rt Hon the Lord Knights CBE QPM CBIM DL
(*Chief Constable of Sheffield and Rotherham, South Yorkshire and West Midlands, 1972-1985*)

When I was asked to contribute a foreword to this book I found myself reflecting, perhaps not unnaturally, on the police training scene as it existed when I first joined the service, now almost 50 years ago. So far as recruit training was concerned it was the general (although by no means universal) practice to provide new entrants with a course of instruction of about 3 months. About 40 of the then 183 police forces maintained training schools of varying size, and the content and quality of the training given also varied widely. Most, but not all, of those forces which had no training school sent their recruits to one of the large force schools; my own training as a Lincolnshire officer, for example, was undertaken at the school maintained by the then West Riding Constabulary at Wakefield.

Almost exclusively the courses were designed to 'teach' the students rather than "train" them. We had to learn much of the law by heart and very little if any attention was paid to our ability or otherwise to communicate with and relate to the public we were to serve. In the light of the circumstances then prevailing, however, these comments should not be taken as a criticism. The police officer of those days, once he left the police station, was effectively 'lost' to his supervising officers and they to him. There were no pocket radios then of course, and except in those few towns where there was a street pillar police telephone system the obtaining of advice or assistance was generally only possible at pre-arranged 'conference points'. The officer therefore had to make most of his decisions on the spot, without recourse to advice, and a detailed knowledge of the law and his powers was necessary more perhaps than it is today if he was not to overstep his authority, a breach of which he was in those days alone accountable for. Respect for and co-operation with the police by the public was taken for granted, underpinned as it was by the social controls of those days such as respect for authority, religion and close community living. Policing was much more of a community matter than often it is today.

The provision of specialist training in such matters as crime investigation and traffic work was only just beginning, and it was regarded as being a matter to be handled generally entirely in the ordinary police schools or at the Headquarters of those comparatively few large forces where specialist work was being performed daily. Refresher training, if it was organised at all, was usually no more than a few hours a year, organised on a divisional basis for those officers who could be spared from normal duties. Home Office involvement in the whole field amounted to little more than gentle encouragement.

In the intervening years of course we have lived through a social revolution which has been accompanied by vast cultural, political, technological and economic changes. The result has been a better educated, more politically aware, more challenging, multi-racial society, with new expectations and attitudes and changed standards of morality, where respect for the police has to be earned rather than simply assumed. At the same time we have experienced increasing crime, often more violent and professional in character, involving kidnappings, bombings and shootings, flourishing fraud and a lucrative market in dangerous drugs. Inevitably these tremendous changes have markedly affected police and policing. They have become much more professional and sophisticated, with radio communications, computers, motor vehicles of all types, forensic science laboratories and the like, and in order to ensure that their forces could properly respond to all these new challenges chief constables have increased enormously the amount of training given to their officers. The chief constable of one large force, for example, listed in his annual report for 1985, in addition to formal recruit training, no less than 49 courses of various types organised in-house for his officers and 86 organised by other forces and organisations. It is estimated that this represented a total average abstraction from normal duty of 190 officers every day of the year. Much of this activity has developed quite empirically with little if any overall strategy or concerted attempts to measure its long-term effect.

The deployment of resources on a scale such as this, more particularly at a time when efficiency and effectiveness are the watchwords, justifies questions touching on such matters as what the effect has been of all this activity, whether as a consequence the police task is being discharged to greater effect and whether the service delivered by the police has improved commensurately with the effort being devoted to preparing the individual officers for their particular tasks at all levels of responsibility. The answers are not easy to come by. Critics of the police would point to the urban riots of 1981 and 1985, the ever increasing figures of recorded crime (and the decreasing percentage of detections) or the figures of complaints against police, and maintain that the level of service given was not acceptable to the community. Such measures, however, are far too general of course—what is needed is an ability to assess much more sensitively individual aspects of police activity. Questions regarding the preparation of recruits for their new duties, the central importance of relationships with the community and the management skills of senior officers formed a large part of the Scarman Report following the 1981 public order problems. Happily some of the answers in these particular areas are now becoming easier to arrive at as a result of research work undertaken in recent years by both academics and police officers, and the papers brought together in this book reflect some of this activity and the new directions already being taken in police training.

It could not have come at a better time. The recommendations of the Scarman Report already referred to led to a major review of recruit and race relations training, and pressure from the more challenging members of the now defunct metropolitan police committees largely led to the Police Training Council in 1984 setting in train an 'over-view' of the whole field of police training. The fruits of all this work are now beginning to appear in the form of new courses and if these are to be successful in producing officers properly prepared for the challenges of the ever changing society in which we find ourselves today, they need to reflect judgements made with a clear recognition of the objectives it is desired to achieve and which can be monitored and tested, rather than on simple professional intuition as was often the case in the past. Consideration needs to be given also to new methods of training such as 'distance learning' and Tutored Video Instruction, both of which have much to offer in reducing the wastage from normal police duty which traditional methods entail, and at a time when the 'corporate approach' to crime reduction is receiving so much attention more thought needs to be given to multi-discipline training.

Changing long-held attitudes and practices, however, is a very difficult and lengthy process and, in discussing some of the fundamental considerations which need to be addressed in developing police skills as opposed to simply teaching law and procedure, this book serves a most useful purpose. It is a very good introduction to a most important area of police activity and I commend it to anyone who is engaged in the training field whether as a practical trainer or as an initiator and planner.

Birmingham,
1st December 1987

Editor's note

The chapters in this book were commissioned with a number of different authors, including police officers, civil servants and academic researchers. All shared a common interest in achieving a better understanding of the training needs of the police service and, in general, were of like mind in regard to the best ways of improving training. The intention, however, was not to produce a totally consistent set of views. Training is a dynamic field, responding constantly to new needs and new ideas, and any book such as this can hope to do no more than present a snapshot of the range of current thinking and activity at a particular time. The authors have, therefore, presented what they personally see as some of the most relevant research findings and the most pressing issues. They do not necessarily represent the official view of any one body with a stake in police training. The book does not, for example, constitute a statement of Home Office policy on the subject, and police officers who have contributed to the book have done so as individuals rather than as representatives of a particular police force. To all those who have taken time to write about their research findings or training activities I am extremely grateful, and trust that the results will prove as interesting to others as they have to me.

1 Introduction

Peter Southgate

This volume is a collection of specially commissioned papers, intended to illustrate current thinking and practice in the field of police training. It provides an account of some of the wide range of work which has been done in this country in the last few years at police training establishments and by academics, consultants and researchers. Some of the papers are descriptive or historical in their approach; some discuss training philosophies and methods; most are concerned with the needs to be met by training and some address the tricky problems of evaluating the impact of training courses.

The Training Structure

Before looking at 'new developments' in training one should pause to consider the base from which such developments have grown. In doing so, however, it would be wrong to assume that there was once a fixed, monolithic training structure and that then, at some crucial turning point, change began to take place. Certainly, turning points can be identified, but training has never been wholly static and there have always been some changes taking place. What is different now is that the pace and scale of change have become much greater and, rather more significantly, the methods, content and style of training are changing. It is important to recognise that there are various levels and types of police training, each with its own problems and concerns, though, in general terms, these remarks about change do apply to virtually all areas of police training. But the training of new recruits to the police service is what tends to be most often in the spotlight. This is understandable because the numbers going through such training at one time are larger than for any other courses, because all officers go through this training, and because it is the stage at which trainees are—potentially, at least—most malleable and susceptible to ideas about how the job should be done. (In this last respect, training is one of the most standardised—and standardising—aspects of policing.) On an alternative view, though, new learning and ideas which develop in the context of training for senior officers may actually have a more significant impact upon the way policing gets done. For they may lead to changes instituted at management level which determine how grass-roots policing is conducted. It is obviously, then, important to take a comprehensive view of training.

As with other aspects of policing, training provision is made partly by the Home Office on a centralised basis and partly locally by individual forces. (In the Metropolitan Police arrangements are slightly different, with all recruit training being done 'in force'.) For some purposes there is also sharing of training resources on a regional basis. Since the end of World War II all recruits to police forces in England and Wales have attended a course known as Initial Training, provided at one of a small number (currently six) of Home Office maintained District Training Centres. This course now lasts 14 weeks, but has varied from ten to thirteen in the past. Until recently probationers returned after about 18 months' service for a further two weeks' 'Continuation Course' at the Centre, but this final course was discontinued in June 1987. The Initial Course covers a range of subjects too wide to summarise easily; the intention is to provide an introduction to all the main responsibilities and tasks of the police constable and to teach procedures, to the extent that the probationer can then begin to perform those tasks under supervision. A considerable amount of detail is included in some of the lessons and associated notes which students receive, but the coverage does not pretend to be comprehensive.

The centres are staffed by officers on secondment from various forces. Since 1969 there has been a Central Planning Unit (now Central Planning and Training Unit); this provides support services to the Centres, particularly the training of officers seconded to work as trainers in the Centres and the design of the curriculum and examinations to be used there.

New recruits are regarded as probationers for the first two years of their service and, apart from the time spent at the District Training Centre, their training is the responsibility of their force Training Department. Traditionally, the pattern has been for the Initial Course to be preceded by a week's Induction Course, and followed by a two-week Local Procedure Course, both in-force. There then follows a ten-week Tutor Constable attachment and then about a year's beat duty under normal supervision arrangements. During this time the force Training Department provides classroom instruction (for 84 periods) covering a similar range of subjects to those dealt with at the District Training Centre, though with the aim of developing more detailed knowledge and understanding.

After the probationary period constables then go through periodic 'development' training. Arrangements for this vary somewhat from force to force, but a common pattern is for such training to be given every five years, with a two-week course being the norm. There has been little standardisation of such courses and, in practice, they have been used as an opportunity to go over aspects of law and procedure which constables find especially difficult or complex, rather than to provide any broader overview of force policy or to discuss current policing problems.

Apart from such courses there are two other main types of training provided; first, that for teaching specialist skills and, second, that for managerial and supervisory officers. Specialist courses are mostly provided in-force or through co-operative arrangements whereby several forces combine resources to provide a course. Some, though, are nationally provided, such as that at the Home Office Crime Prevention Centre in Staffordshire, and the course for Community Liaison Officers in Derbyshire.

Supervisory training for sergeants and inspectors has received considerable attention recently. Over a four-year period a review was conducted jointly by the Metropolitan Police and the Central Planning and Training Unit to study the training needs of these ranks. This has resulted in the introduction of new courses which are currently being introduced.

At the higher management level, the Police Staff College at Bramshill plays the major role. It provides Junior, Intermediate and Senior 'Command' courses (and also a Command course for overseas police officers), a 'Special' course for constables and younger sergeants with clear higher management potential, and a series of short 'Carousel' courses covering aspects of management, planning and development and community relations broadly defined. (There is also an organisational development consultancy service starting to evolve out of the Carousel programme.) In addition, the College sponsors a small number of officers to pursue individual courses of study at academic institutions; individual forces also do this. Those sponsored normally study law or social sciences and conduct research on policing topics.

The development of national policy on police training is shared in a similar way to that on other policing matters, with representation from police authorities, police forces and the Home Office. A series of committees oversees the work of the Training Centres, the Central Planning and Training Unit and the common police services. The top level of representation is the Police Training Council, which advises the Home Secretary on matters related to police training. From time to time the Council sets up working groups and reviews. A major review of Probationer Training was completed in 1973, but the last few years have seen a particularly large number of reports, the most widely known being the Stage II Review of Probationer Training Commissioned at the University of East Anglia (published in 1987), following on from a Stage I Working Party review conducted after the Scarman Report. (Another Working Party of the Council had looked specifically at Community and Race Relations Training.) A Working Party on Post-Probationer Training also reported in 1987.

In its oversight and review of training arrangements, the Council takes the views of Her Majesty's Inspectorate of Constabulary. The Chief Inspector's Annual Report on the police service includes training in its remit, with particular reference to the provision of training facilities and their efficiency. Staff of the Inspectorate are in continuous touch with all training departments and establishments and play a vital role in helping to maintain standards on a continuing basis.

Recent Changes

In his 1981 report on the Brixton disorders Lord Scarman made a range of recommendations about the future of policing and of police-public relationships in particular. Some proposals on training were included, but he did not go into great detail in this area for he recognised that improvements were already in hand. He did, however, strongly endorse the need for them, both at the recruit stage and later in the police officer's career. "Above all," he said in conclusion, "the central theme in all training must be the need for the police to secure the consent and support of the public if they are successfully to perform their duties." (Scarman, 1981). This is the theme which runs throughout the chapters in this book and, indeed, throughout the developments and innovations which are described in it.

As the above reference to Lord Scarman's report makes clear, in one sense the movement in what could be called 'new directions' in police training owes its origins to concerns about difficulties between police and ethnic minorities. Inasmuch as these conflicts were exacerbated by racial intolerance or lack of understanding on the part of police officers, a clear need was for training for greater tolerance and better information about ethnic minorities. Thus the considerable efforts which went—and continue to go—into community and race relations training of various kinds. But there is some difference of opinion as to whether race and community relations training is so unique in the problems it addresses that it should be treated as a separate issue, or whether it is best seen as simply a part of more broadly conceived programmes of training in human relations or social skills. The more extreme advocates of race relations training see themselves as pursuing a crusade against white racism, and even less extreme advocates will argue a need for very directly focused consciousness raising about the subject. However effective such approaches may be with some groups, though, experience suggests that they can run into severe problems of acceptance with the police, and that they must be very carefully integrated into mainstream training programmes if they are not to be rejected as deliberately anti-police and so become counterproductive. Then there is the view that, by running courses called "race relations" or "racism awareness" that a 'labelling' process operates whereby one may help to perpetuate a problem by calling it a problem. On the other hand, if race relations training is treated as something which is, in effect, a sub-category of something broader called "human relations" then suspicions can arise that it is somehow being downgraded in importance and that the 'real' issues—of white institutional racism and so on—are being sidestepped or diluted. Obviously there is such a danger, and it is important that this does not happen.

The Book

The first section of this book contains a series of chapters which approach training with particular reference to community and race relations issues. Martin Lightfoot, Director of the Brunel University Centre for the Study of Community and Race Relations, draws upon his work there in developing courses for police officers. Early on in the Centre's existence police forces were approached to say what their current training arrangements were for community and race relations, and the chapter reports their responses. Following this it goes on to develop a typology of approaches to such training, characterising them under the headings personalised, consultative, organisational, conceptual and permeation, and looking at the likely advantages and disadvantages of each approach.

John Shaw has worked for a number of years in the Department of Extra-Mural Studies at Manchester University developing the now well-established annual programme of week-long 'Holly Royde' seminars. Through his own work, and that of others he brings to these seminars on a consultancy basis, he has encouraged hundreds of senior police officers over the years to think creatively about community relations issues and, in doing so, to look at issues not simply from a narrow law and order point of view. His chapter describes the philosophy behind the seminars and the manner in which they are conducted.

Ray Cochrane and Sue Phillips of the University of Birmingham write about the training of police Community Liaison Officers, based upon their recent studies of the role and training of these officers. Among their many observations are that 'Community Liaison' can mean many different things and that, while the officers for whom CLO training is currently designed are normally of inspector rank, community liaison work is, in reality, performed by officers in various ranks. Two important messages here, then, are that community liaison work is conducted on a broad front within the police, and that, in planning training, one should look very closely at what tasks it is necessary to train people for.

Trevor Hall, Race Relations Consultant to the Home Office, contributes a personal view of the needs of the police service for race relations training. He believes that we need more understanding of how discrimination affects police behaviour, clear objectives for police officers in working against it, an active commitment on the part of senior management and a programme of race relations training which can permeate the whole of the organisation. It is still unclear whether it is attitude change or behaviour change which should be the goal of training. What is clear, though, is the need for professional police behaviour. He outlines several past and current approaches to race relations training, and warns against expecting dramatic changes through training, for the racial problems of society cannot be laid entirely at the door of the police.

Nigel Fielding has conducted research on the formal and informal socialisation of recruits into policing. His chapter shows that police attitudes towards ethnic minorities are, in a sense, a paradigm of attitudes towards other groups perceived as minority and/or deviant. Like other writers in the book he sees a need for a more facilitative approach to training, and for greater correspondence between formal training and field experiences. Ways to achieve this may include drawing the Tutor Constable more consistently into training programmes and making more use of the probationer's own experiences during the training.

The middle chapters of the book deal with various approaches to the challenges now facing police trainers, some of them wide-ranging and some more narrowly focused. Les Poole, Director of the Home Office Central Planning and Training Unit, sets the scene with his account of the work being done at the CPTU in implementing the Police Training Council Strategy. He shows how, in doing this, the CPTU is helping to spread the acceptance of a new approach to training; one which emphasises the learning of skills, rather than the teaching of information, and a greater emphasis upon the human relations side of policing instead of simply learning about legal and technical matters.

Tony Butler (Leicestershire Constabulary) looks at training needs from the point of view of the divisional commander, taking account of the pressures under which modern policing operates and the consequent need for proper planning and management of resources. Training needs should be defined through this process of rational problem definition but, for this process to work the service needs officers who can think strategically and innovatively, who can plan and evaluate and who are skilled managers and communicators. The chapter advocates a reassessment of the divisional commander's responsibilities for training and for a partnership between trainers and operational police officers.

Paul Mathias of the Metropolitan Police gives an account of how the philosophy of training has changed at Hendon over recent years. He chronicles the movement from Social Skills through Integrated Police Studies and Human Awareness Training to Policing Skills. Essential elements of this movement were the evolution of a more open and facilitative style of training, team spirit, staff development and the use of external consultants. The contributions of key individuals who can inspire and move others at the right moment are seen to be vital to the success of such changes.

Mike Plumridge (until recently at the Police Staff College) has, over many years, been involved in the development of management skills within the police service, and his chapter draws upon data from research and working experiences among police managers. He too sees a movement towards new styles of management in response to new pressures upon and within the police service. But he is concerned that the culture and style of the police organisation can limit its ability to respond in a sufficiently innovative and flexible manner, and to take full advantage of the benefits of cross-fertilisation of ideas and experiences between policing and other occupations. Another problem with a traditionally hierarchical organisation is that the most effective learning cannot take place where the training staff are in a position of power and authority over the learners.

Mary Manolias of the Home Office Scientific Research and Development Branch has developed a particular interest in stress in policing. Her chapter draws upon data from an ACPO-sponsored study of this topic, published in 1983, and describes some of the ways in which stress can affect the police officer. Although stress is in one sense the individual officer's problem, it has potentially serious implications for police-public relationships and is, therefore, a management and a training problem. The best approach is seen as a preventive rather than a remedial one, focusing not primarily upon training for stress *per se,* but upon training which will help the officer handle the interpersonal relationships of day-to-day policing more effectively.

The final report on Police Probationer Training by the Stage II Review Team at the University of East Anglia was recently published and many readers will, by now, be familiar with its contents. John Elliott's chapter develops further some of the ideas put forward in the main report, arguing in particular for the use of case study learning. Starting from the now widespread view that social skills training has, so far, been too isolated from training in law and procedure, he suggests that the way to integrate the two sides of training is to combine them in case studies. In doing this it would be essential to draw upon real-life material, so as to overcome the problem of transfer of knowledge from the classroom to the street.

Eric Shepherd, Director of the Applied Psychology Unit at the City of London Polytechnic, has worked with police forces to develop interviewing skills training. He sees these skills as a central aspect of the policing task, which puts demands upon the officer for ability in different sorts of interview at different points in his career. He argues that 'on the job' training, the predominant medium of an officer's interpersonal skills learning, must be improved—by conscious commitment and by the use of appropriate technology and adequate resourcing—to fulfil the same professional criteria as 'formal' police training.

In my chapter with Florence Marden we explore some of the dilemmas facing police officers in regard to the management of calls involving domestic disputes and violence. The chapter is based upon data from the recent RPU study of police-public encounters, upon previous research and upon material and experience gathered in the course of Florence Marden's work in Britain and the United States on police training and counselling. It suggests that there are several ways of looking at the issues, taking account of the self-preservation of the officer, the legal and procedural issues involved, the organisational implications and police-public relationships. We note some of the recent advances made in policing domestic disputes and violence, and consider possible implications for training if real and lasting advances are to be made.

The final section of the book is rather briefer than one would like it to be, dealing as it does with attempts to measure the impact of training. Evaluation of this kind is one of the most difficult and challenging aspects of training, especially where it is essentially an applied skill which is being taught, and a skill which is not generally practised under supervision. Some earlier chapters do also make reference to evaluative work, in particular the chapter by Nigel Fielding, which charts attitude change among officers during their first two years in the police. The chapter deals in some detail with attitudes towards ethnic minorities and, for that reason, was placed elsewhere, but it does also have a bearing upon questions of training evaluation.

Stephen Stradling (University of Manchester) and Keith Harper (Greater Manchester Police) contribute a chapter based upon a study of probationers' attitudes to policing and the public. These were measured before and after their Tutor Constable attachment, providing the opportunity to see whether this appeared to make any measurable differences. Very little impact could, in fact, be discerned. Much of the discussion centres around questions of discretion in police work, and the need for greater priority to be given to teaching this, rather than the more technical skills currently identified in force objectives.

Ray Bull (Glasgow College of Technology) and Peter Horncastle (North East London Polytechnic) describe their work on evaluating the Metropolitan Police courses in Human Awareness/Policing Skills. Using a range of questionnaires, they looked at the impact of this training over the 1982–84 period, concluding that, of the three elements in the training, the most successful was interpersonal skills, followed by self-awareness, with community relations a poor third. The important question, though, was whether this training had any long-term impact; were the skills taught being put into practice? The chapter concludes by outlining further work now in hand to look at this question through observational research.

In the final chapter I attempt to draw together the various threads of the book. This proved to be a less difficult task than might be expected, for there are some very strong and consistent messages and themes which emerge from the contributions.

Many aspects of training are not dealt with directly here, particularly those involving the more technical sides of policing. But, by implication, there are some important points to consider about those aspects. Ultimately, *every* policing activity impinges in some way upon the public as individuals or groups, so that the interaction of the human and the technical is crucial. In the study of organisations the concept of man as machine did once achieve some currency but this approach has long since been seen as totally inappropriate. Policing has always been about dealing with people, and police officers have never been seen as automatons (though some of them might disagree!). It is quite unrealistic to consider legal, technical or procedural activities without taking account of their human context and, in this sense, there is no such thing as police work which does *not* concern human relationships. The extent of this may vary, and also the extent to which it may cause problems; but one of the central strands of current approaches to training is the need to recognise such interconnections and interdependencies.

2 Community and race relations training[1]

Martin Lightfoot

The Background

Closely following Lord Scarman's report on the Brixton disorders, the Police Training Council appointed a working party to "review the community relations training given to the police", and a reference to Lord Scarman's recommendations on the subject was expressly made part of the brief. Members of the working party included representatives of police associations, local authorities, the Home Office, the Commission for Racial Equality and an academic adviser. At around the same time a further working party was appointed to review police probationer constable training, and studies were also commissioned on the handling of public order situations and supervisory and management training. The Report of the Working Party on Community and Race Relations Training was published in February 1983. It contained some 33 conclusions, ranging from recommendations on the principles to underlie future community and race relations training, through specific recommendations for individual ranks in the service, to the training of trainers and the provision of materials. A diagrammatic representation of the recommendations appears as Figure 1. Amongst the recommendations was that there should be a specialist community and race relations resource unit, "possibly at a university", to train trainers and to undertake research and development work. (This unit subsequently became the Centre for the Study of Community and Race Relations (CSCRR) at Brunel University, its remit somewhat widened in negotiations with the University.)

The recommendations were wide ranging, and the report was highly critical of the arrangements then current for community and race relations training within the service. The report concluded:

> There are a number of serious weaknesses in present 'in force' training. Not all forces give training in community and race relations and few give training to ranks above sergeant. The aims of such training as is given are generally unclear and unrelated to the practical requirements of the police service. The most serious defect in the content of present training is that it consists, for the most part, simply of information. A narrow range of methods is used and neither the training nor individual officers are assessed. Training is not organised to maximum effect. Expertise and materials available, while adequate for present training, will not be so in future (*Home Office, 1983c*).

In seeking to make constructive recommendations for future arrangements, the working party was restricted by the limited experience of community and race relations training in this country. On the one hand, it was impressed (and influenced) by developments in other public services which involved intensive

---

1 I am grateful to my colleagues at the Centre for the Study of Community and Race Relations for their contributions to the thinking behind this paper, and especially to Bill Hughes, Richard Joss and Robin Oakley, whose work is directly quoted.

A diagrammatic analysis of the Police Training Council Working Party report on *Community and Race Relations Training for the Police*, prepared by Bill Hughes, Research Fellow of Brunel University and Superintendent, Greater Manchester Police. The numbers in parentheses refer to paragraph numbers of the Police Training Council Working Party report on *Community and Race Relations Training for the Police*.

CONTENT

CRR training must be relevant to practical policing (5.4). Its fundamental aim must be to ensure that the whole range of police duties is carried out in a manner conducive to good relations with all minority groups (4.5).

Academic analysis and information of itself is not enough (4.10, 4.15).

Attitude training can only be effective if taught hand in hand with effective policing skills and vice versa (2.6, 3.6, 3.7, 4.8).	Sensitivity to and knowledge of local conditions are essential (3.5).

Police officers should be given an appreciation of their service role as well as their law enforcement role (3.3).

CONTEXT

CRR training should permeate police training generally and not just be taught in isolation (4.5, 4.19).

All officers up to C/Supt. should receive CRR training regularly (4.14, 5.3).

CRR training should relate to the rank and experience of officers concerned (5.7).	CRR training should be developmental (4.20, 5.11, 5.12, 5.13).

The general principle should be that the needs of officers for training should determine the time made available and not an arbitrary time allocated (2.4).

CREDIBILITY

CRR training should have clear and realistic aims (4.8, 5.2).

Police officers who undertake CRR training should be carefully selected and have professional credibility (5.6).

There should be a substantial involvement from lay speakers who have themselves received training (4.16, 4.17, 5.6, 8.1).

Training methods should be varied and carefully chosen (4.15, 5.5, 8.2), and good quality training aids should be used (4.18, 8.8, 8.9).

There should be lay involvement in the design at courses including advisers from minority ethnic groups (5.6, 8.2).

Officers' assessments should include CRR considerations (4.11, 5.10).

All CRR training should be monitored and assessed (5.8).

sensitisation to issues surrounding (what is commonly called) 'racism' (and also, occasionally, 'sexism'). On the other, it was aware of the distinctive nature of the police service, and cautious about the potential resistance which such techniques might encounter among experienced police officers. Faced with this uncertainty, the working party recommended that further pilot work should be undertaken with 'racism awareness training' and turned instead to the only major example it could discover of 'equal opportunities' training to be undertaken within a disciplined service environment. The Equal Opportunities Management Institute (EOMI) at Patrick Air Force Base in Florida, which is responsible for the training of all equal opportunity trainers throughout the US armed services (including the Coastguard service, but not the police), was extremely influential in guiding the working party's thinking. In some cases, including the necessary length of a course for training trainers, the working party tended to follow EOMI practice in the absence of any experience closer to home (Peppard, 1980, 1983).

The report did not feel it necessary to consider in detail what it was, in precise terms, it meant by 'community and race relations', though it was aware that the tendency to conflate 'community and race relations' with 'race relations' was one to which police officers and the general public alike were prone. This was perhaps especially so since the origins of the working party were so closely associated with the events of 1981 in the inner cities. In practice the working party seems to have adopted a flexible approach. It was aware, on the one hand, that among minority communities themselves there was an insistence that the 'racial' dimension was both potent and urgent. On the other it was aware that many police officers, especially in rural forces, would disclaim the problem as being irrelevant. It therefore quoted and stressed Lord Scarman to the effect that the issue which the service needed to address was race relations in the wider context of police-community relations. In doing so it could scarcely avoid the perception that there were individual qualities—of attitudes, of personal and interactional skills, of human awareness—that were germane to such a context, but which could not be addressed by 'community and race relations' as such. Stressing 'race' too strongly would have diminished the report's credibility with many in the police service; stressing 'community relations' too strongly would have appeared to evade the very issues which they were primarily commissioned to consider, and might anyway have ended up sounding too like 'public relations'; stressing individual qualities and skills too strongly would have risked allowing trainers to sidestep the wider social issues which were seen as a major part of the problem. The report is not strong on the kind of synthesis, or path through the problems, which might be necessary, though it was conscious enough of the difficulties to recommend the commissioning of more research on police-public encounters (Southgate, 1986). This suggests that the working party was alert to the possibility that the most influential factor in police-public relations may be the product of the sum of a host of interactions, many of them very minor in character (Jones and Levi, 1983).

The purpose of this chapter is to review the current state of police community and race relations training in relation to the PTC report and to examine some of the issues as they currently affect the system. In doing so, it will be necessary to refer periodically to the experience of the Brunel Centre, though it is not the intention to consider the operation of the Centre in anything more than an oblique way.

Police Community and Race Relations Training in Practice

In a postal survey undertaken in May 1985, the Brunel Centre surveyed all new initiatives undertaken by forces in England and Wales. (The Brunel Centre itself ran its first course for police officers in November of 1984, so would not be likely to have had more than a sensitising influence on forces by May 1985.) The aim of the exercise was not so much to gain an accurate and comprehensive view of developments, but to highlight certain kinds of development which might merit further examination and evaluation. Nevertheless, and in spite of the inherent limitations of exercises of this kind, the survey did give a general picture of the state of community and race relations training some two years after the Police Training Council Working Party report.

Thirty-six forces responded, and three further forces which did not initially respond did so when they were sent a draft of the report. Forces were prompted to provide details of developments under eight headings, which ranged from multi-agency initiatives, through use of lay contributors to assessment and training materials. For purposes of analysis the replies are grouped under three headings: training methods, the use of lay contributors, and multi-agency training.

Training Methods. Few forces laid claim to any interesting developments in this area, though this may owe something to the nature of the question put. Some initiatives already known to the Centre, such as the Met's use of a language laboratory, were not mentioned. The dominant impression given by forces was that teaching in this area was dominated by didactic, information-based presentations, including the use of 'panels' of lay contributors. However, there was evidence in some forces that innovative use was being made of case studies and small group work. Significantly, most of the forces' responses related to probationer training; almost no reference was made to management or specialist training. The most frequently mentioned exercise was *Lifestyles*, the teaching packs developed by Dr Ken Thomas at Nottingham University. With this and similar material, several forces were working with small group discussion and/or project work to assess the problems encountered by minority ethnic groups.

The most interesting material under this heading, however, came from forces using role play and role reversal. Such techniques included probationers playing the different parties to common disputes, and police officers taking on the roles of professionals in other agencies, such as social services and probation officer, though some forces regarded the reluctance of students to participate and the time-consuming nature of the preparation as militating against the continued use of such techniques. Several forces, too, reported difficulties in running interactive, student-centred exercises given the lack of suitably trained instructors.

Several forces reported use made of computer-aided learning, though this appeared to be confined to command band public order training. However, some forces had been concerned to develop self-paced remedial and revision packages, and the West Midlands Police were experimenting with structured videos of difficult situations which could be used for students to discuss appropriate responses, in the company of representatives from other agencies.

Use of Lay Contributors. Some forces, concerned about the lack of realism in practicals, had sought to involve lay contributors, including in one case the use of black drama students, and in another the use of clerical civilian staff in the training school. Considerable variations were found in the use of lay consultants to advise, formally or informally, on training offerings. One force had appointed a full-time lay advisor, while others relied more on informal contacts and relationships. No consistent pattern could be discerned, and much appeared to depend upon the initiatives—and, no doubt, negotiating skill—of individual trainers. Forces clearly fought shy of close, formal involvement, and a lay involvement on the kind of strong model advocated by the Police Training Council Working Party was not discernible anywhere.

Multi-Agency Approaches. A number of interesting initiatives were reported in the area of multi-agency approaches. The Met were experimenting with a 'pairing' system, where officers were joined with a probation officer to prepare a joint profile of a particular geographical area, while Lincolnshire were engaged on a multi-agency joint study of a large housing estate. Other joint courses for police officers and other agency staff were reported in Devon and Cornwall, Bedfordshire, Greater Manchester, Cleveland, West Yorkshire, Kent, Nottinghamshire, Derbyshire and Leicestershire.

Community attachments appeared to be of three general kinds: short visits, one-way placements of longer duration (two days to several weeks), and full reciprocal exchange schemes. The first of these was the most common; almost all forces have an arrangement whereby probationers spend various amounts of time in contact with different agencies, community groups, churches and temples, youth clubs, and so forth. More ambitiously, some forces, such as Sussex for example, devoted two days on a newly appointed sergeants course to work with other agencies, an arrangement which they reported as being of value in breaking down barriers, appreciating the constraints that others work under and countering stereotypes.

More extended placements were rare, and there appeared to be a tendency for these to be used for officers specialising in community liaison and affairs, or alternatively for cadet officers. In one or two cases a reverse scheme was reported, where trainee social workers or trainees from other agencies spend a period with the police. The most ambitious schemes involved reciprocal placements, though these were often, once again, limited to specialist officers. In one example, that of Norfolk:

'For the past three years, exchange schemes, placements and attachments have been operating between police, probation, social services and educational welfare. There are approximately forty such exchanges taking place each year and, in duration, range from between three to seven days. Despite initial reservations on both sides, this programme has proved immensely valuable and the demand for places is high.'

Developments in Police Community and Race Relations Training

It is clear from the CSCRR survey that significant change had taken place within the service in quite a short space of time. However, the changes introduced were fragmentary in character, with a tendency to be short-lived as experienced trainers moved on to other police duties, and, in both range and depth, forces' offerings in community and race relations training fell far short of the PTC recommendations, though significant progress had been made in the most centralised parts of the system, such as that for probationers and within management development taking place at the Police Staff College at Bramshill.

The gap between the aspirations of the working party and practical action was, however, still extremely large. A major part of the reasons for this is inherent within the structure of the system itself. Some of the features of the system—such as the practice of moving trainers into other parts of the system after a spell of two or three years in training, the low status of training and the lack of a career structure within it, and the reluctance to give credence to lay trainers—are longstanding features, the subject of continuous debate within the service, on which little consensus has been achieved. On the other hand, the police training system is a highly centralised one—though admittedly some parts are more so than others—a feature which of itself creates difficulties in pursuing constructive development.

The features of highly centralised and decentralised educational systems, and some of their consequences, are understood in general terms, though their local application may need some adaptation to the particular circumstances of the police service (see, for example, Schon, 1972; House, 1974; Kogan, 1978; Archer, 1984). In centralised systems, much of the energy of the system is devoted to maintaining central control, and to tending and extending the mechanisms by which that control can be maintained. This tendency, moreover, survives political change, since it is the controlling possibilities of the political system itself that is in question, and which it is in all interests to maintain. On the other hand, in decentralised systems, such as the school system in England and Wales, the activity of the central body is designed to minimise the damage which might be done by innovations which disrupt or undermine central policy. In decentralised systems, therefore, local initiatives and central control are in a state of tension. But initiatives are constantly being generated within centralised systems as well, so that in centralised systems there is a periodic necessity for the central authorities to initiate a controlled programme of change. This requires considerable political and institutional energy; it is therefore slow to implement and spasmodic. Centralised systems are characterised by a 'stop-go' approach to change.

There is a further consequence of this process. In decentralised systems, modifications are constantly taking place, and there is a tendency for decentralised systems to achieve a greater compatibility with their environment: 'since no aspect of it is ever uniform, it can only be matched by provisions which are adapted, or which can be adjusted, to local variations, special circumstances and unique configurations' (Archer, 1984, p. 189). On the other hand, the reverse effect can be observed in centralised systems, in which the discouragement of differentiation, often taking the form of discouragement of specialisation, leads to periodic waves of maladaptation to the external world. Centralised systems are constantly faced with the problem of mismatch between educational processes and the requirements of a changing environment (Jones and Joss, 1986).

(As an aside, it is perhaps worth mentioning that in structural terms, the introduction of the Brunel Centre for the Study of Community and Race Relations amounted to an attempt to mix the modes: here was an institution of a kind favoured in decentralised systems, set up on a freestanding basis within a centralised system. Distinct difficulties might be expected with such an arrangement. They include suspicions of a lack of inwardness with the problems and concerns of the service, and resentment at what is likely to be seen as a failure to appreciate the extent of the progress that has already been made. On the other hand, one might expect that it could encourage a far greater sense of innovation within what Schon (1972) has called a 'family resemblance'. It has been important, for example, within this framework to press for a greater personal commitment on the part of trainers, to resist the conventional model of 'packages' which trainers can simply implement, and encourage local development rather than impose a national one.)

Approaches to Community and Race Relations Training

Few have supposed that there may be ready solutions to the problems associated with community and race relations training. It is more common to favour particular lines of development which it is thought would ameliorate some of the shortcomings identified. Though informed observers, both within and without the service, have many points of consensus concerning the nature of the problem, the training solutions proposed are markedly dissimilar. In broad terms, the approaches can be characterised as *personalised*, *consultative*, *organisational*, *conceptual*, and *permeation*. None of these approaches is mutually exclusive in terms of the practical delivery of training programmes, and many trainers invoke a variety of methods and approaches, partly out of pragmatism and partly as a consequence of the inherent problems involved in the evaluation of any particular approach. However, in some cases, trainers have argued that, perhaps especially in the field of community and race relations training, a consistency of approach is necessary, not simply out of a desire to avoid the transmission of confusing messages, but in order to secure a coherent frame of discourse and relationship within the training environment. In the account of the main approaches proposed, therefore, the concern has been to indicate the likely advantages and disadvantages of the various approaches, and their consequent place in an overall offering, rather than to attempt to isolate preferred models.

Personalised. Personalised approaches begin from the assumption that the only secure method of achieving behaviour change lies within the individual, and involves adjustment or change to the individual perception or personality. It is argued that any other kind of modification (for example, changes in the force discipline or in management or supervisory techniques) can only ever be superficial, effective while the eye of the organisation is engaged, but fruitless in private or unsupervised situations, and, perhaps especially, subject to erosion in moments of stress. Although it is sometimes a subsidiary position of the personalised diagnosis that better methods of selection are required and that the 'screening' of individuals would reduce the necessity for remedial action, it is rare for this position to extend itself into organisational proposals. Central to the position is the proposition that in the last analysis it is the internal working of individuals which is at issue, and which must be the focus of the trainer's attentions. Ethical problems associated with such approaches are rarely considered; it is commonly taken as axiomatic that the mental configurations which the trainer seeks to induce or impose are in some sense 'correct' (Bruner, 1979). ('Racism awareness' is the phrase commonly used, though it is possible to regard the 'personalised' approach as wider than this phrase might imply, loosely as it is often used. For the classic statement on 'racism awareness', see Katz, 1978.)

In its strong versions, the personalised model is aligned with socio-historical perspectives. Racism is a *white* problem, the product of a colonial history, perhaps exacerbated by capitalist systems. Proponents of this position do not see the violent oppression of black people by white people as confined to slavery; nor do they believe that slavery in its strict sense is a matter of past history. There are other, more subtle forms of 'slavery', continuously employed by white people in an attempt to exert and maintain supremacy in all forms of economic and cultural life. Hence, even liberal interventions, in, for example, the school system, aimed at introducing and legitimising black culture, can be regarded as more subtle expressions of the universal determination of white people to dominate black. More recently, even 'racism awareness' itself has been the subject of radical critique (Sivanandan, 1985; LSPU, 1987). Sometimes this is on the grounds that such effort diverts activity from the solidarity of the working class, which is where the real struggle is held to belong. Sometimes it is on the grounds that this *too* can be seen as a further liberal tactic, the more insidious because in appearing to humble themselves before the experience of black people, white people are in fact exorcising a guilt which enables them the more effectively to exert control. On this radical view, 'racism awareness' can be seen as black people inadvertently helping to develop the power and subtlety of the means by which white people exploit them. Hence, in place of impervious, unthinking oppressors, black people now have subtle and thoughtful oppressors. In such radical extensions of the position, attention may be diverted away from the personalised approach, arguing that it is ineffectual and probably counter-productive, and towards strong positive action in terms of greater justice and economic equality.

Many have believed that it is possible to counter what is here called the strong version of the personalised approach by mounting arguments against the various components. For example, it is possible to believe that the position can be countered by insisting that 'colonialism'—the complete dominance of one ethnic group by another on the other's traditional territory—is not the product of (what is sometimes called) the 'colonial period', and that it can be discerned in all periods of historical record, and that moreover there is no evidence that colonialists, or slavers, have always been white. Nor, it might be argued, is the nature of imperialist domination made significantly different, more insidious or even evil, by its association with modern economic organisation. It is possible, too, to question the degree of exploitation, perhaps by pointing to economically successful minority ethnic groups, and the comparative success of similar ethnic groups in different, but still predominantly white, environments. It is also tempting to counter that sympathetic whites should not be manoeuvred into a 'no win' situation, in which positive moves to appreciate the black point of view, and an explicit acknowledgement that attitudes and structures may indeed militate against black interests, can be regarded as themseves further evidence of a white dominance.

All such counters are possible, and almost all the ingredients of this strong version of the personalised approach can be approached with rational approaches of this kind. But (as police officers and others who have tried it know) arguments of this kind are not productive. Indeed, it is probably the case that they miss the point. Whereas such discourse is often clothed in the language of rational argument, and appears amenable to evidence and analysis, the appearance is deceptive. What is being offered is not rational (or not rational in this conventional sense), but a set of emotive perceptions, none the less powerful, but bidding, not for discussion, but negotiation. Rationality, here, belongs more to an assessment of strategy than to reasoned exchange of views.

In its weak versions, the personalised approach adopts a less sweeping account of the white malaise. It is argued that, inherent both in individuals and in the institutions of society are deep and subtle prejudices of which, at the least as a preliminary, white people need to be aware. To this extent at least the phrase 'racism awareness' carries a precise meaning; there is no question but that the 'racism' exists; the problem is to make people aware of it. To this end trainers will seek by various means to make white people more introspective about their own feelings towards black people and more empathetic towards their situations. In terms of its educational implementation this version of the personalised approach is a mixture of the student-centred and teacher/trainer-centred. On the one hand, the trainer comes to the training event with preconceived notions about the inside of the student's head, and moreover some of the most private and personal parts of the head; on the other, the assumption is made that all students have the potential within themselves to recognise and combat prejudicial feelings and behaviour, and that the most the trainer can do is to assist in this process. The dilemma for the trainer is to give encouragement to the student's self-motivation without diminishing the edge and urgency which the confident assumption of prejudice gives to the training event.

The dilemma is illustrated most effectively in the weakest of the personalised approaches, in which the trainer merely seeks to 'explore' feelings about race in a way which does not pre-judge the attitudes of the students. In such contexts it is difficult for the trainer to avoid eliciting representations of (what the student believes to be) the 'correct' version of the attitudes concerned. There is room, it is true, for a degree of parrying and negotiation with the student on what the 'correct' might consist of, but the student knows the situation too well to allow him or herself to stray too far out of the 'frame' which he or she believes is expected. A helpful hypothesis might be that this is a major source of the sense among students that they have "had community and race relations training up to here" or that they "know all about community and race relations". It is sometimes instructive to interpret such messages not in a literal sense, but as an expression of irritation at having to rehearse the skill of conforming to expectations when, in the student's mind, it has already been demonstrated that it is possessed.

The Working Party of the Police Training Council considered that 'racism awareness' merited further exploration and recommended that a pilot study of its effectiveness in relation to the police service should be undertaken. The study, small scale but closely focused, was undertaken by Peter Southgate of the Home Office Research and Planning Unit and published by the Home Office as *Racism Awareness Training for the Police* in 1984. It is worth pausing briefly on this study, since it has been widely, and mistakenly, interpreted as having disposed of the issue so far as the police service is concerned, and also because it underlines the nature of some of the difficulties which the personalised approach involves.

Four such courses were mounted, using external trainers. Southgate himself was only allowed to observe two of them. In an earlier study concerned with probationer training, Southgate (1982) had noted that community and race relations training concentrated very largely on factual information about minority ethnic groups, and to a lesser extent on attitudes, although difficulty was experienced in persuading police officers that relationships with minority ethnic groups might need a different set of attitudes on the part of the police than relationships with the white population. Moreover, the report levelled criticism at the lack of time for community and race relations training, so that 'many issues of fact remain untouched, and attitude is stressed rather than explored' (p.24). Given that this, or something very like it, was the experience of police officers so far as community and race relations training was concerned, it was scarcely surprising that the expectation of the police officers involved in the pilot study was that this was the kind of thing that they were to expect. Beyond this quite basic misapprehension, there was confusion (and some apprehension) over why officers had been selected for the course, and there was the added problem that the course was entirely devoted to race and race relations, lacking the opportunity to relate such work to policing issues of a more general character. Finally, the evaluation was only able to assess the immediate impact of the training: no follow-up of the effect some time after was undertaken.

Hence, not only were these pilot courses of a kind unfamiliar to police officers, they were mounted in a context, and in a way, which was artificial by police training standards. Nevertheless, Southgate did manage to produce some pertinent conclusions. His overall conclusions are that racism awareness could have its place in police training, but only where it was thoroughly integrated into more general, more policing-specific aspects of training, where the objectives of both the teacher and the learner were clear from the start, and where some prior preparation had taken place, with the trainer knowing more about the background and training history of the participants.

The conclusions are careful and seem unexceptional. Michael Banton in reviewing Southgate's racism awareness study in *Police Magazine*, seemed anxious to relate 'racism awareness' to a larger political agenda of which it is held to form a part:

'. . . the current idea of racism is part of a political package. If it is to be used in police training there must be sufficient time in the programme for all the components of it to be properly considered.'

He concludes:

'The PTC should be prepared to support a greater variety of experimental schemes and be ready to back the winners. None are likely to succeed unless they respect the boundary between a person's private opinions and that person's competence on the job. It sounds as if Racism Awareness Training cannot do that.' (Banton, 1984.)

Banton has been quoted to demonstrate the kinds of misgivings which personalised approaches can arouse, even in such a distinguished and experienced commentator. It is evident, surely, that if potent political ideas are present, and that this necessitates the allocating of additional time for the processing of such ideas, this can only be in the interests of substituting an alternative political framework. Nor would Southgate himself, judging from his report, disagree that the boundary between private opinions and competence on the job is an important one, and deserving respect. The premise of personalised approaches, however, is that there is a relationship between these two, and that—at least in some contexts—this relationship may be critical for policing behaviour and performance. Southgate's report leaves both this and the training implication open, but it remains on the agenda.

Consultative. The Working Party of the Police Training Council recommended that, not only should representatives of minority ethnic groups be involved in the delivery of police training, but that they should also be consulted and involved in the formative and design processes of police training. From the text of the report the precise grounds for this recommendation are not clear. The implication seems to be that, since trainer collaborators from minority ethnic groups are likely to be essential to the success and credibility of police community and race relations training, then it would be as well to seek their collaboration in the design process as well as in the role of occasional contributors. Indeed (or so the reasoning seems to go) their contributions are likely to be more effective, and their commitment more substantial, if they felt that they were *collaborating* with police trainers, rather than merely *contributing* to police training. One of the specific tasks allotted to the new university-based Centre in the report was the 'training' of such contributors, actual or potential.

There may be a sub-text here, though, if so, it is implicit rather than explicit. A strand of curriculum development thinking over the past twenty years within the mainstream educational system has been interested in the relationship between the curriculum and the educational organisation's relations with the outside world. Such external organisations might include pressure groups, to be sure, but also client groups of various kinds (educational institutions being commonly characterised by the absence of any single, clearly defined client group).

Sustained attempts to look at the possibility of using such theories to change (for example) the way schools taught about industry by introducing employers and trade unions into curriculum planning processes were undertaken (Jamieson and Lightfoot, 1982). This was in the hope that the quality of relationships would lead curriculum change, rather than the other way round. Of course, training within an instrumental employment culture (such as a police training school) would be a rather different proposition: most professions rely mainly on outside, independent institutions to train their staff. But the benefits of the close collaboration of minority ethnic representatives might have a more profound effect on the police training operation than simply the creation of a more satisfactory 'expert' input into police community and race relations training.

Whatever the truth of this speculation, it is clear that the improved *permeability* of police training to outside influence is a different and potentially separate solution (or part of one). It impacts on the *ethos* of training, and includes the possibility that the enhancement of relationships between police trainers and outside contributors will enlarge the potential scope of the influence of such outside contributors, beyond the narrow 'panel' session or 'lecture' format which has traditionally been favoured.

Difficulties which have arisen from this process are perhaps inevitable in exercises of this kind. Expectations of the degree to which external contributors can participate in the planning process may be aroused to an extent which trainers, for one reason or another, may not feel able to fulfil—though it has to be observed that these expectations are not, in Brunel's experience and observation, greater than those envisaged by the Police Training Council Working Party.

Organisational. It may seem inappropriate to include organisational strategies in a paper on training. Few would question that organisational adjustments have a place in the overall police strategy for community and race relations, but a recognition that training itself has a role in these organisational projects would not be a common conclusion from the simple acceptance of the general proposition. Training, however, impacts on the organisation in a variety of ways:

1. As an expressive function of the organisation it is a key place for the articulation of the normative values of the organisation, implicit or explicit.
2. Its relationship to the rest of the organisation is in a variety of ways a commentary on the climate of the organisation and an index of the degree to which the organisation is open to constructive change and development.
3. The degree of training's integration into the mainstream operational life of the police organisation may be an index, not just of the degree to which the training function is held in regard, but also of the effectiveness of the force's managerial ability to maximise its effective use of human resources.

These issues are prominent for all training functions, but perhaps especially so for community and race relations. Trainers who have attended the Brunel Curriculum Development courses have not often been in a position to influence the organisation in these global ways, and such insights as have been obtained have as often come from informal consultancy arrangements which the Brunel team have undertaken at individual forces' invitation. Comments on this aspect of community and race relations training are therefore speculative; they are worth including because they are potentially some of the most significant and effective changes within the reach of senior police managers.

At one level, the expressive function of the community and race relations training can be simply stated. The force will have—or if it does not, it certainly should have—a stated policy on community and race relations, and perhaps in addition some specific and quantifiable goals which can be transmitted by supervisors and managers to operational officers in terms which are easy to understand, and in which individual roles can be internalised. Trainers will seek to inform themselves of such policies and goals, and will seek to ensure that they are built into training programmes. Thus far the relationship between the training function and the organisation is straightforward. However, the community and race relations trainer will be often and forcefully struck by the fact that, for these policies and goals to be implemented properly within the training function, they will need to be implemented throughout the training offering, and not just within sections of it which are labelled community and race relations. Very little imagination is needed to appreciate the importance of many, perhaps most, of the messages which the force would wish to convey to its officers about community and race relations to training in drugs, CID, traffic, etc. Nor does it seem unreasonable to follow the Police Training Council Working Party in arguing that such training should extend beyond probationer training, which is too often the sole focus of curriculum development. Mechanisms for procuring consistency within a force training system on these matters do not at present exist, unless it be on a purely personal basis between one trainer and another.

Moreover, the thoughtful community and race relations trainer, or training manager, will be struck by the extent to which the messages which the training school transmits in its totality are difficult to reconcile with the kinds of messages which are likely to be embodied in community and race relations policies. Often this dichotomy is more obvious to outside observers than to police officers, though trainers of all kinds can be concerned about the degree to which certain elements of the training offering can be at odds with the deep structure of the training messages themselves.

Organisations, within the police service as well as outside it, differ considerably in the degree to which the training part of the organisation is integrated into some of the key organisational issues. Recruitment has already been mentioned as an issue which impacts on training. An organisational separation between recruitment and training functions may be dysfunctional: who shrewder, more in touch with the issues, the potential and the limitations of recruits than an experienced trainer? Similarly, in considering the issue of assessment of individual officers in training, officers at Brunel have been frequently struck by the similarity between the kinds of collaborative, interactive assessment techniques considered appropriate for the assessment of community and race relations training, and the kinds of techniques in place in most forces for staff appraisal. Training assessments could form an important contributory resource for staff appraisal, including consideration for promotion. Similarly, the appraisal process could provide important information to both trainers and managers concerning the need for training, and there seems no reason why an assessment of the officer's performance in community and race relations matters should not be specifically prompted in the appraisal routine. Certainly, appraisal is often used in this way in industry, and training recommendations frequently result from both regular (eg annual) appraisal and career development counselling.

It may also be worth considering the role of training in the mainstream work of policing. If this seems an eccentric or intrusive idea, one can only point to experience in other professional spheres and in industry which tends to underline the degree to which the interaction between training and operations is a strong mark of both adaptability and client-centredness within organisations. It ought not to be, as it is, an exceptional event for the training department to be asked its opinion concerning some organisational change. Similarly, it ought not be exceptional for training departments to make some suggesion as to organisational development.

Finally, it is in community and race relations training above all that some of the inherent contradictions of police training are most apparent. The East Anglia review team summarise the contradiction in this way:

> Any casual visitor is likely to be struck by two aspects of (District Training) Centre life. The first is the range of the curriculum, its variety of settings and components. It looks like a balanced curriculum, expressing a fairly straightforward logic of requirements. The second impression may somewhat qualify this impression in terms of a different perspective on balance. It looks like a military establishment devoted to the preparation of recruits for subordinate roles in a command structure. Not just because the students and staff, unless engaged in some of the physical activities, are all dressed in uniform and immaculately turned out. Not just because movement about the campus, even by groups evidently on their way to the swimming pool for instance, is clearly regimented. It is more a general absence of casualness, particularly notable in the interaction between ranks, which is clearly governed by rigid protocols of rank recognition. As this is not confined to the interaction between students and instructors, but applies also to at least the visible relationships between staff of different ranks, the impression is of a rather strictly hierarchical organisation in which the distribution of power is a significant and ever-present feature. The visitor, attempting to synchronise these two impressions, might wonder whether such an organisation is capable of supporting and facilitating the range of teaching and learning modes appropriate to its diverse curriculum brief. (Macdonald *et al.,* 1987)

The review team continue to observe that although the Social Skills of Policing lessons (which include most of the elements of community and race relations training within the probationer package) are likely to be less formal, they are not likely to be fundamentally different in character. Indeed, the major difference is likely to be one of a lower level of attention and concentration, even one of boredom, derived in part at least from the fact that this area of teaching is not subject to the regular testing which characterises the law teaching. The review team conclude that:

> the balance of the curriculum is heavily weighted in favour of certain forms of pedagogy consonant with the milieu of command, and that efforts to promote a mixed pedagogy to serve differentiated values and outcomes might be difficult to accommodate without some fundamental change in the Centre environment. (p. 36)

In these circumstances, where trainers do manage to promote effective learning in community and race relations, it ought to be regarded as achievement of a very high order indeed.

Conceptual. The Police Training Council Working Party was critical of the tendency for community and race relations training to consist of information about minority groups. The criticism of such approaches is not aimed at eliminating relevant information—indeed, such information is likely to be of practical use to officers, and hence valued by them. However, where it is relevant it is likely to be strictly local in character, and subject to considerable variations over time. Too strong a concentration on distinguishing features of minority groups may indeed encourage stereotyping. Moreover, it is unlikely to help very much in understanding the dynamics of communities, and will not of itself provide a conceptual framework to enable the individual officers to respond to novel situations, and to construct for themselves a method of working and a self-view which is at one and the same time true to the individual and valid within the context of the organisation (Lipsky, 1980; Argyris and Schon, 1974; Schon, 1983).

For this reason, several commentators have argued that some elements of basic social science shoud be included in police training, and should form a major part of community and race relations training. Two approaches can be distinguished. The first involves the straightforward teaching of social science (Bull and Horncastle, 1983; Das, 1987). An approach of this kind seems common in the United States, and many police trainers have become convinced of the usefulness of basic psychology in the training of police officers. Some have argued that this needs to be extended to sociology and social anthropology.

The grounds for this are various. There is of course some element in it of transmitting the findings of empirical research, on the grounds that this provides a sounder basis for decision-making than the untutored perceptions of individual officers. On the other hand, research in the social sciences (unless it be at the harder end of applied psychology) is rarely of the definitive kind that gives an unambiguous basis for action. Just as, with certain possible exceptions (Ajzen and Fishbein, 1980), research does not reveal any clear link between attitudes and behaviour, so it seems likely that the link between the possession of a theory and behaviour is a tenuous one.

The second approach stops short of social science teaching, but uses some of the techniques available within those disciplines to provide 'frameworks', in the expectation that these can be used to clarify and structure perceptions. It can be distinguished from the straightforward social science approach by its avoidance of overarching structural theories, many of which may be conflicting, and some of which may be contentious.

Outline of a teaching sequence involving a 'framework' approach. Based on developmental work by Robin Oakley at Brunel University.

Understanding Communities

1. Dimensions of Social Organisation

1.1   Structures. Eg class, race, gender. These represent the 'anatomy' of the way in which communities are organised, and how power is distributed; how people group and identify themselves in terms of likeness or common interest and of difference from others.

1.2   Cultures. The ways of life, values and ideas, and the general assumptions that groups share, which shape their behaviour and their social relations, and which they organise to promote and protect.

1.3   Biographies. The 'life paths' or (in the broadest sense) the 'careers' that particular individuals pursue during their lives as they move within or between various structures and cultures.

2. Modes of Social Relationship

2.1   Role Relations. Relating to positions in an organised group or agency (eg trade unions, police) which are task-based.

2.2   Category Relations. Relating to social stereotypes, usually about 'kinds of people' (eg in terms of class, race, culture).

2.3   Personal Relations. Relating to social groups or networks of which participants have a high degree of personal knowledge.

3. Images of Community

Inferring the 'working images' of the community implicit in the operation of professional groups, and the way in which 'problems' are defined and identified.

4. Models of Community

It is possible to draw out, with the use of appropriate exercises, three distinct 'models' of community which represent the three different ways of thinking about communities.

4.1   Model A. This represents the 'ideal' image of community, homogenous and stable, epitomised by the idea of the traditional rural village community, yet alive and well in the thinking of policy-makers and practitioners, both in their work and in their domestic lives.

4.2   Model B. The 'pathological' image of community, the negative version of Model A, in which practitioners commonly perceive the kinds of communities which they find difficult, or with which they are unfamiliar.

4.3   Model C. A more 'realistic' image of community in those areas which prove difficult or unfamiliar, in that it recognises positively the extent of heterogeniety, conflict and change that characterises modern society, and attemps to come to terms with the pluralism and the loosening and challenging of social bonds that all professionals are now obliged to confront.

In each model the key features of structures, cultures and biographies are indicated, as are the predominant modes of social relationship and—crucially for all professionals—the status of 'authority' in the eyes of the public or client group.

As an example of the possibilities inherent in this second approach, one could point to the frameworks developed by Robin Oakley at the Brunel Centre. The key concepts fall into four distinct but interrelated areas: understanding communities, understanding discrimination, understanding culture and ethnicity, and understanding racism. The sequence is important for the process, and reflects a belief that community and race relations need to be seen in a framework of other concepts which encompass the nature of communities in general, and the operation of discrimination. It is only within this extensive framework that the specific features of 'racism' can be identified and understood. A sample of a teaching sequence using this approach is shown in Figure 2. Such an outline, however, needs to be seen in the context of the exercises and teaching styles employed, without which it is merely a 'contents page' for a teaching sequence.

Permeation. The problems associated with the provision of distinct periods of time to deal, in some sense of the word, with community and race relations, combined with the relative difficulty (and possible undesirability) of testing student performance in this area of the curriculum, have contributed to a growing sense among commentators on police training that the most desirable—and possibly the most effective—method of communicating an understanding of community and race relations issues is through the permeation of the curriculum. On the face of it, the argument has considerable force: if such messages were embedded in more instrumental parts of the curriculum, and especially in high status areas, such as CID or traffic, they might be expected to have greater weight and carry more conviction.

There is by now a considerable history of attempts to work 'across the curriculum' in the mainstream educational system, but few curriculum innovations have been found to be more fraught with difficulties and fragile in the face of staff changes and other preoccupations of specialist teaching departments. Moreover, strategies aimed at changing institutions across curricular boundaries are especially vulnerable to insufficient or superficial understanding of what the problem involves (see, for example, Torbe, 1986). The difficulties are enhanced where existing arrangements for the collaboration between departments are few or non-existent. Even in schools, where the same pupils may be taught by a number of different teachers, and where there are clear educational and operational opportunities to develop themes 'across the curriculum' the mechanisms for collaborative policy-making and curriculum development do not exist as a matter of routine, and need to be created specifically for such purposes. How much more difficult, then, within force training schools, where most officers are present for specific courses, with a small number of allocated staff, and where many of the courses involve specialised technical training in which community and race relations issues may be seen as an unwelcome and irrelevant diversion.

In practice, police trainers from Brunel have found that any such strategy needs to be opportunistic in character. It may, for example, be necessary to use working parties, shared events between courses, shared outside contributors and other such devices to secure some measure of community and race relations input into more specialised courses.

Conclusion

The mediation of these various approaches is a subtle matter, and one which depends very much on local circumstances, personal, social and institutional. Assessing the relative stress which should be placed on the skills and personality of the individual trainer, on the character and history of the local community, and the kind of institutional support (or resistance) which is likely to be met is both difficult to do and difficult to evaluate accurately at a distance. However, it is already clear from work done so far that no other, more directed approach would have the same chance of success, unless it were to sacrifice that depth and inwardness of understanding without which the enterprise would not have been worth the effort.

Such an analysis, if accurate, highlights some of the more fundamental decisions which the service has to confront. If such issues are raised in particular by community and race relations training, that should come as no surprise given the distinct combination of the personal and institutional which this area of concern combines. If police training is not to have its value system inverted, with community and race relations training being the core around which technical specialisms can be arranged—and that would indeed be a viable policy option—then the licence for diversification and adaptability accorded to individual trainers will need to be enhanced. If such a process leads to a variegation in training provision (within what, following Schon (1972), has been called a 'family resemblance'), then the way in which management considers and controls its training function will need some appropriate adjustment.

3 The Holly Royde senior police seminar in community relations 1968–1987

John Shaw

The Annual Seminar at Holly Royde has for some twenty years been a fixture in the British police service's calendar. The story of its development is an interesting one, not least because that development has been the result of collaboration between several different interest groups with different but usually reconcilable objectives. While the Police Department of the Home Office has given the seminar official status, it has never taken over sole responsibility for planning and running it, preferring this to be shared with Manchester. Manchester University, on the other hand, through its Extra-Mural Department with its long experience in teaching what can be, and often is, a contentious topic, namely police-community relations, regards certain methodological principles as of absolutely prime importance and is completely committed to them.

The third interest group whose collaboration has contributed to the seminar's development is the ethnic minority population. Through the contribution of successive Home Office race relations specialists to the planning process, and the presence of ethnic minority personnel on the seminar staff, the perception of the police service by members of ethnic minorities has informed our thinking about the nature of management training in this subject. A fourth group whose influence has been considerable, at least in the eighties, consists of various Americans associated with the training effort in race relations and equal opportunity undertaken there in the police and armed services (see Shaw, Nordlie and Shapiro, 1987). This group is epitomised by Capt. M. J. Marriott, USN (Ret.) who made significant contributions to the seminars in the early 80s. Since a recent publication (Shaw, 1987) has described the series from a chronological point of view, my aim in this chapter will be to analyse the series from the methodological angle, looking closely at the sequence of items in the seminar, choice of speakers, community visits, case studies, discussion groups, the use of the learning cycle concept, group projects, action planning, attitude change and seminar evaluation methods.

Choice of training methodology depends upon specified objectives. The latter, in turn, depend upon the existing state of the organisations, ie police forces, which the seminar exists to serve, and upon a particular concept of training which the various parties to the seminar hold. The truth is that there is no commonly shared concept of the role of training. We on the university side of the operation see training ideally as an integrated component in overall organisational development (see Hunt, 1987); some other parties to the seminar probably view training seminars more in terms of the personal and professional development of those who attend. The planning and implementation of the seminars, therefore, reflect this dualism and their content and method swing, not always easily, between the poles of personal enhancement and organisational development. Given the decentralised organisation of the police service in Britain, it is understandable that central government should not wish to demand certain institutional structures from police forces, nor indeed can they, given the constitutional relationship between police forces and central government. Along with Police Authorities and Consultative

Groups (as set up in the Police and Criminal Evidence Act 1984) they can only influence decisions. On the other hand, the seminar planners as a group are always conscious of the fact that individual senior officers whose knowledge and awareness of the race relations dimension of their work is enhanced by attendance at a seminar, should be assisted as much as possible to preserve that awareness on their return and translate it into their post-return decision-making and planning.

One final comment is probably in order before I turn to the substance of this chapter. While, ostensibly, the Holly Royde seminars aim to give senior police officers a deeper awareness of the importance of police-community relations in general, in practice much attention has been focused on the narrower issue of relations between the police and the ethnic minorities. This has been specially so in the aftermath of the civil disorders of the early and middle 80s. It is also a fact that the British police service, especially at senior levels, is predominantly a white male preserve. Thus many of the assumptions which have underlain the planning decisions refer to and derive from a recognition of the attitudes prevalent in a largely white service. Many senior officers, for example, are insulated from the realities of life of ordinary black people in the inner cities; the seminar has to try to dispel this ignorance. In this and in other matters, the planners' assumptions have to be realistic. To admit the existence of personal and institutionalised racism in the service is neither to condone it, nor to exaggerate it. To lay bare our thinking is to run the risk of offending ethnic minority citizens on the one hand, or police officers on the other. To the outraged of either group, I can only plead the defence of necessity, that is, the need to identify the issues both of fact and attitude in the organisation before changes can be brought about.

The Learning Process

The general goals of these seminars were narrowed down in the mid-seventies, viz., to make "senior officers with command responsibilities" aware of the community and race relations dimension of policing, and assist them in their management role. Given that such seminars are bound to challenge many assumptions about effective policing we are, in fact, in a contentious area where there have to be effective teaching/facilitating processes to ensure that the conflicts inevitably generated become opportunities for learning.

In an earlier contribution I stressed the importance of the following aspects of the learning process:

"First, it was essential to provide the conditions for an open dialogue, free from defensiveness. Such conditions are best achieved in small group discussions with guidance by experienced group facilitators.

Second, it was necessary to see the seminar as a developmental process, with each successive stage mirrored in the group behaviour (see Tuckman, 1965). Thus, it was to be expected that resistance would be expressed early on. On the other hand, performance of group tasks would be expected to improve as the process reached its peak in the later stages of the week.

Third, it was advisable, where possible, to use practitioners as speakers more than academics so that the connection between information and its relation to practical situations always remained a central feature of the ensuing debate.

Fourth, for similar reasons, race relations should be placed in a wider social and police context so that its complementarity with other aspects of policing, such as enforcing the law, the constable's discretion and his generally accepted role, be clearly established.

Fifth, the officers' own professional experiences must be related, analysed and reconstructed where necessary. This would probably be best done through the medium of case material provided in advance by participants (Batten and Batten 1965; Patten, 1971).

Sixth, informal social contact between ethnic minorities and seminar participants should be arranged as an essential part of the seminar experience (Shaw, 1987)."

In short, the seminar must take the participants through a rapid learning process and at the various stages of the process, the learning goals must be related to each particular stage. Repetition of the seminar has crystallised this process more and more in my mind.

If we take as our guide a simple 'open system' model (Katz and Kahn, 1966), the following further elaboration of the developmental process can be indicated. The *input* stage is difficult if only because participants usually vary tremendously in their degree of awareness of the importance of community relations issues *vis-à-vis* policing. At the risk of boring those participants with high awareness, attention has to be focused on those with the least, since their resistance and/or ignorance will prove an obstacle to later progress if not dealt with. Thus, an officer of Chief Constable or Deputy Chief rank and a senior Home Office civil servant may be drafted in to assert the importance of policy in this area, the reasons for its adoption, and to identify important issues. As a further contribution to bringing all participants up to a satisfactory level of awareness, speakers from the ethnic minorities and from community groups, whom they meet on visits, identify key issues in their own communities which impinge on police-community relations. In summary, the input stage is about raising awareness, identifying issues, and delineating the main elements of current official policy.

The *throughput* stage of the seminar falls into two parts, namely the identification of specific policing problems in this area and the consideration of varying remedies for these issues faced both by police and the community at large. The boundary between these two parts is, for practical purposes, fairly blurred and necessarily so. In recent years, for example, we have brought in officers from an inner-city subdivision, in particular Chapeltown in Leeds, to tell the seminar about the work they do. We have also for nearly twenty years required participants to bring in case material drawn from their own forces' experience, which, if analysed in detail and reconstructed, contributes to both parts of the 'throughput' process. Also, in recent years, community schemes, such as the Stonebridge Bus Garage Project, have sent speakers to the seminar to underline the view that remedies for the problems of urban life are not solely down to the police to solve. The police service provides an important component of, but not the entire answer to, the issues facing us.

The *output* stage of the seminar is concerned, obviously, with whether the knowledge, skills and attitudes which the participants acquire can be taken back to their forces and divisions. For several years, we have used the idea of group and personal projects as vehicles by which the learning derived from the seminar is crystallised, reinforced and exported from the seminar. A *group* project with the title, for example, of 'Guidelines for Policing an Inner City Sub-Division' is one type of vehicle. Latterly, however, we have moved to *personal* Action Plans in which a participant having identified an issue with which he/she is faced, eg school vandalism, better youth liaison, is enabled to plan several strategies for addressing these issues on return to work.

Previous research (see below) shows that putting learning into practice is difficult, and we are currently exploring means whereby teams rather than individuals may attend, so that 'action planning' can proceed on a more realistic basis with greater likelihood of implementation on return (see also below).

Syndicate Groups

One of our early learnings was the importance of the small face-to-face learning group as the best vehicle by which resistances could be overcome, doubts clarified, learning from peers accomplished and commitment to action after the seminar maintained.

In a recent contribution to the topic of effective learning groups (Smith, 1987), several important principles are set out. First, everyone shall be clear as to why they are there. Group facilitators, chosen both for their intimate knowledge of race relations issues and their ability to work with a group in a non-directive way, encourage their groups, incidentally not more than a dozen persons in number, to begin by expressing their perceived reasons for being present. In this way those who have doubts about the value of the seminar are identified and a dialogue can, if necessary, be deliberately stimulated between them and their peers who hold more positive views. Most often, however, desirable change will result simply from hearing what positive colleagues say in the unforced atmosphere of a good group.

Secondly, syndicate group facilitators shall provide a model for group members to follow. In this particular field, the attitudes and views of the facilitator towards prejudice and discrimination are crucial. His or her own fairness, balance, behaviour and knowledge on the issues concerned will be watched closely by group members and assessed for its sincerity and appropriateness.

Thirdly, groups shall be helped to handle constructively the inevitable confrontations or conflicts which must be expected to arise during training in this topic area. While it has been cogently argued that moments of crisis and confrontation are absolutely crucial to success in modifying inter-racial attitudes (Jones and Harris, 1971), how these conflicts are handled determines whether or not they will simply reinforce the participants' attitudes. The group facilitators' skill depends largely upon their ability to mobilise the progressive forces within the group to challenge and modify expressions of prejudice. Only rarely, when group members refuse to take up the challenge, should the skilled facilitator need to directly challenge the prejudicial views. In my view, while attitude modification is best achieved through the mobilisation of peer group pressure, the facilitator's strength derives from his or her grasp of the issues, understanding of the often misunderstood concepts of race relations, knowledge of the history of the subject in the British context especially, and the ability to impart this knowledge in a credible manner.

Fourthly, facilitators shall assist in the translation into action of the ideas and information gained during the seminar. This relates to the output stage of the learning process, discussed during the previous section, and implies an ability on the part of the facilitators to change from a 'discussion-leading' style to a 'workshop' style as the seminar progresses.

In concluding this section, I would like to mention the importance of the various group tasks and the possession by the facilitators of the skills necessary to accomplish these. Throughout this sequence of seminars, certain demands are made upon the groups. The ability to use case material so that it serves to highlight issues within the service requires the ability to diagnose and then to reconstruct the situations depicted. The ability to lead a discussion so that constructive conclusions are reached is crucial. The ability to give clear guidance during the workshop phase, so that members understand the task required of them and how to do it, is also crucial. Where the group shies away from its task, the facilitators will need to create a sense of purposiveness and of the importance of goal-achievement so that within the limited time available the seminar tasks are accomplished.

The Use of Case Studies

Since I have made several references to these, some elaboration of the concept is called for. We have long recognised that to talk of remedies and solutions to the issues of police-community relations begs the question as to what those issues in fact are. There is still a minority, albeit a diminishing group, among the participants who suspect that a lot of the debate is politically motivated and lacks a firm basis in the realities of day-to-day policing. To debate this thesis in the context of a five-day seminar would be stultifying and unproductive. It is far better to have the participants produce an incident from within their own division or department which has occurred in the recent past and to bring this along to the seminar. This has produced, over the years, a wide spectrum of material which amounts to nothing less than a detailed description of the realities of policing in parts of Britain today. Without attempting an exhaustive classification, topics have included; Law enforcement vs. community policing, institutional racism, racial attacks, using the communication media effectively, inter-racial fights, neighbour disputes, the activity of the National Front, racial discrimination, immigration, incitement to racial hatred and recognition of cultural differences. (Their value, incidentally, for probationer training has already been recognised and the author, along with Eric Seward of the CRE, put some of the best ones into a training package at the request of the West Yorkshire Metropolitan Police.)

Modifying principles already laid down by others (eg Batten and Batten, 1965), we follow a number of guidelines both for the selection of material by the group in the first instances and its use as a training aid. These include: incidents chosen should not be 'success stories', rather they should leave something to be desired so far as response is concerned; identifying marks should as far as possible be removed from cases so that discussion can be franker than it might otherwise be; discussion should be taken through several stages, eg identifying the action or actions taken and the ensuing consequences, assessing the correctness or incorrectness of such actions, suggesting possible alternative actions or procedures, choosing the best ones to follow, and tracing out the consequences likely to follow from these so far as policing the community is concerned.

During this discussion the facilitators' task is to keep the process in mind, but not to influence the content in a specific direction. The professional expertise present in the group will ensure that the case in question will be subjected to detailed scrutiny and that a reconstruction along effective lines will emerge, provided that the facilitator provides a process which respects the principles set out above.

Finally, since the originator of the case is in the discussion group, its authenticity is assured. At a late stage in the discussion, the originator will usually add some explanatory comments or may comment upon the 'solution' to the situation which the group have advocated. One should bear in mind that the object of the exercise is for the group to learn from the experience of the division or officers in question and, with the benefit of hindsight, to find a better or different method of response. At no time is the case used as a stick to beat the originator with; rather the emphasis is on the positive value of the case as a piece of learning material.

Choice of Speakers

Central to the choice of speakers for in-service training seminars for members of any profession is the question of their credibility with the audience. Precisely how credibility is to be defined has been a matter of debate among social psychologists for many years. Hovland and his collaborators (1953) identified expertness, trustworthiness and prestige as key dimensions. Schweitzer and Ginsburg (1966) have also emphasised verbal and presentational ability, dynamism and sensitive concern.

We rapidly discovered that in a contentious area such as police-community relations, there is sometimes an underlying suspicion that the speaker has a political axe to grind or is engaged in special pleading for his own particular point of view. Given that credibility is a characteristic which is attributed to an individual by an observer and is subject necessarily to a degree of bias, there is no sure-fire way of finding contributors who satisfy all participants as to their right to be believed. One can, however, recognise certain important attributes likely to impress most members of a particular professional group.

Foremost among these for a senior police audience is the requirement that the police speakers know the realities of policing areas of high crime, multiple deprivation, multi-ethnic occupation, or potentiality for civil disorder. These kinds of policing experiences endow a speaker with a high degree of expertness and if he or she can at the same time come across as trustworthy and possess, through rank mainly but not exclusively, high prestige, then we have a contributor whose credibility so far as the majority of the audience is concerned will be unquestioned. If the speaker possesses also verbal ability and fluency plus a dynamic or lively manner, then his or her credibility with the vast majority of the audience is assured.

For non-police contributors, analogous considerations apply. Given that the population I am describing is a managerial group, then a speaker's experience of having managed military or civilian departments seems to be more valid than the possession of theoretical knowledge. Here again, manner and method of presentation are also important. Humour, liveliness and what may be called 'business school' type presentations, using relevant audio-visual aids, rather than lectures in the university sense, have greatest impact or effect.

So far as ethnic minority contributors are concerned, the normal considerations of practical experience, sincerity, prestige, verbal fluency, liveliness of style, and relevance apply. However, there is a special consideration also. Since a major concern of these seminars is with police relationships with minority communities in various parts of the country, especially the cities, it is easy for the spokesperson to appear to the audience to be engaged in special pleading on behalf of his or her own group. This is especially true if the speaker is a full-time professional working in the race relations field. Experience shows, however, that if the speaker 'tells it like it is', in other words, tells the unvarnished truth about the situation as minorities find it, then his message will be well received. To be an advocate for one's own and similar groups is not an easy task but it is made somewhat easier if religious and political objectives are put to one side.

Important though it is to choose speakers who are likely to appeal to a police audience if maximum impact is to be achieved, our evaluations have shown over many years that participants usually place a higher value on participative learning than on the didactic presentations. In other words, visits, discussions, case studies, practical projects and syndicate work generally leave the greatest impression on them. Nevertheless, a balanced programme must contain speeches and lectures, as well as other kinds of learning, and these individuals must, as I have indicated, be chosen carefully for maximum effect.

Community Visits

It was mentioned above when discussing the learning process that the 'input stage' is about raising the level of awareness and identifying issues. As part of this, participants visit an inner-city area, including the local Community Relations Council, and talk to members of mosques, temples, community centres and youth clubs. The local police divisional commander is also made aware of our visit and we either visit the station for a briefing or officers visit Holly Royde to brief the participants there. Of particular importance and interest to participants is the balance between law-enforcement and community policing, and how the local divisional commander and his professional community relations specialist manage these two complementary aspects of their work. Members will usually be provided with a document describing the local population, how it is composed, and various other statistics.

Our aim is to provide participants with as full a picture of the locality as possible both from the policing angle and from the point of view of the Community Relations Council and the various community groups. On occasions, we have included briefings from the statutory agencies such as Housing, Education and Social Services, but usually time does not permit. As well as the more formal occasions, the participants also spend an evening having a meal and socialising with local people. By the end of an intensive day, participants have been afforded an insight into local conditions that would take very much longer to acquire 'in real life'.

Experience shows that this visit, usually to Chapeltown in Leeds or occasionally Moss Side in Manchester, is one of the key events in the 'input' stage of the seminar. A degree of empathy and even identification with the local community is acquired, an awareness of the subjective reality of life in the inner cities is gained, and the mood of the seminar often palpably changes after this experience.

However, in order that the lessons of the visit be reinforced and underlined, a debriefing takes place the following morning. In this session, participants are taken through the 'descriptive', 'explanatory' and 'application' phases of the learning cycle. It is an important aspect of the methodology used that the lessons to be drawn from experiential aspects of the programme be consciously drawn out and their possible applications in professional practice be discussed.

Sometimes, very painful encounters are undergone, as has been the case on several occasions when visits have been made to youth clubs, youth training schemes, or hostels for homeless youths. I have already referred elsewhere (Shaw, 1987) to the senior officer who said his visit to a hostel for homeless and alienated youth "was a revelation, for me at any rate, that ethnic minorities . . . have a definite mistrust of the police, a fear of the police and no wish to recognise the police as a potential friend."

From the psychological point of view, it is important that this painful realisation should not just be left there. It can, and usually does, enable the group facilitator to instigate a useful explanatory discussion of the causes and reasons behind such mistrust and alienation from an important section of the populace so far as policing is concerned. This, in turn, gives rise to considerations of the application, in the future, of such awareness; for example, what can be done to build better bridges between the police and alienated youth. Officers can be encouraged to ask themselves "How good is my liaison in my division with such groups?" As has been mentioned above, in the discussion of the role of the syndicate groups, the skill of the facilitator in turning 'pain into gain' is crucial to the success of the seminar as a learning experience. It seems to me that the only educational justification for allowing confrontational clashes and painful encounters is the conscious use of such experiences as the basis for greater self-awareness and improved professional performance.

Group Projects

As the seminar progresses to its 'output' stage, attention switches mainly to the possibility of members being able to export from the seminar, in usable form, the lessons learned from the course. Several methods have been used over the years to facilitate this process. Effectively, the format has to switch from 'seminar' to 'workshop', the latter being a term to describe a project- or task-based situation.

Group projects, in which the syndicate group, as a whole, carries out a task, have been attempted. This may consist of requiring the group to prepare a paper for presentation at the final session. A group task, carried out by officers from different forces policing different environments, necessarily has certain drawbacks as a document on which to act when the individual has returned to his or her own force. It is not for use in a specific situation, hence its main purpose is to draw together the varied experiences of the week, particularly in the latter part when, as indicated above, the presentations are mainly about remedies and solutions. This exemplifies the principle of the 'learning cycle', mentioned above, that the transfer of learning from theory to practice requires an 'application' stage. As mentioned above, we have sometimes found it useful to take a fairly general theme for the group project: eg Guidelines for policing a division or district with a high degree of inter-racial conflict. In requiring the group to enunciate principles, our belief is that these will be of value to the returning officers even in policing situations widely differing in their nature. Having said this, however, we recognise from the case studies that many of the challenges facing police, particularly in the inner cities, are of a similar nature. Hence, there is a convergence of experience and remedy.

As these exercises were of limited value, we have experimented with practical management exercises in which several policing situations are described and the group task is to choose one of these and to identify the management implications. Having done this, the group analyses the situation, decides upon a management response, identifies the resources necessary to carry it out, takes into account the personnel aspect and other realistic considerations, including contingency measures should the original plan fail to be effective.

Clearly, managing the transition from the seminar to the work situation is perhaps the most important process of the whole week. It is also the most difficult since the participants move out of the influence of the staff and their peers and return to a highly variable range of situations. Accordingly, in order to cope with this process more effectively, we have changed in the last three years to a system in which the participant is required to carry out a personal project, which is his or her attempt to relate the content and experience of the seminar to his or her back-home situation.

Action Planning

On the first occasion we used this approach, participants were required to produce an individual paper "on any aspects of police management in the area of equal opportunity and community relations that a participant thinks require attention in his own force." "Seminar staff will be available for consultation, advice and assistance", the programme added.

The effect of such an approach to the 'output' phase is to bring into sharper focus any resistances to the learning task which still persist. One group facilitator commented on the fact that one officer in his group refused to do a plan: "It was impressive to see the group tackle the deviant in the group who refused to do an individual Action Plan on the grounds that it was unnecessary in his case. They did not succeed in changing his mind, but this is what peer group pressure is all about. At least, all but one were on the side of the angels and they tried very hard with the dissenter."

In this case, the solution was to link this officer, who came from a rural area, with a colleague from an area with greater perceived police-community relations issues. In this manner, his learning would continue, if only at one remove from his own situation.

The individual projects, once initiated, achieved a degree of success, being rated by members at the end of the seminar at 7 out of 10 as a measure of their practical value.

Subsequently, with the assistance of Mr Keith Hellawell, the Deputy Chief Constable of Humberside, an authority on management systems in the police service, we have sought to integrate the Action Plans more closely into the fabric of the seminar. By means of a lecture setting out the importance of detailed planning for effective management action and by dint of better briefing by the syndicate leaders about the 'nuts and bolts' of action planning, the value rating of the Action Plan component of the seminar continues to improve year by year.

Experience shows the importance of identifying the various components of an Action Plan, such as overall goals, sub-goals, persons responsible, completion dates, additional resources, and likely obstacles and how they can be overcome.

The use of the final phase of the seminar for an Action Planning exercise throws into sharp relief the extent to which training on race relations and equal opportunity issues is still rooted in raising awareness, rather than in tackling abuses and encouraging firm management action on equal opportunity. The important switch in recent years to greater emphasis on institutional rather than personal discrimination (Feagin and Feagin, 1978), has enabled us to see that improving race relations in organisations is as much a function of management as it is of training. The discriminatory processes of social organisations such as the police will not be reduced unless managerial action is taken. Such considerations underline the importance of senior officer seminars, of which there are all too few.

However, an individual senior officer, even if in effective command of a subdivision or division, must still lead by consent and negotiate the details of new management initiatives with those members of his division to whom he will delegate the task of implementing his plan. The latter's absence from Holly Royde means that an Action Plan is tentative, provisional and problematical. We do know from some follow-up research we have done (see below) that action is taken by commanders subsequent to Holly Royde, but it seems obvious that if divisions or departments were to send groups of people (rather than single individuals), as the Prison Department is now doing, then there is more likelihood of concerted action.

The Role of the Politician

A brief word on this subject. There is, as in many aspects of police work, a political dimension to race relations and equal opportunity. The race relations legislation of the 60s and 70s is an important element legitimising our efforts to bring about social change, especially change in important social organisations such as the police service. Officers of senior rank, therefore, need to know that the views of senior politicians, both in and out of government, support their efforts to alter the situation that obtains, in which an entrenched majority have set the personal, cultural and institutional norms of the service.

How the political spokesman is best used, however, is a matter for debate and experiment. He or she may be used in the input stage to enunciate current policy, an ideal role for a government minister; or at the output stage to concentrate on describing current initiatives and/or likely legislation.

The method we favour at present is to focus on an issue of great public concern, such as immigration, racial attacks, or ethnic monitoring, and to invite a politician with governmental or Select Committee experience to address the political dimensions of a particular issue or issues. A recent successful example of this was when Mr Jeremy Hanley, MP, addressed the seminar on racial attacks. Given his personal commitment to harmonious race relations and his membership of the House of Commons Select Committee on Race Relations and Immigration, an extremely relevant contribution was assured. Politicians differ in their interest in and commitment to race relations and this factor has to be taken into account in the selection of appropriate political contributors as with all speakers.

The Multi-Racial Training Team

John Coffey (1987) in setting out his principles of effective training programmes makes the following statement: "One of the rules of race training required that the training team demonstrate through its composition and behaviour, inter-racial co-operation". This principle is followed at Holly Royde. At the levels of seminar director, consultant, lecturer and group facilitator, the team is multi-racial. Additionally, since the police managerial groups we train are predominantly white, it is important to ensure that within the syndicate groups, the voice and experience of ethnic minorities is heard. This is achieved also through the use of 'resource persons', whose role in the group is to insert into the discussion at appropriate moments correct information about minority cultures and their own experiences, and those of their fellows, so far as discrimination and prejudice is concerned. Many of the misperceptions and misunderstandings of the members about the lives, aspirations and experience generally of the minorities can be adjusted through the give and take of discussion in the syndicate room.

As Coffey states above, the multi-racial composition of the team is not an optional extra but an essential feature of race relations training, to model for the benefit of the participants an inter-racial co-operative situation. Given that the seminar advocates precisely this in the police service, the organisers of the seminar have to practise what they preach. An effective demonstration of this in action is an important component of the overall message.

Coffey goes on to mention the tensions between team members of multi-racial teams which he encountered in his wide training experience in the USA. In our experience, the concept of the multi-racial team is sometimes challenged either by members of the majority or minority groups. While it is certainly true that only the member of a minority racial group can know from experience the full force of discrimination and hence has a dimension of experience denied to a majority person, however empathetic with the minority they may be, the principle of the training effort as 'inter-racial co-operation' must remain supreme.

It is also appropriate to add here that our colleagues in the USA have experienced the realisation that women in many organisations are a minority and that their problems within largely male organisations need to be addressed in forums of the kind we are describing here. As Hope (1987) noted, training "was too black/ white oriented and it did not deal with problems of other minorities and females". Even though such a transition is barely beginning here, the role both of white women and black women has been and continues to be important in the training teams I am describing.

Evaluation

I have discussed elsewhere already (Shaw, 1987) the problems inherent in the effective and meaningful evaluation of training courses, so I will not labour those points again. In brief, the evaluations and measurements of the Holly Royde seminars have been of three kinds, viz., pre-seminar and post-seminar measures of participants' attitudes, measures of the perceived values of the various components of the seminars, and follow-up questionnaires to participants to find out what if any initiatives they have been able to take on return to their division or department.

First, the attitude measures. Before the seminar starts we ask the participants their opinion on the following matters: the importance of the race relations dimension in present-day policing; the need for sensitivity in policing multi-ethnic areas; the awareness of their own responsibilities *vis-à-vis* race relations. We also seek to know their opinions on racial disadvantage in Britain today, and on whether they think that Britain is a multi-racial society.

Certain opinions we sample bear more directly upon the seminar and its methodology, eg how aware are they of their own attitudes and prejudices, how important do they think it is to reflect upon past experience and how helpful do they think the seminar will be in showing them how to make useful community contacts. Finally, we ask them whether they intend to initiate any changes in the community relations dimension of their current policing responsibility and how important they think it is to have an Action Plan in order to make successful changes.

By measuring, through a self-report inventory, all these attitudes and opinions, on a five-point scale both before and after, we aim to see whether the experience of the seminar has affected them, even temporarily. By having participants fill in these inventories anonymously, we try to reduce the element of mere compliance in their answers. Of course, it is not possible to know whether any changes are internalised, ie leading to genuine acceptance of new points of view. This would require follow-up of the individuals themselves and also checking out their changed views with significant others; both of these objectives are outside the scope of the strictly training role we have necessarily adopted.

It is not unusual to find an average movement in the positive direction of between 15% and 20% in the scores on several of the items during the course of the seminar. Sometimes the items showing greatest changes relate to participants' perceptions of society, eg "awareness of the reality of racial disadvantage"; on other occasions the greatest change is in the level of their own awareness of their own racial attitudes; yet again the greatest change may be in the strength of their intention to initiate changes productive of better police-community relations. There is no predictable pattern in these changes. It can be said, however, that usually most items show only a small amount of positive change.

Since, as has already been said, we can only guess whether changes obtained in this manner are due to compliance, identification or internalisation of new points of view (Kelman, 1961), the main value of these readings is to help us to monitor the seminars and, in particular, to note whether differing emphases in the programme from year to year are reflected in the ensuing attitudes. In particular, as the seminars have moved from raising the level of awareness as the main objective to encouraging action likely to improve police-community relations, the average post-seminar score on intention to institute initiatives has usually shown a marked increase.

Second, participants' evaluations of the various items in the seminar programme are always closely scrutinised in order to ensure that programme contents and methods are of value to attenders. As I reported elsewhere (Shaw, 1987), "participative and experiential items . . . ranked, in general, highest in post-seminar evaluation. For example, taking the top of the rank orders from four different seminars . . . no fewer than twelve out of twenty top choices were of (these) items." One or two didactic items or speakers have challenged this trend. In general, however, we have come to rely on the discussion groups, the case studies, the visits and the group or individual projects to make the prime impact upon attenders.

Third, there is the follow-up of the post-seminar behaviour of the attenders. On one occasion, in the early eighties, with the assistance of the Police Department of the Home Office, we asked thirty senior officers to identify initiatives undertaken as a result of attending the seminar earlier in the year. Seven cited specific decisions or initiatives and gave detailed information about these. Fifteen said that they were contemplating changes but had not yet made them. Many of these said that their prior commitment had been reinforced by the seminar. Eight were unable to specify any new initiatives or to say that their attitudes had been significantly affected by the seminar.

These findings have been discussed elsewhere (Shaw, 1987). Suffice it to say here that these findings show the need for greater follow-up efforts, especially with regard to the fifty per cent who were considering making changes in practices, procedures and methods. Any encouragement, support and stimulation might result in greater action. It is clear that in a short seminar designed to encourage, enthuse and stimulate, there is insufficient time to consider the 'nuts and bolts' of successful intervention. If training is to be effective in producing organisation change then it must be converted to post-seminar behaviour by follow-up activity, as well as by paying greater attention to detail during the 'output' phase of the seminar.

Conclusion

There is a belief in some quarters that the entire rationale on which such seminars are based is out-dated and ineffective. Proponents of this view (eg Pettigrew, 1981; Hunt, 1987) believe that racism is not so much rooted in individual psychology more an indirect reflection of conformity with immediate social and other environmental influences. Following this line of argument means that we could without great loss dispense with much of the training presently done; concentrating instead on teaching race relations specialists how to monitor the racist procedures in their departments and advising their commanders on remedial action.

It is possible that the way forward does lie in this direction and, indeed, the pervasiveness of institutional racism necessitates a root and branch approach. However, the divisional commander remains a key figure so far as institutional change is concerned. Organisational renewal requires commitment to it by top management if it is to be successfully prosecuted. This is recognised by those who advocate a 'public health model' of change such as I have just described.

Thus, restructuring the organisational environment so that different practices become the norm is part of the answer. The other, and equally important, part is played by the aware and insightful commander who sees the subtle ways in which his organisation fails to meet the needs of minorities, either as clients, staff or as potential recruits. There is much anecdotal evidence, as well as evidence of a more formal kind (eg Nordlie, 1987), pointing to the key role of the divisional, departmental or regional chief so far as the initiation of change is concerned. One may have well-trained professional staff, able to monitor the relevant indices and to plan a more equitable set of practices, provisions and procedures for a particular department. If, however, the commander, or chief executive, is unconvinced, then progress towards change will be slow. All this suggests that the hearts and minds of these people are crucial elements in the equation. Thus the seminars described in this chapter, wherever they may be carried out, will continue to be essential in the drive to make the police service a social instrument which acts equitably towards people of all races and other minorities.

4 The training of community liaison officers

Raymond Cochrane and Susan Phillips

In this chapter we attempt to do four things: present some ideas relating to training in general; discuss methods of evaluating training provision; point out some training issues which are specifically relevant to the role of the Community Liaison officers (abbreviated to CLOs, henceforth, although in particular forces these officers may belong to Community Affairs, Community Involvement and other Departments or to operational sections); suggest a model for the training of CLOs in terms of content, style, format and staffing. The observations made in the following pages draw upon two Home Office sponsored studies which we have recently completed (Phillips and Cochrane, 1985, 1987). The first was an analysis of the role and function of CLOs, and the second was an evaluation of training provision for the same group. The latter study involved preparing recommendations for improving training.

Training—individual and organisational aspects

Hinrichs (1976) defined training as: "Any organisationally initiated procedures which are intended to foster learning among organisational members in a direction which is intended to contribute to overall organisational objectives".

Clearly there are two perspectives within this definition—one being the individual, and the other the organisation. Taking an individual perspective, training may be seen as a development opportunity because it equips the individual with skills and competencies which enable him or her to improve performance in relation to a specific job. For example, a typist may be given training in word processing, because the office is about to be equipped with up-dated machines, or may be given training in shorthand because it is foreseen that he or she will be promoted to private secretary. It is to this category of training that Lindsay (1984) attaches the term 'remedial development training'. Where learning is task orientated, it is a process of skill enhancement. Alternatively, training may provide opportunities which develop the individual in a less specific way. This involves equipping a person with general attributes—cognitive or interpersonal—which will be of personal benefit to that individual and, it is assumed, of indirect benefit to the organisation. These are not, however, necessarily directly related to a specific post. An example is secondment to study for a degree, or day release to complete professional qualifications. Lindsay calls this anticipatory development.

Training can be seen as a process by which an individual's pattern of behaviour is changed in a direction which suits the organisation. To be effective in this sense, there needs to be both a clear understanding of the organisation's present and future needs (in terms of the skills and competencies it requires of its staff), and of the appropriateness of training content and methods for the achievement of these goals.

Seen from the perspective of the organisation, individual training experiences produce two advantages. First, it is assumed that skills acquired will be required by the organisation at some future date. Much that goes on under the umbrella of 'management development training' falls into this category. It is addressing the long-term needs of the organisation, rather than the current specific job-related training needs of a particular individual. Hence, Lindsay's use of the word anticipatory. It is this type of training which is easily criticised for its lack of credibility. Training is, after all, only one amongst a variety of possible responses to organisational problems, but tends often to be taken as an obvious solution, perhaps because of the positive values surrounding education in general. In other words there is a danger that training is seen as a panacea for organisational ills. It may be that more sophisticated selection procedures, paying more attention to fitting square pegs into square holes (Rowbottom and Billis, 1977; Stamp, 1980), and matching individual style to task requirements would be more realistic or effective solutions to what have been assumed to be training problems.

A neat solution to dilemmas posed by raising these issues is to take the opposite view of training and to gear it to specific job requirements and, indeed, to the specific training needs of particular individuals. This, in fact, limits training to remedial development. In the police service there is undoubtedly a need for training to be linked to job requirements. This has been recognised in relation to recruit training (MacDonald et al., 1986; Nijkerk, 1986), skills training (Shepherd, 1985) , community relations training (Joss, 1986), and management training (Kakabadse, 1984). However, training is also frequently assumed to serve the anticipatory function as well. We have found this conceptual distinction between individual or job-related orientation, and organisational orientation particularly useful in handling inconsistencies inherent in the training provision for a role which has yet to be thoroughly defined, let alone validated.

The failure of police training departments to determine in detail just what specific training should accomplish has been noted by Jones and Joss (1985) among others. The tendency to produce a 'training smorgasbord' was certainly apparent in our review of existing training for CLOs. The problem appeared to stem from an inadequate appreciation of the CLOs' job which necessarily precluded rational analysis of how the training course should be constructed. All too frequently there is a mismatch between training and the actual job, primarily because training is designed in the absence of thorough analysis of training needs, or in the presence of longstanding prejudices about the nature of training and the nature of the job (Jones and Joss, 1985).

In addition it has to be born in mind that policing is a consumer-related activity, so attention needs to be paid to public reactions to the officer once he or she has received training. Public perception of the police has received a lot of attention in recent years (Jones and Levi, 1983; Jones, 1986; Sykes and Clark, 1975; Southgate, 1986; Smith and Gray, 1983), and the advantages of adopting a radically different model of the effective police officer from that based upon the traditional emphasis on decisiveness and technical competence have been advocated by Jones and Joss at Brunel and by MacDonald and his colleagues at East Anglia. Kakabadse (1984) in his management development survey contrasted the responses of middle ranking police officers to those of their counterparts in industry on the importance of having sound technical training. Police managers appear to value this highly, whereas once in a management position the importance of technical training seems to diminish among managers in industry. One reason advanced for this is that the police believe they are unpopular and disliked in the eyes of the general public, and further believe that their image will be enhanced by increased technical competence. The legitimacy of these assumptions has however been challenged (Jones and Levi, 1983; Jones and Joss, 1985). In particular, a question has been raised over the relevance of the technical-expert model to real world situations in which police officers often find themselves, interacting with other people whose definitions of situations/reality differ markedly from the definitions formed by police culture and training.

Developments in the field of community and race relations training at Brunel and in probationer training at the Centre for Applied Research in Education at East Anglia, have developed an alternative view of professionalism based on effective practice, known as the 'reflective practitioner' model (Schon, 1983). The core professional competencies of the reflective practitioner include: an understanding of the boundaries of his or her own expertise; skills in relating to those whose background and experience leads them to view the world differently; and the ability to reflect upon his or her own performance at the interface of these worlds.

The development of skills and attitudes required by the reflective practitioner model involves the activation of self-directed learning processes. It demands a learning style which is characterised by the exploration and incorporation of new material, which in turn depends upon the willingness of trainees to examine their existing cognitive frameworks and to be prepared to adapt or expand their view of the world. This kind of learning obviously has implications for teaching in terms of the content, process and focus of training. While content should be closely related to job needs (in other words should be meaningful), processes should include a teaching style which will encourage the building of links between existing understanding and new material. The focus must be on the learner not the teacher; that is training should be student-centred.

Some writers have made a clear distinction between training and development. They suggest that training is predominantly a mechanistic processes with goals and objectives specified in advance. Here evaluation would be limited to the attainment of highly specific and predictable outcomes. Development on the other hand relates to a more fulfilling experience for the individual which touches the whole person, rather than just the performance of a particular occupational role. Training deals with core competencies, development deals with effectiveness. This distinction however lacks utility when applied to the role of Community Liaison Officer. There are aspects of the job which lend themselves to a training approach; indeed there are specific skills, which for some officers are paramount. Many CLOs are involved in schools liaison work, for example, and these officers may be required to spend a large proportion of their time communicating with school children. There are officers whose natural abilities enable them to perform effectively in schools, but there are others whose performance in the role is dysfunctional (Phillips and Cochrane, 1986). In cases like this, development of self-awareness is inadequate; what is required is the development of specific competence and confidence. Here remedial training in the form of skills training, albeit with a requisite cognitive component is appropriate. However, many aspects of the CLO's role do require broader interpersonal skills, including the ability to deal with conflict and to resolve ambiguities, and the need to understand broad social issues. To perform effectively in these areas an officer requires a high level of self-awareness and a wide behavioural repertoire.

The Learning Process

We may examine the learning process as a series of stages which involve message receiving, storage, response and feedback. All these are necessary for learning if this is to enable the individual to draw on what is stored in the memory and apply it to situations in the environment. Gagne (1985) in his search for a theory of instruction, ie "a rationally based relationship between instructional events, their effects on the learning process and learning outcomes", concludes that different types of learning rely on different internal processes which are facilitated by different instructional events. Skills acquisition for example relies heavily on both individual practice and informative feedback from an external source, whereas learning conceptual or factual material depends on new ideas being incorporated into the individual's already existing structure.

Thomas and Harri-Augstein (1977, 1985) argue that it is of paramount importance to distinguish between learning and teaching. They are convinced that most people "learn how to be taught, not how to learn" and, therefore, usually fail to benefit from learning experiences. In pointing out that learning is not the same as submitting to being taught they distinguish between self-organised learning and other-organised learning. Self-organised learning centres on the individual becoming more self aware with regard to his or her learning processes, and becoming actively involved in bringing about changes in behaviour and experience as a result of learning.

The fact that adults have a store of life experiences is a valuable resource but past experience can either hinder or promote understanding. Hence these experiences need to be engaged if the new learning is to be effective (Henderson, 1985).

Reflectivity thus emerges as being of great significance in adult learning. Cagne talks of the transformation of non-meaningful stimuli into those associated with meaningful information already available to the learner. Ausubel (1968) suggests that to be meaningful, new ideas must be subsumed into existing ideas by being dealt with at a higher level of abstraction and generality through the operation of what he terms an advance organiser. Others refer to schemata as the internal mechanism which provides a framework within which already acquired knowledge is organised and into which new ideas may be slotted, that is they are a means by which ownership of new material may be established. Bruner (1963) talks of predispositions to learning, and uses the concept of 'revisiting' which refers to the process of connecting what we have learned with what else we know.

Thus, the relevance of past experience and the development of cognitive structures which organise what has been learned in ways meaningful to the individual is acknowledged by writers from very different backgrounds. However, variety of background in terms of cognitive functioning or life experience may be seen both as a resource and as a threat to those involved in adult learning. Recognition of the value of experience and its centrality to learning poses a threat to the role definition of teacher, removing the security provided by a prescriptive, information-providing role. Equally, it poses a threat to the learner for whom the learning experience may challenge longstanding beliefs. As Henderson (1986) puts it, adults "nearly always have something to lose in learning as well as something to gain".

The processes of revising existing cognitive structures, the creation of new schemata, the questioning of long-held beliefs, may provoke strong resistance. The hope is that ultimately the opportunities for personal growth may be seen as attractive and embraced enthusiastically, but this is by no means guaranteed. The central feature of this process is that of achieving 'ownership' of information. If the learner/course member, fails to integrate the new knowledge or skills or attitudes within his or her own repertoire, then learning has not taken place. If the CLO returns to work unchanged in any way then the course has been a waste of time and money.

What are the implications of this for content, process and focus? First, it is clearly important that content should be related to the starting point, as well as the job requirement, of each individual; but more of that later. Secondly, the process needs to be one which will enable learning to take place effectively; that is it needs to allow for the building of links between what is already known and the new material. Where skill learning is involved this implies that there should be a development of understanding of the area, an appreciation of what constitutes good performance, and of the cost of poor performance. It also requires the time and opportunity to practice in order to develop confidence and competence using constructive feedback followed by more practice, until a standard acceptable to the *learner* is reached. As far as knowledge is concerned, individual and group work should be provided to encourage new material to be absorbed into already organised schemata, and to encourage the development of new perspectives or patterns of thinking. Development in the area of attitudes is particularly dependent upon the individual having time and opportunity to examine existing attitudes, analyse responses to confrontation, and develop new ways of perceiving and responding.

The Role of the Trainer

Much of the recent work in the field of adult learning has been concerned with examining process and focus so that these ends may be reached. The role of the tutor is central to the discussion. If the focus is to be the needs of the learner rather than the supposed content requirements then it is inappropriate to see the role of the teacher as being solely that of provider of content. Focus on the teacher follows from focus on the learner, and it becomes more appropriate to use the term 'tutor'—someone who may guide into learning, or 'facilitator'—someone who encourages the individual in his or her learning experience.

Once training (or development) is aimed at producing learning or change on the level of personal style, interpersonal skills or in individual values and attitudes, it is imperative that training interventions are conducted by those who have the ability to function on the affective level. Kakabadse (1984), when talking about interpersonal skills training, recognises the need for counsellors who are skilled at helping people to cope with their feelings; Butler (1986) points out that one of the risks of community relations training is that it may lead to the development of a resistance to challenging communications, which can be minimised by selecting appropriate teaching methods; Jones and Joss (1985) advocate a training model which blends teaching information with an understanding of "how that information can be used to understand both social and psychological processes involved in interactions". Interactive teaching methods are necessary if learning is to occur in the effective and behavioural domain. Shepherd (1985) underlines the need for a facilitative rather than didactic form of instruction if the aim is "to develop in the trainee the capacity to synthesise feeling with doing and thinking". Wells (1982), while advocating direct involvement in police training by members of the community, cautions that "contributors should be skilled facilitators in teaching, capable of working with small groups for extended periods". Bull (1986) has drawn attention to the need for trainers to know more about "the principles underlying behaviour", but in his evaluation of Human Awareness Training for recruits to the Metropolitan Police, wonders "whether or not awareness skills can successfully be taught and whether instructors are adequately prepared to cope with the training needs of recruits".

Clearly there is widespread recognition of the need for a facilitative style of trainer to work particularly in areas which have a high affective and attitudinal content. This requires the development of trainers who are not primarily technique orientated but who are able to work with emotions and who have the ability to deal with particular issues as and when they arise. In addition, these people will need a very high level of self-awareness (Plumridge, 1987)—a combination of talents which is extremely rare in any organisation or profession.

Recognition of the need, and indeed consensus over its importance does not automatically lead to a supply of suitably equipped trainers, nor answer the question of whether facilitative trainers need be police officers.

There is, within the police service, a basic organisational problem surrounding the training role which centres on the tradition that to be effective, trainers require 'street credibility'. This is thought to be ensured by selecting trainers from among experienced and successful officers. Credibility is maintained by a system of rotation, ensuring that trainers spend an average of only 2 years away from operational duties. Until recently, training officers received 9 weeks training at the Central Planning and Training Unit, one of the few functions to be carried out centrally. On completion of their training they then, ideally, return either to their forces to work as divisional or force trainers, or to a District Training Centre where they are involved in Initial Recruit Training. (Unfortunately, however, many of those completing the course have not subsequently been involved in training work, a situation which CPTU and HMIC are seeking to remedy.)

Recently, staff at the Unit, themselves seconded mainly for a 3-year tour of duty, have collaborated with educationalists and consultants to develop a wider repertoire of teaching skills than hitherto, in response to the recognition that more versatile trainers are required. There has been a shift from emphasis primarily on the technical aspects of training to emphasising interpersonal skills. A new 11-week course has been developed for police trainers, and there are plans to offer retraining to those already in the system who were trained to the old methods. One goal of the new course is to encourage trainers to "create an atmosphere conducive to active student involvement where positive wide ranging responses and solutions are encouraged" (Poole, 1986). Clearly, officers trained with these goals in mind will be more able to act as tutors, or even facilitators than those trained under a 'right answer' philosophy.

The question of the supply of facilitative trainers is also being addressed by staff at the Police Staff College at Bramshill. Their experience is that though, with time, police trainers may acquire and develop facilitative skills, a 2-year secondment severely limits the extent to which these officers are able to make an optimum contribution as facilitators. It is plain that the need we have identified for the training of community liaison officers is one of current concern to others working within the field of police training. In time, developments in these and other areas, eg the Centre for the Study of Community and Race Relations at Brunel University, may lead to the supply of skilled facilitators who may be used as a training resource for Community Liaison Officers. Meanwhile, in our final section, we advocate a multi-disciplinary approach to the staffing of a national course for police community liaison officers.

Training as a Panacea

Some writers, responding to the present preoccupation with training within the police service remind us that there is a danger in assuming that training is a panacea for all ills, and that if we get the training 'right' then we will end up with the right kind of police force, policing in the right way. Denkers (1986) points out that the underlying assumption of a remedial approach is that there is something inherently wrong about the ideas and mental constitution of the police officer, rather than identifying problems at the level of the sub-culture (see also Brown and Willis, 1985; Butler, 1986). Exclusive concentration on training also avoids admitting that often it is managerial and structural rather than individual shortcomings which lead to malpractice, inefficiency and lack of satisfaction, tempting the individual officer to 'act out' within the community the kind of treatment he or she receives within the organisation. Butler (1986) points out that, though training can help in improving police community relations, there is a danger of "subsuming societal and organisational problems within the individuals who are to receive the training".

Joss (1986) maintains that without a broader definition of police training, moving "away from a model of socialisation towards a model that emphasises training as a part of organisational development", there are very marked constraints on the impact which training in community and race relations can have on relations between the police and communities. He proposes a model of training, closely matching the model we have adopted, which attempts to link operational performance and training at three levels: that of the individual, the unit (micro-system) and the total organisation (macro-system). He points out the need for matching training to both operational need and individual performance, whilst, at the same time, not losing sight of the need to maintain consistency at the level of organisational goals.

There are then, limitations which we would not dispute, to what can be achieved by training; however, these limitations can be minimised by the selection of appropriate training techniques and objectives.

An Approach to the Evaluation of Training

In looking at the training of police Community Liaison Officers we were faced with a basic question—What is the training for? In other words, by what or whose criteria do we evaluate the effectiveness of current training? We were aware that we were not alone in asking this question as we found the same issue being raised by other researchers either explicitly or implicitly.

We could perhaps summarise the issue of the choice of perspective under five headings, closely related to the five levels of evaluation suggested by Hamblin (1974). Whichever position is selected the researcher would find company, for writers on police training may be found operating from each of these positions.

First, the "what for?" question could be addressed at a broad *societal level*. This would force upon the evaluator a need to discuss the purpose of policing, and to deal with the question of what kind of a police force Britain wants or needs in the 1980s and the 1990s, and with what kind of a police force we wish to enter the 21st century.

Second, training could be evaluated in terms of achieving *organisational goals*, which would centre attention primarily on policy-making. By its policies an organisation expresses its goals and purpose, outlines its philosophy and ethos, and describes the kind of image it seeks to project.

The third level at which evaluation could be executed is at that of *the actual job* or organisational role. This requires an analysis of the job as it is perceived by those within the organisation, particularly by the immediate supervisors of those carrying out the role—those who are managing the function.

Fourth, there is the level of the *individual* as he or she operates within the role. Here the need is to consider the skills, knowledge and attitudes which are necessary to enable the individual to meet role requirements as set out before him or her. This perspective would lead to a consideration of what remedial development training is necessary for each individual, bearing in mind that differences in both role requirements and personal experience may mean that training appropriate to one person is not necessarily relevant to another.

The fifth level of analysis is *the training itself*. It implies considering what training interventions are likely to be successful in equipping individuals to perform their particular roles, given their particular levels of skill, the present state of their knowledge, and their prevailing attitudes towards both the CLO's role and different communities with which it brings them into contact.

For our evaluation of the training (existing and potential) of CLOs we adopted a perspective based on levels 3, 4 and 5. In part this was as a result of what data were available, and in part it presented a realistic appraisal of what it is possible for outsiders to achieve in a relatively short period. More of this in the final section, where we advance four areas for consideration—content, style, format and staffing.

The Role of the Community Liaison officer

Much of what has gone before applies to many roles within the police service and, indeed, the training needs of CLOs overlap to a considerable extent with the training needs of many other police officers. However, there are some distinctive aspects of the work of CLOs which point to particular training needs. Before mentioning these, however, it is worth pointing out that CLOs are often given that role after many years service with their force and with many training courses under their belts.

Several authors (eg Jones and Joss, 1985; Plumridge, 1985) see the expectations aroused by previous experience of police training as posing severe limitations on an officer's ability to enter a self-directed learning environment, to seize the training course as a development opportunity, and to engage with the subject at an effective level. We shared these reservations about the deforming effects of traditional police training. While the course which we evaluated had a structure and style which had most of the characteristics of the old style training course, and most of the students were, indeed, old hands at training courses, the in-depth interview data we gathered suggested a greater willingness to engage in self-directed learning and a greater openness to challenge and uncertainty than we had anticipated. So all may not be lost, even for long-serving police officers entering new style training.

Three special factors emerged from our earlier study of the role and function of CLOs which need to be taken into account in providing satisfactory training:

1. In most police forces the role of the CLO is ill defined, therefore one essential ingredient in a training course must be the provision of time and opportunity for course members to develop an understanding of their role. This lack of clarity over the role was also usually associated with considerable ambiguity over the status of being a CLO. It was clear that many operational officers (but not all) saw CLOs as 'non combatants'. This attitude was not entirely absent in the ranks of CLOs either. The uncertainty over role and status threw CLOs back on their own resources or could lead to an unquestioning adoption of the style and practices of their predecessors.

2. There were very wide variations in functions between CLOs operating in different force structures (and there is even evidence of variations within a force), leading to the existence of a wide range of training needs. Our study identified several ways in which CLOs were integrated into their forces, a wide range of ranks occupied by officers doing similar jobs, and an enormous variety of specific tasks which they might be expected to carry out. These ranged from advising the Chief Constable on policy to repairing slide projectors, from dealing with potential riots in Handsworth to addressing the Women's Institute in Solihull.

3. There is need to recognise the importance of matching training style with content. For CLOs, perhaps more than any other group of police officers, it is necessary to engage in reflective practices concerning the role, to develop appropriate attitudes and to achieve competencies in specific skill areas.

All these considerations have particular implications for training style.

Training for Community Liaison Officers

1. Content

Policing occurs within a social context but much police training to date has ignored the significance of this fact. Current reviews of police training (MacDonald *et al.* 1987; Bull, 1986; Bull and Horncastle, 1986; Jones and Joss, 1985) have laid increasing stress on the importance of an understanding of the social context and the value of developing models which may be used by practitioners in the policing field. Such considerations are of particular relevance to newly appointed Community Liaison Officers who so often operate at the interface between community groups or social agencies and the police.

By and large, previous training given to Community Liaison Officers has focused on providing factual information accompanied by some skills training, leaving the attitude component as implicit within the knowledge component. The attitude component is an important dimension for training, though attitudes are not the only precursors of behaviour. Attitude change is a delicate and personal area and one which, if insensitively handled, may have the effect of hardening undesirable attitudes as a defence mechanism. As such, consideration of the attitude component has implications for tutorial style and course format.

Factual information may be used as a means to expose attitudes dysfunctional to the CLO, as well as to provide the necessary knowledge base. The knowledge component should provide an analytical framework in addition to factual information relevant to CLOs' particular area of functioning. The acquisition of specific skills required by their role is important for CLOs, whether the community liaison role is interpreted at one extreme in terms of public relations or, at the other, in terms of bridge building (Phillips and Cochrane, 1985a; 1987). Aspects of the job bring police officers into contact with professionals in different walks of life. Whilst it is acknowledged that skills training available to police officers in these areas—for example, CLOs may find themselves working alongside social workers, probation officers or educationalists—will necessarily fall short of that given within those professions, we maintain that a minimum level of competence in the relevant skill areas should be achieved. Failure to do this will, in the long run, be destructive to the objectives of developing positive contact with the community and eventually have repercussions on the organisation as a whole. Some areas require specific skills, which may occur more naturally in some officers than others, but which may be enhanced and developed with well-designed training, with elements of theory, practice and feedback. All this implies that course content should be approached with 3 components in mind: the provision of factual information, ie providing a knowledge base; the acquisition or development of the particular skills required to perform as a CLO in a given force area; and the examination, fostering and development of attitudes appropriate to the role.

An effective course must include material which will contribute to the development of an analytical model, a framework within which the many facets of modern policework may be understood. As well as a broad theoretical model, CLOs need specific information about the various sections of society with which they build bridges. A course should therefore include information about such communities. In particular, it might include:

—information on historical and contemporary structure and culture of the various groups within our society which are distinguishable by their ethnicity;
—information about other minority groups, distinguishable by means other than their ethnicity, eg youth, women, the elderly, the unemployed, the physically or mentally handicapped;
—information about the structure and function of those statutory bodies with which a co-operative liaison is often sought, eg Education, Social Services, Probation, Local Councils and Councillors; and
—information about current trends in police community liaison, discussion of policy and its outworking in practice, including an examination of individual force goals and an awareness of the variations across the country.

Self awareness is an important component of successful communication. Information-based aspects of the course need to be explicitly accompanied by the development of personal awareness of attitudes towards different groups in society, and an examination of the role of the CLO in relation to such groups.

Specific skills which are frequently required by CLOs include:
public speaking; television and radio interview techniques; committee skills; communicating with young people, particularly school children; preparation of press releases. It is highly desirable that, at the end of training, a CLO should be

comfortable and confident in all of these contexts.

Though made up of many different parts as outlined above, to be effective course content should be presented in a co-ordinated and cohesive manner. Its structure and purpose should be clearly outlined at the outset, and communicating links provided wherever necessary. Course tutors should take responsibility, through discussion with course members, for relating specific content to the objectives of the course.

2. Style

As already discussed, teaching and learning are not synonymous. We are convinced that the training needs of police Community Liaison Officers can best be met in a learning-focused course. When compared with traditional police training methods this kind of training calls for some rethinking and restructuring of approach. It calls for a shift in emphasis from looking to experts to provide the 'right answer' in a classroom setting, to using a variety of information sources as a means of reaching new insights, and a personally satisfying set of conclusions or orientations which will become fruitful in the unexpected and varied demands of the work situations. For example, an important element within a course could be individual project work. The word project is used cautiously here. In our experience the term project as used on police training courses often refers to a piece of individual or group work which culminates in some form of presentation, preparation for which often obscures the research element. Forces may well require some feedback from individuals as a result of project work, but we feel that the course design should support, guide and resource the development of learning and understanding for the individual student. Presentation may, in itself, be a way of providing additional resources for other course members, and this is quite acceptable. However, presentation of project work as a method of practising public speaking should be avoided. Course tutors should be equipped to guide students in their project work, and training centre resources be allocated to support project work, eg library, video and telephone facilities should be provided.

A common complaint on residential police training courses is that of information overload. Attention span can be increased by providing variation of stimulus— lectures, videos, group exercises, video playback, discussion, individual reading and research, as well as visits including opportunities for observation, discussion and reflection.

The process of acquiring knowledge and the development of attitudes are closely linked. Each student attends a course with a personal knowledge and attitude base, in addition to a level of competence in particular skills, and it is into this already existent framework that new material will be incorporated; acquisition of knowledge is not simply a matter of committing facts to memory.

This implies that course structure should allow for information to be presented in such a way that it may readily be utilised by the individual, specifically:

(a) Factual information should be accompanied or followed by periods of reflection. Reflection may be facilitated by discussion in small groups, and by individual study.

(b) Small group work should form an integral part of the timetabled programme, and not be 'bolted on' or expected to occur naturally in the evenings, though fruitful discussion may well continue into relaxation periods.

(c) Small group discussion should be facilitated by tutors attached to the course for that purpose.

(d) Tutors should have access to training resources to which they may direct individuals whose requirements, due either to particular job demands or personal levels of understanding, are not sufficiently met by the formal sessions.

Skills training needs to be carefully designed to include the identification of training needs, ie identify the level of competence already acquired by the individual officers and the standard of performance necessary for the particular job.

Skills training should include elements of theory, practice and feedback, using whatever methods best suit the particular skill. For example, the skill of addressing school children could be developed in the context of some understanding of childrens' needs and outlooks at different stages of development, and of the educational context. Officers needing this training should be given opportunities to prepare and deliver talks, culminating where possible with practical sessions involving young people. Each stage should be accompanied by relevant feedback, so that a sense of increasing confidence and competence can be fostered.

3. Format

The role of Community Liaison Officers exists in most of the police forces in England and Wales. Indeed section 66 of the Police and Criminal Evidence Act 1984 assumes that each police force has local officers who bear this title. However, variations in role, function and policy abound and these variations create particular demands in relation to training provision. If there is to be a common national course of training for CLOs, one feature of it must be a flexibility which recognises inter force variation in rank, structure and role. In addition, this flexibility would allow for individual differences to be accommodated.

Given the diversity of ranks, organisational structures and specific tasks found among CLOs, an argument could be sustained for developing small scale in-force training courses tailored to local requirements. In this way newly appointed CLOs would not be exposed to the confusion of meeting their counterparts from other forces and discovering that their jobs vary in significant details. Each force would be able to impart its own philosophies and tailor training to its own specific need. However, even allowing for a fast turnover of staff, it would seldom be economic to hold courses regularly. The smaller forces, and those with a small number of CLOs, may never reach a moment when it is economic to put on a specialist course, yet their CLOs may well be doing work with high visibility, whose performance has a potential for affecting the attitudes of different groups within a community towards the police—work which if badly done may be destructive to its stated purpose.

On balance, there are considerable advantages in having common training run at a national level (Phillips and Cochrane, 1987). Such a course could support a team of facilitator/trainers, possibly using both police and civilian staff. Relevant teaching materials could be amassed, expertise developed, and evaluation carried out. But, above and beyond the economic and educational considerations, a national course could help to give CLOs a sense of professional identity which might compensate to some extent for their marginality within their own force structures. It would also allow them to work out an understanding of role and purpose in company with officers from very different backgrounds.

The national course should be made up of two elements. A basic core course where ideas about the purpose of community liaison, the nature of communities and social structures, could be explored. With appropriate tutorial staffing, this core element could encompass a small number of themes relevant to all officers involved in community liaison activities, irrespective of specific role, rank, function or prevailing policy. The main aim of the core course should be to encourage CLOs to explore the purpose of their role, and to develop a philosophy which will guide them in their day-to-day decision-making. This emphasis on conceptual development would help to mitigate the confusion arising from a lack of clarity within the organisation about the purpose of community liaison activities. We suggest this basic or Core Training should be mandatory for all newly appointed CLOs, and occur optimally within two, and definitely within six, months of them taking up their appointment.

A core curriculum of one week's duration could consist of the following elements:

(a) An appreciation of the structure and purpose of community liaison leading to the development of a firm conceptual and philosophical base for community liaison work.
(b) A basic social science component relevant to issues which affect society at large, eg social composition of Britain in the 80s, unemployment, the nature of prejudice.
(c) Methods of evaluating the effectiveness of community liaison work.
(d) A consideration of the problems involved in establishing the credibility of community liaison both *inside* and *outside* the police service.

The second element could cater for the variation in training needs, and be made up of a range of consecutive Optional Modules from which individual officers would select according to their particular needs. These modules would vary in length from 1–2 day seminars to a whole week, depending on particular content matched with appropriate style. For one officer the core course plus two modules may meet his or her training requirements, whereas another officer may select four or five modules in addition to the core course.

In view of the nature of their work, it is assumed that CLOs would find the modular structure advantageous, facilitating their continued involvement in the community. Regardless of the nature and number of modules selected, prior attendance at the core course would be a prerequisite, as it is this element which would lead each individual to the development of a philosophy which would then underlie the more specific aspects of their training.

From our knowledge of the variety of contexts in which CLOs operate, we see a clear need for the following options to be made available:

(a) PUBLIC RELATIONS, eg drafting press releases, radio broadcasting, television interviews.
(b) JUVENILE LIAISON, eg juvenile crime, child abuse or non-accidental injury, liaison with Social Services.
(c) LIAISON WITH THE EDUCATION SERVICE, eg the structure of the service, policy on schools liaison, skills of addressing young people.
(d) RACE RELATIONS, eg culture and religion of different ethnic groups, attitudes, racial attacks, problems of adjustment.
(e) YOUTH, eg youth unemployment, sub-cultures, attitudes, communicating with youth.
(f) DISADVANTAGE, eg unemployment, poverty, physical and mental handicap, the elderly.

(g) IN FORCE TRAINING, eg preparing and presenting material to police training courses, informal training, influencing attitudes.

(h) COMMUNICATIONS SKILLS, eg communicating at an individual and group level, committee work, chairmanship, listening skills.

(i) POLICIES FOR COMMUNITY LIAISON (for senior officers), eg politics and policing, the creation and implementation of policy.

(j) CORPORATE APPROACHES TO CRIME REDUCTION, eg Neighbourhood Watch, inter-agency co-operation.

Under this structure officers would be able to develop attitudes, knowledge and skills in harmony with their job requirements, whilst acquiring a firm philosophical base on which to build.

4. Staffing

As our earlier discussion of training indicates, focusing on learning as opposed to teaching implies certain requirements for staffing.

Present staffing of community liaison and many other police training courses assumes that visiting expert lecturers are a valuable resource. However, it has become apparent that training courses for Community Liaison Officers can only be effective by employing a team of skilled facilitators specifically dedicated to the course for its duration. At the time of writing, this requirement may represent a demand on the police as an organisation which it is unable to fulfil. However, we hear echoes of our own thinking coming from other contributors to this volume, highlighting the need for facilitators as opposed to instructors within police training. We see skilled facilitation as being an absolutely crucial requirement for a course of the nature being proposed here. It is necessary to guide course members through their learning experience, not as expert practitioners in the field, but as enablers, supportive to the learning process. It follows that ideally only trainers experienced in facilitation should lead or tutor on a course as ambitious as the one we are suggesting. There is, of course, the possibility of using non-police staffing, which is not without precedent, but there are the fears of lack of credibility once this option is adopted. How well founded this apprehension is cannot be determined, so it is important at least to explore the possibility of a team composed of both police and civilian tutors working together.

On this basis, a small team of trainers carefully selected for the job would be sufficient to provide economic, relevant and effective training for all the forces of England and Wales.

In summary, we recommend a centrally organised, learner-centred approach to the training of police Community Liaison Officers supported by a team of civilian and police facilitators, adopting a modular structure. Exploration of the role itself should form an important part of the mandatory core course, and be supplemented by a range of modules reflecting the diversity of the community liaison role.

Our research began with a specific focus on the role and training of police Community Liaison Officers, but it raised issues common to several areas reviewed in this volume. Although the format for training which we advance relates specifically to the training of police community liaison officers, the key issues of role definition, matching learning experiences with training needs, and the necessity of integrating evaluation and practice in training have wider application. They are of relevance to the service as a whole, indeed they are cornerstones for organisational development in any context.

5 Race relations training: a personal view

Trevor Hall

I write this chapter not as a representative of the Home Office and its policy, but as an individual with some years of experience of race relations in this country. The chapter sets out to focus on the need for:

1. an understanding of how institutional and individual racial discrimination affects professional behaviour in the police force;
2. clear objectives in both policy and practice to enable police officers of *all* ranks to attain the elimination of discrimination and to promote an equitable service;
3. senior management to take the lead in an active commitment to good race relations; and
4. a realistically-timed programme for effective race relations training to permeate the whole police force.

The police service maintains its high reputation for integrity as a disciplined body of officers, but inasmuch as police officers reflect the mores and behaviour of society, they cannot be expected *de facto* to operate in impeccable fashion. What we must recognise, however, is that from time to time certain police behaviours may have accentuated the difference and distance between the black communities and the police. The attitudes which certain sectors of the community may have to the police are not always formed by how they perceive the police in their crime role, but may also be gained from the many other services the police provide for the public.

Lord Scarman in his report on the Brixton disorders of 1981 stated that the objectives of policing include *both* maintaining order and enforcing the law. The problem is that in certain circumstances the law enforcement efforts of the police may so anger the section of the community at which those efforts are directed that people from that community start to engage in collective attacks on the police. Lord Scarman went on to say that:

> The conflict which can arise between the duty of the police to maintain order and their duty to enforce the law, and the priority which must be given to the former, have long been recognised by the police themselves, though they are factors to which commentators on policing have in the past often paid too little attention. The successful solution of the conflict lies first in the priority to be given in the last resort to the maintenance of public order, and secondly in the constant and common-sense exercise of police discretion. Indeed the exercise of discretion lies at the heart of the policing function. It is undeniable that there is only one law for all: and it is right that this should be so. But it is equally well-recognised that successful policing depends on the exercise of discretion in how the law is enforced (Scarman, 1981).

It is a fact that racial prejudice and discrimination whether conscious or not are widespread in our society today. The police as part of our society reflect its

53

mores and habits of thought. But it is difficult to gauge the extent to which the police service is racially prejudiced or to which its practices are discriminatory.

The recent NACRO report on *Black People and the Criminal Justice System* states: "Discrimination in the Criminal Justice System is particularly disastrous since the system is one of the bedrocks on which our society is based. It must be seen to be fair to all sections of the community in the way it works, and unless this is the case, it will not have the confidence of the whole population. Without this, the strong moral imperative which rests on all members of society to remain within the law is lost. Young people, particularly young black people, become cynical about, and alienated from the system which is supposed to protect them equally as it protects other members of society. Their respect for the law disappears, and the temptation to disregard the law increases. The Criminal Justice System as a whole needs to be clear about where it is trying to go, and the steps by which it is trying to get there. It is imperative to convince the ethnic minorities that as far as the Criminal Justice System is concerned they have the same rights—and the same obligations—as any other section of the community, that the Criminal Justice System is there to serve them. Any attempts to achieve this have therefore got to be genuine attempts at reassessment and change and a determination to tackle racial discrimination."

The police is only one part of our Criminal Justice System and any attempts therefore to assist the police to understand how institutional discrimination can affect professional performance should recognise that the issue of racial discrimination is for the whole Criminal Justice System and not just the police.

It is, in my view, a fallacy to assume that the racial discrimination which many black people experience daily and complain of regularly is due partly to their unfamiliarity with our Criminal Justice system. Whether we are speaking of Afro-Caribbean, African or Asian people they all share a common history with our colonial past and an identification with our institutions and systems. What is more, many of the current issues in race relations are located in the experience of those black people born, bred, socialised and educated in Britain.

The Third PSI survey, *Black and White Britain* (Brown, 1984), demonstrated that people of Asian and Afro-Caribbean origins are most frequently discriminated against in employment. Whether it is within the police culture or in employment generally racial discrimination is a part of the fabric of life in our society today, and is an evil which all agencies—not only the police—and institutions have a duty to eradicate.

It is only when the reality of discrimination is faced honestly and squarely that the problems can be effectively tackled. This was the view of the Police Training Council Working Party who in 1983 following the Scarman Report produced the report *Community and Race Relations Training for the Police* (Home Office, 1983c). This detailed and constructive work remains a vital document for all those involved in increasing racial awareness and good professional behaviour within the police service and who believe that race relations training is a vital tool in this process.

It is important to state from the outset that race relations training is not and shoud not be seen to be a panacea—a cure for all. It cannot be expected to bring about dramatic changes in our social behaviour and attitudinal responses. I think it is equally false to project the police officer as the sole agent in society who is responsible for its race problems.

I now turn to race relations training.

Training in race relations for the police must be carefully designed to incorporate:

(a) appropriate content, style and method;
(b) a realistic recognition and use of both the life experience and the professional experience each participant brings;
(c) a realistic recognition of the role of the instructor, and what he/she has to cope with;
(d) the realistic expectations of the training designer;
(e) practicable and sensible action planning designed to improve the officer's professional skills, confidence and clarity, and thus to enhance the reputation of the police force as a whole.

The report of the Police Training Council Working party also suggested that officers at junior and middle management level should be equipped to understand the importance of supervising more junior officers in a manner that reinforces the training they themselves would have received.

Above all else, race relations training must demand that managers prepare, support, check and assist before, during and after the training event all those who receive the training. It needs to recognise that the force is embarking upon an organic process, not a once-for-all curative.

I would like to examine in some detail several of the past (and indeed current) approaches to race relations training in the police service, and to outline a different contemporary focus.

The Black Experience approach asks black individuals to "tell us where it hurts". The dangers here are that the black men and women who are able to express their experience are dismissed as radicals, political extremists, exceptions to the norm, having chips on their shoulders, anti-establishment activists; in other words their experience is dismissed under the guise of "they do not understand the way we do things here."

The Intellectual Approach (and please note that few black accredited intellectuals were invited to contribute to such a development) used mostly white professionals from academic institutions with no recognisable experience of black and mainly urban communities. The distanced structure can be perceived by the black community as devaluing and unsympathetic, by the recipients of the training as politically biased. Again, the approach can easily be dismissed (and thus the issue trivialised).

The Balancing Act sought to apportion responsibilty (or blame?) to both black and white people. Black men and women are involved in training programmes, but are allocated the emotional, the offensive, the painful items on the agenda, and thus are set up to adopt a stereotyped whining role. Once more their experience is dismissed as being unrepresentative. Recipients of such a training style have been known to leave the close confines of the training programme, 'check out' the 'message' with any black people they happen to meet and return confirmed and supported in their initial prejudice or perception. There is no equality of presentation and planning in such programmes—and no real attempt is made to identify experienced professional black persons with an understanding of organisational culture. Too often, course participants are exposed only to the deprived, struggling black groups, to the angry and seemingly aggressive young people.

The Information Focus Approach stemmed from the false belief that the problems arose simply from a white lack of understanding of non-white cultures. So, training programmes would seek to impart certain identified ethnic/religious representatives to present non-controvertible issues and information (arranged marriages, particularly, caste systems) not central to our real problems. What is omitted then is that the contemporary issues are those of black people born in the UK and steeped in current culture, not those from overseas cultures. The native Afro-Caribbean, African or Asian Briton, born and bred in London or Birmingham or Cardiff is not yet perceived to be indigenous to the UK. Again, dismissal and devaluing are at work, and the approach slides past the real problems. In spite of these training programmes and their attendant costs, organisations are dismayed to find that there is little change in the public's perception of them, whilst within the organisations there is a dawning realisation that *institutional discrimination* is at work causing pain. Hence the need for a new approach, for new thinking.

This new thinking places the focus clearly on the role, function and responsibility of management. The rationale is that management clearly is responsible for the ethos of the force and, moreover, that poor race relations is a clear indication of wider managerial problems. For the first time those who attempt to approach seriously the issues around race have to accept that racial discrimination does not stand in isolation from the whole gamut of management problems. They have to be prepared to examine and challenge long-held views, practices, and unwritten codes. The issues raised by an effective race relations training programme will focus on recruitment, selection, training and promotion. Good race relations = good human relations = good management. Undeniably, good race relations means change within an organisation—never an easy prospect, especially if externally imposed and not owned from within the organisation.

Senior management, in order to effect such change, has to demonstrate
(a) an individual understanding of race issues,
(b) a determination to tackle institutional discrimination,
(c) an active commitment to the elimination of racism, and
(d) a willingness to expose itself to new learning.

The management approach, then, is designed to enable senior management to recognise both the nature and the extent of the damage perpetrated through racial discrimination, as perceived by black and white men and women from within and without the organisation.

Dr Ann Dummett in her book *Portrait of English Racism* (1973) states:

A racist society has institutions which effectively maintain inequality between members of different groups, in such a way that the open doctrine is unnecessary, or even if operated partly by individuals who are not themselves racist in their beliefs still have the effect of making and perpetuating inequalities . . . it is perfectly possible for an institution to be racially exclusive in fact without a single word or notice or an internal memo, or a constitution making this plain: it is indeed perfectly possible for it to be racist in spite of written statements and exhortations to the contrary.

Further, managers must ensure that the skills, knowledge and understanding gained during training can be used fully in practice and in policy. It is important that training be offered at all levels and in all forces, not simply for those seen to be on the front line, because of the practice of moving police officers. There must be the recognition that race relations concerns every one of us.

Towards the Future

Nadine Peppard in her 1980 paper *Towards effective race relations training* concluded there are already in Britain some indications that those who have made attempts over the years to give training in 'community relations'—for example, the police service—have themselves come to realise the inadequacy of information-giving training and are seeking to acquire new skills in tackling attitudes. They recognise that the individual cannot react to situations which require flexibility and understanding unless he has acquired some awareness of himself as a person and as someone occupying a particular role and called upon to perform particular duties in relation to others. These indications of some moves forward from the simplistic approaches generally characterising race relations training up to now are encouraging, and there will be an increasing demand for authoritative, detailed advice and appropriate source material. Much good work has been done by many individuals since Miss Peppard first wrote her paper but we are still not clear whether the emphasis in race relations training should be on attitudes change or behaviour change. For my part I believe that it is only through professional behaviour, recognised as such by all, that the issues of race and the police will be positively measured.

6 Socialisation of recruits into the police role

Nigel Fielding

Introduction

There are increasing pressures on the police to adapt to the changing character and circumstances of British society. While public debate continues over the role of the police, research demonstrates that the ability of police management to affect the practice of that role is dependent upon the attitude of the ordinary constable. Independent review boards, community policing schemes and other reforms may stand or fall on their acceptability to those who carry out basic police work. Changes in police organisation aimed at creating a more 'professional' police may have furthered the formal control of the police administration without making everyday police practice more accountable.

The research reported here was designed to measure shifts in attitude to police work and the police occupation consequent on exposure to agencies of informal socialisation. Its broad aim was to document the process of attitude shift on the part of police recruits as they undergo training and early service.

Police training involves brief and highly condensed periods of classroom instruction, drill and physical training, and much longer periods of attachment to operational police shifts. The former can be regarded as agencies of formal socialisation, the latter as agencies of informal socialisation. The research sought to compare the influence of these agencies and to do so in relation to the probationers' experience of police work. It questioned probationary constables while they were involved in formal instruction, when they were on the beat under supervision, and after they had been accepted into the force. Attitude data gathered by survey questionnaire were interrelated with qualitative data from interviews with recruits and trainers and observation of training sessions.

Method

Formal efforts at socialisation are known to be most effective at the relatively early stages of the recruit's career (van Maanen, 1975). With increasing police experience, informal socialisation comes to enjoy higher salience (Harris, 1973). It is the study's aim to examine the impact of the various agencies in the training process by references to attitudes to colleagues, police administration, criminals, the general public and minority groups within it. The contention is that the data on attitude shift reveal that over time novices achieve an individual balance between formal, informal and experiential agencies of socialisation. This implies that there is more variation in working attitudes among constables than is suggested by previous analyses.

Three groups of attitudes were examined. First, attitudes toward work were examined by a survey questionnaire, including matters such as job satisfaction, job security and wages, colleagues as primary sources of friendship, trade union activity, career orientation and promotion. Second, rank ordering exercises, chosen for their sensitivity to change in attitudes over time, assessed attitudes about contemporary policing, which included views on dealing with violence and arming the police, administrative control and supervisory officers, working with partners of the opposite sex, and crime control v. 'social service'. Third were attitudes about contemporary social and political issues which influence policing, including attitudes toward racial minorities, capital and corporal punishment, obscenity, pornography and permissiveness, vandalism and hooliganism, and the use of alternative sentences to imprisonment, also examined by the survey questionnaire. These research instruments were administered to a sample of recruits at a constabulary force training establishment (see below) at induction and at 12 and 24 months after joining.

The principal sources of qualitative data were interviews with a subsample of the recruits, and with police instructors, Tutor Constables, and senior police officers. The interviews pursued selected issues from the survey questionnaire, along with questions concerning (initially) reasons for joining and (subsequently) job satisfaction, satisfaction with the training programme, perceptions of colleagues and the public, and several other issues. Questions about training considered the treatment of police, legal and academic subjects, the use of simulations and exercises, the experience of recruits at the Home Office District Training Centre at which they underwent their Initial Course and the experience of recruits with serving police officers (Tutor Constables and others on their shift). Questions concerning police work itself pursued such matters as arming the police, the recruitment of coloured people, women in the police, the Police Federation, police/public relations and intra-organisational relations (with immediate supervisors, senior officers and officers involved in training). Interviews with instructors, Tutor Constables and senior officers considered their assessment of the recruit training programme, appraisal of recruits, the place of training in the organisation, and their own career and ambitions.

The research was sited at a constabulary force Training Establishment which runs a variety of national, advanced, and in-service courses as well as the in-force element of basic training. Probationers return to the Establishment from the District Training Centre or operational placements/postings for local procedure and other input by local trainers. Four intakes of recruits to the constabulary formed the core sample. The total sample was initially 125, comprising 115 men and 10 women. The mean age was 25. The bulk of recruits were drawn from semi-skilled and skilled manual workers' families. The level of educational attainment was low, with nearly half having less than one 'O' Level pass and only 10 having an 'A' Level. In these respects the sample more closely resembled the educational profile which was at one time customary in the police service, as opposed to the trend toward more highly educated recruits emerging in the recent past. For example, in 1985, 700 recruits nationally had 2 or more 'A' Levels, 1718 had 5 or more 'O' Levels and only 455 had no qualifications (Home Office, 1987).

It was also noted that, largely as a result of a targeted recruiting campaign, an unusually large proportion of recruits had been serving in the military prior to joining. This was so particularly of the first two intakes and, overall, recruits with a military background comprised 42% of the sample. Such a background is common in the USA and some studies (van Maanen, 1975) go so far as to describe it as the norm. Many of the ex-military recruits had been assisting civilian police in Northern Ireland or had been attached to the military police. In the light of their relatively large numbers, previous exposure to uniformed service and experience of policing-type situations, it was worthwhile to compare responses in this group to those from civilian backgrounds. It was hypothesised that the distinction might well be an important predictor of attitudes on the grounds that police service had similarities to military service which would be less pronounced in civilian occupations. In this chapter, the groups are referred to respectively as 'military' and 'civilian' recruits. The study also included police instructors, Tutor Constables from local stations to which recruits were posted, and senior police officers and administrators.

In the light of these particular features of the research sample it is sensible to note that the focus of the study was not on the typicality or otherwise of certain attitudes as applied to the total population of police recruits at a given point in time. Although such studies are common in research on attitudes, there is always a problem in extrapolating from sample to population, and this, among other factors, accounts for the problematic relationship between attitudes and action upon which many applications of attitude studies to policy have floundered. The intention of the present study is to use the attitude data as indices of change over time in the sample recruits, so that the impact of the different stages of training can be examined. While the pattern of attitude shift discussed below suggests that the measures adopted were sensitive to change, it is logically possible that differently constituted samples could show different patterns of change. Against this possibility it should be noted that, whatever the sample, the training regime to which recruits are exposed is broadly consistent throughout the country, and that the comparison of responses by 'military' and 'civilian' recruits in this study may also be taken as a comparison of the traditional and the more recent (more highly educated) recruits. Interestingly enough the more 'illiberal' attitudes are by no means expressed only by older recruits, those with military backgrounds or low education. Nevertheless, in that attitude shift is a worthwhile line of enquiry, it is to be hoped that future research will further examine the relationships between attitude and stages of training so that a fully comprehensive picture can eventually be built up.

A 'realistic' understanding of the police role

The research documented the evolution of the recruits' attitudes during socialisation into the police role. The measures of attitude change were employed as indices of the changing relationship of the recruit to the police role. The data indicate a movement towards increasingly *pragmatic* conceptions of policing as work. This evidence bears out Becker's (1961) analysis of occupational socialisation and the identity change consequent on it. It supports the salience of a distinction between 'instrumental' and 'idealist' elements in the individual's occupational stance. 'Instrumentalism' denotes an orientation to pragmatic aspects such as pay and job security, but also to the equally practical matter of how best to get the job done. 'Idealistic' elements refer to the philosophical underpinnings of the work, for example, notions of service, duty and the superiority of community good over self-interest.

Similar occupations

Respondents ranked a list of occupations according to similarity to the police role. The occupations included teacher, civil servant, social worker, skilled manual worker, military, lawyer, clergy and public relations officer. These were chosen for their reference to pertinent aspects of the police role and in light of their use by other researchers, facilitating comparison (Cook, 1977). At induction the occupation seen as most like policing was "military". The second most similar occupation was "public relations officer". After a year these responses were reversed. The background of respondents suggesting that policing was like military service was checked: the difference in ranking between civilian and ex-military groups was significant at induction but not after a year, suggesting a convergence of view. Cook (1977) administered this exercise to police at different stages of service and also found public relations the most 'similar' occupation.

When means of induction and year one rank scores were tested for significance the most significant shift (at the .001 level) was in the perceived similarity to social work. This was the third occupation most like policing at induction, but after a year was fifth. This is relevant in light of Punch's (1979) contrast between the substantial element of 'social service' work in policing and his observation that such work is held in low esteem by police. The shift may relate to the experience of the recruit with social workers and exposure to an 'occupational culture' which devalues them. Also notable was the insistence on dissimilarity to skilled manual work.

The rank order data were also entered into an MDS MINIRSA program, which locates the 'ideal point' for each individual amongst a 'map' of preferred points (in this instance, job titles). At recruit stage the majority of ideal points were almost equidistant between two main groups: teacher, social worker and civil servant; lawyer, military and public relations. This indicated no strong preferences at this stage, although a greater number of recruits were located nearer the public relations/military/lawyer group. Socialisation into the police organisation and culture is marked by more informed choice. After a year there were stronger choice preferences for social worker, military and public relations. The clustering of teacher, civil servant, social worker and clergy at induction suggested these occupations were seen as similar; a common quality of a 'treatment' or service orientation could be inferred. The clustering of lawyer, public relations officer and military suggested the contrast of 'treatment' with 'control-oriented' occupations. After a year, choices were more discriminating, dividing approximately equally between three groups, those seeing policing as military service, as public relations work, and as social work. Interestingly, however, the largest group saw policing as having similarities to all three of these broad approaches. Socialisation enables novices to eliminate occupations having no similar qualities to policing, but there are divergent evaluations of the relative similarities of those that possess similar qualities. The correspondence of interview data with the survey responses confirmed the reliability and validity of these choices.

Attractions of the job

A shift from social to personal values, which is suggested by a movement from 'idealistic' to 'instrumental' responses, was well expressed by comparison of

61

induction and one year responses to an item ranking certain aspects of the job in order of importance. "Interest and variety" came high on both occasions but at one year there was more spread in the ranking, and the number choosing it as the most important attraction of the job declined slightly. Meanwhile "good pay" rose in importance, being the top advantage for 10% rather than the earlier 7% of respondents. However second and third choices declined. The importance of not just examining first choices was shown by responses on "good workmates", which declined from 3% to 1% as number one, while choice as second most important was up from 13% to 23% and third, fourth and fifth choices largely held. This trend conformed with analyses of socialisation into an 'occupational culture', with which results on 'supervisor who does not breathe down your neck' were also consistent. This was of negligible importance at induction (1% first choice) but increased to 6% first choice after a year, with the third choice score also increasing. The final aspect, "a sense of performing public service", provides a contrast with 'instrumental' aspects, declining from 26% to 22% first choice, with broad consistency at lower levels. These results, particularly the changes in relative importance of 'good pay' and 'sense of public service', support a picture of shifts towards an 'instrumental' approach. Additionally, shifts on "good workmates" and "supervisor who does not breathe down your neck" support the salience of an 'occupational culture'.

Police role and lifestyle

Results from five items concerning the police role and lifestyle also indicated a move towards a more 'instrumental' approach to policing. Tested for significance, the number who felt policing was 'just like any other job' increased from 4% to 16%, and the number disagreeing fell by 13%. The number believing that police should only do what they must on the job increased from 1% to 7%, and the number who disagreed fell by 6%. Those who felt police work should not interfere with private life increased by 10% and disagreement fell by 10%. Respondents who felt one should never stop being a police officer on or off duty fell from 58% to 53%. Similarly, those who put duty before private life fell from the very high figure on recruitment, 95%, to 83% and the number disagreeing increased from 5% to 18%.

A comparison of induction and one year responses was performed by cross-tabulation. Of the 13% who changed their opinions on 'just like any other job', 12% changed to agreement and 1% to disagreement. The only change in response to "only do what he must to earn a living" was a 6% shift to agreement. The 30% change in view on 'work should not interfere with private life' divided into a 20% shift to agreement and a 10% shift to disagreement. For "duty before private life" there was a 16% shift to disagreement and 4% to agreement. Finally, the statement 'never stop being a PC on or off duty' resulted in a 20% shift to disagreement and 14% to agreement.

The degree to which an officer may put duty above private life varies over time as well as among officers. These data from early in occupational socialisation support Savitz's critique (1982) of Kirkham (1979); there are degrees of loyalty to peers, and various countervailing circumstances can negate the high priority normally assigned to supporting colleagues. The assumption of an 'instrumental' behavioural style implies an increasingly pragmatic approach to police work as well as to one's status as a police employee. Such a trend balances 'idealistic' expressions of a sense of duty and service.

Working with minorities

Police attitudes on race have increasingly been used as indicative of their perspective on working with 'problematic' groups generally, including youths and women. Apart from the intrinsic importance of maintaining sound relations with all groups in the population, relations with those who may be inclined to challenge the police (Holdaway, 1984) are worth close scrutiny. This is particularly important to monitor during training in the case of race because of the Police Training Council's belief that "attitudes are as much caught as they are taught" (Home Office, 1983c). This highlights the role of informal socialisation by experienced officers of probationers who may be impressionable or feel that they need to project attitudes consistent with those expressed by those whose appointments are confirmed or who are in a position of authority (Southgate, 1982). Ethnic minorities, particularly young Afro-Caribbeans, do present police with dilemmas of order maintenance. Because they are readily identifiable, attitudes towards them may express the probationer's general attitude towards other challenging but less immediately recognisable groups, such as professional criminals or political radicals. It is important to note that the matter of race is pursued here because of an interest in the way that probationers refine their understanding of the perspective of those who are different to them. The argument is that such an understanding is vital in enabling the officer to anticipate the likely intentions and actions of such people (Fielding, 1984), and that this is in turn vital in their establishing a repertoire of methods of intervention by which conflictful situations can be handled competently (Fielding, forthcoming).

In their 1982 study, Colman and Gorman found that, compared with control subjects, recruits' and probationers' scores were significantly "more conservative and authoritarian, and the probationer's open-ended responses on the death penalty and coloured immigration were rated significantly more . . . intolerant . . . Among the recruits basic training was followed by a reduction in conservatism and authoritarianism. The findings suggest that the police force attracts conservative and authoritarian personalities, that basic training has a temporarily liberalising effect, and that continued police service results in increasingly illiberal/intolerant attitudes towards coloured immigration" (1982).

To other researchers, the Colman and Gorman study illustrated the danger of over-simplification of complex attitudes, particularly as it was reported in the press under the headline "Recruits to police reveal illiberal arm of the law" (*The Times* 24.8.81). Butler's summary of Colman and Gorman's findings show them a good deal more limited than at least the newspaper reports suggested. "The results of the four psychological tests showed that there were no differences between the scores of recruits and the control group on the Rokeach Dogmatism Scale and the Eysenck Social and Political Attitude Inventory and the opinions on the death penalty, coloured immigration and mixed marriages. In fact on the two latter items the average score of the recruits was lower, that is, more tolerant than the controls (Butler, 1982). The higher authoritarianism of recruits on the Wilson-Patterson Attitude Inventory turned out to apply only to females.

The Colman and Gorman study seemed to repeat the problems of definition of

63

the key concept and of the 'normal' response which have plagued attitude research. Further, the psychometric tests themselves seem bizarre, with items such as "Bible truth: Yes or No" apparently peeking through from some dim American farming past when they were devised. The possibility that recruits may have felt obliged to give what they foresaw as 'police' answers was not explored. Two lessons may be drawn from this: first, the need to ask questions which directly address the working concerns of officers, and second, the need for longitudinal data to indicate shift other than by comparison of groups at different stages who may have had a dissimilar career through the organisation.

An item concerning coloured people in the police illustrates the importance of testing for views relevant to policing as opposed to questions about general attitudes. In response to the statement "police should try hard to recruit coloured people"; overall agreement was 28% and overall disagreement 40%, 31% gave a neutral answer. Agreement increased by age (43% in the 30+ age group) and disagreement was strongest in the youngest group (54% against 13% agreement). Before concluding that greater 'bias' is shown in the youngest group the responses were cross-tabulated by previous occupation. Agreement was expressed by 36% of skilled non-manual and 39% of the military group, while only 20% semi-skilled, 19% cadet/student and 5% of skilled manual worker groups agreed.

In sum, these figures show that military experience or higher status occupational backgrounds were associated with more favourable responses to coloured recruitment. For the military group this was due to their experience of similar work. In interviews, respondents with experience as Military Police reported that the Army found it useful to have coloured Military Police (chiefly to deal with coloured soldiers). The research covered several questions pertinent to racial attitudes, including "There should be a stop to coloured immigration into Britain". Strong disagreement was expressed by 2% of respondents, disagreement by 9% and a neutral view by 24%. Agreement was expressed by 37% and strong agreement by 28%. Such a question may well invoke complex beliefs about race, but it is simply noted here that 76% of the former military respondents agreed and 4% disagreed. This compares with 56% agreement amongst 'civilian' respondents. One might expect former soldiers to be more 'biased' and answers to the general attitude questions bear this out, but they turned out to be more favourable to coloured recruitment than their peers. Views pertinent to the work may be more salient in the occupational context even when they contradict general attitudes.

The suggestion that there should be more 'coloured' police can be seen as an essentially segregationist sentiment—coloured recruits would not be used to 'ginger up' white communities but to police their 'own' areas. For example, one officer said: "In coloured areas it would be much better with a load of coloured police because it's easier to handle your own. But in white areas they would be called 'coloured pigs' . . . If a woman comes and marries a man or a man comes and marries a woman . . . OK but I don't believe the same for all the family and relations . . . I don't believe in throwing any of them out but we have got about enough". The feeling expressed was that minority group members who qualify for residence should receive equal treatment, but resources are limited. When resources are limited, entitlement is qualified. As newcomers, minorities do not have the prior claim held by the 'obviously' British.

The tension between this and the need to offer the fair treatment seen as characteristic of 'British justice' was reflected in several of our survey questions. While some half to two-thirds of recuits opposed a partnership of white countries

(47% induction, 52% year one and 60% year two) with the rest undecided (41% induction, 33% year one, 29% year two), about two-thirds at year one and half at year two (65%, 57%) agreed there should be a stop to coloured immigration (24% at year one and 22% at year two didn't know). Significantly, 66% also agreed there should be a control on white immigration. The apparent contradiction of a belief in the need for more minority police in a society one wishes to preserve from further immigration has already been mentioned. It was noted that special circumstances such as the role of coloured soldiers in the Military Police could account for apparently contradictory views. In one recruit's words, "We have had problems when I was in the military police with the coloureds. Until we got our own coloured bobby. He succeeded where we failed. It would help if there was more coloured police. Generally most whites accept coloured anyway. It's the other way round that's the problem". The following interview extract at the induction stage illustrates how apparently contradictory beliefs can be accommodated.

"It's just unfortunate that they're a different colour from what we are, but they talk English and they're the same as us. You get some very nice blokes, I've met quite a few. [In the services?] That's right. They would do anything for you. So as far as I'm concerned we are all equal. [Do you think there should be more of them in the police?] If they have got what it takes to get in the police, yeah . . . [Do you think there should be an end to immigration?] Yes, I do, yes. There's far too many people from abroad coming here now, taking a hell of a lot of houses with the English population homeless . . . [What about sending people back where they came from?] Yes, I'm all for it. I am really. I mean, it *is* England. They are homeless over there, but that's not our fault. I say look after number one, look after your own country first."

It would be hard to deny the officer's ability to ignore the consequences for the individuals to whom he feels positively of the policy he advocates at the close. But with what consequences for policing?

One way that attitudes bear on police action arises from the officer's understanding of the behaviour of people whose culturally-grounded assumptions about respect, assistance, humour and anger differ from his own. A lack of understanding and reliance on stereotypes can lead officers to assume that which must properly be proven. If as a consequence police resources are concentrated on those who are assumed to be responsible for, for example, the bulk of thefts from the person, there is a danger both that culprits who are not members of a visibly distinct group will escape and that the members of the visibly distinct group will become resentful and remote from the police. Home Office research shows that blacks have been most heavily arrested for two offences in which there was considerable scope for selective perception of potential culprits: violent theft, and being a 'suspected person', where the chances of arrest were up to fifteen times that of whites. These figures are so high that they prompt the question whether arrest rates accurately reflect the involvement of whites and blacks in criminal activity and, if not, whether the hypothesis that the suspicions of police bear disproportionately on blacks may account for some of the difference (Stevens and Willis, 1979). In the following response there are several references which indicate the details police use to gauge appropriate action. There is also an indication that the officer categorises groups according to their proximity to a consensual 'norm', sensing that all minorities suffer deprivation in degree of their distance from mainstream values. "Any frustrated minority, be it coloureds or terrorists, it's the same thing. Due to the circumstances they're in. It's partly their fault but partly the fault of society. [Do you think there should be more coloured people in the police?] Yeah. But on the other hand, they sometimes get backlash from their own population . . . You need to have very, very tolerant policemen . . . Certain sections [of the white population] would give black police trouble. There's always the odd Daily Express reactionary mucking about. The white police probably wouldn't have problems with the coloured population, apart from . . . the mob situation. Usually the coloureds [are] . . . very insular in that respect, especially the Asians."

He shows some sensitivity to cultural differences, while another drew on beliefs about coloured minorities to indicate the serious problems to be faced. "The immigrant population tend to think the police are just out to get them. I hope this situation will resolve itself over the next decade . . . There should be more coloured policemen . . . I don't think [whites] would take orders from a black PC. Because they will see him as coming from another country even though perhaps he's been born in this country . . . He probably would have problems being a black PC. He would have to be stationed where there is an immigrant community". The two responses share the underlying assumption that police are not agents of change. The potential of the police to lead the community to a less hypocritical racial politics is not part of their thinking. Further, to police effectively the constable must be 'like' the local public, and evaluate minorities from the perspective of those with whom they will have to work. As the following discussion suggests, dealings with different groups within the public was something of a preoccupation of probationers.

Most of those prepared to consider the position of black recruits adopted a stance that, like women, 'minorities' could be useful to the police in certain specialist roles: "There certainly should be more coloured police . . . [But] miners would probably call him 'bloody wog' . . . It would be a problem for them there. So you've got to use coloured policemen where there are coloured people". There was also a case where experience led a recruit to the idea that a large black recruitment could lead to attitude change, but in the black not the white community:

"You can't help group feeling whether you are a policemen or a black or all Masons. Group feelings exist, genuine feeling, you can measure that . . . You get a lot of trouble with minority groups because they don't understand why you do things . . . They treat him purely as an authoritarian figure, and in a lot of cases they're very freely-expressive people and express themselves by a dislike and a flouting of authority . . . The way to get round it is to have more coloured policemen. The coloured population will see there are people of their own group in the police. They're going to go one of two ways. If it's a very small minority of coloured people in the force they're going to call them Uncle Toms. But if they see larger numbers then they're going to think we can exist with them. They're less likely to think of the police as a white group or a front for the government".

That respondent couched his argument specifically in terms of mutual (mis)understandings. Others explicitly acknowledged their prejudice as a problem they had to work on: "That's something I'm going to have to get hold of. I am prejudiced, not against the people as such but they seem to have a fantastic chip on their shoulder, the coloured youth . . . It's something I'm going to have to come to

66

terms with. But so far, especially living in Moss Side, they're rude, they're arrogant, they have got a chip on their shoulder . . . Coloured policemen? Yes, it definitely helps. They would have more confidence in somebody of their own race . . . Because they tend to think we're prejudiced as well. That's one of the things that gives you the prejudice in the first place." This bespeaks a willingness to acknowledge one's feelings, and the extract bore a particular acute switch from denunciation of black youth to approval of black recruitment. A similar response demonstrates the thoughtfulness stimulated by facing the issue in previous work settings: "[There are] an awful lot [of problems]. You've got your own personal bias, which is built up over years, that you have got to control. You've got to relate to them as human beings before you start to relate to them as a problem. But there are problems and the biggest is that they build theirselves into a community and separate to us . . . But the majority of them aren't that bad. It's like talking about Sheffield Wednesday supporters club. They're a load of hooligans, but the majority of them aren't. I've met a lot of coloured people who did fantastic jobs in the hospitals". Those with some experience to go on endorsed black recruitment but for black areas only, while those without expressed unconcern or guarded attitudes. Black police, it seems, are likely to be alienated from their 'own' community, from the predominantly white areas they would police, and from the police culture the other constables find such a helpful resource.

There were a few responses from people who attributed their positive attitude to their own minority status: "I just look at them as the same as what I am. My parents are Polish. I could be black. Their parents are only the same as what mine are . . . There should definitely be more coloured police . . . It would be difficult [as a coloured PC] because some [citizens] are prejudiced, all the names you get called. [Do you think there should be an end to immigration?] No, not really". Counter-trend results were also recorded in the survey responses. At year one, 56% of recruits endorsed and 28% opposed mixed marriages, while by year two 71% endorsed them and only 12% disagreed. The one year stage also saw the highest level of support for an end to coloured immigration (65%), declining to 57% at year two. By this stage, probationers' attitudes are influenced more by their own policing experiences than by agencies of socialisation (Butler, 1982).

Where contact with minority groups is moderate or slight, the delicacy of the racial issue may make the probationers' manner with minority group people stiffly formal, and aggravate the contacts they do have. This is where training needs to intervene. The several positions which have been reviewed show that the issue is a live one and that probationers are thoughtful about the influence of their policework on minority groups. The grounds are there for training to draw this debate out of the canteen into the classroom. The practice situation is pre-eminently the focus for the detachment of officers' performance from their 'private' views. Beliefs invoked by questions at a general level are unlikely to be as pertinent as the features presented by the situation at hand. Where the suspect's demeanour, the patrol partner's disposition, the ethos of the shift, the nature of the offence and attitude of the victim all lend themselves to racist action, the officer's general beliefs on race may be relevant. Contemporary training appears to acknowledge only such gross cases.

Offenders and officers

There is also evidence that, while probationers do not excuse the responsibility of offenders for their actions, neither do they see them in an unrealistic light. First, there was an extreme uniformity of view regarding the statement "Criminals are sick people who need treatment". There was a concentration of responses in disagreement with this at year one and, indeed, 52% were in strong disagreement; the very small neutral figure (4%) is also noteworthy. The 'inverse' of this statement was the equally direct one that "Criminals should be hated". Exactly half the sample disagreed with this at year one, and there was 30% neutral response. While respondents do not excuse infraction neither do they believe it clearly represents evil in its perpetrator. The responses to the two items suggest the application of an occupational perspective—police see criminals as responsible for their actions and, therefore, as fair targets for enforcement, not as atavistic misfits.

The realistic trend in images of significant groups in the probationers' experience is also borne out in attitudes toward the police organisation. Responses to the statement "The police administration are out of touch with the ranks" show there is substantial perception of a gulf between management and ranks after the first year. Only 1% strongly disagreed, and 10% disagreed, while 22% were neutral; 42% agreed and 26% strongly agreed, so the bulk of the sample perceived the gap, a quarter strongly. This does not mean that the tension between idealism and instrumentalism has been dissolved. An index was the response to "A Police Constable's behaviour must be exemplary at all times". Overall responses ran from 28% strongly agreeing and 38% agreeing through 23% neutral, 8% disagreeing, and only 3% strongly disagreeing. After a year there were still a lot of 'idealists', but these figures do not represent the 'military' group, 16% of whom believed police behaviour need not be exemplary at all times, compared to 6% of 'civilian' respondents.

Debate and differentiation

The research findings were clearly relevant to the evaluation of conventional training. The pattern of attitude shift revealed the impact of training, its limits, and the varying influence of formal and informal elements of the training process. Overall there was a shift towards attitudes identified in previous research as distinctive of police occupational culture, but the present analysis emphasises that convergence is not absolute and a trend towards similar attitudes is not universal. People can be insulated from the effects of occupational culture by a variety of factors, eg, their previous education, experience similar to policing (such as military service), or the conscious design of police trainers. Furthermore, 'the occupational culture' is hardly as solidary and monolithic as it has often been depicted (see Fielding, 1987). It is desirable that there is diversity of opinion, not because the majority trend is necessarily undesirable, but because such diversity could be drawn on quite explicitly in training to provoke learning which would better prepare probationers for the flexibility they will need to display in routine police work. Society is complex and the role of training should be to make plain that there is diversity and that police officers should be ready for it, respecting it within the limits of the law and their practical discretion.

There are good grounds for arguing that recognition of the need to take account of people with differing perspectives and cultures is initially quite strong in recruits. For example, there is their early idealism and attitude toward social service. They perceive a diversity of police tasks and emphasise 'variety' as an attraction of police work. Patterns in the shift on various attitude items suggest substantial variation in views among probationers, even at the end of the probationary period. There has been a tendency for studies to fasten on the more gross changes in attitude, particularly those which suggest an intolerant, or even 'authoritarian' response. Such items occur in our data, too; for example, at induction some 24% agreed that most criminals prey upon society, but this mushroomed to 65% at year one and 68% at year two. Before one builds a case around such data it is worth examining not only several dimensions of the crime and punishment issue but also the size of counter-response. Probationers consistently and strongly agree that prisons should be places of punishment (88% induction, 93% year one, 86% year two). Further, around half (53%, 60%, 56%) endorsed punishment even if it did not fit the crime. However, about a third (36%, 23%, 32%) did not agree; they would not take things that far. This indicates a point of division among probationers, upon which training could capitalise. It could, for example, base discussion sessions around sets of case studies or imaginary scenarios posing different degrees and dimensions of 'wrongful arrest'.

Similarly expressive of diversity were views towards social services. It is widely argued that policing includes considerable social service work but that this is disliked by constables. Police generally display little regard for social workers (Punch, 1979). The pattern of response to the idea that 'social workers defeat justice by helping the criminal' suggests two things. First, there is a strong shift toward the view which is uncharitable about the effects of social work. The majority, 65%, disagreed with the statement at induction, but the disagreement fell, to 20% at year one and 25% at year two (with 58% and 47% agreement respectively). However, the second point to make is that both the counter-response, and the dip to the minimum disagreement at year one, suggest dimensions of response which are important to training but easily lost when one is preoccupied with the magnitude of the shift to a relatively harsh perspective. The counter-response still leaves fully a quarter of officers completing their probation who do not dismiss the efforts of social work with offenders. Moreover, the 'dip' implies that the view taken at the end of the first year's probation is an extreme. At the end of this first year, recruits have undergone their longest exposure to formal training (the Initial Course at the District Training Centres), followed by a sequence of specialist attachments, Tutor Constable attachment, and short returns to force training establishments for further formal training. In the year, they have experienced the contrast between formal and informal (on-the-job) training most sharply; it is during this year that the 'reality shock' of the recruits' first exposure to the work, and fit between it and what training taught them to expect, occurs. The second year views better represent the views new officers bear when their perspective is on a police career and some of the controversies of policing are resolved for them. Another instance was opinion on whether "criminals should be hated", where 77% did not agree at induction, and this dropped markedly to 50% disagreement at year one while returning to 69% disagreement at the end of probation. A number of individual attitude items show such a dip, with the second year response building back up to the earlier view, but at a reduced level, and the year one score showing the sharpest impact of views expressive of a jaded, hardbitten occupational culture.

Another line of argument may be applied to results which seem less equivocal. It is necessary to remember that attitudes are complex and cannot be captured by single items. The fact that, for example, a steadily increasing number did not think the treatment of criminals is too harsh (77% induction, 88% year one, 94% year two) does not close the matter. This item addresses the balance of punishment and rehabilitation. As we have seen from an earlier item, recruits believe prisons should essentially be about punishment. However, when one focuses on the issue of rehabilitation, one finds much less adamant and decisive views, with about a third agreeing that prisons confirm offenders in crime rather than rehabilitating them, a third disagreeing and a third unsure, both at years one and two.

Informal and formal socialisation

Recent attitude studies have acknowledged the non-linear course of police socialisation. Bennett (1984) advocates modifying the "socialisation hypothesis" to "employ the socialisation model's concept of directional change, yet instead of positing cumulativeness, focus upon the discrepancy between academic training and actual field experiences and behavioural expectation". Harris (1973), van Maanen (1975) and Niederhoffer (1967) suggest that field experience following academy training produces a state of reality shock. Expectations generated in formal training are often radically altered once the recruit begins actual police work (Bennett, 1984). As Bennett implies, the variability of early field experiences— notably, in our study, the Tutor Constable posting—drives recruits apart. Recruits initially move into line in the 'academy' but this is counteracted by field experience. The initial exposures to the realities of police work isolate rather than immerse recruits in the occupational culture. Bull (1986) has documented the resistance by experienced officers to ideas advanced by training and initially adhered to by probationers in their early field assignments. While there is a movement toward similarity of view and values in training, later in probation it is challenged by the very different experiences probationers have in the field. If the views and values promoted in training are positive while field experiences are negative, then this is clearly problematic. It implies the need to more closely 'manage' the probationers' attempts to make sense of their early field experiences.

Attitude research has increasingly highlighted 'environmental' factors over 'personality' factors. Butler and Cochrane (1977) point out that police spend much of their time with people at their worst: "It is not surprising if the corrupt, sordid, violent and acquisitive nature of man's inhumanity to man should shape his view of the world . . . The factors within the police environment strongly influence the course and direction of police occupational socialisation". The implication is that the influence on outcomes of everyday policing incidents are numerous, and a fixed measure of their weight cannot be assigned. Butler and Cochrane acknowledge this: "In the almost total absence of official guidance and direction, [the officer] is left to his own standards of discretion, being guided by the informal codes which exist within his immediate work group and the occasional 'hints' he may perceive as emanating from the policymakers". While law is an overarching constraint, it is also another source of ambiguity. It all leaves the probationers highly vulnerable to the idiosyncratic interpretations of others who are significant for them (the Tutor Constable, a sergeant, a strong-willed partner) but not necessarily to other probationers. The probationer is in a confusing and dangerous situation. Training may not be able to provide clear guidance but it could help probationers express the disparate demands and build confidence by the cross-fertilisation that comes from trading experiences.

There is no intrinsic value in studying attitudes; they are primarily useful as an index of change on the individual's part where that change can be related to some process the individual is experiencing. It is mistaken to aim at changing the probationers' attitudes *per se*; it is questionable whether underlying attitudes can be changed even in severe programmes of indoctrination (Becker, 1961). There is no merit in persuading individuals to adopt particular attitudes, but there is a great need to sensitise them to the existence of alternative attitudes on the part of others so they can grasp that their actions will need to take account of the different starting assumptions which others have.

There is no doubt that police hold strong views on many issues. But the nub of the matter is their relevance to actual behaviour. It is telling that the relationship between attitude and action is one of the most problematic in social science. Studies of experienced officers confirm there is no direct relationship between the attitudes expressed towards 'attitude objects' and police behaviour towards them. Thus, when Cruse and Rubin observed 1059 police/citizen interactions over a six-month period they found "a wide difference between attitude and behaviour, particularly in the areas of racial differences and attitudes. That is, while policemen might express highly prejudiced attitudes, they were rated as having behaved in an even-handed fashion with citizens . . . Programmes aimed at changing attitudes may not be as essential as programmes aimed at increasing the consistency and professionalism of police behaviour" (Cruise and Rubin, 1973). It is vital that training programmes provide for frequent 'debriefings' by which probationers can review their experience on the street and their observations of the various working styles of other officers, in the training setting, if the goal of consistency in practice is to be pursued.

The particular importance of formal and informal agencies of socialisation depends on the balance of training and operational experience. Formal organisation may be most persuasive at the earliest stage of induction, but the research indicates the limited duration of this influence. The 'idealistic' orientations of raw recruits begin to take on the 'instrumental' edge of veterans after one year of service. Their instructors often emphasise the value of street experience over the lessons of the classroom. Interview and observation data show that even within the formal socialisation programme the 'occupational culture' exercises a substantial influence. It is unreasonable to expect the influence of formal socialisation to be direct; individuals choose what they think valuable from the different approaches on offer. But once the recruit has earned the rewards the training school can give, by passing the various examinations, more tangible and longer-lasting rewards are on offer from other sources.

The 'stage model' of occupational socialisation should not be interpreted as a rigid one. The heuristic value of models of occupational career should not lead to the assumption of linearity. Occupational socialisation is a process of identity transformation and the stages do not have an inexorable dynamic (Manning, 1975). Issues such as whether to seek promotion, opt for a specialism, and remain in the force must be decided. One's self-identity can be crucially influenced by the role one performs at work. The results of the research illustrate the resilience of the recruits through the increasing instrumentalism of their approach to police work. The rising influence of the occupational culture, and the mediation of the culture by the recruits' own experience, accounts for the continuing ability of recruits to define policing as they do.

Training

The research data confirm that training has an impact on recruits, but also that its purchase declines as the corresponding impact of police experience increases. The police culture is pragmatic and puts great emphasis on 'commonsense' and 'experience'. But police seem unaware that, logically, these two qualities contradict each other. If policing is 'all about commonsense', why do people have to experience police work before they can understand it? Police work is a great deal more than 'commonsense'. This, and the brevity of the period when formal training can have peak impact on probationers, bear implications which police trainers should take to heart.

First, the structure of recruit training needs to interleave formal training and periods of field experience more intensively than at present. After the Initial Course, the Tutor Constable attachment need not be a block. Further, if probationers were brought back to training during this attachment for short (one- or two-day) seminars, their Tutor Constables should also attend. Trainers could focus on work of the sort probationers are practising (eg, injury accidents or car stops) to draw on the very recent experience of probationers with their tutors. Thought should be given to extending the Tutor Constable attachment, with frequent, short 'debriefings' and discussion seminars, at the expense of observational placements in specialist sections. Exposure to the work of CID or enquiry desk could wait until year two. If the objection is raised that the greater incorporation of Tutor Constables in training would deplete manpower, it should be noted that the reliance of shifts on inexperienced officers is already recognised as a problem and this would have the benefit of improving the quality of service the public received. As to the tutor's temporary absence, that is the cost of obtaining a better-trained probationer who will more quickly be able to take up the reins once training is completed.

Second, the practice in some forces of assigning a 'personal tutor' from training to liaise with the probationers while on attachments should be standardised. This is vital not only for its value in identifying problems as soon as possible and affording the probationer an image of the organisation to contradict the embittered views sometimes held by the experienced, but in making the Tutor Constable feel part of the training enterprises. There is strong evidence (Fielding, forthcoming) that Tutor Constable assessment of probationer performance is unsystematic, problematic (constables regard it as supervisors' work to perform staff appraisal) and not closely reviewed by the Tutor Constable's supervisors (so that unreliable judgements remain invisible). The incorporation of Tutor Constables into training is an urgent need and could provide a subsidiary means to disseminate innovations from training to the 'shopfloor'.

Third, training has for too long concentrated on rote learning at the expense of understanding. The great importance of legal input means that training the memory will always be a component of recruit training, but this need not be the model for imparting all that probationers need to know. Both mode and content need to change. The mode of the seminar should be preferred over the formal lecture wherever possible if probationers are to be kept on the right side of the 'learning curve'. What is intended is not just the 'question and answer technique' but a more genuinely discursive approach; debate and discussion need to be encouraged and bouts of questions and answers are not sufficient as a device to bring about a more interactive session.

Content is the main point, though. At present training programmes present social science material in a largely exhortatory way, as shown by interview responses where sociology lectures were seen as seeking to minimise the size of the coloured population. The image of social science is that of the 'do-gooder' discipline, exhorting constables to be nice to people they know little about but probably dislike. Social science could be used in a more applied way, to help recruits understand appropriate interactional tactics, how policing is actually done in multicultural situations elsewhere and so on. One may again take dealing with ethnic minorities as a type case for situations where officers must cope with the unfamiliar. Social science in training has a lot more potential uses than gingering up officers' 'views on race', where the fit between such broad beliefs and later action is highly problematic. Firmly attached to empirical policing examples, the 'right' course of action could be validated in terms of police practice and not in terms of 'good' racial sentiment.

Applied research on police work has moved a long way in the last decade. Trainers no longer need to be so concerned over 'theory' and the 'big issues'. The bulk of contemporary social research on policing concerns the nitty gritty of police work: interrogation and interview techniques, verbal and non-verbal interactional skills, negotiation and bargaining skills, deployment strategies and assessment skills. If trainers, and their probationers, still occasionally find the data controversial, it can only improve the quality of debate.

7 Police training: a skills approach

Leslie Poole

Training Strategy

Future developments in police training will be influenced to a significant extent by the following statement by the Police Training Council:

"Our actions are ultimately directed towards helping police officers develop the knowledge, understanding, skills and attitudes required to meet the needs of policing, present and future" (Police Training Council, 1985).

Does this herald a major change in police training? If so, how can it be implemented?

As the Director of the Home Office Central Planning and Training Unit, it is my responsibility to train police officers as trainers nationally, and to design, examine, and validate training courses throughout England and Wales except Metropolitan London, for all officers up to the rank of Inspector. For the more senior ranks, similar responsibilities are assumed by the Police Staff College. So far as constables, sergeants and inspectors are concerned, the task of transmitting the aim of the Police Training Council into a training strategy for future action rests primarily with my Unit.

The questions raised must be "Why is this change necessary?" and "How can it be achieved?" What must be clear from the outset is that the programmes we have embarked upon and will devise will be experiential. That is, they will be committed to developing all four elements—understanding, skills, attitudes and knowledge—which are all so essential to tackle policing in the 1990s (Further Education Unit, 1987). In all these respects we will be endeavouring to develop and build upon practical experience to produce a more competent and professional police officer.

In common with other writers in this collection of papers, my concern is how police training can impact on police/public relations. Implicit in the rationale of the Police Training Council's statement is the recognition of the need to develop such relationships. Policing a community and motivating and organising a workforce are analogous in many respects, particularly so when police officers are seen as managers of resources making autonomous and often independent decisions on the street. Many of the skills for both tasks are transferable. For instance, managers in both situations have to weigh up differing courses of action, examine all the implications, ask questions, process that information, delegate tasks, seek support or back-up, solve problems, make decisions, communicate those decisions to others, exercise discretion and apply policy or law. How these elements are handled and the judgement applied can very much affect sources of public dissatisfaction with the police.

The values and style of management of the most successful managers in industry are, I suggest, essential also for modern police managers. The best industrial managers have been those who demand high standards, are concerned with top quality service to their customers and have a high level of caring, consultation and discussion with their own workforce; who pass on information and both give *and* receive constant feedback on results; who can cope with frequent change, have a positive attitude and are supportive of new initiatives. Such concerns distinguish successful organisations from those that have foundered (Goldsmith and Clutterbuck, 1984; and Peters, 1982). The extent to which police organisations will be successful in the future must surely depend on such major issues as quality of service, concern for people within the organisation, willingness to take on new information and involvement of workforce and community in implementing change.

Can the attitudes and skills required by the manager of resources be developed or enhanced in police training? What is certain is that the development of these skills will not occur purely by chance. Partly, it can be tackled in training providing that certain assumptions are reconsidered.

First, there is the belief that training is mainly concerned with the inculcation of knowledge, and that a British secondary education teacher-centred model is still suitable for vocations such as the police (Education 2000, 1983). Second, the assumption that the appropriate skills for policing cannot be learnt at least in part within the training environment (Hind, 1986). Finally, it is often assumed that technical knowledge—in the police instance, legal knowledge, or an in-depth knowledge of management theories—is indicative of superior performance in an occupation. In fact, the most effective individuals in an organisation are likely to be those with a particular set of attitudes, high motivation *and* a good level of knowledge (Klemp, 1977). The most effective police officers and managers depend, significantly, on a high level of interpersonal ability and well-developed human skills. Most of those skills can be developed given an appropriate format and environment (McClelland & Winter, 1969).

Constables constantly say that their job is about applying the law in diverse circumstances, about helping others, negotiating, handling confronting situations, resolving issues, talking to people, assessing problems, making instant decisions, responding promptly to situations and dealing with stress in themselves and others. Many varied incidents require skills when dealing with people, knowledge and application of the law in its social context and helping in the solution of problems within the community. In asking where such skills and application were gained, the response has invariably been "through experience" or "by accident". Whatever else it might have been, it was not formal training that provided the opportunity to develop those skills. Most police officers were taught the law and experience was expected to do the rest. I believe, and research in education and other organisations indicate, that we can do better than that.

Is the academic training model adequate?

The major emphasis on training police officers has been to give them a thorough grounding in law by means of formal lesson presentation. We cannot, of course, criticise all police training in the past for adopting such a format. Why should police training historically have differed from the standards and approach which have prevailed in secondary school education? Whilst primary and junior education have, in many respects, been innovative, even creative, in involving questions of open learning, experimentation and a supportive environment, unfortunately secondary education has been far more restrictive. It has primarily been geared to university entrance and academic learning. Little concern has been expressed until recently about teaching life skills, preparing young people for a real and rapidly changing world and for a career which will probably not be for life (Education 2000, 1983).

Hitherto, the secondary education system has predominantly been concerned with the pursuit of factual knowledge and methods of assessment based on paper and pencil tests, centred around the repeating of information in order to gain entry into the university system. Teaching has been similarly concerned with the delivery of that information. The extent to which this approach fits vocational training, such as that for the police, is seriously questionable. It might well be asked to what extent university entry standards which relate to around 10% of the population should dominate or determine overall standards and training methods throughout vocational education. The reasons for retaining this model are particularly weak in relation to policing. The task itself is so involved with extremes of life and human behaviour in such diverse social situations that the workforce are primarily concerned with experience and practicality, not theory and classroom examinations.

Pouring in information in many types of vocational training does little to develop the skills and application necessary to carry out the job. "If you present information, information is what the students acquire . . . in discussion at least something has to go on in the students' minds before they speak" (Bligh, 1986). Even in purely academic terms, the levels of learning progress from recall, through comprehension to application and analysis.

During the past twenty years, the police service has tinkered with management training, social studies, social skills, community relations, race relations, human awareness training and other approaches. In the main it has adopted an academic model and school orientated teaching to achieve results (Poole, 1986). It has presented isolated packages of law, psychology, management, race relations, etc. The impact of this type of training on street level policing and the internal organisation has been relatively minor. As an example, successive generations of Metropolitan officers have learnt verbatim and been tested on a paragraph concerning their "attitude to the public". This requires them to recall that a police officer should "look on himself as the servant and guardian of the general public and treat all law abiding citizens, irrespective of their race, colour, creed or social position, with unfailing patience and courtesy" (Metropolitan Police, 1987). Good intentioned and wise as this advice may be, the impact of that learning on the behaviour and attitudes of officers might best be judged by reference to complaints statistics.

Only recently have training programmes been evaluated in an attempt to ensure that police training responses affect operational performance and the behaviour of officers on the street. The 2½-year project evaluating the Human Awareness Training programme in the Metropolitan Police is one such example. The programme itself is concerned with human skills as well as technical skills and is based on three fundamental strands involving self-awareness, inter-personal skills and community relations. Success in the latter, it is suggested, is dependent on development of the other two areas. The evaluation is in response to demands generated by the service for more effective training. The impact on police complaints has been analysed and a 17% reduction found in complaints against officers who received this module as part of their basic training (Bull, 1986). This finding reinforces the view that this training can and does impact on relations with the public.

Like many other organisations in the past the police service has pumped in information on management; covering such theories as those of Maslow (1954) and Herzberg (1966). But those theories have little effect on management techniques which are applied within the organisation subsequently or which produce the best managers. Similarly, with social skills of policing or community relations, the fact that officers can distinguish between repressed or sublimated aggression in a classroom or a textbook has never helped them deal with situations in practice, or given them strategies to reduce the confrontation where arrest is not called for. So it appears that while knowledge of community relations, West Indian history or geography is helpful in a contextual sense, regurgitating that knowledge is not likely to improve the community relations process or the interface between police and public on the street. In the same way, rote learning of police powers or the law never ensured correct application of it, or any concept in some officers of how it might best be applied. Intricate knowledge of the distinction between grievous bodily harm with or without intent is of little consequence in de-escalating a violent situation or in affecting an arrest. This type of knowledge, of whatever sort, underpins practical application and can develop understanding, but it does not provide the means to achieve solutions or the opportunity to practice the skills. In terms of developing community relations strategies, efforts to do so without developing awareness of self and skills in interacting with others are unlikely to be fruitful. Failure to integrate those skills thoroughly with the technical content is also likely to prove ineffective. (For an historical perspective on developments, see Poole, 1986).

Such ventures as Human Awareness Training were a response by the service to major changes in society and to reports proposing a significant change of emphasis (Scarman, 1981; Smith and Gray, 1983). New demands are constantly being made on the service and we can only anticipate that the rate of change will accelerate more rapidly in the future. Frequently discussed matters such as terrorism, air and sea hijacking, hostage negotiation, drug taking, solvent abuse, computer frauds involving millions of pounds, police firearms tactics, riot shields, flame proof overalls, police support units, rape crisis centres, victim support schemes, neighbourhood watch or multi-agency approach, were all unfamiliar twenty years ago.

How can we accommodate, in our professional training, the effects which the wider world and technological advance are having on British culture and, in its turn, the police service? Are we merely responsive to them or can we be more proactive? For example, racial conflict, satellite communications and media coverage are but three areas where actions and reactions are constantly at issue. Thus, Asian groups will demonstrate in Bradford and London within a few hours of events occurring on the other side of the globe. This, in turn, affects policing and the attitudes of the police organisation towards the press and Asians alike.

Of course, legislation has changed to deal with new problems, but there must also be personal and managerial adjustments to cope with changes which also affect our own lives. The nature of our society and the people in it inevitably provide not only changing community demands because it is a different public, but also affect the managerial view of what the police responses should be to those changes. The organisation itself must be substantially affected if it is to deal with changing demand and not adopt a traditional position that is out of touch with that change and the conflicting pressures to which police officers are subjected.

A practical, skills approach

Policing is a task founded and rich in experience. It has traditionally been geared towards action rather than academic theory. Far more functional then, to build on that approach and attempt to link the best of the experience with the more appropriate academic disciplines, rather than to adhere to a dysfunctional academic model of training for the police service.

For instance, how can the experienced criminal investigator dismiss the expertise of the psychologist in such areas as non-verbal communication, proxemics or kinesics on the grounds that those words are jargon and that the psychologists' practical experience of the right kind is negligible? In fact, those investigators themselves use similar techniques, perhaps unknown to themselves, but do not categorise their practices verbally. What is unfamiliar is the awareness of the process and the language in which it is disguised. To effect a realistic bridge between those two professionals will help to reduce substantially the time taken to acquire this so called 'experience' and become a more effective investigator. The police service cannot afford to disregard any means which might enhance investigators' effectiveness and, as an example, new courses in interviewing skills are incorporating this academic expertise.

If we accept that policing is so experientially based, then it will be no surprise to realise that the Central Planning and Training Unit is making extensive endeavours to make its training experientially based as well. To share experience, be it of life or policing, extensive opportunities must be given to deal with issues and resolve problems, using role play or simulation. This involves the creation of a learning environment which is participative and student-centred. Certainly, if police officers are going to have to deal with constant change—and that seems inevitable—then they should have the opportunity to develop their ability to learn and go on learning throughout their working life. That learning is developed by real experience and structured opportunities to consider and build on that experience.

Similarly, if police work is to solve problems and make decisions, as officers suggest it is, the training must provide open-ended situations in which those skills can be developed. In the same way, if their capacity to communicate, their general attitude and their ability to handle people are such crucial elements in dealing with incidents, the public and subordinates, then adequate provision must be made in the classroom to develop their inter-personal skills (Hind, 1986). That can no longer be accomplished by adhering solely to a 'talk and chalk' method in a legally based curriculum. It must be done using a variety of teaching methods in a training situation which aims to develop skills as well as knowledge, emphasises the practical nature of the task and incorporates opportunities to review and build upon the experiences of both trainer and trainee.

In a society where, since infant school, most of us have been accustomed to learning by being talked at by someone in a teacher role, who possesses all the knowledge and delivers it to the subordinate student, it is predictable that moving out of that strait-jacket and making a significant change is likely to be unfamiliar, and may be a painful process.

Functions of the Central Planning and Training Unit

Having discussed the rationale and need for this change of emphasis, how does this fit in to the practical context of the current work of the Central Planning and Training Unit (CPTU)?

Police training is being subjected to a number of reviews. In Probationer, Post-Probationer, Sergeant and Inspector Training and Promotion Examinations strenuous efforts are being made by many inside and external to the police service to improve the quality of training to make it more relevant to the daily task and to help the service maximise its human resources.

To match the Police Training Council's strategy, the thread running through all these reviews is a need for a more student-centred approach to learning, involving a lot of active participation. The demand is for the creation of more open-ended learning situations where problems can be shared and discussed, acted out in role play or simulation, or put on video and the performance analysed. This involves the development of many teaching methods to enhance the repertoire of the police trainer. It must develop skill without sacrificing knowledge. To do so the trainer needs to facilitate learning by others in a number of ways including giving them information. This will enable students to tackle simultaneously the four areas of the training strategy of skills, attitudes, understanding and knowledge.

Inevitably, this means a major change in the use of classroom time to develop skills and apply the law within the context of the community; in effect, to develop the manager of resources on the street referred to earlier. A major step towards meeting this need for skills-based training was to commence a new course for police trainers of 11 weeks duration in 1986. The course is geared towards a 'management' model of training, emphasising the acquisition and development of knowledge and skills in police officers. The course includes a variety of teaching methods designed to develop inter-personal skills, rudiments of counselling and assessing human performance. It also includes problem solving and elements of learning through experience. Students are encouraged to see themselves as 'learners' who will continue to learn throughout the rest of their service and beyond. In practical terms the course should have significant benefits in building co-operation between forces, District Training Centres and CPTU. Since early 1987 all trainers have spent one week of their three weeks' teaching practice in-force with classes other than Initial Course students. This, we hope, will help to encourage new developments in training when officers with experience can come face to face with experiential learning.

This training course is the main thrust of the work of CPTU. It forms a sound basis for anyone who fills any training post in which dealing with people or making sensitive judgements is an essential element.

The Unit continues to run specialist courses for drill, physical training and self defence. It is also responsible for designing national curricula and providing audio visual support for non-specialist courses for all ranks below chief inspector. Hence, we are writing courses for public order training. At the same time we are examining and developing the Stage II recommendations on Probationer Training, (MacDonald et al., 1987) in so far as they are consistent with the Police Training Council's strategy.

Presently, the CPTU syllabus for the 2-year probationary period in all forces (except the Metropolitan) and at District Training Centres is predominantly legal and technical in content. It is geared primarily to the learning of the law through

79

classroom lecture, supported by some practical exercises and some social skills lessons (which are not integrated with the mainstream of the curriculum). My Unit prepares the examination questions for Training Centres based on the legal content of the syllabus. Marks achieved in written examinations are the major method of assessing potential to become police officers.

For the future, we envisage the first 8 months of the 2-year probationary period will be a sandwich course. It will interlink theory with practice by interspersing periods of police duty with formal training. The emphasis will be on debriefing and utilising that practical experience and relating it to both legal knowledge and human skills using student-centred teaching methods. The syllabus will fully integrate the legal, interpersonal and community dimensions of policing. A variety of appropriate learning tasks will be devised to achieve this integration, and ensure that the themes will be geared towards the development of those practical abilities which are essential to all effective police officers. Assessment methods will extend far beyond written tests to include practical performance, in order to produce a profile for students indicating their personal strengths and weaknesses in the critical areas of ability required to do their job.

There is also a full-time team of six officers, half provincial, half Metropolitan, who have designed the curriculum for a new Sergeants' Course and are presently constructing a new Inspectors' Course. More so in supervisor training than constable training, there are rarely right or wrong answers to given management situations. There is no formula which, when applied, will result in an appropriate response in a given situation (Management Review Team, 1987). The aim of this management training programme is to have a realistic perspective and situations in which the student can test out various possible solutions in a supportive environment. The purpose here is to learn from the classroom experience with support and guidance from a trainer and not to produce 'the only solution' or to avoid making mistakes at all costs for fear of ridicule. This style of training is already being attempted in some forces and the differing teaching styles are very much in line with the aims of our new eleven-week course for trainers.

Training for prospective supervisors pre-supposes that the examination which qualified them for that post (plus subsequent in-force interviews) adequately fits officers for the post of sergeant or inspector. The Promotion Examinations are now being questioned from a variety of sources as to what exactly they are testing, their relevance to policing and the emphasis on pure recall of information *vis-à-vis* comprehension, application, managerial potential or decision making skills. Consequently, the Promotion Examinations Unit which forms part of CPTU is now engaged, on behalf of the Promotion Examinations Board, in reviewing the examinations structure. Over the next 2 years we are looking at a more practical style of examination particularly related to the police officer's practical and operational management role. This is likely to be geared to the specific abilities identified by the Sergeant/Inspectors' Review. This project will take the Examinations Department into entirely new areas of assessment of candidate ability which are already being tackled in the medical profession and progressive management in industry, but by few others.

My team are involved in the preparation of a central curriculum for post probationer training which the staff associations and CPTU anticipate will meet national demands. The legal element—updating on legislation—would be separated from the core of the course and provided in a simplified form, explaining the law in straightforward language with graphic interpretation. Less turgid than the legal textbook and less time consuming than formal classroom presentation, these notes can form the basis of a training session in person or on video, according to force practice. The core of the syllabus will be prepared at CPTU in accordance with an agreed syllabus tackling matters of national and general concern. Matters of local concern are best dealt with on a local basis. Such a model involves CPTU being less prescriptive in its role and more responsive to forces' needs. Agreeing the outline of a course and producing specimen exercises for each component and establishing, through monitoring, that courses are meeting the agreed basic criteria will be the tasks for the future. Hence the CPTU role is to co-ordinate central training in a more systematic but less directive manner and to update material on an ongoing basis and to evaluate its effectiveness.

The whole question of update and review of training is a matter which in the past has been left to ad hoc meetings to resolve, usually years after courses are manifestly out of date. The recent appointment of a number of additional staff to my Unit to evaluate and monitor national training material and to assist in piloting and validation, should alleviate the need to update courses long after they are known to be defunct. This, in effect, is a quality control function for the Unit. Constant review and monitoring, regular contact with force training departments and the three representative organisations will, I believe, ensure a much more dynamic response to constantly changing needs in society and the service and enable prompt changes to be made to materials and syllabi. We are anxious to develop relationships between the Unit, the various forces and the District Training Centres in order to encourage a better trust and communication for the benefit of the service. In doing so, we hope to encourage best practice throughout the service with CPTU the centre of a 'wheel' evaluating contributions and suggestions, servicing and disseminating best practice to others.

Another area new to CPTU is the development of materials and expertise in the educational sphere. Presently, our legal research facilities are well established and, I believe, held in high regard. But, if the police service is not to operate in a vacuum and is to remain reasonably on target with its training, it must also keep in touch with developments in vocational, professional and management education in other fields. This aspect of our role is just beginning to develop.

Sustaining change and its purpose

One of the difficulties in coping with the management of so many major changes is the need to keep interested parties in touch with what is going on. Dealing with innovation, implementing change and apprising everyone of the process still requires that the existing system be serviced until the new developments can be put in place. It inevitably requires a willingness by all those affected to deal with the change and be supportive during the time that the two systems are operating in tandem but, sometimes, apparently, at variance. The need to remain constructive, objective and open-minded is of primary importance and, provided that the common goal of producing a first-rate police officer remains our ultimate joint aim, then we will be capable of dealing with the change.

If training is to have credibility in its design and real impact on policing it must utilise the street experience of operational officers and promptly respond to their needs and those of the community. Training, *per se,* has little value and is a very costly process if it is out of line with service and community needs. It is essential for the Unit to be pragmatic and up-to-date in its provision of national training packages by taking account of recent events and developments. Constructed packages for whatever course, rewritten every 7 or 8 years will give CPTU no credibility, give the service no confidence in its efforts and, above all, will not give the operational officer what he must have.

The message from police officers is clear. They want the skills, knowledge, abilities and understanding to be effective in their role and improve the interface with the law-abiding majority of the public they serve. The Central Planning and Training Unit is dedicated to meeting those demands. When our training impacts on improving the human face of policing in Britain then we will indeed have made a 'real' contribution.

The encouragement of officers of high quality to become trainers will assist this process, but that can only be a realistic objective if the skills required to become an effective trainer reflect those required in the operational sphere. Emphasis on the right attitude, the best image, adequate knowledge, practical and human skills and police experience will give training the credibility it should have, whether that training is in the classroom or on the job. What must be constantly be borne in mind is that the changes being made in training are not merely taking place for change's sake. The goal is to improve the relationship between police officers and the community and to make a realistic contribution to effective and practical policing by developing human as well as technical skills.

8 Police training for the 1990s: the divisional commander's perspective

Anthony Butler

Commanding a police division presents many challenges today, and there is no evidence the job is going to become easier in the next decade. The divisional commander's primary responsibility is to use the resources at his disposal to provide the best possible service to the people who live and work on his division. The most valuable resources are the personnel under his command, and if they are to respond to the demands of policing today, they have to have the appropriate knowledge, skills and attitudes to perform effectively. Training has a key role to play in ensuring officers and civilian support staff have these knowledge, skills and attitudes. Therefore, from the divisional commander's perspective, he requires a training system to provide such personnel. However, the pressures are such that he is going to expect far more from his staff in the 1990s. Every day spent by one of his staff in training is one day less in operational policing or time spent by a civilian employee in supporting operational officers. In other words, divisional commanders are expecting training departments to develop more efficient methods of training to produce the same results but in less time—give better value for money. Occasionally, cynics have been known to suggest that divisions are there to provide the training department with people to fill their classroom. This is an overstatement, but in the future training departments will have to ensure they have due regard for the training needs of their customers—the operational commanders and their staff.

This chapter will be looking at the role of training in helping divisional commanders solve basic policing problems in the next decade. The challenges of policing in the years ahead will only be met by high quality personnel, trained in response to needs identified by operational commanders, and by training methods which minimise the amount of time they spend away from productive work.

In recent years there has been research to elicit the significant differences in the operational and managerial responsibilities of sub-divisional superintendents and divisional chief superintendents. As a consequence, there has been a redefinition in some forces where the responsibilities of the latter officers have been distanced from operational command with consequently greater emphasis on what has been termed 'inspectorate' functions. The issues discussed in this chapter are not affected by this distinction, because the theme is one of improving the quality and reliability of service to the public by improving the knowledge, skills and attitudes of officers. This responsibility is equally applicable to chief superintendents in traditional operational command or in roles which emphasise their monitoring, co-ordinating and staff-development functions.

* The views expressed in this chapter are those of the author and do not necessarily reflect the policies of his present or previous forces or of the police service in general.

Policing in the 1980s

Before looking towards the 1990s and possible training developments for the coming decade, there is a need to establish a context. This will be done by looking at policing landmarks during the present decade and attempting to identify training opportunities which have been grasped and those which need to be further developed and continued into the years ahead. There are a number of dangers in making assumptions about historical events which occurred in the recent past. It is very easy to identify some issue as having immediate importance but, in the longer historical context, the same event may prove to be of only minor concern. With this proviso, three events or trends appear to stand out as policing landmarks.

(i) Scarman Report

On any analysis the urban riots of 1981 had a substantial impact on many areas of policing. The Scarman Report on the disturbances whilst not covering all the issues was, in itself, a landmark event: one simple message which it gave chief constables was that policing in the future must reflect the needs of the community being policed. It was no longer appropriate for local police commanders to make assumptions about what was good for their community and then deliver that product. This was in no sense an abdication of operational policing responsibility, but was simply an extension of the consumer politics which had been growing during the previous decade. One of the consequences of this view was Section 106 of the Police and Criminal Evidence Act 1984 which obliged police forces to make arrangements for obtaining the views of people in their area about matters concerning the policing of the area.

If the consumers' needs were going to take a higher profile, then Scarman questioned the abilities of the police to deliver. The delivery of community-sensitive policing, in Scarman's analysis, depended on the recruitment of the right people into police work and their subsequent training and management. Unfortunately, the only evidence submitted to Scarman in relation to police officers' attitudes during training was of dubious quality (see Butler, 1982). However, it was clear that probationer training would benefit from a detailed review. Scarman also pointed to the need for senior officers to be made aware, in a more formal sense, of the difficulties of policing multi-racial and deprived populations and the complexity of managing police operations in such circumstances. One of the consequences of this observation was the establishment of the community relations training initiative at Brunel University.

(ii) Public Order Operations

The recommendations made by Lord Scarman were essentially looking towards the longer term for the prevention of public disorder and the improvement in police-community relations in those neighbourhoods where they were being strained, possibly by insensitive policing, but more likely by the oppressive combination of social, economic and racial deprivations. In the shorter term, the police service recognised that outbreaks of public disorder had taken a quantum leap by both the violence shown to the police and the resort to weapons such as petrol bombs. There followed a thorough national review of public order tactics which led to improved training and contingency plans for co-ordination of large numbers of police officers in response to outbreaks of public disorder. The miners' dispute demonstrated the thoroughness of these preparations. The political implications of the policing of the miners' dispute may be subject to debate, but what is clear from that year is that the police were not overwhelmed by the sheer force of numbers deployed during the dispute.

Unfortunately, the disturbances in Birmingham and London in 1985 did, once again, demonstrate a shortcoming in police training and preparation. In these events, it was not the individual constables and sergeants who were ill prepared. The shortcomings were in two areas: first, the rapid build-up of manpower was hampered by inadequate mobilisation plans and, once the manpower had arrived, communications difficulties in the field caused problems of co-ordination. The second major problem, however, was the lack of training and preparation of ground commanders.

(iii) Operational Effectiveness

The police service was rather slow initially in realising that public sector financial restraint included itself. The first hint came in 1982, when the then HM Chief Inspector of Constabulary alerted chief constables to a particular question for the coming inspection round. This question was concerned with the chief constable's identification of operational policing priorities, the deployment of resources to attack these problems and, the sting in the tail, the degrees to which chief constables had established appropriate procedures to evaluate their achievements. This initial hint was followed very closely by the circulation of the draft version of what was to become Home Office Circular 114/1983. This draft was greeted with less than enthusiastic response by some chief constables perhaps who saw it as an interference with their operational prerogatives and, in some cases, were dismissive of the need to introduce into the service such concepts as effectiveness and efficiency. Since the publication of that circular in November 1983, few if any chief constables would now claim that value for money, operational effectiveness, and political accountability are not on the agenda. In terms of landmark events the ripples, if not tidal waves, are being felt throughout many forces where organisational changes have been quite radical in response to the demands for greater cost effectiveness. There have been substantial increases in the number of civilian support staff recruited to police forces and the use of new technologies such as dictation equipment, word processing and micro computers have all brought with them managerial problems to be solved.

Divisional Commander's Responsibilities

The three watershed events of the Scarman Report, the escalation of public disorder and demands for operational effectiveness, have threads running through them which provide a link. From the divisional commander's perspective in dealing with public order, whilst the events leading to the disorder and the actual incident are traumatic and pose significant problems, they are thankfully relatively rare events. Indeed, Scarman would argue that by developing an appropriately sensitive and accountable police service, many of these incidents could be either anticipated or prevented. For the remainder of this chapter the technical aspects of dealing with public disorder, such as the provision of training, equipment and the application of specific tactics will not be considered further. That is not to discount the impact of public disorder, but this will be implicit in other issues which will be examined in detail.

There are some interesting similarities to be seen when considering the government's Financial Management Initiative and Scarman's plea for more accountability and improved management and training. Scarman argued for these improvements from the point of view of a better police service; the Financial Management Initiative assumes at least the maintenance of the existing service or an improved service, but is seeking this goal whilst at the same time constraining public resources. In this environment, the principal responsibilities of divisional commanders has been to continue to provide a service of high quality and reliability in the face of rising demand on his manpower and, in some cases, real reductions in those resources.

Quality and reliability of service will continue to be an issue for divisional commanders into the next decade, together with a number of subsidiary but related responsibilities:—

1. The achievement and demonstration of a policing service which is locally sensitive and accountable.
2. An ability to think and plan strategically.
3. The development of innovative and novel solutions to policing problems.
4. The integration of increased numbers of civilian support staff.
5. The exploitation of new technology both to improve operational effectiveness and as a means of providing information for decision making. The ability to get the maximum effort and contribution from those resources avaliable.
6. The ability to monitor and evaluate performance and innovation on a continuing basis.

Quality and reliability of service

Whilst many of these responsibilities have traditionally fallen to the divisional commander, there is a new emphasis on accountability and value for money which pervades all of them. For example, there has always been a responsibility to provide high quality and reliable service; however, the new dimension is the need to establish the criteria on which the standard of service will be judged and, thereafter, be prepared to measure it. The context of this paper is training in the next decade, therefore, unless it can be demonstrated that there are some shortfalls in the quality and reliability of service and the other issues raised above, then there are no reasons to change current practice, in short, no problems to solve.

One way to approach this question of current performance is to consider one divisional commander's own experience in a large urban police force. Over a period of five years the number of calls received by the division has increased by nearly three-quarters. In the same period there have been no additional police officers or cars. All calls, whether received at a central control room servicing the whole force or at the sub-divisional stations, are recorded on a computerised command and control system. This system is operated by a sergeant at the sub-division who is responsible for despatching officers to deal with the caller's requests or incident. During this period of increasing workload, no formal policy has been defined to establish guidance as to which calls can and should be dealt with over the telephone, or diverted to other agencies or bodies, or simply not given any police action. As a consequence, there have developed informal systems and practices simply to cope with all the calls coming in to the system. This has led to some useful and effective innovation. It has also created considerable stress for the sergeants because they do not have any formal policy on which to rely when members of the public make complaints about such matters as delays in response. Furthermore, there are times when some calls do not receive a response when there is a need.

Things have now reached a point where it is not a matter of managing calls through some graded response arrangement; there simply are too many calls for the officers to deal with. The quality of the service given is more and more coming to depend on the time of day, shift or the number of previous calls received. In effect, the quality and reliability of service has become subject to random and arbitary events and decisons.

When these points are raised with sub-divisional superintendents they are unable to suggest criteria on which the standards of service to the public can be measured. However, when more detailed observations are made of the officers who are receiving calls, there is evidence of ways in which the service could be improved by more courtesy and more effective communication strategies. Information from callers is being lost because officers seem unable to ask the right questions.

In summary, the problems are:—
1. The handling of calls has not been the subject of strategic policy-making.
2. Quality of service is not established at a policy level.
3. Current standards of service are random and arbitary.
4. Improvements to the handling of calls may be inhibited by the quality of existing communications skills in officers.

Sensitive and Accountable Policing

When the problems of increased workload and static resources were raised with a group of experienced constables and sergeants they suggested the answer was to 'educate the public' to expect less. This approach raises two issues: first, it implies a notion that the customers will have to accept what is given to them and that any resistance can be overcome by 'education'. The second more important point is the implication of a paternalistic relationship with the public: they, the public, are not going to be part of the debate of how the police will manage increasing workload and static resources; they will not be offered options as to what elements of the service could be discontinued. The implication is that the police will decide what is 'good' for the public, and then educate the public to accept it.

At the command level, consider the following example. At a meeting of a police consultative committee, the chairman is criticising the police:—

"We have been raising these community problems for some time and all that happens is that you tell us what the police cannot do because there are not enough men. You have choices as to how you use your men and you have not explained why some cannot be used to deal with our problems. When we talk about taking our own action, having residents patrolling some of the areas at risk, you accuse us of being vigilantes."

These two examples provide evidence of the same problem:— All officers need to accept the contribution of the consumer of police services to the design of those services. This realisation is equally important for both the officers providing the service and those of more senior rank who are responsible for developing policy. The aim is to show policing to be sensitive and accountable to the needs of the community.

Strategic thinking, innovation, planning and evaluation

Strategic thinking is the key to improving the performance of the sub-division. A simple test which the chief superintendent can use is to ask his sub-divisional superintendents, "On what criteria do you want me to judge the improvements you have made to the quality of service delivered by your sub-division in 12 months' time?" The depth of the answer will demonstrate the quality of vision and commitment. In pursuing the question further, plans will need to be drawn, and these provide an opportunity to judge the quality of leadership and understanding of police effectiveness.

Strategic thinking is essentially a process of rational problem identification, analysis and choosing options for action. Consider an example of this process in action:—

The sub-division is confronted with a large increase in the number of thefts from parked cars. There are two concentrations of these crimes, one around a sports centre and another in a public car park. The superintendent proposes to use a crime prevention campaign and uniformed patrols to reduce these crimes. The divisional commander then asks questions about the proportion of cars left unlocked, or that have valuable property on display, and what is the predominant means of entry to the cars. The data available does not include the figures showing how many cars were insecure, or whether property was left on display. However, the analysis does show that the majority of property stolen is fitted to the vehicles, namely radios and stereo equipment, furthermore there is an increasing tendency to break the windows of cars to gain access. There are insufficient officers to deploy them on a regular basis to the two car parks in a preventive patrol tactic, but of more significance is the evidence that when this tactic has been tried in the past, the offences have been displaced elsewhere.

There is less chance of solving policing problems when their true nature is unknown because of an incomplete analysis. In this case there is little point in making a major effort to get people to secure their cars if criminals are simply going to break windows to steal. To plan to use manpower without first establishing its availability is naive, and to adopt tactics which have unwelcome consequences is hardly professional. The process of rational problem solving also requires proper objective evaluation, and when the starting point is unknown or vague because the initial analysis is incomplete or slipshod, subsequent measurement of effectiveness is impossible.

When the sub-division was forced to reconsider the analysis of known facts, they realised the need to take an innovative approach to this problem. As a consequence it was argued that the random time and geographical distribution of these incidents made the single approach of targeting the offences inefficient and too manpower intensive. However, the targeting of the relatively few known or suspected criminals active in this type of crime was likely to be more efficient and require less manpower. A plan was made which included detailed crime analysis linked to criminal profiling and surveillance training. As a result of careful preparation, within 10 days of the start of the operation five of the targeted offenders had been observed breaking into cars and stealing property. When arrested they admitted more than 50 other similar offences.

The difference between the first approach and the second exemplifies the chief superintendent's problem. He has to ensure the resources under the command of his superintendents are used to the maximum effect. He requires senior officers who:—

—will look forward with vision and imagination, rather than backwards;
—will be able to think strategically and develop policy accordingly,
—will recognise the need to employ rational problem identification and solution techniques to their planning; and
—will be capable of measuring their operational achievements and undertaking objective evaluations of the results.

The 'People' Dimension

Understanding the notions of standards of service within a framework of sensitivity to community needs, and the application of rational management methods are prerequisites for making progress in the delivery of police services in the next decade. But there is another essential ingredient—the 'people' dimension. It is essential for managers to understand that they will only be as successful as the extent of the commitment they can achieve from the people they lead. This is the 'people' dimension. It is likely there will only be very small increases in police establishments in the next decade. The case for such increases seems to become increasingly difficult to justify to the satisfaction of the Home Office. In this situation, the husbanding of manpower to achieve the maximum results will become more, rather than less, important. The divisional commander requires managers who are capable of releasing the full motivation of the people they command.

Civilianisation and New Technology

To a degree, the changes of approach to issues of quality of service, sensitivity, accountablility, strategic vision and innovation, are simply differences of emphasis in what have been traditional policing methods. However, the significant increase in the numbers of civilian staff, particularly into areas which have traditionally been regarded as only capable of being undertaken by police officers, are real changes of substance. The same point can be made in relation to new technology such as micro computers and word processors. The full potential of these new personnel and the exploitation of new technology require new management skills and basic knowledge. For example, officers in supervisory ranks are trained in respect of police discipline procedure, but there seems to be a very limited knowledge of civilian staff conditions of service and discipline procedures. There is also a need to recognise the subtle differences of style required for the management of civilian support staff, and to recognise their personal and career aspiration within an overall personnel policy.

The major strides which have been made in recent years to increase the power and potential, and reduce the cost, of micro computers opens major opportunities to increase the effectiveness of police operations and massively increase the efficiency of administrative systems. The extent to which police forces will be able to grasp these opportunities will depend on the degree of imagination and understanding of these systems by police managers. The requirement for strategic planning assumes decisions being made on the basis of facts and their objective analysis. All police forces collect mountains of facts and figures about their work, but how many senior police managers use micro computer modelling to assist them to use this information to make strategic decisions? The divisional commander requires people in his management teams who have some basic understanding of computer systems and the opportunities they present. Computer literacy is now a requirement in police managers.

These examples provide some cause for concern because there is prima facie evidence of gaps in the knowledge, skills and attitudes of officers at several levels which are inhibiting improvements in the quality and reliability of the policing service delivered by the division. A primary concern of the rest of this chapter will be examining ways in which these gaps in knowledge and skills can be addressed. Before moving towards proposals for solutions it will be useful to examine the general trends in training provided in the force.

Force training today

There is no doubt that the world in which police officers are expected to work has changed dramatically since 1981. One might expect that these changes would be reflected in the training provided by force training systems. To pursue this proposition, the training courses of a large urban police force provide the following useful case study. Two related themes will be emphasised: first, the investment which is made in various forms of police training; second, the return which can be measured in terms of the everyday needs of the divisional commander confronting the problems described in the preceding section.

The case study will consider the training courses provided during 1986. In-force training for probationary constables used 8965 man-days in addition to the time the officers spent at the district training centres. To show the drain on operational resources represented by this figure, it is the equivalent of more than 36 officers being engaged full time on training throughout the year. Probationer training has recently been the subject of a searching review on behalf of the Police Training Council (Macdonald *et al.*, 1987) and therefore will not be considered in detail here, except to make the point that the employable cost, that is the cost of salaries, rent allowance and all other overheads of these officers, was just short of three quarters of a million pounds for the year.

General training for constables in the force covers three areas, refresher training, courses for beat officers and tutor constables. This training accounted for 6855 days. Pre-promotion and refresher training for sergeants accounted for 2140 days and training for inspectors accounted for a further 2050 days. Public order training, which was primarily for constables, sergeants and inspectors used a total of 4440 days. Training in the use of the computerised command and control system, the PNC and teleprinters accounted for 2387 days. It apparently requires the same amount of time—five days—to bring a constable up to date in his five-yearly refresher course, as it does to learn how to operate the PNC. Training for criminal investigation officers accounted for 3350 days. All these training courses account for 21,222 days. or the equivalent of more than 86 police officers full time over the year. However, there is still one massive area of training which has not been listed: this is driver training, and it accounted for 16,601 man-days or the equivalent of more than 67 police officers during the year.

Sergeants received 15 days of training immediately prior to promotion and then received another 5 days at five-yearly intervals. A sergeant who attended a course in 1986 had not received formal training since 1981, that is before Scarman, before Home Office Circular 114/83 and before the introduction of the annual setting of operational objectives on the policing by objectives model. With these major changes in mind, how was a course held in 1986 viewed by a sergeant?:—

"I think the two weeks was a chance to relax, get away from the pressures of the sub-division . . . From what I recall it was mainly going over new legislation . . . they spent a lot of time on drinking and driving law. This was not very interesting to me because I had spent the past three years on the Traffic Division and was up to date on this . . . We had some visiting speakers but they were not very relevant. For example, someone came to talk to us about community relations. It was the sort of lecture they give to probationers about customs, religions and so on. We had had it all before and there was nothing new in what he had to say . . . As far as management topics were concerned we didn't have any. We were asked to give a four-minute talk about our own sub-divisional objective for the year on the first day of the course. I think it was a way to get everyone introduced. But after that we never talked about objectives again during the two weeks."

This course has now been replaced with an annual one-day course which takes place on divisions and includes constables.

There is no facility for periodic refresher training for inspectors. After the initial post-promotion course and development course, inspectors are left to engage in self-development if they are so motivated. In terms of commitment, training for inspectors represents fewer man-days than refresher training for drivers. In fact, 7.7 times more days are spent annually on driver training than on training inspectors. The promotion opportunities for inspectors to rise above this rank are very limited and as a consequence, there are many inspectors on divisions who may spend over 15 years in the rank without any further training in areas of management development.

The overwhelming emphasis of current training is on the delivery of basic services. There is little or no apparent recognition of the need to ensure that existing resources are used to their best effect by developing the conceptual skills and attitudes of managers. This is not because forces do not have a commitment to training. Indeed, the reverse seems to be the case: for example the recommendation for training for operators of the HOLMES system is for an initial course of four weeks followed by refresher training at the rate of two days per two months. The problem seems to be a lack of vision and understanding about the contribution training has to make to enable police forces to meet the challenges of the next decade. Perhaps this apparent lack of vision and incisiveness could be overcome by a clear statement of current problems facing the force and an agenda for action where training can make a contribution to the solution of those problems.

The overwhelming conclusion which can be drawn from the force training profile is the emphasis it places on the 'doing' of police work, and the very limited reference to the areas of conceptual skills and attitudes. Earlier in the chapter, reference was made to the demands on divisional commanders to respond to the challenges presented in policing in a new era of 'value for money'. The primary responsibility of the chief superintendent to ensure the quality and reliability of service, it was argued, was inexorably linked to six subsidiary responsibilities. All these responsibilities were examined from the division commander's perspective, to establish if there were any deficits in the knowledge, skills and attitudes of his officers. Training departments are founded on the assumption that the ability to do work effectively depends on the individual's knowledge, skill and attitude. Therefore, before moving to the final part of this chapter, it will be useful to summarise the apparent deficiencies in knowledge, skill and attitudes which were identified from day-to-day policing experience.

1 The quality of police response to calls has suffered in the face of increasing workload by a failure to develop strategic policy to pre-empt the problem, and a failure to develop a means of objectively defining and measuring appropriate standards of service. On the level of service delivery, improvements are being inhibited by the communications skills and attitudes of officers and civilian support staff receiving calls.

2 The reluctant acceptance of a consumer orientation by senior managers, operational officers and civilian support staff is inhibiting the full development of a policing service which can be demonstrated to be sensitive to community needs and also producing hard quantifiable results.

3 Officers with managerial responsibilities must be visionaries who are capable of getting to the heart of the problem by a rational system of problem solving. Their leadership must be exercised on the basis of striving for clear goals with no doubt in anyone's mind that results will be measured.

4 The effective managment of resources demands people skills to realise the full potential of the staff.

5 To further the effective management of resources, there is a need to integrate civilian support staff into the total efforts of the division.

6 The complexity of policing, the volume of information gathered and the demands for decision based on facts rather than assumptions, requires a recognition of the contribution which can be made by new technology, in particular, computers.

Force training in the future

The problems facing the divisional commander illustrated by the case examples point to various training needs. But the review of current force training raises serious questions as to its capacity to meet these needs. Therefore, there is some value in re-appraising current training strategy with a view to developing training for the future.

Training should not be seen as an end in itself—it has a purpose. This purpose is to make the force effective in meeting its obligations which, in the main, can be defined as the maintenance or improvement of its standard of service. The value of training has to be seen against this criterion. If training does not make a difference to the quality and reliability of service delivered, then it is redundant. Consider, for example, the value of driver training. To meet the demand for value for money, the training department should be able to demonstrate a clear link between the level of driving standards demanded and some output measure such as rate of accidents per mile driven. The measure would have to be statistically sound to control for other variables such as weather conditions, time of day, traffic volume and personal characteristics of the driver such as age and so forth. When all these variables were established, then the value of driving courses could be measured. In the absence of these criteria, standards set by the driving school are arbitrary. The same argument holds true for all training. There is a requirement for its value to demonstrated. There must be established relationships between the training given and the quality and reliability of police services delivered.

Defining Training Needs—for today

Despite the watershed developments of the past few years, a significant proportion of training needs will remain largely unchanged. The role of training departments in respect of these continuing training programmes is to be able to sustain them on the basis of objective task analysis and to be able to assure members of the force, HM Inspectorate and the police authority, that training is delivered in the most cost effective way.

Text books on the management of training describe the use of needs analysis or task analysis to establish training requirements and objectives (Davies, 1971). Task analysis is one of the primary sources for the identification of training needs, and therefore it is vital to ensure its reliability and validity. Unfortunately, there are some examples of very inadequate task analysis, which can lead to expensive mistakes in the design of training schedules.

In 1984, a report was prepared concerning the management training needs of sergeants following an analysis of a nationwide questionnaire survey (Franklin *et al.*, 1984) The questionnaire listed 96 tasks, and respondents were asked to indicate the average frequency with which each task occurred, and score the task on a range of 'difficulty' and 'personal importance'. There are some questions as to the quality of this research which raise doubts about its value as a basis on which to design management training for sergeants. The survey did not establish a baseline of knowledge, skills and attitudes which one would assume sergeants possess as a prerequisite of being promoted, and as a consequence the questionnaire contained many tasks which a constable—rather than a sergeant—would be expected to undertake proficiently. It would be unrealistic to assume that all training throughout an officer's career had to start from the same point and not build on previous training and experience. The questionnaire also contained many examples of poorly defined tasks, thus making the definition of subsequent learning objectives difficult.

Having established the repertoire of relevant tasks with sufficient clarity to enable training objectives to be written, the next question which has to be asked in the development of training is "where should or does a person learn to perform this task?" The proficient performance of a task is likely to be achieved in most cases through a combination of formal classroom learning and on-the-job training and experience. Therefore, the next step in the task analysis is to establish the proportion of the knowledge, skills or attitudes of the task learnt in the classroom. Finally, the task analysis must give some assessment, independent of the person responsible for undertaking the task, as to how well it has to be performed. If a task is required to be performed by law according to specific criteria, then the scope for deviation should be non-existent. However, for some tasks it is not at all critical if they are not performed to perfection although, in an ideal world, they would be; but the world has to compromise because the cost of perfection is often unrealistic. Therefore, judgements have to be made about the value of training when the criticality of performance is well below 100 per cent. The survey of sergeants did not include any data which could be used to measure the proportion of learning which needed to be achieved in the classroom of the criticality of the proficient performance of the task.

The power of this approach to task analysis in the development of training programmes can be found from another example. In 1982, the New York City Police Foundation undertook a review to validate the recruit training curriculum of the New York City Police Department (Lubans, 1982). The Foundation used the services of Lubans Associates, a specialist consulting organisation,to undertake a task analysis of the work of patrol officers. The study was based on a questionnaire designed after extensive observational field work with patrol officers. Two identical questionnaires were produced; the first elicited responses from patrol officers to establish the frequency with which they performed the tasks. The second questionnaire was completed by sergeants to establish the proportion of the task that was learnt in the formal training sessions compared with the proportion learnt on-the-job, and the criticality of proficient performance of the task. This method requires the careful determination of task selection rules. For example, a task may be performed very infrequently, but when it is performed it has to be 100 per cent proficient; discharging a firearm would be such a task. Another task might be performed more frequently but would not be a disaster if it was not performed to 100 per cent proficiency, for example, completing an accident card involving a dog. Using this method, the survey established that 20 per cent of the existing recruit training curriculum was redundant. The survey also identified a significant number of tasks which were performed by patrol officers and which were not taught in recruit training. The recruit training curriculum had been defined by an 'expert panel' consisting of 10 patrol sergeants who were asked to list all the tasks undertaken by patrol officers. They listed about 100 tasks. The observations of patrol officers at work which preceded the questionnaire identified more than eight times as many tasks. In another study involving 11,000 state police officers, it was found that one third of the tasks taught in the recruit training course were not even performed by the officers and a third of the tasks actually performed were not the subject of any training. The study demonstrated significant training redundancy and a significant lack of training for some tasks.

The evidence of the past few years would suggest police forces are not very good at predicting training needs for the future. In 1980, a review of community and race relation training given at district training centres revealed this point. Social change had overtaken the training and rendered it virtually redundant. (Butler and Tharme, 1981.) At force level, training departments have a good record at identifying the training implications of new legislation, but perhaps are not as effective at responding to the more conceptual training issues. As an example, in a large urban force, it seems almost inconceivable that a training course held in 1986 for sergeants who had not received formal training for 5 years, would only spend a few minutes out of a two-week course on the topic of sub-divisional objectives. The force had been using the system of the rational management of operational policing, using goals, objectives and action plans, since December 1983; however, the training department had not implemented any training on this topic.

It would be too easy to lay blame at the door of training departments for their apparent lack of vision. This would compound the problem because the responsibility lies with senior managers who should have the wider vision of the future shape and role of the force. In recent years training has had a very high profile in relation to the training of recruits and probationer constables, but even here it has had a narrow perspective, mainly associated with race and community issues. Unfortunately, economic pressures have tended to develop a siege mentality in many senior managers; the focus and energy has been consumed in making excuses for not doing things when it could have been more productively channelled into efforts to create opportunities for their officers on the street to improve their service. To achieve this end, the strategic importance of training should have been higher on the agenda. The six problems for the divisional commander which have been identified earlier in the chapter require a strategic response by the force. They all require a conceptual conversion of managers, which will only occur if the force creates a climate which is receptive to the development of this approach to police work.

The features which will distinquish the successful forces of the future will be the extent to which their management has been able to generate more effort from their existing staff and thereby improve the quality of service. This is not a 'treadmill' approach to management where staff are pushed to the limit. It is, in fact, a realistic recognition of the human condition, building on the self-motivation and dedication which is a feature of the young men and women who join the service. They are entitled to expect police forces to train their managers to create opportunities for them to give of their best, not simply struggle from one crisis to another, compensating through their own initiative for the lack of thought and vision of the officers above them.

The Role of the Training Department

At its very basic level, the role of the training department is to satisfy the needs of its customers who can be categorised as falling within three broad groups: the executive management of the force, the divisional commanders and individual force members. The executive management should, in the normal course of their responsibilities, define a strategic vision for the force. This vision will imply certain characteristics about the style, organisation and management methods of the force. The divisional commander will have to take the vision within the context of his current operations and formulate tactics to enable the vision to be achieved. In both cases training requirements are likely to be identified as the need for new knowledge, skills and attitudes become apparent. Traditionally, developments in training have been motivated by needs identified by management, with a consequent neglect of individual personal development needs. The exception to this rule has been the courses which are held for officers studying for their promotion examinations. It seems curious that training departments do not serve a further need for officers seeking to learn the skills of a new rank to prepare themselves for selection. It can be argued that this is done for them when they are successful in being selected but there are other good professional reasons why officers might seek to avail themselves of training to improve their own personal effectiveness. Training orientated to simply passing promotion examinations seems to be missing the wider point of self-development.

As an earlier paragraph observed, training has not been very high on the agenda, therefore the development of a strategic plan for training, from a managerial and personal development perspective may require the training department to act as a catalyst and innovator. In fact there will almost certainly be some requirement for them to establish a research and planning capacity.

The developments suggested here in relation to the role of training departments will not occur without the conscious efforts of the officer in the chief constable's management team who has a responsibility for training. There is also a need to establish a framework in which the process can be nurtured and developed. Such a framework could be based on an annual development plan. The plan would define those current training needs which were already known and produce a training programme with performance criteria. Where training needs were less well defined the plan would provide an outline strategy for research into training needs and methods to make the training process more efficient. The plan would show how it was linked to the overall force development plan.

There is a need for departments to become committed to annual reviews of training in conjunction with their customers, and then publish an annual development plan setting out how they are going to respond to changing needs. It is on this basis that they will become accountable in value for money terms. In the long run, training departments should be established as cost centres. Their style and range of courses should be directly related to the quality of service they provide and the demands made on them by the force. For example, if some forms of management training could be obtained more cost-effectively from an external source, or through the division using its own resources, then the money the division saved by not using the training department should be capable of being ploughed back into the operational work of the division.

Staffing and Innovation

The challenges facing training departments as they move into the next decade should not be underestimated. Two practical implications are immediately apparent, first, there are questions about the qualifications and experience of the trainers, and second, innovation will make a large contribution to improvements in the efficiency of training methods.

Despite the involvement of civilian staff in teaching at the Police Staff College since its foundation and Home Office policy encouraging the use of civilian staff, there is a remarkable absence of civilian staff from many force training departments. In one large urban force there are 96 police officers engaged on training (excluding officers on firearms training), at a current annual cost of £2.2m at 1986/7 salary levels, and no civilian teaching staff. Two points raise serious questions about the wisdom of such a policy. First, there is a two-year turn-over in the secondments of police officers to the training department which induces substantial costs in training the trainers, and also holds the level of expertise and competence at an artificially low level. Second—and this may explain why there are significant gaps in the training provided—the force does not have access to staff with professional management training expertise.

Many of the challenges facing operational police officers will only be overcome through imaginative solutions; similarly, the issues facing training will require an equal share of innovation. The very nature of innovation requires the people facing the problem to actively seek the solution; however, some suggested new approaches could be considered.

With the increasing involvement of civilian staff in areas which have been formerly undertaken by police officers, for example police station enquiry office work, and the appointment of higher grade civilian staff to managerial positions, it makes sense to develop joint training programmes. Not only are there many similarities in the conceptual skills and attitudes required to be effective managers, but such a development would break down some of the remaining prejudices against civilian support staff, and thereby aid their total integration.

A major constraint on the effectiveness of formal training is the apparent difficulty of translating classroom learning into work situations. This is especially true of the sophisticated conceptual skills increasingly being required by middle and senior managers. One of the least recognised benefits of a system of rational management such as the policing by objectives model, is its ability to act as a training medium (Butler, 1984). New management challenges are both creating training needs and simultaneously creating training opportunities. Police forces should harness these opportunities and raise the status of professional knowledge and skills. This can be done by innovations in training methods. Some of these approaches could be considered:—

—Maintaining an appropriate level of day-to-day knowledge by uniformed officers could be ensured by on-the-job briefings. A system of 'roll call training' has been used successfully in the United States for many years (Butler and Skitt, 1974). The introduction of such a system would also show the importance the force attached to professional knowledge.

—Officers seeking promotion should be encouraged to prepare themselves by personal development supported by a formal career development system. The training department would need to prepare suitable material and make it available on demand.

—Training could be made more efficient by the wider use of new technologies such as videos. As an example, the development of a strategy of distance learning could be used for both roll call training and personal development.

Concluding comments

This chapter has tried to portray a view 'from the street', setting training within the context of the demands being made on divisional commanders as they endeavour to continue to provide a reliable police service to their community. It has been argued that watershed events in this decade have, and will continue to have, consequences far into the next decade. It seems certain that resources, and particularly manpower, will not grow at a rate commensurate with increased demands for police services (Butler, 1987). Therefore, the means will have to be found for achieving more from existing resources—improved productivity. The police are not alone in this; there is a growing literature and recognition in business of the significant contribution the skills and attitudes of individual managers can make to releasing the latent potential of their staff in the pursuit of improved performance (Peters and Waterman, 1982). This additional resource will only be released, and productivity thereby improved, when the reasons for suppressing its contribution have been identified and understood. For example, a reduction in the number of man-days lost through sickness will create additional productive resources, but the reasons for officers taking sick leave may be complex and a strategy has to be developed to reduce sick days (Butler, 1987).

The review of the operational problems of the divisional commander concluded by identifying six issues all of which have a significant impact on the productive potential of the divisional commander's personnel. These six issues were inter-related and centred around the ability of the executive management to demonstrate leadership and vision in confronting the social challenge. Key elements of this visionary leadership would be shown in the setting of policies which had a consumer orientation emphasising quality and reliability of service. As an example, it was pointed out there was a need to define standards of service in such police activities as responding to calls from the public. The vision would also have to deal with the deficit in 'people skills', which inhibit the co-operation and the co-ordination of the efforts of all staff which would include greater integration of police officers and civilian support staff. Finally, there has to be an appreciation of the benefits which can be achieved from innovation, particularly the use of information technology.

The second part of the chapter was concerned with developing the training department to make training for today more efficient, to plan ahead for tomorrow's training needs, and in achieving these two ends, to consider the appointment of a core of professionally qualified training staff and innovations in the means of delivering training. The reader might be inclined to see this chapter as some kind of recipe for training departments to tinker with current practice and make marginal changes here and there. If this interpretation is made then the reader has missed the underlying point. Training is too important to be left entirely to the training department. Essentially, training is a fundamental responsibility for all managers who should see the personal development of their staff as a priority, because it is only through the people who work for him that improved service will be achieved. As a consequence of the current approach, which emphasises training as an organisational problem-solver, there is an absence of an understanding of the limitations of what training can achieve. This point has been well described recently by Chatterton (1987), in relation to the training of sergeants, and has been discussed elsewhere in relation to police community and race relations training (Butler, 1986). Both these papers argue that no amount of training will compensate for inherent structural inconsistencies within the force organisation and management, or somehow blind officers to the realities of their experience of police work.

Thus, the points proposed in this chapter argue for a re-assessment of the divisional commander's responsibilities for training, and look towards the development of a partnership between professional trainers and operational practitioners. The partnership would be based on a few simple principles:—

—The divisional commander has a responsibility for delivering the service to the public.

—Improved productivity will be the key to future success and training has a key role to play in the personal development of staff to achieve this improvement.

—Training departments must be based on a consumer-driven philosophy, the consumers being operational police officers.

—Training departments have a responsibility to make their own systems as cost-effective as possible, which will include changes to staffing policy, a recognition of the training needs of civilian support staff and the methods of delivering training.

—Training departments should develop a capacity to be a central consultancy resource to divisional commanders.

—The identification of training needs and priorities should be a joint venture between the training department and their customers.

If there were simple solutions available to solve the challenges currently facing the police service, then they would have been implemented. As this is not the case, it is unlikely that one idea will achieve this end. Therefore, the most this chapter can hope to achieve is the raising of questions and a contribution to the debate. What is beyond question is the need for a partnership approach between trainers and operational practitioners. This chapter seeks to propose options for developing this partnership.

9 Paving the way for philosophy and practices at Peel Centre, Hendon

Paul Mathias

It has been said by many that there are two certainties in our lives, those of life and death, the great equalisers of our time on earth are the beginning and the end. These statements mirror our lives in the police service; these have a start and a finish and the certainty remains that we will all go through these processes. For many the most traumatic is the beginning because it heralds new anxieties, new demands, confronting events of which we have no previous experiences on which to draw, making new relationships, subscribing to new rules and values and placing ourselves in a spiral of change. There seem to be very few police officers who are unable to recall their first days in the police service, and most have a general schema of the time they underwent their training course. It represents a major life event in terms of starting a new job, a job that starts with training. Starting in the police service means starting at training and training to start.

As such, for the individual and the organisation, the start and the training provided become crucial. Immediately, questions are raised as to what is meant by training, who will be the trainers, where will it take place and who are to be the trainees. These and other questions have been raised in recent years by policemen themselves, academic and other consultants, the Home Office and by critics of the service. It may be regarded as encouraging that the Metropolitan Police, as this period of unrest and change unfolded, were not prepared to play a passive role, but undertook an active part in responding to and stimulating change. The willingness to acknowledge and accept the need for change, to plan and prepare for it, and a commitment to undertake the processes necessary to achieve change were all vital elements.

In order to reflect and represent the changes that have occurred in Metropolitan Police training and to indicate the philosophy and practices now pursued there is need to present a short historical background. Up until the early 1960s training in the Metropolitan Police followed a general pattern, whereby an individual would receive a general introductory course, usually of ten to twelve weeks' duration, at the Central Training Complex at Hendon. The training would be provided by other police officers and the overall programme would be co-ordinated by police. The material used was presented at a basic level and was totally orientated towards the role of the police officer. It was trainer (teacher) centred, knowledge based and located in conventional school and classroom settings. Staff employed in these settings were themselves provided with initial training which preached the basic techniques of teaching, but in an environment which perpetuated a rigid and one-dimensional type of training. It is fair to acknowledge that role play as a technique was used to good advantage, and that individual staff brought their own imagination and variety to this sphere of training. However many staff used the tool of role play without fully understanding its purpose and potential. Also, the flair brought by an individual to the training scene would flicker and at the most be short term. Too much variation or innovation would disrupt or derail the vehicle of training from its rigid and fixed path. There was little opportunity to sustain vision, experimentation or evaluation. People knew what would happen as a result of applying what the training provided; it was predictable, safe and besides it had always worked. Perhaps, unkindly, it was training for the masses, mass produced. The individual might well have felt on occasions that he or she was being pressed into a mould and placed on an assembly line where further bits were added. The notion of individual differences, the needs of the student or the organisation, styles of teaching, planning, aims and objectives, evaluation, and many others, had little visible sign of life at that stage.

Any training provided beyond the initial stage at this time bore similar characteristics in its approach. Whether specialist, promotion or driving courses, or generalist, continuation or first aid training, it remained knowledge based and teacher centred. Another possible weakness common to all training provided was that it was the responsibility and preserve of those assigned to Training Branch. A possible exception was the phase of learning beats whereby an officer from the station you were first posted to, acted as an adopted 'parent' who received you for eight hours and then returned you to your own isolation. This detached form of 'sitting by nellie' was prone to a number of disadvantages, with the young trainee incurring most of the penalties. The 'parent' constables received no training themselves or clear direction on their role; often they were only months older in service than the trainee, they provided no objective assessment of the trainee nor actively contributed to his or her development. For the trainee it may have felt like the blind leading the blind, being subjected to a succession of 'parent' constables, some supportive but others openly hostile, limited helpful feedback, enduring menial tasks, practical jokes and other initiation rites. Some fared very well, some never really gained the experience, confidence and momentum to progress as far as was needed, while some were very unhappy when confronted by circumstances which allowed no use of the training given. Such experiences, coupled with the training period provided, meant that for the individual officer training was a passive affair, often with no apparent results, unrelated to the work place and capable of generating negative emotions. These insecure and negative attitudes often appeared to be absorbed into the culture of the organisation.

At this period events within and outside the police service were changing in significant ways. Many of the social changes following the second world war had either sufficiently established themselves or permeated their way through to allow a greater number of people to feel comfortable, content and capable of seeking greater fulfilment in their lives. Service industries were expanding, leisure activities increasing and homes were better equipped with appliances. Transportation, in terms of vehicles and new roads and motorways, had improved and increased. Television was reaching far more homes and making people aware of what others had and what they should expect themselves. Economically, people and industries were financially stable and everybody was being assured that they had never had it so good. An example of the significant changes occurring can be illustrated by the growth of computers at this period. In the 1950s there were fewer than 1000 large computers in use in America, almost all owned or used by Federal Government Departments. By the mid-1960s the figure had risen to 30,000 with a large majority used in industry and offices! Even further expansion in micro-electronics had allowed expression in terms of science, technology and management, that virtually matched intellectual comprehension. Computers permit the military to design more versatile and lethal weapons, they are being used on motor vehicles to reduce fuel costs and increase safety and in the medical world it is predicted they will help restore vision to the blind by decoding visual information from artificial eyes.

Major computer contracts involving special budgets, buildings and technical skills are now part of the pattern of modern police forces. It is unthinkable now to imagine the police service operating without computer assistance, technical surveillance devices, protective equipment, vehicles and a host of technological support equipment. Equally, the role of the police has been subjected to examination concerning the manner in which they use this equipment, handle the additional information generated and move away from the traditional traits associated with policing. The apparently more critical examination and expectation of policing by an increasingly better informed and educated audience has been matched by a self-evaluation by the police of themselves. The demand for change, the response to change and the understanding and handling of change were all processes that started to gather pace during the late 1960s and early '70s.

Training was well suited as a vehicle for coping with and managing the different dimensions of change. An early reflection of this was the introduction into the Initial Training programme during 1971/2 of a two-week segment entitled 'Social Skills Training': a recognition that police training was not solely about knowledge of the law but involved considering the social environment in which it would be practised. This new element was presented as a two-week package at the beginning of the course, was factually orientated and stemmed from a sociological perspective. It encountered many now familiar problems, such as lacking set objectives for achieving training, evaluation of the programme, giving feedback to students, and supplying back-up material. However, it clashed sharply with the traditional approaches followed in training at that time. But the seeds for change had been germinated by this important phase; this was not a stage of new training failing, but an important period of development. Not only were new elements of training initiated by police themelves, but they exposed many of the issues that would need to be addressed if training was to be the engine house of change. The police themselves were aware that, although change was needed, it would not be provided or undertaken by others, but was their responsibility. Even in the early days there was a sense that the police would have to tackle and 'own' the problems themselves, a fact recognised as a vital component in any change process, (eg French and Bell, 1978, Hackman and Shuttle, 1977). Other factors were also central to ensuring development within training. The need to identify individuals to present the new social skills programme revealed the importance of involving key personnel; the support of individuals outside the organisation to act as consultants who would analyse, design, evaluate and train those involved was also nurtured; finally, the need for good support material was also evident. It was not just simply a question of what new material was required, but of what was the most advantageous way to presenting it and from what perspectives—that of the police themselves, or from those who were the victims of crime or in some other way interactive with the police. This undoubtedly encouraged consideration of whether other organisations or educational establishments had training programmes suited for transfer or adaptation into Metropolitan Police training.

Those early tentative steps might now, on reflection, be seen as essential and elementary in permitting the processes of change to take place and gain hold. Any faster progress, while possibly meeting the wishes and demands of certain critics, would have been difficult to sustain and may well have evaporated. Certainly, sufficient key individuals both within and outside the organisation had not been identified and were not available to stimulate changes in training. There was no space, natural breaks or latitude in police training that would allow a new scheme to be introduced.

Government policy throughout the '70s was to bring the Metropolitan Police to its establishment figure. Success in this meant increased numbers of officers to be trained, and all training resources were directed to that end. Increased numbers of newly trained officers caused training to be subjected to objective and subjective examination by those directly involved in training and others. It revealed how ill-prepared on occasions the force was, in general terms, to accommodate the high influx of new officers. Any spare capacity that existed in the training department needed to be given over to specialist training in subject areas such as the operation of new technology and dealing with terrorism. In respect of the former, new computerised communication systems were being planned and contracts drawn up, while in the latter the IRA bombing campaign in the United Kingdom, hi-jacking of planes and public order events, such as Red Lion Square, prompted new skills to be urgently provided. In addition, the unrest and turmoil in the Metropolitan Police in the mid-'70s worked against effort being put into training or development of the right environment for cultivating new approaches to training. Allegations of widespread corruption, lack of true professionalism, inadequate senior officers, lack of co-operation between sections of the force and a lack of direction culminated in a fragile period for the Metropolitan Police. A time of diminishing public support and co-operation, falling morale and the emergence of articulate critics is perhaps not the best time to change training. More so when that change is only an idea without the foundations or structures to ensure its survival. The Commissioner of this period, Sir Robert Mark, pursued immediate and positive action in attacking corruption and bringing the force together as a whole unit, rather than a collection of competing and conflicting groups. This, together with coping with national and international terrorism, drained much of the energy of the organisation. It is interesting to note that Sir Robert did agree to the recruitment of women cadets into the Cadet School, which was to assist in nourishing the flow of women into the service. (It was also noticed that the women cadets affected an improvement in the behaviour and manner of the male cadets.) Furthermore, the number of coloured officers rose from 1 to 80 during his period in office, and the cause of better race relations was nurtured further in the organisation. Two other factors from this period deserve brief mention. First, the media which Sir Robert was prepared and able to use and, secondly, the recognition that people needed to be able to function as a team as well as individuals. These themes were to become pronounced features of the new approach to training.

In many senses the scene was now set for the introduction of the new philosophy and practices to training. The organisational structure, unity and common purpose shared by the greater number of its members, and the environmental changes to the culture of the organisation offered signs that time was right for such movement. The exploration, if tentative and superficial, of many of the elements of a new approach to training meant that many of the ingredients were known and partially available. What was needed was some catalyst to bring them all together. While the true explanation may never be known, several key events occurred during the late '70s and very early '80s which may, in isolation or combination, account for the surge into the present state. The Scarman enquiry into the Brixton riots of 1981 made a series of recommendations regarding the police, many relating to the type of training provided. A number of key individuals, policemen and consultants from a number of fields, were assembled and available for appreciable periods. Another factor was that the students undergoing training had experienced a more flexible approach to education and training for themselves. It has also been argued that the changes occurring within the organisation, as outlined above, raised the status of the Training Branch and provided it with the authority to direct and control new approaches to training. There are undoubtedly other factors that created the momentum that was to allow Metropolitan Police training to respond to pressing demands from inside the force and contribute to training elsewhere. Whatever the true sequence or full range of factors that were responsible, significant developments took place during the 1980s, such that it is now possible to clearly describe the philosophy and practices which emerged. It has not always been possible to identify a coherent philosophy in the past and 'practices' might have been read as 'a practice'. A clear policy and common understanding and direction are part of the advances made in training.

The philosophy of training which now prevails has the following features:

(a) Development of the individual is a principal tenet and individual differences are recognised and honoured.

(b) The promotion of team activities and organisational goals so that working with and for others becomes natural.

(c) The acquisition and practice of skills are as valued as the quest for knowledge.

(d) A full range of teaching techniques should be employed both to cater for individual learning styles (Honey and Mumford, 1983) and to ensure the achievement of learning.

(e) There should be immediate, accurate and helpful feedback on performance and the means to modify or improve such performance if necessary.

(f) A positive environment for learning should be created in which learning becomes fulfilling and promotes self-learning and development.

(g) The emphasis should be on the student and not the teacher and that role should be active rather than passive.

(h) Training must be validated and found reliable and be the subject of on-going evaluation.

(i) Creativity and experimentation should be encouraged and supported at all opportunities.

(j) The lessons of training should be capable of transference into the work place and the views of the client should be sought at every opportunity.

(k) There should be a continuity of themes and approaches in all aspects of training.

(l) Training should provide as much for the affective domain of feelings and behaviour as it does for the cognitive domain of knowledge.

In summary, training should be student centred and presented in a range of styles aimed at developing the individual and promoting the concept of self-development.

It is unlikely that today any of the principles listed above would be questioned. But even five or six years ago training might well have been teacher centred, with rote learning, lectures and formal examinations as central parts. It would have been difficult to determine any provision that took account of individual differences, or subject matter that permitted any breadth or depth to issues beyond those which were clearly police matters, such as legislation, arrest techniques and police support services. To any observer with prior experiences of police training it would have been easy to comment that basically the training had not changed since they undertook it.

If philosophies are carved out of experiences, needs, hopes and expectations, how are they introduced into training and how are they maintained over time and translated into reality? What are the practices that allow the achievement of the philosophy and what is their relationship? Do practices lead to the formulation of philosophy or is it important to identify the correct philosophy and then build the practices to enable their reality and fulfilment? The experiences of Hendon will show that the relationship is complex and involves a mixture of interaction. Undoubtedly some practices need establishing to clarify the philosophy which in turn defines and determines further practices.

Two early philosophies of the late 1970s were that training should be student centred and that greater emphasis should be placed on the social skills needed to police societies, groups and individuals. Much of this stemmed from the awareness accumulated by individuals within the police service since the early 1970s. Key individuals were posted to Training Branch during the late 1970s and early '80s and were able to bring their personal experience and abilities to bear in such a way as to conceive and conceptualise new directions. Not only were these key individuals able to articulate, present and promote this new philosophy but they were also able to detail the mechanisms and practices to achieve them. The Research and Planning Unit was established to plan and structure further training strategies, provide the resources needed to research and design training programmes and evaluate them. Credibility and status were given to this Unit with a line command system that allowed heads of sub-units to report to and consult directly with the Deputy Assistant Commissioner for Training; decisions could be made swiftly, without protracted passage through other branches. It was a resource which existed for use by heads of different training branches (eg Cadets, Promotional Courses, training in the field); an early and perhaps primitive system of quality control was also provided and a co-ordination point for external consultants was established. On a much wider scale it illustrated that training needed planning and that there were many different components that make up a training programme. It might be prudent to note that our experiences have shown that consultants who are willing to present programmes, rather than purely design them, and who endeavour to relate to the culture of the organisation prove most cost-effective in terms of developing and directing training programmes. Not only does this allow projects to be carried through to fruition but permits, in this instance, police officers involved in training the opportunity to practice, experiment and gain confidence with new approaches. Good consultants provide good role models, displaying the awareness, empathy and sense of self-development that will in due course be sought from the trainee. Contained in that last statement is an indication of the qualities required of potential and practising trainers, their role in encouraging development of others and, by inference, the crucial nature of their role as trainers in the whole process. The part played by staff is vital and will be described below, after brief mention of another aspect of the pattern of events occurring at the time.

While the whole of Metropolitan Police training, through its range of generalist and specialist training, was alive to the changes that were occurring, the new philosophy and practices could not be introduced en bloc. Certainly a blanket approach would have had much to commend it, but was quite unrealistic in terms of the resources and organisation required to achieve it. As many other organisations have found, (eg Beer and Huse, 1977; Walton, 1974; Hautaluoma and Gavin, 1975), effective change can occur when there are opportunities to establish an experimental 'unit'. This scope to confine and concentrate resources can create the supportive environment to pilot and monitor the new philosophy and practices being undertaken. A natural choice for the Metropolitan Police of such a section or unit was the Initial Training Wing. Through the influence of the Police Training Council, the Scarman Report, and Dr Alec Maine, Educational Advisor to the Force, this wing was prepared and primed through internal exploration of new approaches by the staff themselves. Organisationally, the advantages of involving those with long-term future employment, relatively free from cultural tradition and with recent experience in educational backgrounds which made them receptive to new practices, were also attractive.

The Initial Training Wing, for a twenty-week training programme for those first joining the service had, by the early 1980s, already introduced a number of minor changes. There was an improved knowledge base to existing lessons, increased use of role play, attempts to improve the quality of assessment of students and consolidation of the new element of training addressing attitude and behaviour known as "Policing Skills". All these factors, particularly Policing Skills, demanded proved staff training. If training is to produce officers who are more aware of themselves, aware of others, with positive attitudes and a range of responses to select from when dealing with incidents, then these attributes need to be demonstrated and displayed by staff. There is nothing more inconsistent and conflicting if the philosophy preached is not matched by the corresponding practices. The management team assembled in Initial Training at this time was strong in terms of experiences, conceptional thinking and commitment, and they recognised the need to enlist the support and contribution of the staff.

However, the staff both demanded and deserved appropriate training experiences themselves. There is little point availing themselves of opportunities to learn new practices if the philosophy from which these emanate and to which they relate is not understood. Good communication is essential so that a network for exchanging information and common goals is identified and available data is shared. The management team within Initial Training at this time co-ordinated all the communication activities, made themselves available and accessible for queries and were totally honest about information received and given to others. During 1984 all the staff spent a weekend in a seminar at the Police Staff College so that early teething troubles could be resolved, philosophy restated and fuller commitment pledged. This weekend not only confronted personnel and group difficulties but showed how effectively as individuals and as a team they were performing. It also demonstrated that the process of providing better staff training needed expanding. The practice of a selective group of trainers presenting the new approaches to training was not sufficient. Not only was it preventing the full integration of new ideas and systems but the students could clearly identify two distinct approaches, namely a knowledge and a skills approach. The tactic of providing a catch-up programme, built round the new policing skills element for existing staff and added to the basic technique course for new staff members, lacked long-term viability. Although it had succeeded in making staff more attuned to their training needs it failed to allow them to develop themselves. It was, therefore, supplemented with a task analysis of the role of a trainer which revealed key functions and exposed the limitations in staff training at this time, notably in areas such as formulating aims and objectives for lessons, different teaching styles, assessment and facilitation skills.

Accordingly, a staff development programme was designed and piloted. Built on a three-stage model of introductory, intermediate and advanced phases, designed to permit reflection, practice and development of skills, knowledge and attitudes on a cumulative basis. The actual philosophy of training was outlined and explained in the introductory course; together with the means and rationalisation to achieve them. This programme also provided plenty of feedback facilities, in the art of giving and receiving tutorials, the use of assessment sheets on the prospective trainers as strategies for self-development. The training of the trainers was undertaken by a group of proven police trainers, supported by external consultants, who possessed the credibility, confidence and personal commitment to succeed with a vital component of change to a new style and system of police training. If staff are to be innovative, student centred and able facilitators, as well as providing fast, accurate and usable feedback, able to counsel and empathise with others, and themselves present the right attitudes and appropriate behaviour, then these qualities must be developed within a training course. They will not occur or evolve by chance or good fortune. The accreditation of the staff training programme at the Hendon College to the City & Guilds (London Institute) Teaching Certificate has added a further seal of approval to this scheme and provided much valued personal satisfaction to those officers entering training. The training function is now accorded a status and credibility much sought after by others in the organisation.

There is little doubt that the renewed approval and vitality found in training attracted prospective applicants for employment within this area. Not only was there a comprehensive and widely acclaimed training programme available, but the job analysis had provided the profile of attributes and personality characteristics sought. Criteria could be established for the selection process which would be fair and desirable for both the individual and the Training Branch. Other practices already implemented now fully supported the philosophy set for training. The objective set by senior management in the initial training wing to recruit staff to the set establishment figure had been pursued vigorously and had been achieved by late 1983. Strategies for effecting this had included targeting those with previous teaching experience, and from minority groups in the service such as ethnic and women officers. The eventual ratio of ethnic and women officers at present on the training staff exceeded that found in the force as a whole. It not only attracted very capable officers in terms of professional and personal experience, but provided very visual statements in terms of philosophy, equality and opportunity. Endorsement of the philosophy of considering the individual and what he or she might contribute to training had been made with the employment of constables as trainers since 1982. No longer could teaching skills only be acquired by the acquisition of rank, but they were open to anyone willing to submit themselves for examination and found to possess or have the potential to develop the necessary skills.

Having gained sufficient and suitable staff, with a purpose-signed staff training and development programme available, the next task was to ensure a regular flow of the best officers available to undertake training. A scheme to structure their selection and recruitment and lead to better equipped staff was devised. This involves one day Assessment Centres which set a number of objectives for 8/10 potential staff to work through. Personal files are obtained from the station or offices where they are currently working. Added to these are the assessments made by a panel of observers who monitor and mark morning activities of writing an essay on a topical subject relating to the police service, participating in a discussion group, appraising a lesson and planning a presentation. All of the tasks provide the opportunity for potential staff to demonstrate the qualities needed at Hendon: communication skills, ability to handle diverse concepts and issues, skills of working in a team, sensitivity to the feelings of others, facilitating opportunity for others to express themselves and giving and receiving feedback. With the right array of tasks and properly trained observers, all these attributes can be elicited and tested. The afternoon comprises an interview with two or three panels of interviewers. Here the onus is on the individual to express her or himself and flesh out their personal profiles—strengths and weaknesses, things they have done well, personal action plans for the next twelve months, force and local philosophies where they currently work and how they are putting them into effect. For the interviewers the task is to listen, concentrate, and occasionally prompt or probe.

Members of the interview panel and observers of the morning activities then assemble and score prospective staff on the criteria that have been set. The different activities undertaken enable a reliable and valid profile to be assembled which indicates those suited and with the potential to develop as trainers. All candidates, those accepted and those rejected, are provided with feedback on their performance. Thus even those not accepted learn what their perceived strengths and weaknesses are and how they might develop or improve them. For many it might be the first specific mirror on how they are seen by others. The exacting demands of the Assessment Centre do not discourage applicants from submitting themselves as candidates; they see it as fair, open and appropriate and as allowing them to be judged as a person. Highly relevant when considering that, as training staff, they will need to assess others as people and as police officers, and they will be responsible for developing the skills of others to handle and manage people. Presenting the right role model is crucial if we want to produce the correct attitude and behaviour in our officers. If those charged with presenting the new philosophy do not put it into practice, then negative behaviour, disharmony and disenchantment will result. Fortunately some excellent role models, in all ranks, have become associated with training, and the introduction of Assessment Centres has served to recruit more of them. It was not necessary to advertise, for officers already successful elsewhere in the organisation were applying for training and many are encouraged by the prospect of developing themselves within training. The balance has swung towards selecting out rather than selecting in. People want to be trainers and to be part of the new philosophy and practices.

The task of selecting what to include in the training programme and what to leave out was an important issue. The tendency had previously been for new legislation, concerns identified by the public or pressure groups, and 'showcase displays' whereby support units,—eg forensic, firearms and traffic—gave presentations of what they did, to be added to an already bulging programme. This was stifling and stagnating the programme, so that as much energy of the staff went into managing it as into actually training the students.

The new philosophy demanded that emphasis be given to students learning more about themselves to allow them to be more aware of others, to providing the opportunity to practise skills and communication, listening and empathy, to allowing time for receiving feedback and counselling, and to giving scope for students to direct their own training programme. The notion of 'pruning' the programme had crept in during the early 1980s and it was revised at regular intervals. This created breathing space for brief periods before new legislation filled it up. The programme needed greater flexibility and the ability to respond to the needs of the student. The Training Manual designed and introduced in 1979 had been intended as a teaching aid and not a restrictive method of teaching by rote. It had become the latter due to failure to ensure that the principles behind it were properly presented to the staff and students. Reflecting the mood of confidence and openness felt by those involved in the Initial Training phase, there was, though, a readiness to confront this failing. Acceptance of the Training Dual as a tool, together with the freedom to plan and present lessons, meant staff and students could manage the available time more effectively. As long as staff ensured that lesson aims and objectives were met, then the method and techniques employed were at their discretion. This caused questions to be asked such as "What is the best method for presenting this lesson?", "Can part of it be pre-read?", "Can the students tackle it in large or small groups, getting together in a plenary session towards the end?", "Do the individuals in this class need class teaching on this subject or can it be learnt and reinforced with private reading?"

While this management of the syllabus was occurring at the micro-level, similar scrutiny and analysis was taking place at the macro-level. Senior management were determining: what subject material needed to be covered within the initial course; what subjects could be presented during other phases of training; what was educationally achievable during the early stage; what could be entirely pre-read or perhaps covered by 'distance learning'; and what was no longer relevant. For example, the force policy of cautioning drunks meant that the system of using drunkenness offences as elementary arrest cases needed reviewing, while the movement towards criminal cases being conducted by the Crown Prosecution Service caused an examination of the training geared to preparing and presenting cases at court. Many traditional police subjects could be gracefully retired, condensed or amalgamated with other lessons. At the very minimum many required a clinical overhaul as to the relevance of the lesson objectives, the accuracy of content, variable methods of presentation and how the lessons were able to promote and prepare for the development of force policies and Training Branch philosophies and practices. It is regarded as essential that, at the earliest opportunity, each student is introduced to and taught how to interact with the policies and plans of the organisation. The training, at the initial stage, needed to be adapted to allow this to take place. If we want the spirit and processes of self-development to continue post training, then the concepts of the role of the individual as a member of a team and unit of the organisation have to be established at this early stage.

The training programme that evolved had never been structured to include set objectives, self-appraisal, flexibility of approach or responding to central themes that could be transferred into future training courses. These were accepted as weaknesses and steps taken to resolve them. These included the creation of a manual writing team charged with reviewing, rewriting and re-assembling a new programme of training, a complete up-date and enhancement of the Policing Skills element of the programme and provision for the programme to be evaluated. These steps, along with a number of others, have permitted a more realistic, flexible and manageable training programme to evolve, capable of meeting the demands of modern policing and reflecting the new philosophies of training.

It should not be overlooked that this is an expensive task to undertake in terms of manpower, time and diversity of the work involved. For the Metropolitan

Police it is a full-time task monitoring new legislation, integrating force policy and taking account of issues raised by pressure groups and other agencies who seek an input into police training. Training videos, exercises, books and research have to be perused to see if new material can be gleaned and added to our programne. A liaison must be maintained with academics, trainers in other organisations and police officers in other forces to share and exchange good practice, research results, experience of pilot schemes and other initiatives or projects. The Metropolitan Police Initial Training Wing have a proven and respected record of helping other training units—particularly in local authorities and other police forces—in establishing and developing their respective training programmes, whether in explaining philosophies, demonstrating good practices, providing them with material, visits to Peel Centre or staff training courses. Members of London Regional Transport, London Ambulance Service, Hertfordshire, Nottinghamshire, Surrey and West Midlands police forces have attended such courses.

It is, however, time consuming to practice these philosophies and, without doubt, easier to have less elaborate philosophies which rely on traditional methods of training, syllabus design and content. If, though, training is to respond to change and play a role in directing that change then there has to be an acceptance of and commitment to the issues outlined above. If there is a desire to develop others and prepare them to develop themselves, then the unit charged with undertaking this must express and display the desired philosophies and practices themselves. They must be dynamic in developing themselves and their training programmes. To this end the Initial Training Wing at Hendon have continued to pursue new projects, submit themselves to scrutiny and try to predict future trends.

In addition to the projects on staff training, selection and recruitment of staff and reviewing training programmes there have been other initiatives. These include:
(a) designing an assessment of the Policing Skills element of the programme, argued by many as an impossible task;
(b) enhancing role play situations and practicals so that they become reliable and valid learning experiences in themselves;
(c) developing a scheme whereby projects are undertaken with community agencies by groups of four students who then make a presentation to their colleagues and prepare a paper;
(d) allowing the subject of discretion to be practised and assessed; and
(e) supporting a study with the Police Foundation to evaluate how training is transferred into the work place.

This last project has involved batteries of questionnaires to probationers at key stages of their probationary period, observational studies of police officers during tours of duty and a soon to be conducted telephone survey with people who have sought police assistance. The study will address a crucial question about our training programme: is it usable in the work setting? (A fuller account of this study by Bull and Horncastle is to be found elsewhere in this volume.)

There has been a ready response to requests to hold ourselves up for examination. Not only have we been willing to participate in many different areas such as Home Office reviews, seminars, conferences and working parties, but the keenness to invite others to witness our philosophy and practices has been widely encouraged. Visitors from many fields, pressure groups, and other police forces, other countries and the media have all examined our training at close quarters. The most searching investigation is often from the media who, on some occasions, have possibly set out to discredit it, but have come to acknowledge the changes and progress made. The positive power of the media is not to be underestimated in developing a heightened awareness of personal performance, and the promotion of philosophies and practices to a wider audience who, in turn, may alter their perceptions and expectations so as to provide a more conducive environment for these approaches to be consolidated. It is pleasing to record that the representatives of newspaper, television and radio companies have scrutinised the whole package and reported in a positive manner in subsequent articles and programmes. One benefit of this contact has been the willing supply of material to the Initial Training Wing and collaboration from the BBC Education Department to produce 'race awareness' material. Publicity of this nature benefits not only training, but the force as a whole.

Anticipating change is part of building for the future and recognising trends that will have an impact on subsequent progress. The following are some of the questions that are being addressed:

—How are the future key personnel to be identified and brought into training?
—What skills are going to be needed by future senior management?
—Are highly skilled and expensively trained trainers only to be employed for three years or should their services be retained for longer?
—Should Training Branch have its own promotional system?
—Should training be undertaken by non-police staff?
—What subject areas need to be covered?

Earlier lessons on perceptions, attitudes, communication and group influence have been supplemented by material on stress management, discretion, racism and the police, empathy and non-verbal communication, while material is being prepared on sexism, domestic violence, encounters with people and on new legislation. Identification of new and relevant subject areas remains vital to ensure that changes of policy and emphasis are quickly accommodated by individuals and the organisation.

Informed predictions of the answers to questions such as those above will allow a proactive rather than reactive approach and stimulate the controlled development of the whole force. The integration and continuity of training courses and the transition from training into the work environment are other key areas for future development.

10 Management and organisation development in the police service: the role of Bramshill

Michael Plumridge

"Culture is a pattern of basic assumptions—invented, discovered, or developed by a given group as it learns to cope with its problems of external adaptation and internal integration—that has worked well enough to be considered valid and, therefore, to be taught to new members as the correct way to perceive, think, and feel in relation to those problems."
(Edgar H. Schein *Organisational Culture and Leadership*, 1985)

"Culture is the key to understanding service. An organisation's cultural orientation has implications for every aspect of its operations and its internal and external relationships."
(R. Harrison *Organisation Culture and Quality of Service*, 1987)

This chapter examines the problems facing police organisations in adapting to a rapidly changing environment, the implications for leadership, management and organisation development in the police service, and the present and potential role of the Police Staff College in assisting in these processes.

My hypothesis is that at a time when the pressures upon police organisations are greater than ever before their culture and style obstruct the kinds of flexible and innovative responses which are necessary for their adaptation. As they operate in an increasingly turbulent and changing environment, I will suggest that a training approach will need to give way to a developmental one at the levels of the individual, the group, and the organisation. Moreover, the prime focus of that development has to be the ways in which police organisations learn to cope with their problems of external adaptation and internal integration. The issue for Bramshill thus becomes less of "what ought it to be teaching?" but rather "how can it enhance the learning process for individuals, groups, and whole organisations in order to enable them to learn from, and to adapt to, whatever situation confronts them?"

My perspective upon these issues is distilled from my personal attempts to facilitate the learning of several thousands of police officers, several work teams and some police organisations over the past 19 years, three of them whilst at Brighton Polytechnic and the remainder at the Police Staff College. A further source of my perspective is personal research which consists of:

(a) a research study which elicited the perceptions of their roles of some 180 officers, from 7 police forces, in middle and upper-middle management positions; and

(b) the response of some 2000 officers attending Bramshill courses over the past 5 years to instruments used to test their perceptions of the style and culture of their organisations.

The final influence upon my perspective is that of thinkers and writers, too numerous to record individually, on police and other organisations.

What then can we observe happening to organisations in general, and to police organisations in particular, in relation to their environments? The rate of economic, social, political, cultural and technological change is such that the pressure points on all organisations keep moving, thus demanding the most sensitive outward vision and market research (Schon, 1972). It is no longer possible for an organisation to survive simply by calling upon its past experience or by continuing to do better and better those things which it has always done, whatever its reputation. Most organisations have found that they have had to scan their environments in an ever more fine-tuned and sensitive manner and, instead of asking themselves "just how good are we at our business?", having to ask, "are we in the right business?" (Argyris and Schon, 1974). This is a difficult and disconcerting question for those who have risen to their positions of high status and influence on the strength of long experience of tried and trusted methods, for it apparently threatens their own competence, authority and security. The higher they rise in the organisation the more omnipotent, omniscient, omnicompetent and certain they are expected to be, not only by themselves and by their colleagues but also by subordinates who, in bewilderment, constantly 'look for a Moses to lead them to the promised land'. If things go wrong they can then conveniently blame 'top management' as that is a softer option than taking personal responsibility for the health and effectiveness of the organisation.

Just as important for organisations as the rate of change in their environments is the nature of their clients. Thanks to cultural change and technological advances in the media clients are better informed, more demanding, and more articulate. These phenomena in their turn bring about the need for rapid, accurate and sensitive responses. The era of large organisations appears to be passing as centralised bureaucratic control becomes ever more dysfunctional in providing such responses, and the era of 'small is beautiful' (Schumacher, 1973) appears to be dawning.

Pressures for change in police organisations

Such changes are having an immense impact upon police organisations, calling into question their nature and their values and, hence, the ways in which they are managed. The service has had to contend with a host of ambiguous and often conflicting demands from central government, local government, the 'public' and interest and minority groups. While, on the one hand, there are pressures to develop sensitivity through 'community policing', on the other hand there are forces pushing in the direction of para-military style operations in order to contain public disorder. Central and local government are pressing hard for cuts in public expenditure, value for money, and the effective and efficient use of resources in the context of a continuing increase in criminal and deviant behaviour in society. As modern technology has ensured that the police come under the constant scrutiny of the media (any dramatic event with police involvement is carried 'live' into almost every home) there has been a growing and vociferous debate upon the accountability of the police.

There are developing signs that such pressures are beginning to shape a professional code of best policing practice on an international scale, but particularly in the Western democracies (Skolnick, 1986).

Learning systems

The true test of the capacity of an entity to adapt, be it an individual, a group, an organisation, or indeed a whole society, is not so much whether, or how quickly, it can learn new ways, as whether it is a *learning system*. In other words, how well developed is its capacity to monitor its environment and to invent new ways of responding effectively, through its own behaviour, to the demands made upon it? Such responses require high levels of sensitivity and awareness, not only to its environment but also to its own values and judgements and to its own feelings and behaviour.

If such learning is to occur certain preconditions are necessary. Not only must it have a strong sense of both identity and autonomy, but:—

1. It must recognise, and be committed to, the need to constantly develop, learn, and change.
2. It must know that it doesn't know.
3. It must possess the humility, willingness and capacity to seek both new perspectives and help.
4. It must be committed to creating space for reflecting upon and reconstruing its own attitudes and behaviour and the environment in which it is operating (Kelly, 1963).

These dimensions are totally interdependent and if any one of them is not functioning it is unlikely that the necessary learning and change will occur. These will be vital factors to consider and apply when we come later to reflect upon the processes of management and organisation development.

The processes of organisational change and the preconditions for effective change have been well documented elsewhere (Beckhard, 1969, Beckhard and Harris, 1977, Bennis, 1966, French and Bell, 1978, Greiner, 1967). Suffice it to say at this point that there has to be a widely shared feeling that change is necessary, together with a shared vision of the future which captures the hearts and minds of those involved, ie there must be a high level of ownership and commitment. If the 'reality' of the organisation is to be shared multidirectional communication needs to be open, honest, and effective. If reflective learning is to occur each individual needs a personal sense of identity, purpose, autonomy and self-worth if he is to accept both personal and collective responsibility for outcomes of behaviour; furthermore, the organisation must approach problem-solving in a constant mode of action-research, ie it must not be assumed that wisdom lies in certain quarters but not in others.

If real change is to occur in the style and culture of an organisation it has to happen at five different, yet interdependent, levels (Kuykendall and Roberg, 1982) if that organisation is to become a true learning system:—

LEVEL 1   Changes in the structure, systems, rules, procedures and patterns of communication.

LEVEL 2   Changes in the ways of monitoring and assessing the effectiveness of performance and behaviour.

LEVEL 3   Re-evaluation of the vision or purpose of the organisation and a constant reformulation of corporate strategy.

LEVEL 4   Re-evaluation of inter-group and interpersonal relationships in order to meet organisational needs.

LEVEL 5   Re-evaluation of individual and group values in order to adjust to new goals and behaviours.

Changes in police organisations

Police organisations have been slow in learning the lessons gleaned from the study of change processes in other kinds of organisation. One of the main reasons for this has been that "books which do not have the word 'police' in the title seldom find their way into police management training programmes. Police are reluctant to look at management ideas which are not marketed specifically as police management" (Panzarella, 1984). As Bradley, Walker, and Wilkie (1986) have said, there has been the greatest difficulty in getting police officers to recognise that they *are* managers, a phenomenon well known to the author of this paper who struggled against this reluctance throughout the 1970s. Even at Bramshill there has been a remorseless reluctance to see management and organisational issues as the prime overarching perspective within which all other disciplines and perspectives contribute; "Management Studies" is still viewed as one approach among others and different from Administration, Environmental Studies, and Police Studies. Hence the organisational learning concerning the above five levels of intervention has been a slow re-inventing of the wheel. Until the appearance of Home Office Circular No. 114 of 1983 virtually every change programme in police organisations had stayed firmly at Level 1. That circular, however, pushed police organisations very reluctantly into Level 2 in considering how to measure performance. Many are still stuck there, but for others it provoked the realisation that Level 2 could not be approached in a vacuum, that is, performance cannot be measured until Level 3 (clearly defined goals and, hence, tasks necessary to achieve them) has been attained. In yet fewer forces the sheer difficulty of developing the kind of teamwork and collaboration among top management spurred them to the realisation that in order to achieve corporate goals Levels 4 and 5 would need to be tapped.

The advent of Home Office Circular 114/83, taken together with the Scarman Report (1981), the PSI Report on the Metropolitan Police (Smith and Gray, 1983), the Report of the ACPO Working Party on *Stress in the Police Service* (Manolias, 1983), reports on forces by management consultants, and studies of the roles of Divisional and Sub-Divisional Commander (Males, 1983; Plumridge, 1983) and of the policy-making and dissemination process (Nutley, 1987), have all combined to produce a maelstrom of activity in police organisations around the processes of management and organisational development. Unfortunately these events all followed so rapidly one upon the other that police organisations were unprepared to cope with them and theory was often applied in very ill-considered ways (Doyle and Tindal, 1987). The kinds of approach necessary to manage them, ie the five levels of intervention examined above, required a new philosophy and style of police management, and a new set of skills for the implementation of change and the development of a learning system.

The new philosophy required was a change from a top-down controlling style, in which 'managers' behaved largely as supervisors implementing bureaucratically imposed policies, to a supportive, developmental style in which the different levels in the hierarchy carried out differentiated functions but encouraged and developed a learning climate within the organisation, devolving autonomy as far down in the system as possible, and providing care and support both to organisational members and clients. This would mean that there were three types of role needed to allow the organisation to perform effectively, namely Integration and Direction Giving (policy formulation and vision building), External Monitoring (policy support), and Operational Planning and Actions (internally monitored) (Garratt, 1987).

Until very recent times almost every police officer spent the whole of his working life at the Operational Planning and Actions level and took a very dim view of any colleague who did not. It is, however, interesting to note the number of forces who are currently, if belatedly, sprouting 'Policy Support Groups' under a variety of guises. A few are even removing functional responsibilities, such as Operations, Administration, Personnel etc., from their ACPO level officers, in order to allow them to become the vision builders, integrators and direction givers. The skills, however, which are required for vision building, integration, direction giving, external monitoring, policy support, and internal monitoring have, in the past, received scant attention in training programmes which have been dominated by operational planning and actions. Furthermore, a training ethos tended to produce a controlling, supervising, authoritarian style of management rather than a supportive, developmental, coaching and counselling one which is more the province of a developmental, and particularly a self-developmental, ethos. When faced with handling the five levels of intervention police forces have found that they have some graduates with the necessary research skills to operate in policy support groups at Levels 1–3, but not enough of them. Levels 4 and 5, however, present a quite different problem in that there are very few police officers with skills and experience in the applied behavioural sciences who can help others to reflect upon and revaluate their feelings, values and behaviour. So far as operational managers are concerned, a whole new philosophy and style of management needs to be both espoused and practised if police organisations are to become true learning systems. The recent spate of management literature spearheaded by *In Search of Excellence* (Peters and Waterman, 1982) and *The One Minute Manager* (Blanchard and Johnson, 1982) have outlined this new philosophy, but perhaps its fullest exposition is presented in Bradford and Cohen's *Managing for Excellence* (1984), with its thesis that the traditional concept of 'Manager as Hero' leads to over-responsibility on the part of managers and actually results in subordinates performing at levels far below their capacity. They say that 'heroic' managers fail increasingly to live up to the ideals that they should know at all times what is going on in the department, they should have more technical/professional expertise than any subordinate, they should be able to solve any problem that comes up (or at least solve it before the subordinates!), and they should be the primary (if not the only) person responsible for how the department is working.

Their conclusion is that "The most paradoxical and frustrating trap for the heroic manager is that greater effort exacerbates the problem. While increasingly Herculean efforts are demanded of the leader, the abilities of subordinates are further ignored, causing frustration and weakening of motivation throughout the department. Heroism sets up a self-defeating cycle." They say that the effective manager is the developmental manager.

Style and culture of police organisations

Ironically, middle and upper-middle managers in the service have recognised the need for such a shift in philosophy and style, but have felt powerless to bring it about. Over the past five years some 2000 officers between the ranks of inspector and chief superintendent have completed Roger Harrison's 'Organisation Culture' questionnaire (Harrison, 1972) as the basis of a workshop on 'Organisational Options'. This questionnaire elicits ways in which respondents experience and perceive their organisation and what kind of organisation they would personally prefer and consider to be appropriate.

The four basic cultures are:—

TYPE 1 'POWER' culture or Autocracy with a dominant central figure in whom power is invested and retained.

TYPE 2 'ROLE' culture or Bureaucracy whose features are impersonality, rules, procedures and an hierarchy which is strictly adhered to.

TYPE 3 'ACHIEVEMENT' culture or Matrix form in which power shifts according to the nature of the current task to be performed, task teams are chosen on the basis of experience and expertise, and a premium is placed upon interpersonal and intergroup skills.

TYPE 4 'SUPPORT' culture or Professional Association/Community which represents a federation of individual skills and needs bound together by a shared mission and set of values.

The results obtained from this questionnaire over the five-year period 1982–6 were as follows:—

The Organisation		Type 1 'Power'	Type 2 'Role'	Type 3 'Achieve-ment'	Type 4 'Support'
As Perceived	1982–84	33%	53%	13%	1%
and Experienced	1985–86	36%	48%	14%	2%
As Preferred	1982–84	10%	11%	77%	2%
and Required	1985–86	—	8%	84%	8%

From this table we can see that the majority of respondents perceived and experienced their organisation as primarily a Bureaucracy, but with a strong flavour of Power. On the other hand, most of them saw an Achievement culture as more appropriate.

The picture of the culture as experienced by respondents has changed little during the period to 1986. However, the picture of the preferred culture has changed in that in 1984 21% actually preferred a controlling (top down) culture, ie Power and Role; in 1986 that figure is down to 8% while those preferring achievement and support cultures has risen from 79% to 92%

A further piece of evidence of the present culture comes from a study which the author carried out in seven police forces between 1981 and 1983 of the ways in which middle and upper-middle managers perceived and experienced their roles (Plumridge, 1983). A similar study was carried out in another seven forces at the same time, but using a different methodology (Males, 1983). Both studies produced remarkably similar results and the organisational profile which emerged was one where:—

1. The structure was rigid and much energy went into preserving roles, departments, rules, procedure, committees and tradition. It was hierarchical, valued deference and conformity, and adhered to the chain of command.
2. The atmosphere was impersonal, formal, suspicious and very action centred. Communication was restricted in its flow, was downward, and feelings were hidden and repressed.
3. Decision-making and policy-making stemmed from the top with little participation from below. Decisions were not to be argued with and there was a clear distinction between policy-making and policy execution.
4. Management values and attitudes were concerned with controlling personnel through the sanctions of coercive power; caution towards risk and errors—the latter were to be avoided and were punished; self-sufficiency and hence a closed system concerning sharing resources or seeking help; low tolerance of ambiguity and conflict; order was held to be important and must be imposed, thus giving a false sense of security in an uncertain world; activity and reactivity—ie business—were preferred to proactivity and reflective thought, and perceiving as unacceptable the expression of doubt, fear and uncertainty, which were seen as signs of weakness and incompetence; firmness and decisiveness were seen as essential.

Development needs:

This profile does not seem to be compatible with the needs of a flexible, learning system (Knowles, 1983) which were outlined earlier. Nor is it likely to meet the needs of those seeking an Achievement or a Support culture. This is becoming increasingly recognised and many forces are now beginning to do something about it. One of the greatest problems to be overcome, however, is the notion that while police work, and hence police management, take place 'in the real world', ie in police forces, management development is something quite different which takes place elsewhere and under a separate system of management. It is important to recognise that the majority of management development issues cannot be resolved at the individual level, ie by sending an individual on a course. It is not just a question of giving people more knowledge or more skill; moreover, it is not just a question of helping them to understand their job better. The main issue really concerns the ways in which people work together in an organisation; it is the interaction of particular people, around particular tasks and problems, in a particular organisational setting and climate, ie culture (Margerison, 1984). Therefore, management development needs to be seen firmly within the context of organisational development and organisational culture. It is of interest to note at this point that in police organisations top managers usually see middle managers as the problem who therefore need 'training'. Conversely the middle managers see top managers as the problem and feel that it is they who need the training. Both are, of course, right, but what is really required is for the two groups to work together at developing their skills and effectiveness in working together. This argument, of course, applies to all levels in the hierarchy in any single organisation, and this is the focus of organisation development. It is often said that a true learning system is one which can both talk to itself and to those in its environment.

Thus the challenge for centres of education and training is how best to manage the connection and the interface between themselves and the management and organisational strategies of their client organisations. The demand for relevant 'courses' or programmes in these institutions will always be high while organisations operate in turbulent environments and hence need to change. The problem for them is that they are costly to run and the need to 'fill bedrooms', under pressure from accountants, usually reduces them into a diet of 'bread and butter' programmes which are apt to become a production line mass-producing products which are not sufficiently sensitively negotiated and designed to meet particular customer needs. The larger and the more bureaucratised the institution becomes the more it is prone to serve the needs of its members at the expense of those of its clients.

There is an urgent need to design tailor-made management and organisation development programmes and to determine whether their application results in learning which is congruent with the organisational circumstances in which it is to be applied. The assumption upon which most police management development has hitherto been based is that because all police forces are essentially doing the same job general courses which prepare officers for a particular rank can be attended by officers from a wide range of police forces. While in no way wishing to deprecate the cross fertilisation of ideas across forces which such courses encourage, one should challenge the above assumption. Police forces may all be doing a similar job, but even there considerable variations exist. More importantly, however, they vary greatly in the ways in which they organise themselves, the policies they pursue, the methods they employ, the roles performed by their managers at different levels, and in their style and culture. Hence, the transfer of learning from general courses becomes highly problematic.

To return to the need for tailor-made programmes, the immediate need is to find criteria upon which the success of such programmes might be assessed. In his paper entitled 'Management Development as the Key to Organisational Renewal', delivered to the First World Congress on Management Development in 1981, Professor Gordon Lippitt posed the following questions concerning any contemplated plan for management and organisation development:—

1. Is it based on an articulated value system in which the purposes of an organisation are clearly related to the public it serves?
2. Does it take into account essential needs at the present state of organisational development?
3. Is it based on the realities of future change?
4. Is it based on well-defined organisational objectives?
5. Is it based on examples of successful and unsuccessful executive performance in that particular organisational system?
6. Is it designed to change or reinforce individual attitudes as well as to develop applicable skills and knowledge?
7. Is it in all respects specifically designed for the particular organisation, group, or individual?

8. Is it to be professionally created and implemented? (NB. It is such a complex field that more harm than good can be done by the inexperienced or unknowledgeable.)
9. Is it supported by the leadership practices and climate of the organisation?
10. Does it provide for evaluation in terms of long-range organisational goals?
11. Is it designed ultimately to strengthen rather than to weaken the individual's commitment to the organisation?
12. Is it designed to produce greater capabilities in initiative and creativity in the individual?

These questions are for the organisation, and those responsible for its management to address. But what of the individual learner? As I have explored elsewhere (Plumridge, 1985) a learning or developmental organisation can exist only when the vast majority of its members develop both the will and the skill to become self-directed learners. Before any individual can do that he needs the help of skilled and caring others in order to be able to identify and recognise his own skills, strengths and deficiencies, develop his awareness of those skills at which he needs to work, actually *want* to develop them, and know how he can set about doing so, ie know what resources are available to him and how to use them.

Hence the self-directed learner (Mumford, 1980) is no longer dependent upon being trained by the organisation but has developed in *himself* the following capacities:—

*   to clarify his own vision and goals
*   to establish effectiveness criteria for himself
*   to measure his own effectiveness
*   to identify his own learning needs
*   to plan personal learning
*   to take advantage of learning opportunities
*   to review his own learning processes
*   to listen actively, and in a caring manner, to others
*   to seek and accept help
*   to encourage unwelcome information
*   to take risks and tolerate anxieties and ambiguities
*   to analyse what other successful performers do
*   to know himself
*   to share information with others
*   to review what has been learned.

Moreover, by developing these capacities for himself he is then in a position to help others.

The situation within the service, then, is that it has been, and is likely to be, faced with a constantly changing environment. Its traditions and style have served it well, but no longer seem to provide the speedy and sensitive responses which are needed. Studies conducted among middle and upper-middle managers show that they appreciate a need for a change in style and approach. Several police forces are beginning to address these issues and are increasingly seeking help in attempting to do so. The problem is that such help costs the kind of money which, at present, they can ill afford, and their own internal support systems are ill equipped to mount the kinds of management and organisation development programmes which are necessary. A further problem is that there have been so many changes in the law and in government policy in recent years that the service has become preoccupied with mounting courses to explain these, rather than address the more fundamental issues of developing learning skills and a learning organisation.

Bramshill during the 1970s

What then has been happening at the Police Staff College at Bramshill to reflect, respond to, and anticipate, these events in the service?

Throughout the 1970s police officers were beginning to display an interest in 'management', but it was an interest laced heavily with scepticism—something which they thought they 'ought' to know about rather than as something which inevitably and inherently embraced their role and, indeed, their whole organisation. At that time there was little occurring in their environment to encourage rigorous self-examination, as various surveys of public opinion invariably awarded them high ratings in public esteem. They were entitled to believe that they 'had it right' To approach management development in such circumstances was rather like trying to draw the attention of a marathon runner to health hazards which may be awaiting him in later years!

Bramshill at that time was staffed by two discrete groups and most of its courses were divided into two distinct halves, namely the 'academic' and the 'professional', the former was preoccupied with raising the level of understanding of society, the latter with policing skills, tactics, and strategies. The nature of police organisations and the roles, skills, attitudes and values of individual police officers received scant attention. The fact that each 'student' received a predetermined programme of 'inputs' followed by seminars, and was reported upon by staff to his chief constable in terms of how he had responded to that programme, meant that while many students enhanced their insights and conceptual ability concerning the world in which they operated, few developed the ability to learn how to learn in the broadest sense, ie by looking at themselves and developing self-awareness, creativity and proactivity. The period was dominated by self-confidence which was reflected in a training, or moulding, approach at all levels from the training of probationer constables to the training of aspiring chief constables. Bramshill courses were, on the whole, in the best tradition of staff colleges geared to 'instrumentalist' ends of preserving and reinforcing 'the way we go about doing things' in the confident belief that such approaches have served the organisation well in the past and were likely to continue to do so in the future. It was, however, clear that, even in that period, an increasing number of officers were returning from Bramshill or force supported courses at universities posing more fundamental questions about the nature and style of their organisation, the directions which it was taking and whether these would suffice to meet future needs.

During that period in the 1970s many attempts were made to introduce 'best practice' from the wider world of management and organisational development. These occurred mainly on Senior and Intermediate Command Courses and included:—
1. Sessions conducted by leading thinkers, writers and practitioners in the field of management and organisation development.
2. Joint workshops with senior managers from a wide range of organisations.
3. Exchange attachments with managers from other organisations.
4. Intensive self-discovery and interpersonal skills workshops.
5. Team-Building and project planning workshops of one week's duration run

by internal consultants, kindly 'lent' to the College by Shell and ICI.

It is difficult to estimate the impact of such ventures, which were enjoyed at the time but which were 'phased out' in the late 1970s.

These innovations were intended as an antidote to a surfeit of learning 'about' management and as a means of developing managerial skills. It had long been discovered in other organisations that there was usually a wide gulf in the case of each individual manager, between his 'espoused' theories, ie those theories which he claimed that he believed in, and his 'theory in practice', ie his typical behaviours as witnessed and experienced by those working with and for him. The reading of books, the writing of essays, and attendance at lectures may, or may not, have influenced his espoused theories but they did little to affect his theory in practice.

The world of management development had discovered that it was only in small learning groups (of maximum size of 10–12) that actual behaviour, together with the values and attitudes which underpinned it, could be surfaced and worked at. Furthermore, if group members were to give honest and open feedback to each other in a caring and supportive manner, a high level of trust was necessary. In order to help individuals to learn self-awareness and ways of adjusting their behaviour, *and* to relate the processes occurring in the learning group back to their work situation, a high level of both knowledge and skill is required of the management developer/facilitator. As I will be using the term facilitator frequently in the remainder of this chapter I will define the role as one which empowers and enables the learner to take over responsibility for his own learning, ie to become a 'self-directed learner'. This concept derives from the work of Carl Rogers (1967, 1983) and of Dewey (1913), and demands, as Gibran (1980) has said that the teacher "gives not of his wisdom but rather of his faith and his lovingness".

During the 1970s there was not much facilitating taking place at Bramshill. The smallest courses numbered 30 and the largest (at one time) 144, these being broken down into 'syndicates' of 10–13. As, for most of that time, there were only 3 management developers on the staff, skilled in facilitating such learning, and as they were usually given a maximum of one week out of a total of 12 or 24 weeks with each course, relatively little impact was made upon changing theory in practice, ie behaviour. 'Management' was seen as just another subject to be 'inputted' alongside many others on courses, and the ambitions of most course directors stretched little further than inviting along one or two eminent management 'lecturers' to deliver a two-hour 'input' on management/organisation theory laced with prescriptions and exhortations towards 'better managerial practice'; as a further concession to the 'subject' each student would be expected to produce one 3000 word essay on management during his course!

As several attempts to increase the number of professional management developers on the staff failed, attempts were made to convert the police syndicate directors into facilitators in order that they might build upon the work done by the three management development specialists during the rest of the course. This strategy enjoyed very limited success as the training period allowed for such staff was two weeks and, in any event, their role as writers of reports (ie judges) on each student undermined their role as true facilitators; not surprisingly, students were reluctant to open up their real selves to possible development. Moreover, the course designs did not lend themselves to student centred facilitative approaches.

The most significant advances during that period of the 1970s came on the Special Course. As that course then lasted for 12 months the management development team were given four continuous weeks in which to work with them in a very learner-centred manner; under such conditions considerable personal development, in terms of the individual's values and skills, and his capacity to work as an effective team member, took place.

New strategies at Bramshill

The watershed came at Bramshill in 1980 in the guise of Sir Kenneth Newman who arrived having wrestled with the complexities of commanding the Royal Ulster Constabulary. He was able to switch the focus to the problems and strategic issues facing the British police service. Such thinking at Bramshill preceded the traumatic events of summer 1981 and their various sequels. Corporate strategy became the central theme of the Senior Command Course. In 1981 Sir Kenneth commissioned two research projects, one conducted by the author of this paper and the other by the Home Office Police Research Services Unit, into the roles of Divisional and Sub-Divisional Commanders—the two studies to run independently and in parallel, in order to attempt to identify the core learning needs. The results of these studies threw into question many of the service's managerial practices and myths. In the same year the College, anticipating the needs of forces for an infrastructure of skills to support a corporate and strategic management approach, launched the Carousel Programme and the Rolling Programme. The former was a range of short courses focusing on current policing and police management problems requiring new skills, which proved to be immediately popular. The latter was a form of action learning, involving six forces at a time contributing a team of two middle-ranking officers and a problem they would like to be researched; the objective was to develop the skills of managing a research project, data-collection and data-interpretation over the period of one year. Two such programmes were run between 1981 and 1983 involving 12 forces. The evaluation showed that the participants had learned a great deal but several of their Chief Officers felt that their problem had not been 'solved'.

Also in 1981 the College added much more rigour to the selection and training of its staff. A profile was constructed of the kinds of personality most likely to make effective facilitators. Henceforward all applicants were subjected to a 3-day assessment centre and, if they passed it, a four-week induction programme in facilitation skills. The assessment centres consisted of a battery of psychological tests/profiles, followed by a series of group exercises and tasks observed by a panel of experienced staff members, an individual interview, and feedback to all applicants on their personal profile which had emerged during the 'centre'. Those who were accepted brought their profile to the induction programme as the basis of their personal development as staff members, those who were not usually found it to be a useful data-base upon which to build personal action plans.

In 1982, anticipating Home Office Circular No. 114 of 1983 which emphasised the need for 'value for money' and the effective and efficient use of resources, the College sponsored a series of workshops run by Val Lubans, co-author of the book *Policing by Objectives* (Lubans and Edgar, 1979). These included one each for the senior management teams of Northamptonshire, Lincolnshire and the Metropolitan police forces (during Sir Kenneth's first week as Commissioner!), the HMIs and senior Home Office staff, and Bramshill staff.

Unfortunately, under pressure from government for 'value for money' the simpler, more seductive dimensions of his message were received (ie the mechanics of Policing by Objectives) but the preconditions for its success which he advocated (ie the need for an open, participative culture) were largely ignored (Doyle and Tindal, 1985). Also in 1982 the lessons learned from the 'Yorkshire Ripper' case, and the subsequent internal report led to the setting up at the College of the SCIMITAR project (Serious Crime Investigation—Management, Intelligence, Training and Resources) and the series of 4-week courses for Assistant Chief Constables (Crime) and 2-week courses for Detective Chief Superintendents. A further trend in police forces led to the devolution of autonomy to Sub-Divisional Commanders which left Divisional Commanders seeking a new role. This phenomenon led to the launching of a new 'thin sandwich' programme for Chief Superintendents entitled ODAS (Organisation Development—the Associated Skills). The first of these attracted 16 chief superintendents from 14 forces, two forces providing a pair each. It is of interest to note that, upon their return to their forces, individuals were too vulnerable to the prevailing culture to make an impact, but the two 'partnerships' proved to be durable, sustaining and effective. The lessons learned from this pilot programme coupled with those from Rolling Programmes Nos. 1 and 2, were to have a profound effect when both ODAS and the Rolling programmes were relaunched, with a very different design in 1986. Also in 1982 the radical review of the Special Course commenced, leading in 1985 to the introduction of a much shortened 'sandwich' course, with a very far-sighted and meticulously planned developmental programme. The ODAS and Rolling Programmes will be described more fully later in this paper as examples of what might be done to help police forces to help themselves in becoming truly learning systems.

The newly designed Special Course consists of three main phases, a Preparatory Course (one week), Part I (3 months) and Part II (4 months) one or two years after substantial experience as a sergeant. The Preparatory course introduced participants to the idea of strategic thinking in relation to operational effectiveness and the ownership of ideas in order to enable participants to see what they have to do in order to make ideas come alive. They then return to operations knowing that the programme will have a strong skills/personal development focus.

The aims, objectives, and methods of Part I have been analysed elsewhere by my colleague Robert Adlam (1986). Suffice it to say here that it is notable for the quality of the individual self-development/action plans which it produces. These action plans are reinforced by the training by the College of individual supervisors (an officer from the student's own force) to act as coaches and counsellors, reconventions at the College and visits by College staff to the 'student' in his work location. The response of the individual to his own perceived needs engenders a strong commitment to the action components of the plan (Boydell and Pedler, 1981). Part II of the programme, which follows one or two years of self-development on the job, has the following focal issues:

1. to sustain and enhance the process of strategic thinking in preparation for strategic management;
2. the management of a 'delivery' culture and the management of the interface between 'management culture' and 'street culture'; and
3. managing the problem of an organisation within an organisation ie the police within the community.

The philosophy underlying this programme has also been described by Robert Adlam (1986).

The year 1984 saw the service searching avidly for new solutions to new problems. The aftermath of the Scarman Report (1981), Home Office Circular No. 114 of 1983, Home Office Circular No. 8 of 1984 (stressing the need for a multi-agency approach to crime prevention and crime reduction) and the Policy Studies Institute's Report on the Metropolitan Police (Smith and Gray, 1983), to say nothing of the BBC series on Thames Valley Police and the debate on police accountability, rate-capping in local authorities, and reports on police forces by highly reputable management consultants, all weighed heavily upon the minds of police policy-makers. College staff were kept very busy responding to requests for both information and help and trying to keep track of and in tune with, the multitude of studies and initiatives being undertaken within the service. In 1982 a new Commandant, Mr Barry Pain had arrived and was wrestling with the problem of how to respond effectively to the needs of the service. It became increasingly apparent that the College could never meet all of the demands and that not only the wisest, but also the most effective, course of action for it was to help forces to help themselves.

The search for new approaches to corporate management led the College to mount a series of three-day conferences during 1985 and early 1986 for ACPO ranking officers and heads of Management Services departments under the heading of "Supporting Strategic Management". At these conferences both problems and innovative approaches to them were shared and they became a forum in which forces could help each other to help themselves. They also led to the revitalising of the ODAS and Rolling Programmes and to the introduction of a new Carousel Course entitled "Support Skills for Management Development". All of these programmes are founded upon the philosophy of developing the skills of people at all levels in the organisation in

(a) diagnosing the sources of organisational malfunctioning such as
    (i)   a lack of clarity of purpose,
    (ii) communication difficulties,
    (iii) misdirected energy,
    (iv) lack of creativity or thoroughness in decision-making,
    (v)   ineffective team work; and
(b) developing their skills in helping the learning of both individuals and groups, and in intervening sensitively and effectively in problem situations.

In this way, it is hoped, groups of officers at different levels in any organisation will form supportive and developmental 'networks' capable of helping the organisation to become a true learning system, and to manage change effectively.

Before discussing these initiatives more fully perhaps we should pause to take stock of developments on the mainstream command courses. Since 1982 the Intermediate Command Course has been steadily building upon the results of the research project into the roles of Divisional and Sub-Divisional Commanders. The eleven-week programme commences with two weeks devoted to the fundamental skills of learning, self-awareness and self-development, communicating effectively, creative problem solving and team-building. The rest of the course has become increasingly learner-centred by offering a number of simulations and projects in which those skills can be applied and tested. Meanwhile, the Junior Command Course has been subjected to some quite radical changes. In late 1985, when the course lasted for 22 weeks, the Police Training Council decided that, in future, it should be attended by all chief inspectors upon promotion (some 500 plus per annum), leaving Inspectors Development Courses to be run regionally. This would mean some six courses per annum, each with 84 members, and each course of

7 weeks' duration. A change of such magnitude called for a total reappraisal of content and approach and retraining of tutorial staff. Hence, 1986 became a transitional year for that course with one 16-week course at the beginning of the year, and another at the end of the year. In the period from May to September replanning and retraining of staff took place. Most importantly, however, the nature of the course was changed and, following lessons learned from the new-style Special Course, became much more learner-centred and developmental. In future the course itself will concentrate on self-awareness, learning how to learn and to develop oneself and others, simulations and exercises. It is anticipated that much of the knowledge-based content will be available in 'distance learning' packages that the learner can work at in his own time and at his own pace. Such methods will bring it more into line with best practice in other organisations.

In order to round off this section on Bramshill's response to the management and organisation development needs of the service I will return to the initiatives pursued since the conferences on "Supporting Strategic Management" in 1985/6. Lessons learned from earlier forays into organisational development via ODAS and the Rolling Programme during the period 1982/4 were reassessed and developed into new programmes. Prominent among these lessons were:—

1. Attempts to develop individual self-directed learners are unlikely to succeed unless they form the basis of a firm contract with those responsible for the culture and style of his real work environment. The end product must be 'owned' by those who want the ensuing skills, attitudes, and values transferred into the workplace, and who will support and encourage that transfer.
2. It is vitally important to concentrate upon the ways in which an organisation goes about planning and performing its tasks, and particularly upon 'people processes', ie the effectiveness of all interactions between people.
3. It is important to ensure that a group of people from the same organisation undergo, together and simultaneously, the same developmental experience. In this way, a support network is formed within the organisation which can continue the mutual self-development process, and is of great potential help to top management in working with reality and developing change programmes.
4. Such support networks must cut through the hierarchy and be representative of, and helpful to, all levels within the organisation. Courses which focus on one level in the hierarchy do nothing to build up trust and open communication between levels, an essential ingredient for organisational health and success. This means that top management must be part of the developmental network.
5. Unless the network forms around the notion that every human being has the right to define, own, and solve his/her own problems it is unlikely to develop a learning system.

Thus the ODAS programme is a 'thin sandwich' programme extending over 6 months divided into a number of modules which help participants to take stock of their current organisational situation, take stock of their own skills, develop new ways of looking at and auditing organisational health and effectiveness, and develop new skills in intervening effectively in order to assist organisational change.

Each programme consists of teams from four forces, preferably geographically adjacent in order that they may continue to interact and help each other. Each team consists of an assistant chief constable, a divisional commander, and the head of Management Services or Training. The team which runs the programme consists of an organisation development consultant, a practising deputy chief constable and two members of Bramshill's management development staff. That team is supported by a Steering Group, chaired by a chief constable, which negotiates the initial contract with the chief constable or deputy chief constable, as sponsor, of each participating team, and helps him to consider ways of using his team at the end of the programme, gives help and support to the team running the programme, and debriefs all participants at the end of the programme.

Hence the ODAS programme is aimed at helping police forces at policy-making and senior executive levels.

The Rolling Programme is aimed largely at middle and upper-middle management in support of the ODAS programme. In this programme four members of the Bramshill management development team give 30 days consultancy or training to any single police force which requires help in implementing a change programme. The focus of this activity is to enable that force to develop itself by developing internal consultancy/facilitation skills in a group of officers who will then constitute a potential support network which can be of help to the policy group in managing change.

These two programmes are, of course, both labour intensive and expensive, and can reach only a few forces at a time. The resources of Bramshill are such that there is little prospect of their expansion in order to embrace more forces. It was therefore important to develop a Carousel course which was aiming at self-help, namely "Support Skills for Management Development", which aims to help force training officers and sub-divisional commanders to develop consultancy/facilitation skills in order to enhance learning processes in all those with whom they come into contact.

What, then, has been Bramshill's contribution to meeting the needs of the police service, and how should one begin to evaluate it? At the very least one can say that it has been a common meeting ground for police officers, not only from Great Britain, but from around the world. Even if the staff have contributed little individual officers will have gained a great deal from such meetings in helping them to see many other perspectives on policing than their own. That in itself, however, would scarcely justify the collective investment. The role of the academic (civilian) staff can all too easily be underrated, sneered at, or even dismissed by the more 'macho' and pragmatic among police officers. As Robert Reiner has said (1985) the culture is "very pragmatic, concrete, down-to-earth, and anti-theoretical . . . Police officers are concerned to get from here to tomorrow (or the next hour) safely and with the least fuss and paperwork. This makes them reluctant to contemplate innovation, experimentation or research". In such circumstances those who attempt to encourage a helicopter, or long-term view, or indeed to pose 'WHY?' type questions, are apt to be given a hard time. Nevertheless, increasing numbers of police officers are now becoming active in such pursuits themselves, and more of them are setting such examples as Chief Officers. To what extent Bramshill can claim any credit for that is a matter of speculation, as compared with the effects of recruitment, external and internal pressures on the organisation, and changes in societal mores. It is, however, fair to say that the civilian staff have often played the role of the police officer's conscience and, even if he did not always like what he heard, the police officer could not always ignore it. Their focus has tended to be upon the often denigrated 'service' approach to policing, rather than upon 'crime fighting', and upon a systems approach to the organisation and its environment rather than a mechanistic one.

On the very positive side the development of the Carousel programme of short courses, and the mounting of short conferences for senior officers on topics of mutual concern and interest, have been an undoubted success. They are, however, uncomfortable bedmates with the longer term traditional 'command' type courses because they require great staff versatility and flexibility. The more these 'mainstream' command courses become developmental programmes the more they demand the constant presence of facilitator/tutors, thus rendering them inaccessible to the short course programme. The latter is oversubscribed in terms of applicants by three to four times and demand heavily outweighs supply; it has already introduced far more police officers to Bramshill and to the notion of their own self-development than have the command courses. The other success has been the newly designed Special Course as witnessed by the high level of motivation and commitment of its members and the high ratings they are achieving in in-force appraisal schemes.

Unresolved issues

Perhaps the greatest problem for Bramshill is the lack of clarity of its mission, for without that it is really not possible to create a vision of its future nor a meaningful evaluation of its past. The expectations of its clients are very varied, ambiguous, ambivalent and often conflicting, and hence it faces many paradoxes.

Officially the role of Bramshill is to "produce from within the service its own future leaders"; but if promotion is conditional upon College attendance, and if the kind of leader is not specified, then the fact that a very high proportion of its students attain senior ranks becomes a self-fulfilling prophesy. In fact, in recent years, a considerable proportion of ACCs have not attended the Senior Command Course. In order to evaluate the effectiveness of that course one would have to demonstrate that those who did not attend the course were not so effective as those who did. Even that, however, would be an insufficient evaluation of the course itself, but would be rather an evaluation of the selection procedure *for* the course. The newly designed Special Course is of a different order in that it contains an in-built audit of the growth and development of the individual and of his effectiveness as a junior officer. In these circumstances one is bound to ask "what *kind* of leaders does the police service require?", and, "Is Bramshill creating that product?" All this assumes, of course, that such a 'product' would meet the needs of every police force in the country, whatever its circumstances. If such a product cannot and should not be defined then the main recourse should be to turn to the Special Course solution, and strive to create highly effective and flexible learners. Whilst the College has probably been very successful, in the longer term, in building a 'critical mass' of potential change agents in senior management this strategy tends to be too slow to cope with short-term service needs. Moreover the impact has been largely upon the espoused theories of senior managers rather than upon their theories in practice, as we have discussed elsewhere in this paper. It is these very skills of managing the change process which have been introduced only in very recent years and, as the last 'development programme' received by senior officers is the Senior Command Course, the new initiatives in the short course programme, which we have discussed, have been a necessary complement to command type courses. Bramshill has a huge responsibility in developing leaders whom Schein (1985) describes as 'culture managers'. Such leaders must be capable of stepping outside the culture of their own organisation, even as they continue to live within it, in order to involve their professional colleagues, at all levels, in achieving insights into its cultural dilemmas, and to be genuinely supportive and participative in their approach to change. Hence, our management development processes must nurture 'creative individualists' who possess high objectivity and tolerance of deviant points of view. In the final analysis the more rapidly things change the more dependent we are on leaders to manage the changes; no externally assisted organisation development programme, however sophisticated, can effect such fundamental and rapid cultural change. If Bramshill is to be the focus of developing such leaders it will require facilitators of the highest calibre on its staff who are able and free to encourage and support the most uninhibited forms of reflection, self-discovery, experimentation and creativity which build emotional and intellectual strength and sensitivity. In order to achieve that its staff will need to be exemplars of those very qualities.

The above paragraph introduces most of the unresolved issues facing Bramshill but these are increased and exacerbated by the diverse expectations of its clientele. The introduction of the Carousel programme, the developmental style of the Special Course, the organisation development thrust of ODAS and Rolling Programmes, and the imminent opening of the Simulated Operations Complex, have, for the most part, moved away from the notion of "producing from within the service its future leaders" and are addressing what is, for most Chief Officers, their most important issue, namely "where and how can I obtain help to enable me to develop a more effective and efficient organisation?" In these circumstances what is Bramshill to be—a staff college, the policeman's university, the centre of higher police training, a management and organisation development centre, or a resource centre? Many of these expectations make conflicting demands upon it in terms of strategy, clientele, methods, resources and staffing (ie in terms of the types and members of staff required for each of the above functions).

Staffing and the many problems associated with it is, in fact, at the heart of the unresolved issues facing Bramshill. With the days of purely knowledge-based courses, ie lectures to large audiences, passing in favour of learner-centred developmental programmes staff need to be very highly skilled facilitators and dedicated full time to the group for which they are responsible. Such a role requires a particular kind of personality profile which is at present relatively rare in the police service, and even these officers, when carefully selected, required lengthy training and experience in order to develop the necessary levels of competence and confidence. The problem is compounded by the fact that conditions of service at Bramshill tend not to attract many applicants of the right potential calibre, and a period on the staff is often, very unfairly, seen as a setback to their careers. To act as a facilitator to a developmental programme is highly developmental for the officer himself, for helping others to learn is the surest method of self-development. Furthermore, the two-year period of attachment to College staff grows increasingly inadequate as the expectations of students increase and as does the complexity of programmes in response to these. It might indeed be time to question whether the balance of two police members of staff to one non-police member ought to be reversed if the requisite levels of knowledge, skill and versatility are to be attained. Because there are no specialist careers (and this is not to suggest that there should be) for police officers, it may well be in the best interests of the service to employ far more experienced and skilled management developers/trainers who have been trained in a variety of other organisations. The service has been relatively slow in discovering that there is a wide range of professional skills available to them; it has all too often, attempted to convert police officers into 'instant experts' on almost anything; in spite of the fact that it has taken others years of investment in order to become experts. The management of police organisations becomes increasingly challenging and increasingly complex and demands the skilled help of those many other professionals in such fields as financial management, managing computer systems, information technology, corporate strategy, research, psychology and other behavioural sciences, management and organisation development, and human resources management. All of these 'disciplines' are represented by professions, and expertise in them requires many years of development, application, and experience to acquire. No police officer, for the sake of his career as a professional police officer can afford to spend more than 2 to 3 years in any one of them; he is therefore unlikely, and should not be required, to reach the levels of proficiency which are so essential. Already, several forces are employing full-time 'civilian' experts in finance and computing and an increasing number are engaging part-time consultants in management and organisation development and psychology. As the need for such help grows so Bramshill will need more professionals of this kind as a proportion of its staff; their help is becoming even more essential, not only in the running of courses, but also in terms of consultancy help to forces. This has been the pattern in other public service organisations.

So far as management development in the police service is concerned, the most pressing need is to build a network in all police forces of skilled facilitators/consultants capable of helping individuals and groups and indeed whole organisations to reassess their effectiveness, diagnose the source of problems, and develop new methods, skills and behaviours by means of reflective learning. In this way self-directed learning skills are likely to be developed, thus creating true learning organisations. The Police Staff College, the Metropolitan Police Resource Centre at Hendon and the Central Planning Unit could form the hub of such a network and be responsible for the basic, refresher, and advanced programmes for these facilitator/consultants.

A closely related unresolved problem so far as staff are concerned is that of the conflicting roles of staff members as both assessors and judges, in the role of report-writers on students, on the one hand, and as facilitators/developers on the other. The second of these roles conflicts directly with the first as it is virtually impossible to develop the levels of trust and openness which are necessary if people are to share their learning/development needs in the form of doubts, fears, anxieties and hopes. Also, of course, the whole point of developmental work is to develop self-directed and self-monitoring learners. The contrast between learner behaviour on assessed and non-assessed programmes has been highlighted by the recent developments of the Carousel programme and the newly designed Special Course. On the former, when students know that there is no report back to their force their behaviour rapidly becomes open, spontaneous, trusting and experimental. The problem was not so easily dealt with on the Special Course as it had a history as a 'command' course, and hence of 'secret' reports going back to Chief Officers. The suspicion has gradually been overcome by separating out the processes of 'assessment for development' and 'assessment for the purpose of taking promotion decisions'. The former process, ie 'assessment for development', involves only those people directly committed to the development of the individuals, ie the learner, his 'supervisor' (development) in force, and his Bramshill tutor/facilitator; these are the only ones with direct access to his individual development needs and his personal action plans. The latter process is dealt with in the normal way by his line managers who monitor his progress on the job and compare his performance with his peers. Hence the first principle concerning staff in a developmental programme must be that in order to create a trusting and open learning climate one needs to separate out the assessors according to whether their role supports the developmental process or the promotion system. Assessment is necessary in both cases but in the former it is owned and acted upon by the 'learner' or self-developer, whereas in the latter it is owned by the organisation. In order to make a start on the self-development process one needs a personal skills, attitudes and values profile, and that is best acquired through a professionally run assessment centre.

One further issue concerning staff and their capacity to help the development of others is that of power and status. A learning climate conducive to the development process cannot be built when staff are placed in a position of authority and power over the learner because such a learning climate is built by sharing responsibility, developing individual autonomy and learning together in a genuine learning community. So long as staff take decisions on behalf of the learner the latter cannot experiment, reflect and learn. Hence in a learning community a hierarchical management structure is extremely damaging and dys-functional and controllers have to be converted into supporters and helpers. Furthermore the facilitators themselves are very vulnerable and need a great deal of support and counselling if their confidence and competence is to be maintained and developed. Helping individuals in groups to develop their self-awareness and skills is a very testing experience and the vast range of emotions, attitudes, behaviours, and interactions with which they have to work forms a constant challenge to their competence, stamina and personal development. This makes them very vulnerable to stress and 'burnout' and requires constant care and help from their support system. They certainly cannot sustain their effectiveness for long periods without time out for reflection, recuperation and renewal. Facilitation of learning is a very different role from that of the pedagogue who reiterates the same syllabus, lectures and seminars many times over.

Finally, in considering Bramshill's unresolved issues one cannot avoid reference to its exclusivity. All of its students, with the exception of a few civilians employed by police forces, are police officers, as indeed are the majority of its staff. Earlier in this section we discussed the need for leaders to be 'culture managers' who are 'capable of stepping outside of their own organisation, even as they continue to live within it (Schein, 1985). That is a well-nigh impossible feat for a Bramshill student as it can be a very risky process for him in career terms to question with any profoundity the collective established 'truths' about how police officers 'ought' to think and behave. The whole process of assessing and reporting upon the performance and potential of students, ie police officers on courses, is heavily laced with existing assumptions and values about what kind of a person a senior police officer ought to be. These are the very kinds of assumptions which are liable to be questioned, or challenged, by fellow learners who are not police officers, nor imbued with the culture. Whenever we have experimented with interfacing police officers with people from other occupations or walks of life such questioning has been very developmental for all concerned, but it is sadly a relatively infrequent occurrence.

Hence the key unresolved issues for Bramshill can only be posed as a series of questions. What is its proper role to be if it is to be of maximum help to the police service and the public it serves? How are its activities to be evaluated in terms of its helpfulness to its clients? Who are its clients? How can it best diagnose client needs and respond speedily, sensitively and accurately to them? How can it create a learning climate and a management system which encourages personal, group, and organisational enquiry, experimentation and discovery? Where and how can it find the kinds of staff who can create such a supportive and experimental learning climate in order to develop a sensitive, enquiring and creative police service capable of responding to the varied challenges, expectations, and opportunities which confront it?

11 Training for stress

Mary Manolias

The reader's first reaction on finding a chapter on training for stress is that it is likely to be somewhat superfluous. Surely all that can be said about stress has been said before and there is already an abundance of training packages on the subject on offer? It is certainly true that stress is a topic which has suffered from gross over-exposure during recent years. As so often happens the effect of this has been the opposite to what was intended. Rather than alerting people to an alarming and increasingly common problem, too much publicity has tended to act as a turn-off. There are many people, senior police officers amongst them, who feel that far too much fuss has been made about stress, and it is very easy to sympathise with their viewpoint. It is becoming almost impossible to pick up a newspaper or magazine without finding some reference to stress. The credibility of stress as a real threat has been further undermined by presenting it as a modern 'bogeyman' as if it was something that had only recently come into existence. In certain respects this is true, but man has always had to contend with fear and anxiety and there has never been an age when life was free from stress. In the past people lived and survived under conditions that would appal most of us. They even seem to have achieved some degree of happiness and contentment under those conditions. However, stress was usually linked with real physical danger or other serious threat. What has happened during the recent past is that, while many of the old very real threats that have plagued the human race down the centuries have been overcome, they have been replaced by different and less direct pressures. Many obvious improvements have resulted from man's endless battle to control his environment. Technological advancement has provided remedies to many diseases, the means to ensure adequate supplies of food and other benefits. At the same time it has imposed an increasing number of unnatural constraints. Many of those constraints have become a normal part of life; for example, living at great distances from our places of work and having our activities ruled by the clock. Normal they may be, but certainly not natural. Man has created a range of quite artificial stressors for himself. At the same time many of the social structures, such as the family, the stable social groupings that existed in the neighbourhood and the work environment, which provided his main sources of emotional support, have been slowly eroded. The end result has been to leave him more vulnerable than ever to the pressures on him. The situation is further exacerbated by the fact that Western society today is in the throes of a major social upheaval. Changes are taking place at an ever faster rate, and there no longer seem to be any certainties about the future.

Research has shown that change is a major stressor and can constitute a real threat to health. Holmes and Rahe (1967) produced a "social re-adjustment rating scale" which scores major life changes according to their risk to health. It is interesting to note that even seemingly desired changes such as marriage or outstanding personal achievement carry quite high scores. The theory is that all changes require energy for readjustment. Whether they are good or bad, imposed changes are generally resented. When such changes are made in the workplace they are usually accompanied by a severe drop in morale. In a study of stress management facilities in thirty-two major UK organisations (Shipley and Orlans, 1983) the majority of respondents cited change as being the greatest source of stress at work.

As is always the case, there are those who have been ready to capitalise on the problems of society and there has been a mushrooming industry in stress management courses. These are mostly aimed at the high-powered executive, although the research provides substantial evidence to show that it is the blue collar worker who is the more prone to suffer the effects of stress (Cooper and Smith, 1983). The menus on offer on such courses are generally very similar. They usually emphasise the relationship between stress and cardiovascular disease, make much of the 'A' type personality, ie the thrusting ambitious workaholic, and provide an introduction to relaxation techniques which may include meditation. Often the main difference between courses is their cost. Some are extremely expensive. Stress management courses are at best generally only an introduction and awareness raising exercise, but they can be a grave disappointment to anyone expecting real answers to their problems.

Most of the techniques on offer can provide short-term relief by raising the level of stress tolerance, but they are no more truly effective than taking an aspirin to cure a headache. The palliative helps the sufferer to keep going although he is unfit, but the true problem remains.

Possibly the main defect in the stress package approach is that it artificially separates stress from the ongoing processes of life. Isolating stress as a separate entity certainly facilitates the production of a neat training package, but in doing so succeeds in trivialising a difficult and important issue. No intelligent person can be expected to take the threat of stress very seriously if he is told there is a cure available in six easy lessons. Stress management programmes are not tailored to the needs of the individual and they do not help the man on the street who is seeking an answer to his own particular problems. Such programmes leave it up to the individual to translate the principles expounded and fit them to his own needs. But if it is to acquire meaning, stress training must be linked to personal experience. This is a particularly important consideration in the training of police officers since their occupation encourages a practical attitude towards learning. They often display a tendency to dismiss theory unless it is shown to relate to real life.

Defining stress

Defining stress in a meaningful way is one of the major hurdles in stress training. Most people think they know what is meant by the term and are certainly able to recognise feelings in themselves which they associate with the word. The classic definition of stress does not seem to match this intuitive understanding. Hans Selye (1975) originally defined the stress reaction or General Adaption Syndrome (GAS) in physiological terms. What he was describing was the organism's reaction to extreme threat when the body is prepared for fight or flight by the release of large quantities of adrenalin into the circulatory system. Selye gives a lucid and accurate definition of traumatic stress. It is the one most frequently cited on stress management courses. Few of us will ever experience this extreme pure stress reaction in a lifetime, but from those who have we know it to be significantly different both in quality and quantity from the normal stress experience.

Normal stress may be more easily understood if it is defined in different terms. For instance, substituting a word such as 'dissonance' for stress in this context might help to clarify the situation to a certain extent since it removes the more unfortunate connotations that the word stress has acquired. This would also obviate the need to use such inappropriate terms as 'good' or 'bad' in relation to stress. It would be possible to talk about the degree of dissonance instead. Although juggling with words may help to arrive at a better definition of stress, the everyday experience of stress is so inextricably bound up with the ongoing problems of life that it is probably most easily understood and dealt with in terms of those problems. In short, learning to understand and cope with stress is neither more or less than learning to understand and cope with life.

Following this line of reasoning, it would appear that the most productive approach to training people to deal with the negative effects of stress is by equipping them with appropriate skills for handling those situations or tasks which are perceived as stressful. In some cases this can be done simply by training them in the correct routine procedures or by providing a framework for successful action. As far as the police service is concerned this aspect of training is already quite well handled in some respects. However, for the most part stress-related training will be concerned with life skills such as communication, human awareness and active listening skills. A great deal of interest is already being shown in these by police training establishments, where the main value of such skills is seen to lie in their role of helping to improve relationships with the community. So far they do not seem to have been seriously considered as having an equally valuable role in improving relationships within the police organisation, although one chief constable was heard to remark quite recently: "We are putting all this training effort into improving police community relations. Isn't it time we turned the mirror on ourselves?" If those skills are to be used for the purpose of preventing stress it will only mean a minor shift of emphasis in the training programme and introducing an awareness that their field of application can be wider or differently directed than was originally intended. By adopting such an approach stress training can be smoothly incorporated into other areas of training and will generally be inseparable from them.

High stress occupations

It is generally assumed that policing is a high stress occupation, although the evidence can never be absolutely conclusive since there are few reliable objective methods for measuring stress. Nevertheless findings from stress research carried out in the United States do tend to support this assumption. For example, there are studies demonstrating that as an occupational group the police are prone to abnormally high suicide rates (Nelson and Smith, 1970) and mortality rates, (Blackmore, 1978), and are more susceptible than average to stress-related illnesses (Fell et al., 1975).

In this country the police service was recently selected as one of a number of high stress occupations to be the subject of a special study* conducted by a

---

*A report can be expected in the early part of 1988.

committee set up by the Health Education Council (now the Health Education Authority). The other representative occupations selected were nursing, teaching and social work. It was observed that all those groups could also be described as boundary keeping occupations, that is they all functioned at the interface between the established order, represented by mainly the government and the Civil Service, and society in general, and that they were expected to represent the policies of that order in their dealings with society.

During periods of social stability the organisation of such groups is fairly fixed and often becomes institutionalised. In times of change like today they are subject to pressures from both sides and become a form of social shock absorber. The existing order seeks to preserve stability and maintain the status quo via the controlling activities of these occupations which, in consequence, become targets for the expression of discontent in those sections of society caught up in the effect of change. When the pressures from both sides become sufficiently strong the organisational structure is disrupted, creating an internal climate of uncertainty. The resultant stress engendered in the personnel can be regarded as a kind of barometer of the tension in society at large.

The reader will already have noticed that the professions mentioned are all service occupations and that their work involves close interaction with other people. The coping mechanisms employed by those groups and the ways in which stress was expressed were all seen to be very similar.

In contrast to organisations which had a tangible end product and where high stress levels were reflected by decreased productivity, stress in the person-centred occupations was expressed in their relations with the client group.

This phenomenon was reported by Isobel Menzies as long ago as 1970 when, during her study of nurses in a major teaching hospital, she noticed that nurses attempted to cope with high levels of anxiety by distancing themselves from their patients by a process of depersonalisation. For instance they would often talk about patients by bed numbers or diseases: "the liver in bed 10" or "the pneumonia in bed 15".

There has been surprisingly little published research on this area of interaction, but all the HEC committee members recognised it as a feature of the organisation with which they were most familiar. Distancing between the occupational group and the client was the most commonly observed expression of stress and was invariably viewed as having a disruptive effect on the relationship between the two groups. However, it was thought that there might be even more disturbing manifestations of stress, for example in the teaching profession where frustration might find expression in the classroom, or in hospitals where it may be a major contributory factor to errors in patient treatment. In the United States many police psychologists believe that there is a direct connection between stress and police brutality and are able to produce evidence from case histories in support of this claim (Meredith, 1984).

It would be presumptuous to assume that a parallel situation exists in the UK, since there are marked dissimilarities in background conditions. For instance the police here are not routinely armed, (the exception to this being Northern Ireland) and the UK has not yet experienced the same degrees of urban decay or racial tension that can be found in the US. However there is little room for complacency. Past experience has shown that, in this area, where America goes Britain generally follows.

Police coping

In both the British and American police coping strategies are expressed through a unique operational style. Distancing is usually combined with another related coping mechanism, denial; ie a refusal to acknowledge the reality of unpleasant or distressing events. These together are further coloured by the aggressive police cult of masculinity to give the resultant well-known 'macho' style. Many police officers acquire this style very early in their careers. It is sanctioned by the culture, and the probationer is generally anxious to conform in order to win acceptance from his fellow officers. It is further encouraged by the media, particularly television, which has portrayed the 'macho' style officer in numerous enjoyable productions from 'Z Cars' to 'the Sweeney'. The general public too plays its part in supporting this image through an unconscious expectation that the police officer can cope with anything and everything.

The 'macho' style has at least one positive advantage; it does help the young recruit over many of the early hurdles of police work. Unfortunately, it easily becomes second nature and an accepted part of the officer's persona. When this happens the public image is carried over into his or her private life with potentially disastrous effects on the officer's home life. The most commonly recorded effects are a block on communication between the officer and his spouse, the development of a suspicious attitude towards all members of the family and an insistence on an almost military style of discipline in the home. Within the work situations the main adverse effect is to reduce effective communication within and between all levels of the hierarchy.

Many police officers are undergoing a change of attitude and starting to reject this stereotype. They recognise that there are alternative and better ways to cope with the effects of pressure, but it may be quite a long time before the results of this change become evident. The main obstacles to reform in this area are the apparent effectiveness of the coping strategies incorporated in the 'macho' style and the ease with which they appear to be learned. However, this effectiveness is only partial and there are some events so shocking that such defence mechanisms fail to work. This is clearly seen to be the case after traumatic incidents or dangerous riot situations. The Manchester air crash and the fire at the Bradford football ground triggered severe after-effects in a large proportion of the officers involved. Once his defences are breached the hardened police officer is often found to be inadequately prepared to cope with the distressing emotions engendered by such events. Evidence is coming to light that these same defence mechanisms can occasionally break down in quite unexpected circumstances when an officer is dealing with an incident which, although distressing in itself, eg a cot death, are a normal part of police routine. This problem is currently being researched by the author.

The mechanics of coping strategies are not yet fully understood and consequently it may be too early to start encouraging a wholesale abandonment of the kind of strategies associated with the macho style of operating. No doubt both denial and distancing have a part to play within a wider repertoire of reactions. In some circumstances denial seems the only appropriate reaction. However, training can offer alternative strategies for protecting the officer from the adverse effects of distressing incidents whilst also allowing him to function as a warm and fully human being.

Police stress research in Britain

In the United States police stress has been recognised as a problem for many years and existing research in this area would probably fill a library. It is usually given priority on police training programmes, and many forces employ their own psychologist who is not only responsible for stress training and other psychological aspects of police training but is also available to offer a counselling service to officers. Frequently, induction courses and stress training are also offered to officers' spouses since it is recognised that they have an extremely valuable role to play in providing the right kind of emotional support. There is much that the UK can learn from the American approach to police stress provided we are selective.

In this country concern over police stress is a relatively recent phenomenon. It was mainly the Police Federation which took the lead in alerting forces to the growing number of stress-related illnesses, nervous breakdowns and other abnormal forms of behaviour induced by stress. In 1981 ACPO (Association of Chief Police Officers) set up a working party to examine the problem and report back on their findings. The assistance of the Home Office Scientific Research and Development Branch was sought in conducting the required research. This resulted in a wide ranging study involving a total of 81 police officers together with a team of specialist advisors, each of whom was able to offer some particular expertise in the area of stress. It was recognised that, although the police themselves had sufficient personal experience to provide the answers in this enquiry, they required independent assistance in order to probe sufficiently deeply if they were to understand and uncover the root causes to their problems.

The project took the form of a series of seven workshops, each of which produced its own detailed report. The workshop process itself engendered great enthusiasm amongst the participants; the degree of involvement was such that any distinction between ranks and between police and civilians totally disappeared. Everyone worked together as a united team and the discussion was extremely frank. It is interesting to note that one of the recommendations of the final report was that "Consideration should be given to a wider use of the workshop method" in order to encourage "the exchange of ideas, schemes and information within the Service" (Manolias, 1983).

The initial or directing workshop set the scene and was followed by five parallel and subsidiary workshops each of which concentrated on a different aspect of the problem. The final workshop collated and reviewed the contributory data to produce a final report. The study was completed in the space of a year and a summary of the conclusions and recommendations which was submitted to ACPO Council during the later part of 1983 was accepted without reservation.

Recommendations relating to police training

One of the subsidiary workshops was devoted exclusively to the topic of training for stress. A motto devised by a group of the young constables who took part was

"Competence breeds confidence and confidence breeds competence".

It could well serve as the theme for all stress-related training.

The final recommendations relating to training are listed below and can be roughly grouped under four main headings: general health, probationer and constable training, management training and traumatic incidents.

General
health

— Education in the underlying principles of good health should be made available to all police personnel.

Management

— Those constables selected for promotion to the rank of sergeant should receive training for the post before they are appointed. Courses for other ranks should occur as soon after promotion as possible.

— Before promotion to each rank there should be training in management skills, which should be related to the social skills training currently being developed for constables.

— Specific skills of interviewing, communicating and listening should be taught on all police management courses which should preferably be in short repeated inputs. Emphasis should be placed on the necessity to recognise that police officers are as vulnerable to stress as anyone else since stress is a common human experience in response to pressures of varying forms.

— Regional training centres should provide regular pre-promotion courses, starting with the rank of sergeant.

— Police managers should be regularly exposed to training with non-police organisations.

Trauma

— The training of new recruits should prepare them for the initial operational encounter.

— Training should offer practical strategies, based on skills training for coping with traumatic incidents as they occur: for example, conflict management techniques. Such training should also be offered for more experienced officers.

— All supervisory officers should receive appropriate training to increase their awareness and counselling skills.

The commentary which follows discusses some of the recommendations and makes further suggestions for stress-related training.

General health

It is interesting to note that the recommendation relating to training in the principles of good health makes no reference to the word stress.

Courses in health education should certainly be a routine part of all probationer training. The concept of stress will be more acceptable within the police culture if it is introduced in conjunction with information on general health and physical fitness. This approach also provides an opportunity to underline the importance of exercise and of maintaining a high standard of physical health in combating the effects of stress. Other aspects of stress that might be discussed during a general introductory course are a simple explanation of the physiology of the stress reaction and the effects of adrenalin, an introduction to stress management techniques and some discussion of stress in everyday life. If there is sufficient time and interest the role of support systems including colleague support and some discussion of coping mechanisms might also be included.

The work environment should encourage officers to build on the foundations laid down in training by providing time and facilities for physical exercise and the practice of relaxation techniques, and ensuring that a healthy balanced diet is available in the police canteen. There should also be an active policy to discourage smoking and the excessive intake of alcohol. These last measures are likely to prove unpopular but the success of the government's anti-smoking campaign over the past few years should encourage management to be firm. Additional back-up in this area might come from lectures by visiting speakers and information sheets on particular aspects of health care together with occasional articles on health-related matters in the force newspaper.

Ideally, all levels of police training should include some input on health which would not only remind officers of the general principles of health care and the importance of following them but could also focus on the special health care needs associated with different age groups or stage of career.

It is worth noting that the Look After Yourself (LAY) Project, an offshoot of the Health Education Authority*, exists to offer advice and supporting educational material on all aspects of physical fitness and stress. Some forces have already called on its services to assist in running fitness programmes. LAY is willing to tailor its input to meet particular occupational requirements.

Probationer and constable training

It is generally agreed that policing is a task for mature individuals and certainly many current problems and, consequently, training requirements might simply disappear if it were possible to recruit older individuals with suitable life experience into the job. As it is, most recruits are in their late teens, or early twenties. The higher educational standards required from today's recruits make it more likely that they will come from the kind of home where educational achievement is valued and that they may have had a fairly sheltered upbringing. The service puts more responsibility on these young shoulders than they feel ready to assume, and it is greatly to their credit that they seem to cope as well as they do. Of course, the public expectation of certain actions by the uniformed police officer, for example that he will always take charge in a crisis, exerts such a strong social pressure that it is easier to try to meet it than to avoid it. The young officer nearly always attempts to rise to the occasion.

There are a number of senior officers who will say quite openly that the service is going soft, and that today's probationer is over-protected, but this is largely because they do not realise just how much the beat has changed from their own experience of it. Not only is it physically a more dangerous place, but the people

*LAY Project Centre, Christchurch College, Canterbury, Kent CT1 1QU.

140

on it have less respect for the police uniform and are more ready to question the officer's authority. At the same time requirements for greater police accountability and new legislation such as PACE have imposed increased restrictions on all his actions. For most young officers their greatest fear is of making a mistake or of being unable to cope in an unfamiliar situation. This can often lead to their becoming over-officious and using their uniform as a protective barrier to help cover their own uncertainty, a strategy which certainly does not help to improve relations with the public.

Mistakes are both understandable and inevitable given the demands and diversity of the task. The system makes no allowances for them. In the past there was less likelihood that errors would be noticed. If pressed, most senior officers are able to come up with stories, often amusing, of things that went wrong during their early days on the beat, but if members of the public were there to see, either they did not realise the officer was acting incorrectly or they had too much respect for the uniform to question what was happening. Today the probationer has to work with a public which is much better informed, more prepared to question and often hostile. Complaints against the police, both justified and unjustified, are increasing every year.

Although the Initial Training courses for constables are relatively short, the probationer constables who took part in the workshop had no particular wish to see them extended. Instead they felt they would get far more benefit by learning through experiencing, provided they had the backing of instructor supervisors and were given the opportunity to analyse and discuss their street experiences.

Management training

The report identified management, both in style and structure, as being the greatest source of stress in the service, and the following quote recorded during one of the workshops heads the Section of the report dealing with management style.

"There is more stress in the nick than out on the streets".

The message contained in the recommendations concerned with management training is quite clear. It is that life skills training, at present directed mainly at smoothing interaction between the police and the public, is equally important for relations within the organisation. The methods of training and the benefits accruing from such skills form a recurrent theme throughout this book, emphasising their fundamental importance in good police training.

In addition, it should be remembered that although police managers have more direct dealings with other police officers than with the general public, any stress that they may generate is reflected outwards and the ripples may well spread beyond the boundaries of the service environment. Training which can help to reduce stress within the organisation is important, not only because it assists the system to function smoothly, but because it ultimately affects the quality of interactions with the public. The police manager also has a direct involvement in interactions outside the service. Despite having fewer and less intimate contacts with the general public than the beat constable, his role in promoting a positive image for the police service is just as important. In many respects his task is easier than that of the beat constable but there are still aspects of it which require attention during the training. The transition from ordinary police manager to semi-public figure comes gradually as an officer moves up the promotion ladder, but at each step along the way there is a variety of public appearances. It is true that most of those are very mundane events such as neighbourhood watch meetings, school visits or talks to the women's institute, but because policing as an occupation attracts more than its fair share of public attention they must all be regarded as important pubic appearances.

The quality of police television presentations has improved greatly over the past few years. The presenters on "Crime Watch" for instance are as good as any professionals. However, there are still occasions where an officer being interviewed appears to be as stiff and wooden as Toytown's famous Ernest. It is difficult to understand how men who are normally confident and eloquent can become so surly and inarticulate on the screen. Despite the need for them to exercise great caution over what is said it does not really explain why they give the impression that it is a gun rather than a camera that is being pointed at their heads. Politicians often have even greater need of discretion but for the most part this does not appear to inhibit them one bit. On the contrary they all appear to blossom whenever a television camera is present.

The general improvement in quality can probably be ascribed to the growth in the use of closed circuit TV by training establishments. These are used on a large number of courses so that practice sessions can be recorded and then played back to the class for analysis. Whatever the course is supposed to teach, the students gain an additional benefit from being forced to take a critical look at the way they appear and interact in a group situation and so improve their own public image. There are also a few courses which actually train officers for television appearances, although not every officer is destined to become a TV celebrity.

It is suggested that training for this public element of the police role should build on the social skills training given to probationers. Training and practice in additional accomplishments such as public speaking and running public meetings would be given at a level appropriate to the officer rank and designed around the range of tasks he might be expected to perform. The police service attracts more media time than any other occupation and police officers need many of the same kinds of skills as those who choose to make a career in public life. However, it would create a false impression of the requirement if this was referred to as public relations training, since skills in this area are peripheral to the main tasks of policing. The emphasis given to them in training should continue to reflect this.

Traumatic stress

In the recommendation on the training of recruits the words 'initial operational encounter' were only substituted for 'traumatic incident' after very careful debate. Although it was recognised that the probationer was likely to have quite serious difficulties in coming to terms with the more horrifying and disgusting aspects of police work it was felt that unreadiness and uncertainty over taking the correct action were the greatest sources of anxiety accompanying any new experience.

Training can and does help in such cases although it is impossible to prepare the recruit adequately for every possible eventuality. Most officers, for instance, will remember that training carried them through their first experience of a serious road traffic accident, because there were well-established routines to be followed. The shock came afterwards, but at the time they were able to cope.

Some tasks are less well defined or more difficult to prepare for than others. One example is the delivering of death messages. This is a duty that nearly all police officers dread however hardened they see themselves to be. Few other duties provide the opportunity for such intimate contact between the police officer and private individual and it is important that they are handled with tact and sensitivity. When a person is in a state of extreme distress the normal barriers are broken down and the way he is treated at this time will leave a deep and lasting impression. Of course there is no formula for delivering a death message or any way of knowing how the unfortunate recipient is likely to react. Training however can help the police officer to understand something of the process of shock and grief, as well as exploring and coming to terms with the emotions such situations arouse in himself. The mixture of anxiety over his own emotions combined with embarrassment at having to cause real hurt can create barriers that may prevent him carrying out this important task as well as he might. Probably because it is a difficult area it has been largely overlooked in training. However, one force is now running a series of one-day workshops on the topic and at least one other gets training from a professional counsellor. The courses are at present aimed mainly at experienced officers rather than at probationer level. They have been well received and those who have attended feel they have benefited considerably.

Training can also make a significant contribution in preparing officers for high stress events such as riots, shooting incidents and major disasters. Police training centres already put a lot of effort into the production of realistic simulations in all these areas. These simulations not only provide officers with the opportunity to practice different scenarios so that they are familiar with a repertoire of possible routines, but they also allow them to explore possibilities and outcomes that they might not have otherwise considered. Even more importantly it helps to develop their confidence for the times when they will have to face these situations in reality. Despite its merits some recent real life experiences seem to indicate that this practical approach does not go far enough. The gaps in preparation might well be filled by borrowing from a range of techniques employed by sports psychologists in coaching athletes for peak performances. These techniques concentrate on the mental side of preparation for stressful events. The athletes are first taught to control their anxiety or arousal and to maintain it at the required level for achieving peak performance. They also rehearse mastery and coping skills for the particular challenge they are preparing to meet. In mastery rehearsal the trainee is required to visualise each stage and possibility of the event at the same time describing aloud what he sees. His description is taped so that he then has a record of his ideal actions which he uses as a prompt to mentally rehearse the scenarios over and over again on his own. Coping rehearsal follows a rather similar pattern with the trainee being required to imagine the full range of inappropriate or disturbing thoughts and feelings which might be aroused during the event in question. As he articulates each inappropriate thought he commands himself to 'stop' and substitutes a positive thought which is targeted towards the desired attitude goal. These methods have already been tested out on police training courses in the United States (Rotella, 1984) with very encouraging results and since the techniques are known and used by British psychologists there seems no good reason that they should not be adopted here.

The final recommendation that appeared under the heading of trauma was that all supervisory officers should receive appropriate training to increase their awareness and counselling skills. This directive presents a particularly challenging task for police training since it is difficult to define the cut-off point between improved management skills and amateur psychotherapy.

The intention behind the recommendation is to enhance existing managerial skills by improving communication and facilitating interpersonal relationships. The area of training covered will be mainly listening skills and empathy which are essentially the same skills as those employed in professional counselling. They are deceptively easy to learn but at a basic level they will not equip the supervisor to treat the emotional or psychological effects of staff problems, although they should enable him to handle these areas with greater sensitivity. There can be no instant experts in counselling: professional counsellors need a degree of insight and experience that takes many years of supervised training to acquire.

Trainers will need to spend time teaching supervisors how to recognise the signs of stress and how they can use their new skills to provide help and support to staff with stress-related problems. They will also need to teach them to distinguish between situations which call for practical assistance and those where it will be more appropriate to provide passive support, to understand the limits of their counselling role and how, when and where to refer staff for more expert help.

As with all areas of human awareness training, the teaching of counselling skills can expose areas of vulnerability in the learner. Not only is the quality of the training important but great care must also be exercised in the selection and training of the trainers themselves. Ideally no one without recognised professional skills in counselling on psychotherapy should be required to train such courses. This is clearly an unrealistic goal. A possible compromise might be to have a qualified professional attached to each training centre to supervise all areas of human awareness training, to provide ongoing training to teaching staff and individual counselling for staff and students alike.

The above emphasis on caution is not intended to discourage current efforts at training in those areas but is an attempt to highlight the possible pitfalls so that they can be avoided. There is a very real need for the improvements that are being attempted, and the benefits far outweigh the disadvantages.

Progress and benefits

It is encouraging to note that attempts have been made to implement all the training recommendations of the 1983 stress report. However it was the responsibility of individual forces to introduce them in the way best suited to their own requirements and, in consequence, there is still no clear national policy on stress-related training. In all quarters the development of stress training programmes has been far slower than was originally hoped. Certainly this was not due to any lack of enthusiasm but was rather the inevitable outcome of a combination of uncontrollable outside factors, such as cut-backs on resources, the introduction of new legislation affecting police procedures (mainly the Police and Criminal Evidence Act) which demanded a very considerable training input, and the year-long miners' strike which brought much of police training to a temporary standstill.

Despite the slow start elements of stress-related training are now included in most police training curricula. There is generally a high level of interest in the area, and stress-related inputs to training are probably being expanded as fast as possible within current constraints. It is also probably true to say that most forces are also still finding their way in this area, and it may be some time before they discover the approach best suited to their needs and the training settles into a pattern. In any event stress training input has been unable to keep pace with the growing pressures on the service. These have increased very considerably both from within, as a result of the restrictions on resources and the effects of the legislation already mentioned, and from without due to higher crime rates and the growth of violence in society at large. It would consequently be unreasonable to expect there to have been any observable benefits as a result of stress training inputs. Nevertheless, there have been a number of improvements which are certainly partially,* though not exclusively, attributable to training in this area. One of them is a new openness amongst young officers, who seem prepared to discuss problems and feelings about the job with supervisors and with each other. This would be unheard of only a few years ago. Even more significant is the very definite change in the attitudes towards stress throughout the service. Until quite recently it was common practice to dismiss stress as a sign of weakness. This attitude undoubtedly still prevails in certain quarters but it is rarely openly expressed. Most managers today are quite genuinely concerned about the effects of stress on their staff.

Of course, such changes cannot be measured objectively and more substantial proofs of the effectiveness of stress-related training may eventually be required. So far the only sources of such evidence are the employee assistance programmes that are widely operated throughout the United States. Stress training *per se* never forms more than a part of these programmes which are mainly aimed at improving employee well-being, through the provision of a counselling service. The success of such programmes has been demonstrated in terms of impressive savings in health care costs. Examples which are taken from a report by Audrey Newsome (1985) are the University of Missouri with 7,000 employees which reported savings of $68,000 plus a 40% decrease in the use of health benefits after introducing such a programme, Scovill Manufacturing with 6,500 employees which achieved savings of $186,000 and Dupont with 16,000 employees which saved $419,000. One such programme which put the emphasis on training rather than counselling is "Staywell" run by Control Data (cf. Cooper, 1986), its main concern is to encourage good health practices in its employees. Staywell has five component units: they are smoking prevention, weight control, cardiovascular fitness and stress management. Each employee entering the programme is individually screened and issued with a personal action plan aimed at reducing his or her specific health risks. The programme has proved extremely popular and between 65% and 95% of employees across the different Control Data sites have participated in it. No specific data are available which relate to improvements from the stress management unit alone since this was invariably followed in conjunction with other component units, but careful monitoring of all programmes show very positive results overall. It has been shown that employees who undertook the cardiovascular fitness programmes and successfully reduced their hypertension levels had less than half the health care costs of those who had not followed the programme. Exercise training programmes also showed excellent results with participants having 30% fewer health care claims and half the time spent in hospital than did non-participants.

*Other factors here probably include a more widespread firsthand experience of high stress events and media interest in the aftermath of major disasters and their effects on those involved.

Where next?

Although the recommendations of the 1983 report are as valid today as when it was written, pressures on the service have increased enormously. This is reflected in a general sense of unease throughout the organisation, and a realisation that things are not functioning as they should. Low morale and ambiguity over the role of the police are manifested in expressions of discontent which find their targets in poor leadership, inefficient procedures, management and, at times, particular hapless individuals. The most vociferous critics of management are found at middle management level amongst superintendents and chief superintendents. At the heart of the problem is a system whose design no longer matches the changed demands on it. The present inability to cope can no longer be hidden from the public. Television has highlighted the difficulties experienced by the Metropolitan Police on a number of occasions and it could be inferred from press interviews with the last Commissioner Sir Kenneth Newman that the force was unable to do little more in the face of rising crime than monitor its occurrence. His frequent requests for greater manpower, had they been met, might have eased the problem but they would not have solved it. Despite the obvious deficits in the present system, no one seems to be clear how it should be changed. In an article on police training Louise Brown (1983) remarks that "there appears to be no consensus of opinion as to what the police's role in modern society should be either by the police organisation, the community or the police themselves".

It is clear that a long period of uncertainty lies ahead. Can training do anything to help the service and the individuals within it to prepare for this future? At the individual level it can encourage the development of greater flexibility and more open attitudes. The techniques employed in games and simulations* can be particularly helpful here. Police training establishments already make extensive use of games and simulations but this particular aspect of their use has not been fully explored. Traditionally, their main value has been seen to be in the areas of role play and practical realistic exercises. This particular application is considered significantly important for a centre to have been purpose built at the Police Staff College to accommodate this type of exercise. It is hoped that they will expand their repertoire to include other kinds of simulations. One of the most powerful applications of the methodology is in challenging deeply rooted attitudes and helping to change them. Two particularly good examples of games designed for this specific purpose are "Bafa bafa" and "Star Power". Bafa bafa is concerned with the interactions between two imaginary alien cultures and players are involved in the prejudices and frustrations occasioned by the interactions between them. Star Power allows participants the experiences associated with unmerited and total power or powerlessness.

The uses of games and simulations in exploring unforeseen outcomes has already been mentioned in the context of training for high stress events, but this application can be equally valuable in other contexts. Make-believe scenarios provide a safe environment in which to explore new ideas and cross conventional boundaries, so providing opportunity for personal growth at the individual level and, at a general level, for exploring the implications of future developments in a more unrestricted

*Two organisations whose purpose is to promote these methodologies are ISAGA (International Simulation and Games Association) and the British based SAGSET (Society for the Advancement of Games and Simulations in Education and Training).

146

and imaginative way than would otherwise be possible. Their potential use in planning actual change should not be overlooked. One of the more ambitious applications attempted in this area was a UNESCO Project to involve a total community in the development plans of a small offshore island in the Mediterranean which was about to open itself to tourism (Bracco, 1984). All sections of the population, from fishermen to representatives of the government departments concerned, took part in a large-scale simulated planning exercise. The outcome was a workable development plan agreed by all parties. Sadly the plan was never realised since it clashed with the vested interests of certain powerful factions at work behind the scenes.

Training also has a part to play in the management of change. Some police training centres are already taking an interest in this topic and particularly valuable work is being carried out at the Police Staff College and in the Management Development Unit at Hendon. This is an area of study that needs to be expanded and much can be learned from other sources such as management colleges, university departments and organisations like the Tavistock Institute* which has been running regular conferences on organisational change for several years.

There is already a genuine desire for change within the police organisation together with numerous positive ideas about its future direction. If these are backed by the right training the changes which lie ahead need not be feared. They can be seen as an exciting challenge and an opportunity for improvement and growth.

*The Tavistock Institute of Human Relations, 120, Belsize Lane, London NW3 5BA.

12 Why put case study at the heart of the police training curriculum?

John Elliott

The Stage II Review's recommendations

The Final Report of the Home Office sponsored Stage II Review of Police Probationer Training, (MacDonald et al, 1987) recommends the establishment of a 31-week modular Foundation Course to replace the existing Induction, Initial, and Local Procedures Courses. The proposed new course interweaves periods in Home Office District Training Centres (DTCs) with Field Observation and Training placements. Module 1 (4 weeks) would take place in-force and provide an opportunity for recruits to observe how the police organisation works. Module 2 (10 weeks) would take place in a District Training Centre and enable trainers to build on the observational experience gained during Module 1. Module 3 (5 weeks) would constitute a Field Placement to a Tutor Constable for the purpose of observing the work of an experienced and competent patrol officer and gaining some direct experience of patrol work under his or her supervision. This module would enable probationers to reflectively apply the knowledge and abilities they developed in the previous modules. At the end of this Field Placement the probationers would return to the DTC (5 weeks) for a debriefing and a further opportunity to extend the range and depth of their learning. They would then go, after a week's leave (Module 5), into Module 6 (5 weeks) for a second Field Placement with a Tutor Constable in which they would be prepared to patrol independently. Module 7 (1 week) is a Final Course in a Force Training Centre aimed at debriefing the probationers on their Foundation Course experience and assessing their fitness for independent patrol and future training needs.

The Review team believed that a modular Foundation Course of this kind could close the existing gap between theory and practice, highlight the importance of self and social awareness for high quality operational performance, ensure a more gradual and controlled immersion into the occupational culture and realities of police work, integrate the acquisition of legal/procedural knowledge with the development of social skills, promote greater partnership between central and force trainers, and unlock creative potential throughout the probationer training system.

Perhaps the most significant recommendations about the design of the Foundation Course relate to the curriculum in the DTC modules:

— the curriculum should be reorganised to produce a greater integration of legal and procedural knowledge and social skills;

— the integration proposed should be realised through a core curriculum of case studies which raise issues about the interpretation and enforcement of the law, the police role, and the organisation of policing in society;

— the current social skills and community relations curriculum should be abandoned in favour of an integrated core curriculum based on case study materials;

— case materials should be selected in terms of their usefulness as exemplars of frequently recurring, typical or critical policing situations;

— the information and evidence contained in the case materials should enable probationers to study real operational situations in depth, with a view to clarifying and diagnosing practical policing problems and identifying and evaluating alternative policing strategies.

These recommendations are grounded in the Review team's analysis of the 14-week DTC course. We argued:

1. that the teaching of social skills and awareness was too isolated from the teaching of law and procedures to facilitate its transfer to real operational situations, where it needs to be integrated with the legal/procedural components of problem-solving and decision-making;

2. that the teaching of law and procedures failed to develop transferable knowledge because it was insufficiently contextualised in terms of real examples of policing situations.

It is certainly the case that instructors drew on practical examples of the application of legal/procedural knowledge. But these examples usually represented hypothetical rather than real situations and were described almost entirely in terms of legal and procedural attributes. Such teaching reinforces 'black and white' applications of the law which fail to take into account the complex psychological and social factors officers need to consider when making decisions about whether, when, and how to enforce the law in a particular situation. DTC trainers often argued that responsibility for translating 'black and white' applications of law and procedures into context-sensitive ones resides with Tutor Constables during subsequent on-the-job training. But we found that, whereas trainers often saw the transition from the DTC to the 10-week Tutor Constable attachment as an opportunity to build on the basic knowledge acquired in the DTC, many probationers experienced it as a rather traumatic, abrupt and discontinuous experience. Remarks like "you have to start learning the law all over again" express this discontinuity between a curriculum which transmits 'black and white' applications and a job which requires context sensitive judgements. Such an experienced discontinuity requires probationers to 'unlearn' much of what they learn in the DTC rather than to build on it.

We concluded that the transfer of learning from DTC-based training to the job required a better match between the DTC curriculum and real policing situations where knowledge and skills need to be applied in relation to, rather than in isolation from, each other. Our proposals for a core curriculum of case studies of real policing in the DTC modules constitutes an attempt to both bring this better match about, and to ensure greater continuity between classroom-based and field-based training. From January 1986 we commissioned field researchers to generate case materials from observations of a range of policing situations, and interviews with participants. We then edited and organised the material for use in probationer training. It was intended as a foundation collection which trainers could later develop as they gained experience of handling case materials.

Since we made these proposals they have been subjected to considerable controversy within the police service, particularly amongst trainers. The controversy is not so much about whether case study has any training role or function: the issues revolve around the aims of case study learning and the centrality attributed to it by the Review team. The main lines of argument can be summarised as follows:

The Survival Kit argument: In the early phases of training the primary need of probationers is that they acquire the basic legal and procedural knowledge they are expected to apply on the streets. This body of knowledge should be at the core of any programme of initial training. Case studies can be a useful means of assessing and reinforcing that knowledge once it has been acquired. The problem with the Stage II proposals is that they marginalise the learning of basic law and procedures.

The Methods argument: Case study is simply one method alongside others in the trainer's repertoire of educational methods. These other methods—eg role play, simulation, skill development exercises—may be equally or more effective than case study in achieving the same objectives. The choice of method should remain with the instructor and not be prescribed from a central source.

The 'Technical Efficiency' argument: Case study learning is a very time-consuming process, particularly when it is based on the lengthy, complicated, and unstructured case materials the Stage II team have produced. Other long processes might be equally effective and far more efficient in their use of time.

The 'Lack of Precise Objectives' argument: The outcomes of case study learning on the basis of the kinds of materials Stage II has in mind are not at all precise, or clear enough to provide a basis for the effective transmission and assessment of the specific knowledge and skills which police officers need to do their job well.

The 'Contamination' argument: Case materials gathered from real policing situations can pass on to impressionable young recruits erroneous beliefs about law and procedures and inappropriate attitudes and values, all of which could be difficult to subsequently rectify. The contaminating effects of real case materials can only be avoided by either selecting only those which unambiguously constitute examples of good policing or constructing fictional materials which nevertheless possess the quality of 'realism'.

In this paper I shall look at each of these arguments in turn.

Case study learning and 'the need to know' law and Procedures (the Survival Kit argument)

The Stage II proposals in no way undermine the view that probationers need to acquire a basic knowledge and understanding of the law and procedures they will need to use and apply as patrol constables. If the metaphor of 'the survival kit' refers to what an officer needs to know in order to survive in a police organisation then perhaps legal and procedural learning objectives should dominate the police training curriculum. However, all their achievement can ensure is that an officer meets organisational criteria of technical efficiency in identifying and processing offences. Such an officer may satisfy minimal standards of competence but this doesn't make him or her a good police officer. Cross-professional studies into those abilities which characterise successful performers and differentiate them from merely average ones have concluded that basic subject knowledge is not one of them (Klemp, 1977). Good officers do more than enforce the law in a technically competent manner. They also have a responsibility to the public to enforce it in a manner which minimises the possibility of future crime and preserves the peace. Good policing is defined by social criteria linked to this wider interpretation of the police role. This is constitutionally acknowledged through the concept of the constable's right to exercise discretion in the application of the law to particular circumstances. Part of what it means to *understand the law,* as opposed to merely knowing it, is that an officer has developed the capacity to judge its applicability in a variety of different circumstances. And this implies more than a capacity to simply recognise the objective legal attributes of the situation and which procedural rules need to be followed within it. It implies a capacity to grasp all the factors in the situation which need to be taken into account in deciding what to do.

I suppose one could argue that the aim of classroom-based training should be simply the provision of an organisational survival kit in the form of a technically proficient police officer. The aim of producing a 'good officer' should be left to the organisation through its on-the-job training. We have heard this argument justified on the basis that the abilities which constitute 'good' as opposed to 'technically proficient' policing can only be learned through direct experience. This is why the 'social skills of policing' curriculum in DTCs, based as it is on theoretical concepts drawn from the behavioural sciences, was so frequently dismissed on the grounds that the objectives mismatched job requirements which can only be learned from direct experience. The direct experience argument makes a valid point: namely, that the social awareness and skills of good policing can only be learned through experience of real life situations. But probationers can experience real situations in other forms than through direct experience. They can indirectly or vicariously experience them through either observation or the study of case materials. Case study is in fact a form of experiential learning involving systematic reflection upon either direct or indirect experience of particular practical situations. From the standpoint of the Stage II recommendations case study lies at the core of the learning process throughout the modular Foundation Course. In Module 1 it should involve reflecting about observational experience, while in Modules 3 and 6 both observational and direct experience of particular situations provide the basis for reflection. In the DTC Modules 2 and 4 case study learning is grounded in vicarious experience provided by case materials.

In conception then there is a continuous learning process to be fostered throughout all the different training settings of the Foundation Course. It follows from this that the same abilities can be continuously developed and assessed through case study learning across these different settings, including that of learning to sensitively apply basic law and procedures in particular circumstances. If this is the case then there is no good justification for confining curriculum aims in DTC and other classroom settings to the acquisition of a 'survival kit' of technical knowledge. Such knowledge should be acquired and applied in a broader context of job-related aims. Building the DTC curriculum around a core of case study material does imply severely reducing the dominance of a learning process which fosters recognition and recall learning. Such a process will be subordinate to one which integrates its knowledge outcomes into the reflective study of real policing situations. But this will not marginalise the learning of legal/procedural knowledge, in the sense of neglecting its value and significance for the job of policing. In fact, it will do quite the reverse, by contextualising that knowledge in a form which not only deepens the probationer's understanding of the law but renders it more usable in real policing situations.

The best way of linking the acquisition of legal/procedural knowledge with the process of case study learning was not prescribed by Stage II. For example, relevant factual knowledge may be acquired prior to, interactively with, or after the study of a particular case. How it is processed—whether through 'reading', 'didactic teaching', 'computer assisted learning'—is also left open. All these are matters for experiment by trainers.

Case study is a learning process and not a method (The Methods argument)

The term 'Case Study' can be used in either a 'process' or 'product' sense. In the first sense it is a process of handling case evidence aimed at understanding a particular situation or event. In the second sense it is a product of this process, ie a report or account of the situation grounded in case evidence. Some police trainers have come to associate case study with a particular educational method. Sometimes the process of case study learning is associated with a method of handling case evidence: namely, paper-feed simulation exercises. But this is only one of a variety of learning methods which can be used to develop understanding of a situation or event. Other police trainers have come to associate 'Case Studies as products' with particular methods. For example, a short case report can be used as a method of 'triggering' a general issue for discussion or as a method of illustrating the application of a general rule or norm of behaviour. These illustrative uses of case studies can be distinguished from using them to develop understandings of situations in all their particularity and complexity.

The Stage II Final Report views 'Case Study' as a process of developing an understanding of a particular operational situation or incident on the basis of case materials and reports. It does not prescribe a particular method for handling such material. The material can be used to develop understanding using a variety of methods, eg brainstorming, whole class discussion, individual and group projects, role plays and simulation exercises. These are not alternatives to using case study materials but ways of using them to foster the development of understanding. It is the use of case materials, and not any particular educational method, to foster understanding which the Stage II Report prescribed as the core of the training curriculum. The choice of methods for studying particular cases is indeed the responsibility of the trainers.

Case studies and illustrative examples (the 'Technical Efficiency' argument)

The 'technical efficiency' argument is based on the assumption that the value of using a particular case of police practice for training purposes lies in its power to illustrate or exemplify instances of the application of a law, procedure, norm of conduct, skill, or psychological/sociological theory. Information can be abstracted from real cases to illustrate such instances, and thereby deepen understanding of the legal, procedural, ethical, and theoretical knowledge students need to acquire. However, the argument points out that there is little reason to suppose that illustrative examples abstracted from real cases are any more effective and efficient as means of fostering such understanding than fictional examples derived from hypothetical situations.

152

The Stage II team did not view the core curriculum of case materials and reports primarily as illustrative examples selected to foster certain pre-specifiable objectives in the form of knowledge, skills, and attitudes to be acquired. The case materials and reports should not simply be derived from real cases of practice but also satisfy the criterion of *realism*. They should depict policing situations as they are experienced by the officer(s) responsible for taking intelligent action within them. They provide a 'vicarious experience' for those who are not there of what it is like for those who are. What confronts police officers are complex, unique sets of circumstances, which require particular and concrete responses to the practical problems and dilemmas they pose. From this practical point of view policing situations need to be understood holistically and synthetically as complex and concrete entities in their own right. 'Practical understanding' is a form of cognition which grasps situations holistically from the point of view of practitioners responsible for taking practical decisions about them. Case studies and materials which satisfy the criterion of realism are those which primarily portray situations as objects of the *practical* rather than the *theoretical* understanding.

The studies commissioned by Stage II are rich in narrative detail, portray events in context by relating them to the social environment in which they are set and to the organisation which frames the police officer's response to them, and attempt to represent practical issues and problems from different points of view, eg from the points of view of offenders, members of the public, and the police. Such case studies aspire to portray policing situations both in *comprehensive* detail and in *depth*.

Given the fact that police trainers frequently view case studies as illustrative examples of legal/procedural knowledge, skill applications, norms of conduct, and theoretical ideas, it is small wonder that those produced by the Stage II team failed to satisfy the criterion of technical efficiency. To give students a mass of information to handle, and then to ensure that the process is structured to illustrate particular knowledge objectives, is far more time consuming and risky in terms of coverage than giving them material which is carefully pre-structured in advance to illustrate the objectives. Of course, the trainer can work through the Stage II materials in advance and 'chunk it up' into examples. But lesson preparation is far less time consuming if the trainer is given pre-selected and structured examples to illustrate the objectives, or simply left to cull examples from his or her own experience of practical policing, eg to select from the total situation only those elements which illustrate breathaliser procedure.

What police trainers need to appreciate is that case materials designed as a basis for developing a 'practical understanding' of a particular policing situation cannot be structured by pre-specified categories of knowledge and understanding, whether this be of specific laws, procedures, skills, ethical norms, or behavioural science theories. In order to avoid confusion we need to distinguish Case Studies from Case Examples. The value of a core curriculum of case studies resides in its power to portray something of the reality of actual policing situations as they appear to police officers and others involved. From the latter point of view such situations need to be understood in themselves in all their complexity, concreteness, and uniqueness, and not simply as instances of abstract categories of things.

At this point the reader might well ask why recruits need to develop such an understanding of cases when they have not directly experienced them as practising police officers. Surely, the only learning which can be transferred to the job from studying cases is a knowledge of the specific laws, procedures, skills, norms and theories which can be abstracted from them?

In order to respond to this objection we need to look at the relationship between the development of practical understanding and theoretic understanding. The latter can play a role in developing a practical understanding of cases. Concepts and ideas learned from a variety of subject matters can be eclectically applied in the analysis of case material. The particular selection of concepts and ideas will depend upon the analyser's theoretical knowledge of various subjects, and his or her ability to discern their relevance to the case. This kind of eclectic analysis can then form the basis for synthesising all the significant elements of the situation into a coherent picture of the whole. It is this holistic understanding of particular cases which integrates disparate theoretical knowledge by contextualising it and thereby rendering it practically useful. The holistic meaning grasped in practical understanding cannot be reduced to the sum total of the theoretical knowledge which it integrates. The contextualising function of case study learning explains why the Stage II Review claimed that its proposed core curriculum would bring about the integration of legal/procedural knowledge with interpersonal and social awareness.

Studies of professional decision-making in complex, fluid, and unique social situations suggest that competent practitioners draw on stocks of professional knowledge which are derived from past experience of cases. (See Schon, 1983.) This experience is not stored in the memory as sets of abstract understandings. In recalling past experience practitioners do not abstract theoretical knowledge from the practical cases to which it is applied. It is the 'holistic picture' which is recalled and subsequently drawn on. In a present situation the professional selects, from his or her repertoire of stored cases, those which appear to resemble it in some respects. He or she then compares and contrasts the present with past cases. In doing so elements of theoretical knowledge incorporated in holistic understandings of past cases are tacitly drawn on. Of course, the present situation may contain aspects whose significance eludes past understandings. In order to grasp their significance the practitioner will need to acquire new theoretical knowledge to apply to the case. This will then be integrated into the synthesis which is made of all the significant elements of the case, and stored in the memory in this contextualised form.

It is by increasing the range and variety of practical understandings of cases that practitioners develop their stock of professional knowledge. This is normally done through reflective practice. But in the early stages of their careers much can be done to develop the foundations of professional knowledge through using observational experience and the vicarious experience provided by case materials. One does not have to wait until trainees have direct experience to begin to help them to contextualise and integrate knowledge in a practically useful form. This process can be accelerated through observational experience (as in Module 1) and the vicarious experience provided by a core curriculum of case materials (as in Modules 2 and 4).

Assessing case study learning and the 'problem' of defining objectives (the 'Lack of Precise Objectives' argument)

One of the things which worries police trainers about the kinds of case materials envisaged by the Stage II team is that they do not indicate specific and measurable learning objectives to guide instruction and assessment. They want a general aim like 'developing an understanding of practical policing situations' to be broken down into more specific outcomes in the form of desired student behaviours. In other words they want those student behaviours which indicate a correct understanding as opposed to a misunderstanding of the situation spelled out.

Unfortunately, real life human situations cannot be analysed in these terms. They are open to a variety of interpretations "all of which may be equally valid theoretically and which the facts equally fit, and when this happens there is no way we can say which explanation is the most correct" (Pye 1979). This doesn't mean that some interpretations cannot be assessed as better than others. Runyan (1984) has listed a number of criteria against which alternative understandings can be assessed:

1. "their logical soundness", ie whether an interpretation is logically consistent with the evidence cited in its support;
2. "their comprehensiveness in accounting for a number of puzzling aspects of the event in question";
3. "their survival of tests of attempted falsification", eg whether future events, which an interpretation would lead one to expect, fail to occur;
4. "their consistency with the full range of available relevant evidence" or with "more general knowledge about human functioning or about the person in question";
5. "their credibility relative to other explanatory hypotheses".

Having applied such criteria one may still be left with a number of credible and plausible alternatives. One reason for this is the sheer complexity of human situations. The range and quantity of evidence one needs to consider in order to decide between different interpretations is vast, and not all of it will be accessible to those trying to make sense of the situation as a whole.

For example, let us take a law enforcement situation which is a clear case of criminal damage to the property of an ethnic minority family. Simply grasping the objective legal meaning of the situation is not sufficient as a basis for deciding upon a course of action. After initial investigations the following facts are known:

a. This incident is one of a number of recent cases of criminal damage inflicted on ethnic minority group members in the area.
b. A racist slogan was scrawled on the damaged property.
c. Racist slogans appear frequently on property and buildings in the area.
d. A witness provides evidence which suggests that the offenders were not members of the ethnic minority group of the family.
e. The witness cites evidence to suggest that the behaviour of the offenders was motivated by 'a sense of grievance' directed towards this particular family.
f. The family are well known in the community and appear to arouse hostile reactions amongst its members regardless of their ethnic origin.

Items (a)–(d) appear to suggest that the offence is a case of 'racially motivated crime'. However, items (e) and (f) together do not obviously fit this social interpretation of the situation. They suggest instead that the criminal act was motivated by a 'sense of grievance' towards this particular family. Which interpretation then is correct? One could argue that the first interpretation is in fact consistent with all the known facts. The fact that the offenders were 'airing a sense of grievance' is not in itself inconsistent with their crime being 'racially motivated'. What would make their behaviour inconsistent with the first interpretation is evidence that they normally express their grievances towards others, regardless of ethnic origins, through acts of criminal damage. However, one doesn't have access to such evidence. Also, the fact that hostility towards the family is manifest in all sections of the community is not in itself inconsistent with the first interpretation. There is no evidence that members of the same ethnic group would express their hostility through acts of criminal damage, whereas item (c) suggests that people who are not members of that group do.

However, one could argue that the second interpretation is also consistent with all the known facts. Although a number of acts of criminal damage have been perpetrated against the property of people who belong to the ethnic minority, this doesn't necessarily imply that any or all are 'racially motivated'. One might be able to find evidence to show that members of this minority normally air their grievances by damaging each other's property. The fact that a racist slogan had been scrawled on the damaged property doesn't imply that this occurred contemporaneously with the other damage. It could have been done prior to or after the damage was inflicted. The frequent appearance of racist slogans on property and buildings could in fact suggest a strong possibility that this particular slogan was scrawled quite independently of the other damage inflicted. Finally, one can argue that the fact that the offenders were not members of the same ethnic minority doesn't necessarily imply 'racial motivation'. The fact that the family tend to 'offend' other people generally supports the interpretation that the situation is simply a case of a 'sense of grievance being aired' towards this particular family.

One might conclude that, although the view that the act is a case of 'racially motivated crime' has a surface plausibility, the alternative interpretation also emerges as somewhat plausible after an assessment of the known evidence. Certainly far more evidence needs to be gathered before the latter can be ruled out completely. The assessment has indicated something of the ambiguity of much of the existing evidence and the complexity of what might at first be seen as a straightforward case.

Even if people achieve access to all the relevant facts of a case (a rare state of affairs in everyday life) this may not be a sufficient basis for agreement about the correctness of a single interpretation. Which pattern of meaning people ultimately select to interpret all the available facts will not just depend upon those facts, but upon their social values and basic beliefs concerning human nature. There can be no value-free interpretations of the social meaning of human acts and situations even when these are derived from so-called theoretical disciplines like psychology and sociology. The issue depicted above, for example, may ultimately rest on different ideological beliefs about human nature and ethnic identity which are incapable of refutation solely by appealing to the facts.

One might question whether social, as opposed to legal interpretation, is important for the police role. In relation to my example could one not argue that it is sufficient to understand that an act of criminal damage has occurred in order to proceed with the investigation and arrest? However, 'racially motivated crime' threatens public order in a way which 'airing a sense of grievance' towards a particular individual does not. Inasmuch as the police have a responsibility to maintain public order they need to be able to anticipate the consequences of social acts. And they cannot do this without interpreting their social significance. Social interpretation also guides the investigation of suspects and their arrest. If an act of criminal damage is a case of 'racially motivated crime' the officer will tend to look for suspects known for their racist opinions and activities. If it is understood as 'airing a grievance' the officer will search out suspects amongst the social contacts of the victims.

The complexity of the case materials envisaged by the Stage II team reflects an aspiration of *fidelity to real life exeperience* and the desire not to limit and circumscribe in advance the range of understandings which can be constructed on the basis of the available evidence. If it is inappropriate to structure such materials in terms of specific content objectives then on what basis can trainers select learning activities which will enable probationers to develop their understanding?

The Stage II team were of the view that a process of case study learning aimed at developing understanding is best defined in terms of procedural rather than outcome criteria. From the kind of analysis supplied above of the nature of understanding one can derive a number of criteria for what will count as a worthwhile learning process, eg:

Students should have opportunities to:

i. express, defend, and develop their own interpretations of policing situations;
ii. discuss a range of different interpretations to their own;
iii. assess alternative interpretations in the light of standards of reasoning and evidence;
iv. clarify the values and beliefs which underpin their own and others' interpretations;
v. search for evidence which is relevant to issues of interpretation;
vi. propose and evaluate action strategies.

From such criteria one can derive a set of procedural principles for guiding the interventions of trainers in the learning process. The Stage II Report sets these out as follows:

1. The aim of 'instruction' should be to facilitate a learning process in which recruits are invited to reflect on their responses—interpretations, judgements, decisions, actions and reactions—to the situations they are presented with.
2. The task of instructors as facilitators is *to manage* the process of reflection, and their ability to do so will depend on the extent to which they have been operationally reflective police officers, rather than on their expert knowledge of the law.
3. Instructors should encourage individuals to question their own interpretations, judgements and decisions in the light of alternatives.
4. Instructors should encourage a reflective discussion of alternatives, in which individuals attempt to understand each other's views, in contrast to an argumentative discussion in which individuals are primarily concerned with defending their views.
5. Instructors should give individuals equal opportunities to articulate and explain their own views, and to question others about theirs.
6. Instructors should ensure that individuals can articulate their views without fear of having a chain of thought interrupted, or of being 'put down'.
7. Instructors should ensure that the right to express a minority view without fear is protected.
8. Instructors should ensure that relevant knowledge or opinion, which is being neglected or poorly represented by members of the group, is introduced and considered.
9. Instructors should ensure that individuals have opportunities to develop and build on each others' contributions so that the discussion progresses organically but coherently.

10. Instructors should protect the freedom of individuals not to contribute verbally to a discussion if they so choose.

11. Instructors should foster critical standards in the reflective process by asking questions which require individuals to:
    —clarify or elaborate their views;
    —provide a deeper or more satisfying explanation of a view;
    —reflect about their views in the light of evidence;
    —assess the validity of alternative views in the light of the available evidence.

12. Instructors should refrain from using their authority-position to promote their own views on the presumption that they have expert knowledge which is not open to question.

13. Instructors should only introduce their own views in a context where the recruits are able to treat them as potentially problematic.

14. Instructors should refrain from reinforcing in an uncritical manner any of the views expressed in discussion. Such reinforcement would discourage self-criticism amongst recruits.

15. Instructors should refrain from pressurising for a consensus outcome of discussion. A rational consensus can only emerge in a context of free and open dialogue.

16. Instructors should refrain from imposing a predetermined plan or pattern on the process of reflective discussion.

17. Legal/procedural information and other kinds of factual information should be selected by instructors and/or students in terms of the question:
    'what information is relevant to the case?'
    The primary motive for introducing legal content should be the *need to understand* particular cases in terms of their legal and procedural 'significance, and not just the *need to know* chunks of legal and procedural information.

The process criteria and principles outlined above provide guidance for instructional decisions and their evaluation. Guidance on these matters does not depend on having specific content objectives in mind. So far, however, the process model outlined has not provided any guidance, as the objectives model does, for assessing learning outcomes.

Although the Stage II Report rejects the appropriateness to case study learning of specifications of precise content-linked objectives, it does acknowledge the importance of developing certain core abilities through the long process. Such learning outcomes are often called 'process objectives' to differentiate them from objectives which specify what is to be known and understood about the content.

The Stage II Report outlines six core competencies which appeared at the time of writing to have considerable face validity:

The ability to interpret and apply the law in a manner which is sensitive to the social and cultural contexts of policing situations.

The ability to investigate including (a) observational skills in discriminating those aspects of situations which are relevant to making informed and valid judgements, and (b) interviewing skills of eliciting authentic accounts from suspects, witnesses, and colleagues.

The ability to participate in free and open communication with suspects, witnesses, and colleagues.

The ability to represent/report incidents and situations according to criteria of accuracy, fairness, and relevance.

The ability to evaluate the social effects of general policing policies and strategies.

The ability to self-monitor one's own performance and conduct in the police role.

They were not viewed as 'objectives'. The term 'objective' was not used because it implies a learning outcome which is highly specific, measurable, and fixed. Indeed, the Stage II team rejected the idea of 'process objectives' because it believed that goals linked to learning processes rather than learning content cannot be broken down into specific, measurable, and fixed student behaviours without distortion. We shall return to this point later.

In retrospect we felt that this list incorporates two quite distinct ways of describing abilities. The first four are descriptions which refer to job functions implicit in the police role. The job of policing requires officers to 'enforce (or apply) the law', 'investigate crime', 'communicate with suspects and witnesses', and 'report incidents'. These functional descriptions are different in kind from the last two statements. The latter do not refer to police officers' job functions, but to the qualities which, in the opinion of the Review team, enable them to perform their functions well. One must distinguish *functional* from *generic* statements of abilities. Generic statements refer to those common personal abilities which distinguish good from less satisfactory performances.

Functional descriptions of desired professional abilities are on their own inadequate as a basis for the formative assessment of learning outcomes. They provide no criteria for diagnosing learning difficulties. The fact that a probationer's 'ability to investigate' is poor provides no indication of how it can be improved. But if one knows that this can be explained by an inability 'to discover patterns in large amounts of disparate information' then the trainer has some guidance on how to improve his or her performance.

In the light of these considerations we need to ask how case study learning can foster the development of those personal abilities which are generic to good patrol policing. Within the UK we have had virtually no systematic research directed towards discovering exactly what these qualities are. This is partly because police training is only now beginning to change away from a system dominated by the pursuit of legal knowledge objectives. However, McBer and Company in the USA have conducted extensive research aimed at discovering personal abilities which are generic to good practice in a variety of professions. One of the outcomes of this research, (see Klemp, 1977, Spencer, 1979), has been the discovery of common qualities which are generic to good practice across the professions, including the police. It is significant that 'knowledge of subject matter' has not emerged as a defining characteristic of good practice. "Perhaps the most consistent . . . . yet counter-intuitive . . . finding that we have discovered that the amount of knowledge of a content area is generally *unrelated* to superior performance in an occupation and is often unrelated *even to marginally acceptable performance*. Certainly many occupations require a certain level of knowledge on the part of the individual for the satisfactory discharge of work-related duties, but even more occupations require only that the individual be willing and able to learn new things" (Klemp, 1977).

Most recent attempts in the UK to identify a broader spectrum of abilities as a basis for police training, have adopted one or more of the following approaches:

a. *Task-Functional Analysis based on research into the tasks people perform to fulfil their job functions.*

   As I have argued, this knowledge, even when well-grounded in research, gives us no information about the personal qualities which enable people to perform their tasks and functions successfully. As Spencer (1979) has argued, Job Tasks/Function Analysis has limited usefulness in the quest for generic qualities because "the unit of analysis is the job, not the person who performs the job well". Spencer goes on to point out that detailed lists of job tasks are of little use "without supplementary information about the competencies a superior job incumbent uses" to accomplish the tasks successfully.

b. *Theory-based selection.*

   The existing probationer training package on the 'Social Skills of Policing' (SSOP) is an excellent example of an attempt to identify the social and interpersonal skills involved in policing tasks from such disciplines as psychology and social psychology. From the fact that police officers have to exercise leadership functions it is assumed that the skills involved in exercising such functions can be derived from psychological theories of leadership which have neither been derived from, nor tested in studies of effective leadership in police organisations. Similarly with communication functions, where it is assumed that communication skills can be derived from humanistic psychological theories of interpersonal relationships. As Spencer points out such theory-based approaches "lack supporting empirical data to show that the knowledge or skill characteristics they posit are in fact related to on-the-job performance". We simply should not assume that theory-derived skills and techniques can be transferred as generic components of effective performance in real life policing contexts.

c. *The views of experienced and expert practitioners.*

   If the highly articulated theories of academics should be treated sceptically as a basis for identifying generic abilities, so also should the intuitive and commonsense theories of expert practitioners. An expert panel can quickly generate check-lists of personal qualities like 'courage', 'knowledge of the law', 'commitment', 'loyalty' which reflect idealised images of professional identities derived from the folklore of the occupational culture but, as Spencer again points out, may or may not be related to the personal qualities which constitute effectiveness in the job.

Having pointed out the limitations of these approaches to identifying the abilities of the good patrol officer and, by implication, to identifying a broader set of training goals than legal/procedural content knowledge, I am not arguing that such approaches have no value. The information they generate can suggest hypotheses to be tested against studies which focus on the abilities successful officers exercise in handling the operational situations they encounter. To my knowledge such studies have not been systematically carried out in Britain. All we have to go on at the moment is American research. The abilities which this research has identified as generic to successful performers in all occupations involving judgement and decision in complex social situations fall into three major categories:

—conceptual abilities
—interpersonal abilities
—impacting abilities
Brief descriptions of abilities in each category are as follows:

Conceptual abilities

1. The ability to synthesis diverse and complex information in terms of thematic consistencies (patterns of meaning) which link parts to wholes, and to communicate these insights to others.
   This ability is thought to be crucial to successful performance on problem-solving tasks.
2. The ability to understand the different sides of a controversial issue.
   This conceptual ability is linked to (1) because it is involved in resolving problems posed by discrepant and conflicting information. Those who lack this ability tend to take sides, thereby denying the validity of one or more points of view. Such people make poor negotiators. Those who have it have a capacity to facilitate solutions to issues and thereby resolve conflict.
3. The ability to learn from experience by reflecting upon observations of one's own and others' performances in the work situation and inductively translating them into a practical theory of how such performances can be improved.
   "This skill relates, first, to being involved and participating in an experience, and second, to analysing one's behaviours in the context of that of others." (Klemp, 1977.)
   This ability is perhaps best described by the phrase 'self-monitoring' because it pin-points the essentially self-reflective stance of those who are able to learn from experience.

Interpersonal abilities

4. The ability to empathise accurately with the thoughts, feelings and other mental states of individuals.
   This ability is thought to underpin successful communication with others. It means not taking behaviour at face value and responding in these terms but coming to grasp the deeper concerns which lie beneath the surface of an individual's behaviour, and thereby make a more appropriate response to it.
   'Accurate empathy' is a generic competence which explains successful performance in all those professions which require individuals to play a helping role in constant face to face encounters with the public, and engage in team work with colleagues. Klemp carefully distinguishes 'Accurate Empathy' from the formation of 'Affiliative Relationships' where individuals relate to others by sharing feelings in a context of mutual attraction and trust. The ability to share feelings is best described as sympathy rather than empathy. Accurate empathy is not based on trust, liking, or reciprocity of feeling. Its context is not that of a personal relationship but of a relation in which one person is able to penetrate beyond the surface features of another's duct to diagnose the concerns which underly it.

5. The ability to promote feelings of efficacy in another person.

   Kemp clarifies three dimensions of this interpersonal skill. The first consists of a belief in the other person's capacity to achieve something worthwhile with support and encouragement. The second consists of actively helping another to be more effective. And the third consists of the ability to control impulses and feelings which, if expressed, would make another feel powerless and ineffectual; eg of hostility and anger.

Impacting abilities

A person may possess all the abilities listed above but rarely exercise them because (s)he lacks the motivation. Klemp argues that occupations which involve getting others to do things are populated by people with high power motivation, ie who have a high need to influence and have impact on others. Public service occupations require individuals with high power motivation but who are committed to exerting influence for the sake of the goals of the service rather than for personal gain. Few would disagree that power motivation of this kind is desirable within the police service. Klemp claims that a number of abilities are demonstrated by successful performers with higher power motivation and commitment to organisational goals. These are:

6. The ability to learn interpersonal networks and use them in performing occupational tasks.

   The behaviour of the individual is influenced by the network of personal relations in which (s)he is situated. One is unlikely to have an impact on his or her conduct if one is unfamiliar with this network and unable to relate to other members of it.

7. The ability to discern and develop a shared set of values and goals with the individuals one wishes to influence.

   Such individuals are able to discern areas of consensus at a level beyond that of apparent disagreement or conflict.

8. The ability to identify coalitions within the workforce at all levels of the hierarchy and assess their value in achieving organisational goals.

   Effective individuals join and ally themselves with coalitions that are orientated towards the goals of the organisation.

9. The ability to think of oneself as proactive—a determiner or cause of events— rather than as reactive—a passive victim of circumstances over which one has no control.

According to Klemp this proactive ability is critical for influencing and making an impact on others. Without it the other impacting skills are insufficient to ensure effective performance.

Research into 'Generic Competencies' has tended to use a 'Critical Incidents' interviewing technique combined with sampled observations of work performance. Those who have been identified by their supervisors and peers as average to very good performers are asked to describe in narrative detail how they handled one or more difficult and complex work situations. The interviewers do not pre-structure their questions but ask them responsively to probe the interviewee's account of his or her handling of the situation. The interview data is then analysed with a view to extracting those competencies which are generic to the very good performers and thereby differentiate them from average performers. This analysis can then be cross-checked by observing the performance of some individuals in both categories.

Inspector R. Shadforth and myself, on behalf of the Probationer Development and Training Team at the Home Office Central Planning Unit, are undertaking a small-scale feasibility study, using a similar methodology, aimed at identifying the 'generic abilities' of patrol constables. Twenty-four constables, covering a range of policing environments, and identified by their supervisors as averagely to very competent have been interviewed. (Supervisors were not asked to identify below-average performers.) The analysis of the data is in process at the time of writing. Although, like most of the 'generic competency' research, we are interested in what distinguishes the very competent from the averagely competent performer we are also interested in identifying any competencies which all the interviewees share. It is already clear that many of the cross-professional abilities cited above are central in the performances described by the interviewees. In particular we have noted that 1, 2, 3, 4, 5, 6, 7 and 9 recur frequently in the interview data elicited from patrol constables designated very competent by their supervisors.

Let us examine the relationship between a process of case study learning aimed at 'understanding' and the generic abilities we have described.

In developing an understanding of particular policing situations it is clear that officers need to draw on the three conceptual abilities outlined. The possession of at least some ability to synthesise diverse and complex information, understand an issue from different angles and to self-monitor one's own behaviour in the context of others are necessary conditions of developing understanding. One might doubt whether this is true with respect to self-monitoring. Surely understanding precedes decisions and actions. But this is not the case with respect to practical understanding. An initial interpretation of the practical significance of the situation can only be tested by self-monitoring the actions one undertakes in its light, and assessing their consequences. Such monitoring provides a basis for readjusting one's initial understanding. Even in the context of studying case materials 'insight' can be deepened by exploring various action possibilities through role play and simulation exercises, or even testing them out in the imagination. Such explanations all draw upon the ability to self-monitor one's performance.

The process of case study learning not only depends upon the possession of such conceptual abilities but provides the means of developing them further. They constitute both pre-conditions and outcomes of case study learning. Thus it is possible to assess the quality of the outcomes of such learning using generic abilities as criteria rather than content objectives.

Although case study learning rather obviously provides opportunities for developing conceptual abilities, its provision of opportunities for developing abilities which enhance the quality of a person's interpersonal relations and impact in situations are perhaps less obvious. So let us consider case study learning in the context of direct experience and involvement in a practical situation. In order to assess or interpret a social situation a person needs to gather evidence which is not obvious or even readily accessible. Other people are the major sources of such evidence and in order to gather it from them it is necessary to communicate with them effectively. The abilities listed—'to empathise accurately', and 'to promote feelings of efficacy in another person'— as generic characteristics of successful communicators are important personal qualities a person needs to draw on as (s)he seeks to understand a practical situation. And as (s)he seeks to understand through interpersonal transactions with others these qualities are, in turn, developed further. In the context of direct experience and involvement, interpersonal as well as conceptual abilities are developed through the process of case study learning.

When the experience of cases is mediated through case materials the information has already been gathered and assembled by someone else. The student's access to the people involved is indirect and there is normally no opportunity to engage in face to face interaction with them. In spite of these restrictions case materials which are constructed to provide a vicarious experience of a situation and, thereby, satisfy the criterion of realism, will provide 'thick descriptions' of human conduct in which surface behaviour is portrayed in the context of evidence for the emotional states which underpin it, eg explanatory accounts elicited in interviews with the person and others who have dealings with them. Inferences about people's emotional and mental states, drawn from such case descriptions can be tested through a discussion of alternative understandings of the behaviour in question and simulated episodes which attempt to imaginatively reconstruct it. Case materials, constructed according to the criterion of realism, will therefore provide opportunities for the development of empathy in the same way that good literature portrays fictional characters in ways which invite the reader to empathise with them.

The kinds of case materials produced by the Stage II Review team also provide opportunities for students to develop the ability to promote feelings of efficacy in others. Klemp (1977) pin-points the three aspects of this ability I have already outlined. Case materials which provide 'thick descriptions' of human conduct enable students to examine the positive as well as the negative qualities, of the person(s) concerned. The initial focus will tend to be on the negative aspects of behaviour with accompanying feelings of hostility or anger. But human conduct rarely displays unambiguously negative qualities and the presentation of comprehensive evidence about this usually reveals the ambiguity. Such evidence can support the belief that the person(s) involved have the capacity to achieve something worthwhile with support and encouragement. This 'insight' can then provide a basis for controlling the initial feelings of hostility and exploring suggestions about how, for example, a police officer could handle the situation in a way which enhances rather than diminishes the capacities of those involved to do something worthwhile. These strategies could then be explored through role play. While observing police recruit training in Denmark I noticed that recruits were always invited to evaluate a role play exercise against the criterion "Did we leave the situation as an improved state of affairs for the members of the public involved?"

So far, then, hopefully, I have indicated how case study learning utilises and fosters both conceptual and interpersonal abilities that may be generic to successful patrol policing. Finally, let us examine the relationship between case study learning and the development of 'impacting abilities'. The development of understanding in relation to a particular case will involve students in examining the decisions and interventions of the police. It will suggest alternative decisions and courses of action, the likely impact of which can be assessed through getting students to design and carry out role play and simulation exercises. It is in this context of imaginatively acting out alternative decisions that opportunities are given for the development of those abilities which underpin making an effective impact on the situation. It could be argued that such abilities are not so much involved in developing understanding of a case as in applying that understanding to practice. But I have already argued that a practical understanding of a particular situation is tested by assessing the impact of decisions people take in its light. The assessment of impact brings about readjustments to the prior understanding. In other words, case study learning aimed at understanding is a form of Action Research (see Elliott, 1985) and not a form of research that can be detached from action. I would therefore conclude that the possession of impacting abilities is a condition of deepening and developing an understanding of cases, and the abilities themselves are enhanced in the process.

If case study learning utilises and fosters conceptual, interpersonal and impacting abilities which appear to be generic to good policing, then we have occupationally relevant criteria for assessing the quality of such learning without having to resort to content objectives as outcome measures. But this does not, in my experience, fully reassure many people concerned with assessing the learning outcomes of case study. The attraction of 'content objectives' for those involved in educational assessment is that they are measurable. In attempting to broaden the range of assessable learning outcomes assessment technologists will want them specified in measurable form. This is why they prefer to retain 'objectives' language when talking about the assessment of process-linked outcomes. The idea of 'process objectives' conveys the impression that one can specify 'process goals' in terms of quite specific behaviours which can be precisely measured. With respect to the kinds of generic abilities specified above assessment technologists will want to specify them in terms of behavioural descriptions ('indicators').

The problem with this approach is its behavourist assumption that no significant distinction can be drawn between behaviour and the patterns of thought which underpin it. Either statements about the latter can simply be reduced to statements about the former (naive behaviourism), or their referents can be correlated so that statements about a thought pattern refer to dispositions a person has to behave in certain ways (dispositional behaviourism). Modern assessment technologists in the field of police training tend, in my opinion, to be dispositional behaviourists, and, therefore, will want to analyse generic abilities in terms of their behavioural correlates. Such a stance is radically inconsistent with the basic rationale for focusing on the 'generic abilities' of successful performers as a basis for professional training and assessment. D. C. McClelland (1973), who has played the leading role in developing this rationale, claimed that tests "aimed at assessing the capacity of a person to make a certain kind of response" have very little predictive validity in the sense of predicting how well that person will actually perform in a real life occupational situation. He explains this in terms of the complexity of real life situations:

"... life outside tests seldom presents the individual with such clearly defined alternatives ... is much more apt to be characterised by operant responses in the sense that the individual spontaneously makes a response in the absence of a very clearly defined stimulus."

Tests which measure the achievement of behavioural objectives assess what McClelland calls respondent rather than operant behaviour, ie a behavioural response to a clearly defined stimulus. But respondent performance cannot predict operant performance, and it is largely the latter which is required of patrol officers in real life policing situations. Therefore if we follow the logic of McClelland's argument for police training, any model of assessment structured according to behaviourally defined objectives will be operationally irrelevant to a significant extent. The whole point of identifying generic abilities as a basis for assessment is that they explain successful operant responses in real life situations. They enable practitioners to construct their own responses in complex circumstances where what is required is far from clear. Any attempt to define them in terms of action-correlates either for purposes of curriculum planning or assessment is totally misconceived. It is quite inconsistent with the espoused aspiration of current police training to turn out officers capable of making independent and wise decisions in sensitive and complex policing situations.

Generic abilities cannot be defined in terms of their performance outcomes. "How then can they be assessed?" some may ask. This is a problem for the behaviourist assessment expert but not for the person who without question and quite intuitively, assesses his own and others' conduct by fitting 'the bits and pieces' of behaviour into the patterns of thought which underpin them, thereby giving them coherence and meaning. These patterns are inferred from evidence of the wide range of behaviours a person displays in the circumstances. The evidence is not only gathered from observations of behaviour but by asking the agent to reveal the thinking which underpins that behaviour, and asking other participants about its meaning and significance for them. In developing procedures for assessing the development of 'generic abilities' in police training we need to make this natural, commonsense process more systematic, not by developing an elaborated technology for quantifying behaviours, but by helping trainers to improve the quality of their natural judgements and inferences from observable and subjective data about student performance. What needs to be systematised are procedures for gathering and processing evidence in a form which increases the possibility of making reasonable and valid inferences about the quality of learning. For example, procedures and methods need to be developed for economically sampling, processing, and recording qualitative data derived from self, peer, and tutor assessments of learning. There is a considerable amount of literature now in the area of qualitative educational assessment which police training can draw on.

Much of the evidence needed to assess generic abilities can be gathered during the course of the normal learning process. Assessment does not have to depend entirely on the construction of special tests. But inevitably the full integration of learning and assessment processes restricts the extent to which the systemisation of assessment is possible. The integrated approach will need to be supplemented by specially constructed test situations in which sufficient time can be devoted to adequately and fairly sampling students' learning. But the test situations for assessing generic abilities will need to closely resemble the learning tasks in which such abilities are developed. This does not rule out 'pencil and paper' tests, but their construction will be very different from tests structured to elicit pre-defined responses. Lyle M. Spencer (1979), for example, provides two examples of specially constructed 'paper and pencil' tests of generic abilities. The first asks subjects "to compare and contrast two conflicting statements or analyses of a situation or set of data". This test is designed to assess the ability to discover meaningful patterns in "large amounts of confusing, conflicting data, and cite specific data to support one's inferences".The second example is a test of accurate empathy and asks subjects "to make an appropriate counselling response to a taped or live statement by a 'counsellee' ". Such pencil and paper tests inevitably simplify and abstract from the complexity of real life situations to a far greater extent than a learning process based on the kinds of case materials envisaged by Stage II does. Case materials could be used as a basis for constructing 'simulated job performance' tests, which according to Spencer "are more predictive than operant paper-and-pencil tests". Spencer also claims that peer and superior ratings of job incumbents have greater validity than pencil and paper tests.

All this points towards a way of profiling the development of generic abilities throughout police probationer training which incorporates:

(a) trainers, peers, and self-assessments based on evidence gathered in the case study learning situation, whether the case is directly experienced (on the job learning), or indirectly experienced through observation or activities based on case materials;
(b) observers' assessments of simulated job performances;
(c) operant pencil and paper tests.

How does one help probationers cope with 'the canteen culture'?
(The Contamination argument)

One of the strongest objections police trainers have to a curriculum which focuses on real cases of policing is that they can provide negative examples of practice. The recruit observing how police officers actually work during the In-Force Modules of the proposed new course, or looking at case materials in the context of a DTC classroom, will discover a few police officers who are ignorant of the law, who bend or ignore procedural rules, who participate in a 'canteen culture' which transmits and reinforces 'undesirable' attitudes towards the public. The fear of many trainers is that the study of concrete policing situations will contaminate impressionable young recruits with the ignorance, malpractice, and undesirable attitudes which, not infrequently, they believe characterise police behaviour. The objection rests on a profound distrust many police officers in training roles have of their operational colleagues. Indeed, the Stage II Review found, when interviewing central service trainers, that the desire to 'purify the service' sometimes constituted a motive for entering training.

One of the major functions of DTCs as they existed pre-Review, and still do to a large extent, is the 'purification' of recruits. Through a process of conditioning which stamps out the expression of individuality, induces obedience to rules and supervisors and emotional dependency on peers, 'self' is reconstituted in the form of a model police officer: smart, polite and formal, controlled and disciplined, obedient and loyal. The removal of recruits and their trainers from their normal life situations where their behaviour is influenced by a wide range of social influences, to an almost total institution where they are cut off for the major part of the week from family and friends, and even the world of policing, facilitates this purification process. This kind of central training experienced by recruits in DTCs operates on what we have called "the slippage theory": namely, that the product of the conditioning process operating within the protected DTC environment will counteract the negative influences of 'the canteen culture'. It is hoped that the process will ensure that when recruits 'go out there' the slippage will not be great. This 'theory' continues to underpin the ethos of DTCs in spite of evidence that not all trainers are totally convinced that it works. For example, in some DTCs probationers returning at the end of their probation for the Final Course are isolated from the Initial Course students to avoid contamination. Trainers talk about the scruffiness, lax standards etc., of Final Course students. But if the training had worked in the first place this degree of slippage, according to the theory underlying it, should not have occurred. One suspects that the theory is retained because a better alternative has yet to be demonstrated. It is hard for police trainers to see a case study based curriculum as a possible alternative way of handling the 'contamination' problem. But this is precisely what it is from the perspective of the Stage II team.

Police officers tend to assume that one sorts out problems of behaviour by externally controlling it. Hence, contamination effects can be reduced by behavioural conditioning techniques. Even 'self-discipline', from this perspective, is the internalisation of rules and norms which are initially externally imposed and reinforced. From the perspective of the Stage II Review contamination effects are more appropriately reduced by enhancing recruits' capacities for self-direction. Self-directed behaviour is not a conditioned response to a pre-defined stimulus but a reflective response which draws on personal capacities for discrimination and judgement in particular circumstances. It is the exercise of these capacities which enables police officers to respond to a situation in a manner which is consistent with professional goals and standards, and to resist negative aspects of the occupational culture. They are the types of capacities I have already outlined in discussing generic abilities which are capable of development through case study learning. Such learning is the means of developing those personal qualities which will enable young police officers to resist social pressures to engage in malpractices and adopt unprofessional attitudes. It is the alternative approach to the 'contamination' issue.

An emphasis in training on the development of the kinds of personal qualities I have referred to is supported by current research into attitude change. For example, research suggests that people who are high in self-monitoring ability are better at changing their attitudes and behaviours than 'low self-monitors'. This is because 'high self-monitors' suspend their response to a situation until they have assessed it. In processing information they become aware of inconsistencies between their understanding of the situation and the attitudes which initially predisposed them to respond to it in a certain way. They will then decide upon a more appropriate response which will in turn lead to shifts of general attitude. 'Low self-monitors' cannot separate their general attitudes from their behaviours in this way. Their attitudes totally determine their response to a situation, unmediated by reflection. 'Low self-monitors' appear to lack those cognitive abilities which would enable them to resist the influence of undesirable attitudes on their performance.

The Stage II Final Report summarises its training aspirations for police probationers through the idea of 'The Reflective Practitioner' (Schon, 1983). From this idea one can derive an alternative theory for handling 'the contamination problem'; namely that the development of those cognitive abilities which underpin self-directed behaviour enables police officers to best resist negative aspects of the occupational culture. This theory is not only supported by academic research in the field of attitude change but by research into the 'generic competencies' of successful policing.

If the Stage II approach to the 'contamination problem' provides a more credible alternative than the behavioural conditioning approach currently employed, then police trainers have no cause to worry about introducing case materials which portray negative aspects of policing, providing the learning process into which they are introduced genuinely encourages the development of those cognitive abilities which are 'generic' to good policing.

Concluding remarks

In this paper I have attempted to meet the major objections which the Stage II Review team encountered to their proposals for giving case study a central place in police probationer training. In addressing the major oppositional arguments I have attempted to develop a coherent theory of professional development for future police constables.

Much has been said about the importance of the constable's professional role as key decision-maker and resource manager at the interface between the police organisation and the public. Some senior police officers believe that organisational changes are required to support this role if it is to become a reality. Certainly, many constables become cynical about their own organisation. They do not experience the 'back-up' support and trust which would enable them to operate as responsible professionals. Instead they often experience patrol work as labourers at the bottom of a rank structure which offers few rewards and acknowledgements for wise judgement and responsible action, but plenty of punishment for mistakes. They often feel they have little influence over how their organisation structures their work. The effectiveness of a truly professional training for police probationers will depend upon the willingness of police organisations at the operational level to reassess the role and status of the patrol constable within them.

13 Developing interviewing skills: a career span perspective

Eric Shepherd

> There is nothing in the whole universe that can be more effective than a man or woman's daily behaviour can be.
>
> Walt Whitman (1860)

Efficient and effective interviewing: the foundations of public confidence

In every police-public encounter the public and the police service expect the police officer to manage the exchange—to conduct an interview, ie controlling and directing the conversation whether it be to obtain, to pass on or to clarify information (Russell, 1972). There is a direct link between public perceptions of how an individual officer has fulfilled this everyday core task of interviewing and the degree of confidence within the community that the police in general can be counted upon to be correct both in bringing their specialist knowledge to bear and in handling people (Southgate, 1986).

How an officer brings his or her range and depth of specialist knowledge to bear provides an insight into the *efficiency* of the police service. How an officer handles the person, how he or she treats and talks to the individual, provides an insight into the *effectiveness* of the police service—how mindful it is of the effects of its behaviour not only upon the individual on the 'receiving end' but the contribution of this interview to wider perceptions of policing in the eyes of the public. It is possible to be efficient but at the same time to be entirely ineffective (Metropolitan Police, 1985; Shepherd, 1984).

Interviews which fulfil social, moral and psychological, as well as legal, criteria are efficient and effective. They generate faith in a service to do what is 'right' by the law and what is 'right' by the person, who like everyone (including the officer) has the right to be treated with common decency and respected as a person.

This chapter does not offer a prescriptive view of the 'what' and 'how' of police interviewing. It seeks to relate interviewing as the core skills area of policing with a number of issues and themes raised elsewhere in this text. Summarising the factors put to the test in the interviewing process lays down a framework for understanding the emergence of inadequate and inappropriate interviewing within the police service. The emergence of such interviewing can be related to the organisational culture of the service, particularly its perspective on formal and 'on-the-job' training. A career span perspective on interviewing development would obviate these shortcomings.

Interviewing: the factors involved

Police officers who manage police-public encounters are essentially 'street managers'. The term 'street' captures a fundamental social reality. The identity of those with whom the officer is obliged to converse is immensely variable in terms of age, social, psychological, and legal status, as well as ability and willingness to communicate and to co-operate, in situations of variable complexity, physical and emotional arousal, antipathy and conflict of all kinds (Southgate and Ekblom, 1984).

The term 'manager' is apposite. The course of the interview is the outcome of the officer bringing to bear a personal and professional frame of reference—to define the situation, both in terms of thought and action (Ashworth, 1979; Berger and Luckmann, 1967; Southgate, 1986). How officers define the situation is crucial to judgements of efficiency and effectiveness. Three fundamental factors contribute to this defining process: the officer's analytical skills competence, the officer's interpersonal skills competence, and the officer's self-perceptions (Figure 1).

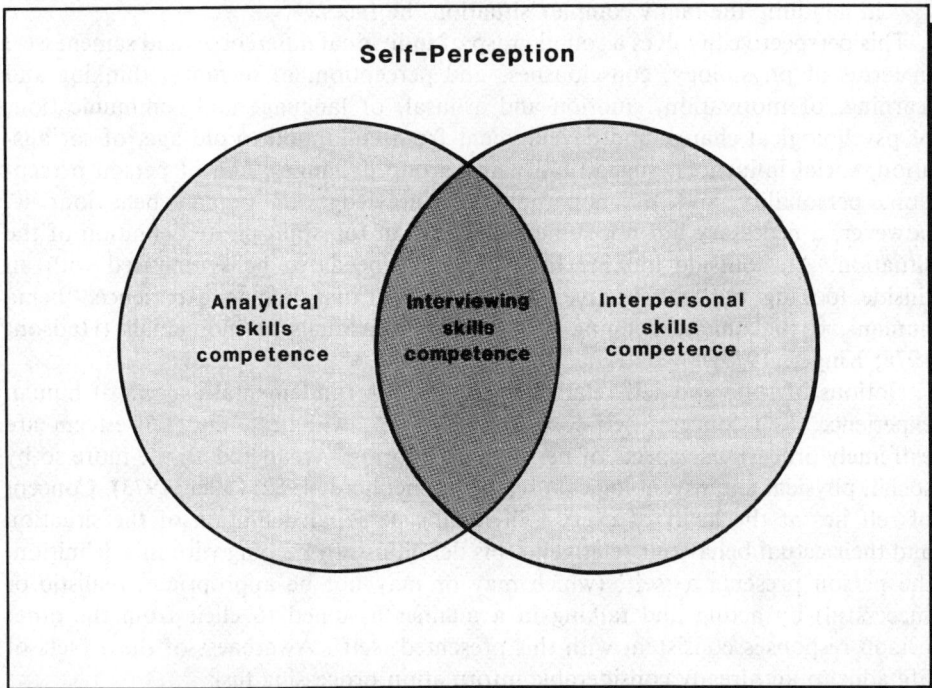

Self-Perception

Analytical skills competence | Interviewing skills competence | Interpersonal skills competence

Figure 1. Factors contributing to an officer's definition of the situation

Analytical skills competence

The police service as an occupational profession "controls a body of expert knowledge which is applied to specialist tasks" (Elliott, 1972). Whilst the level of expert knowledge will be variable between and within individual officers both the public and police management require (and assume) an officer to have sufficient knowledge to define a situation in terms of law and procedures. However, the situation is much more than an abstract legal and procedural puzzle.

The difficulty arises because human beings are involved. The situation has personal significance. It can be a *routine* or a *ritual*—another incident of a particular type. It can, however, be a *drama,* an event challenging an individual's capacity to cope (Hopson and Adams, 1976; Morris, 1972). To emerge as sensitive as well as sensible in defining the situation, an officer needs to recognise the human element—the psychology of human behaviour and human experience.

Every police officer has to cope with the challenge of coming into contact with literally 'anybody'—where anybody refers the entire spectrum of humanity, people of different ages, with differing 'legal' status (victim, offender, witness, bystander, innocent enquirer), of differing status and role, from different social, cultural and economic backgrounds, at different stages and levels of development, with different capacities to communicate and to process information, in different physical and mental states, each responding differently to the prospect, the pressures and the implications of a situation in which they find themselves invited to converse, or initiating conversation, with a police officer (Southgate and Ekblom, 1984).

Policing is inevitably applying psychology. As Russell and Beigel (1982) noted:

"The professional police officer must learn to view behaviour from a perspective similar to a behaviour scientist's in order to insure maximum efficiency in handling the many complex situations he faces."

This perspective involves a sound grasp of individual differences (and samenesses) in terms of physiology, consciousness and perception, of memory, thinking and learning, of motivation, emotion and arousal, of language and communication, of psychological change and development from childhood to old age, of socialisation, social influences, suggestibility and group dynamics, and of person perception, personality and psychopathology. Knowledge of human behaviour is, however, a necessary but not sufficient condition for appropriate definition of the situation. An 'outside looking in' perspective needs to be synthesised with an 'inside looking out' perspective: acknowledging that human experience, 'being human', is the unique defining property of individuals as individuals (Hudson, 1978; Kinget, 1975).

Notions of self, and self relative to others, are fundamental aspects of human experience. Self-concept, self-consciousness, self-awareness, and self-esteem are extremely precarious aspects of personal equilibrium—rendered all the more so by social, physical and psychological pressures (Shepherd, 1982; Ziller, 1973). Concept of self lies at the heart of every individual's personal definition of the situation and their actual behaviour relative to this definition. In keeping with this definition, the person presents a 'self' (which may or may not be appropriate, realistic or successful) by acting and talking in a manner assumed to elicit from the other person responses consistent with this presented 'self'. Awareness of these facts of life adds to an already considerable information processing task.

Information processing skills are necessary at both the micro- and macro-level (Shepherd, 1986a, b). Attention, observation, listening, comprehension, auditory and visual memory are crucial to process the discourse as a stream and as a totality. What is said and done and how it is said and done by all participants constitutes a mental text to be worked upon to detect inconsistency, vagueness, ambiguity and contradiction, signs of arousal, resistance, truth, evasion, deception, and readiness to co-operate.

Information handling potential determines the extent to which an officer can make sensible judgements, can make flexible and constructive decisions, and can make use of his or her level of interpersonal skills competence.

Interpersonal skills competence

An essential prerequisite for a skilled interpersonal performance is consciousness of the 'what' and 'how' of verbal and non-verbal conversational behaviour: turn-taking phenomena, the need to adjust relative share of talking time, the distinction between subjective and objective questioning and the types of question and questioning sequence associated with these, the questions which access affect and fact at different levels of recall and cognitive process, destructive conversational behaviour (overtalking, interrupting, minimally responding) and associated disruptive styles of listening, active listening and behaviours signalling concentration and comprehension, and of the link between types of listening behaviour and assertive behaviour in its constructive and destructive forms (ie responsible assertiveness in contrast to dominance, aggressiveness or submissiveness) (Shepherd, 1987a, b).

Interpersonal skills competence means monitoring and adjusting conversation relative to personality, arousal, and, importantly, perceptions of the relationship. What is said and done and how it is said and done by a participant to a conversation sends a powerful meta-message to the other as to what kind of relationship exists, or is desired to exist, between them (Fisher, 1980). The specialist knowledge and tasks of a professional, in addition to the powers invested in his or her role, imply the pre-existence of an *up-down* (superior/subordinate) relationship in which the professional occupies the up position.

Up-down relationships emphasise deference, based upon difference and psychological (if not social) distance (Southgate, 1986). The net result is enhancement of the professional's self-esteem at the expense of the other person, whose opportunities for expression (let alone self-expression) are constrained. In contrast *across* relationships are characterised by conscious effort to overcome these barriers. A professional's preference for one type of relationship rather than the other is itself a reflection of his or her self-perceptions.

Self-perceptions

Across an individual's entire career span, but most particularly in the earlier years, he or she develops notions of self which act as a "career anchor" (Schein, 1978). Three types of self-perception constitute his or her *occupational self-concept*: (1) self-perceived talents and abilities (based on 'successes' and getting it 'right' in the eyes of the organisation); (2) self-perceived motives and needs (based on (a) opportunities for self-testing and self-diagnosis, and (b) feedback from others); and (3) self-perceived attitudes and values (based on actual encounters between self and the norms and values of the organisation or work setting).

According to Schein an individual's self-perceptions guide, constrain, stabilise and integrate on-the-job behaviour. They represent the officer's personal people-handling philosophy for getting the 'job' done—a set of core assumptions concerning roles and role-expectations particularly with regard to status, rights and obligations (Southgate, 1986). These assumptions founded upon how an officer views himself or herself determine how reality is perceived, how the situation is defined, the conversational relationship aspired to, and the degree of personal and professional competence reflected in any interview.

Interviewing skills competence

Although there are many ways in which the structure and process of an interview have been conceptualised, any interview comprises two basic ingredients: *content* and *conduct*. Content refers to the issues and topics covered; conduct refers to the way content is covered.

To obtain, pass on or clarify information content in a professional manner demands conscious and explicit processes of problem-solving and decision-making to produce a mental framework mapping out

(1) The nature of the 'problem' to be resolved (however approximate or provisional).
(2) The objectives to be achieved.
(3) The degree of flexibility (highly structured, semi-structured, unstructured).
(4) The type of relationship.
(5) The conversational format (a 'script' fulfilling basic conversational requirements, eg GEMAC—greeting, explanation, mutual activity, close (Shepherd, 1986a, b)).
(6) The topics/issues to be covered.

Such framing of content is essential. Complexity is more apparent than real. Negative reaction to the breadth of the task is indicative of people who have never been prepared to prepare for the interviewing task. Most interviews are weak in content. As Goodale (1982) commented interviews are:

"more likely to fail because of poor content than because of the interviewer's weakness in conducting the interview. This is true because people do not take the time or have the knowledge necessary to plan an interview systematically."

To transform a logical framework into a smooth, *apparently* unstructured conversation demands conducting skills. To obtain, pass and clarify information sensibly, sensitively, and skilfully requires the implementation of a systematic sequence of information processing (initiate, listen, focus, probe, use) (Goodale, 1982) within a conversation which fulfils common-sense criteria for acceptability and 'psychological bridge-building' (Shepherd 1986a, b).

To achieve this information processing and conversational skills are put to the test: observing, memorising, avoiding subjective questioning, funnelling questions phrased to discriminate affect and fact and to take account of the interviewee's age, intellect and psychological state, controlling and rewarding the interviewee's participation. In sum, finding facts and minding feelings.

Problems with interviewing

Frameworks for content are most readily mapped out and applied in *structured encounters,*

"those which cannot be planned thoroughly but which require a 'procedure' to be followed, eg dealing with an RTA, where certain things like casualties, HO/RT/1's, an obstruction have to be dealt with" (Metropolitan Police, 1986a).

These encounters contrast with *unplanned* and *planned* encounters which challenge the officer's competence to frame content and to be professional in conducting the interview. Poor content and conduct can be expected, but not necessarily condoned, in *unplanned encounters,*

"which are spontaneous and have little or no structure to them, eg the Police Officer who is stopped in the street and asked for local directions" (Metropolitan Police, 1986a).

Inadequate or absent framing of content and unsystematic, insensitive and unskilled conduct are inconsistent with professionalism in *planned encounters* where

"the final result or outcome may depend on the interpersonal skills of the Police Officer and often in practice relate to interviews with witnesses, victims or suspects" (Metropolitan Police, 1986a).

Officers clearly have fewest problems in defining the situation in structured encounters. Problems and objectives are more readily recognised, with objectives able to be achieved through the application of a relatively inflexible, pre-determined 'procedure' in a highly structured conversation founded upon implicit acceptance of an up-down relationship with equally implicit expectations concerning conversational rights and obligations. There is a distinct possibility of an efficient outcome. There is an equally distinct possibility of alienation—rendering the interview entirely ineffective.

Absence of a framework in spontaneous encounters may, if the officer acts unthinkingly and thoughtlessly, also alienate. However, officers experience the greatest difficulty not when they are under the pressure posed by spontaneity of encounter but when they actually have time to plan for the encounter—whether with a suspect, a victim, or a witness. Although difficulty is experienced in framing content and conducting interviews with all three, least difficulty surrounds suspects—particularly those who are charged and are in custody. The category of the offence gives some guidance with respect to necessary points of evidence, and conversation is constrained because the relationship, rights and obligations are much more readily recognisable. Interviews with victims, complainants and witnesses are seemingly much harder, more anxiety inducing in their demand for conscious thought and action in terms of applying analytical and interpersonal skills.

The result is that all too many officers enter interviews with an alarmingly narrow definition of the situation. Based on a cloudy conception of the 'problem', no antecedent thought as to how the interview will be begun, an all-too-common outcome is an interview which fails to fulfil both efficiency and effectiveness criteria. Poor initiation, meandering and frequently disconnected question-answer sequences, subjective questioning, inappropriate phrasing of questions, failure to listen to answers, disruptive listening and conversational styles, problems with observation and memory, inability to detect change in the interviewee's verbal and non-verbal communication—all operate to obstruct the emergence of accurate, reliable accounts (or any account at all) with tangible effects upon clear-up rates, police morale, and public confidence.

Public confidence is eroded most of all by first-hand experience or second-hand experience (gained through everyday conversation and media coverage) of interviewing which demonstrated an absence of a respect for the interviewee as a person. People 'know' implicitly what philosophers (Downie and Telfer, 1969; Kant, 1964/1785; Peters, 1966) and senior police management (Metropolitan Police, 1985) have found it necessary to spell out explicitly: respect for persons as ends in themselves is fundamentally a respect for law itself. This is a universal expectation whether it be in the context of requests for assistance, traffic offences, stops particularly to effect searches, and crimes against the person and property.

In 1983 the effects of such first-hand experience or second-hand knowledge of instances of inappropriate interviewing were reflected in a Policy Studies Institute (PSI) survey of 2,420 Londoners. A quarter of those surveyed believed officers *often* questioned people inappropriately, using unreasonable pressure or threats. A further 27% believed police officers *occasionally* questioned in this manner.

Whilst under a half believed fabrication of evidence, violence on suspects held at police stations, excessive use of force on arrest and false records of interviews at least *occasionally* happened, about one in ten thought these kinds of misconduct *often* occurred (Smith, 1983; Smith and Gray, 1983).

Prior to and since the PSI report public concerns have focused upon three issues:

(1) Inappropriate assertion/aggressiveness, creating or increasing tension particularly in situations of actual or potential conflict, such as stops in the street.

(2) Oppressiveness and insensitivity to psychological and emotional needs and vulnerabilities of interviewees, particularly the potentially (if not actually) difficult or resistant interviewee, especially the young, the mentally handicapped and the alleged victims of sexual offences.

(3) The pursuit of confessions prejudicing the quality of investigation. The 'cough' (confession) becomes an over-riding aim, a tangible mark of success which increases the risk of overlooking manifest vaguenesses, ambiguities, inconsistencies and contradictions in the accounts of interviewees, as well as increasing the likelihood of false confessions, particularly those likely to create an illusion of clear-up—false admissions of offences to be 'taken into consideration' and false admissions arising from prison visits.

Depressingly these interact to produce a climate of doubt concerning the content of statements and the manner in which these are obtained: doubt within the community, doubt within the judiciary and doubt within officers themselves about getting things 'right' in interviews.

With the advent of tape recording under the terms of the Police and Criminal Evidence Act 1984 and with increasing devolvement of beat crime investigation to uniform officers, more and more interviews within the framework of ostensibly planned encounters are being monitored both as within-force initiatives and as part of central government funded research projects. Already a number of worrisome trends are identifiable. A disturbing proportion of interviews are brief in the extreme. Furthermore, all too many officers are seemingly unready, unwilling, or unable to measure up to the tasks of framing content or fulfilling the principles of interview conduct to derive an adequate account, or to probe an account, even from the most co-operative interviewees.

Arguably, the encounters in question are those which put an officer's investigative and conversational skills most to the test. Whether the inadequacies observed in these interviews arise from a lack of confidence, competence, or both, compounded by anxieties and apprehensions about being monitored, it is impossible to say. However, a recent radio programme (British Broadcasting Corporation, 1987) on the effects of the Police and Criminal Evidence Act highlighted interviewing problems experienced by officers in unmonitored, *structured* encounters. The requirement under the Act to give personal identification and justification for action was perceived as a block upon efficient policing. The 'right' kind of relationship could not be signalled. Giving this information constituted a loss of face, humiliating the officer, rendering him or her not only unable to investigate but unwilling to investigate at all.

The common factor throughout is occupational self-concept: self-perceptions arising from experience of a working culture which has produced generations of officers who struggle to define the situation appropriately and yet interview dysfunctionally.

The origins of dysfunctional interviewing

Coping with change and the development of personal competence are integral to the process of being socialised into the job, which is progressively perceived as an *organisational culture:*

> "the pattern of basic assumptions that a group has invented, discovered, or developed in learning to cope with its problems of external adaptation and internal integration, and that have worked well enough to be considered valid and, therefore, to be taught to new members as the correct way to perceive, think, and feel in relation to these problems." (Schein, 1985).

According to Jelinek, Smircich and Hirsch (1983) culture, another word for social reality, is both product and process, the shaper of human interaction and the outcome of it, continually created and re-created by people's ongoing interactions. Conversation—purposeful and casual—is the predominate medium for learning, passing on, and changing the organisational culture. How police officers talk to each other in police-police encounters creates the culture as a set of norms, *organisational oughts* (van Maanen, 1976) concerning goals, processes and relationships.

Socialisation through conversation exposes an officer to eight crucial "norm influence areas": (1) leadership modelling behaviour, (2) the work-team culture, (3) information and communication systems, (4) performance and reward systems, (5) organisation policies, structures, resourcing, and procedures, (6) training and orientation, (7) first-line supervisor performance, and (8) results orientation (Silverzweig and Allen, 1976). Conversations passing on organisational oughts about how to talk to people occur within two training systems: the formal training system and the informal training system of learning on-the-job.

The formal training system

Formal training has distinct advantages and distinct disadvantages. The agents of socialisation—the trainers—are trained for their task. They are grounded in 'learning' psychology, analysing the requirements for learning and designing instruction for learning (Gagne, 1977). The training centre or school is constructed as a social reality which passes on images of the goals, processes and relationships—norms—which are to be taken as consistent with the occupational oughts of the job. Problems arise because learning in such contexts is, as with other professions, cast in categorical terms. Student ability and talent is measured by the extent to which he or she gets it 'right' in terms of 'knowing' and applying typologies (types of problem; types of solution) in the problem solving and decision making tasks posed in simulated encounters with the 'public'. Characteristically the type of relationship represented by the conversations between instructor and student (up-down) are carried over into practicals whose content and conduct are illustrative of the 'real world'.

For most police officers training meant (and still means) rote learning of categorical knowledge of law and procedures, fostering decision making of the black and white, correct/incorrect kind, in structured encounters which encouraged narrow definition and constrained courses of action. Equally narrow was the range of information processing skill developed in training. Skill implied recall for facts learned from lessons, books and notes, not ability in the necessary skills to make sense, solve problems and make decisions in real world situations. Crucial skills of observation, listening, visual and auditory memory, detecting changes in behaviour—essential to directing and controlling conversations—were not addressed.

Instruction in the essential psychology, to help students make sense of people, to understand human behaviour and human experience was extremely limited. Notes and lessons referred to supposedly important facts concerning things called 'id', 'ego' and 'super-ego', as well as 'self-image', 'groups' and 'stereotypes'.

Having grown up in a talking and hearing world, students were assumed to be good enough if not good conversationalists. Instruction in 'communication' and 'barriers to communication' topped things up—but never touched upon conversational facts of life. Students were left to develop competence in areas deemed to be important—listening and assertion (though the quiet were exhorted to 'speak up'). Good enough conversationalists were exposed to 'interviewing' instruction in the form of the "four Cs", the "seven Ws" and a paradoxical recommendation to 'plan' to be "suitably flexible to allow for conversation flow" (Central Planning and Training Unit, undated).

Getting it 'right' in the interviewing contexts of the classroom and roads immediately outside the classroom was thinking in categories *and* stereotypes, following 'procedure' to get the 'right' answers in a question-answer ritual: a ritual conducted in a manner to ensure an up-down relationship to fulfil the officer's needs and the norms for police-public encounters ('right' self-image = reliance on authority/power = maintaining face = interviewer credibility). Formal training developed minimal competence to direct and control conversation by keeping on top of structured encounters. It was the task of the informal training system—'on-the-job' training—to develop this competence further and to extend it to managing unplanned and planned encounters.

The informal training system

'On-the-job' training is fundamentally observational learning. It is an entirely respectable and efficient way of passing on skills—particularly highly routinised, mechanical skills. Its other terminology—'learning by Nellie' or 'sitting by Nellie'—refers to the origins and the identity of the trainer, the woman on the production line, perhaps operating a machine, in the factories of the last century. The trainee or novice learns by observing the skilled operator as he or she *models* appropriate performance, imitating this performance whilst being observed by Nellie, who breaks down the task into its smaller components and provides feedback on the right and wrong elements of the trainee's performance—during or after the performance.

The simplicity of the learning sequence and its industrial origins—manipulating, machinery, objects and materials—have created within the minds of many organisations dangerous assumptions about simplicity and competence when it comes to 'on-the-job' training. There is the common assumption (that undervalues the complexities involved) that every task can be reduced to a readily observed, readily implemented *simple* sequence of steps. This might apply to machine minding but it certainly does not apply to talking to people with minds. Directing and controlling conversation to find out facts whilst minding feelings stretches analytical and conversational skills to the utmost.

A second common assumption has it that since everyone learns *simply, simply* everyone can teach, ie that experience equals both expertise and the expertise to teach. A moment's thought would lead to the rejection of both assumptions on common-sense grounds. A problem for police officers across the age, rank, role and seniority spectrum has been that both of these assumptions have been the basis for this approach to 'on-the-job' training, enshrined in the attitudes and actions of generations of 'on-the-job' trainers.

'On-the-job' training implies more than one trainer. The officer's manager, responsible for setting performance criteria and monitoring 'job' performance, is crucially responsible for ensuring the officer is trained to fulfil expectations. This involves taking on the role of trainer as well as assigning suitable peers to take on the training function.

Given the importance of 'on-the-job' training it would be logical to assume that peers and managers were motivated to assume their important training roles. Logic would dictate that the organisation would ensure trainers were indeed competent in the skills to be passed on. Observing a trainer who is an unskilled interviewer, who possesses an inappropriate occupational self-concept and who lacks the necessary breadth of basic analytical and conversational skills, means at best the trainee learns nothing and at worst he or she learns to act incompetently. Logic again would argue that trainers were trained for the training task, competent in the necessary instructional skills involved: observing the trainee's peformance, identifying key elements, analysing these elements, selecting and packaging teaching points relative to the trainee's level of development, and, mindful of the psychological make-up of the trainee, pitching the feedback appropriately. Again, logic would suggest that trainers create the conditions for learning in committing time and engineering opportunities to model behaviour, to monitor the trainee's performance and to provide feedback. Finally, common-sense would argue that 'on-the-job' training can only be effective if the trainee is seen as a total person, with trainers directing and controlling conversations to provide the form of workplace counselling to fulfil the trainee's identified needs (Hill, 1981).

Unfortunately, logic has not been reality. The fact is that 'on-the-job' training in the police service has been almost totally unsystematic. Assumptions of simplicity and competence compounded by absence of motivation and the requisite skills, have created a culture in which the identity of Nellie could be somebody, anybody, or nobody. For all too little time and on all too few occasions, Nellie has been somebody who chooses, or is chosen, to fulfil the specific functions of trainer. On occasions, Nellie is anybody available to 'look after' the trainee. Trainers (untrained to fulfil their important and difficult task) in both of these situations have resorted to instructing by issuing instructions. The most common of these is to 'watch how I do it' and, when the interviewing task is completed, to exhort the trainee to do it 'that way'. This side-steps the complexity of the training task— overcoming any lack of motivation to instruct and any lack of observation, analysis, identification, integration and feedback skills.

Given the fact that trainees have the greatest difficulty in identifying key elements within the stream of verbal and non-verbal activity and physical action they are witnessing, and given the fact that all too many Nellies give global extrinsic feedback (tending to give diagnoses of performances in holistic terms—'right', 'wrong', 'not bad', 'good enough') the crucial fine grain learning points to develop analytical competence and conversational competence are missed.

All too many Nellies, particularly the incompetent, the indolent, the unwilling, and the unthinking, claim that interviewing skills cannot be taught. They relegate the acquisition of these skills to *intuition,* an ability to be developed (how is never specified—beyond observation), but once possessed will act as a guide as to how to proceed with any interaction. As Royal and Schutt (1982) rightly comment, intuition is merely judgement coming to the surface with apparent spontaneity. It is, indeed, derived from prior observation of similar situations. However, it highlights the greatest weakness of observational learning: in the absence of a skilled trainer, conclusions are drawn without an examination or evaluation of all the factors involved. Furthermore, it creates situations when intuition fails, when all that is left is a "disguised guess" (Royal and Schutt, 1982).

Disguised guesswork characterises officers who were left increasingly with nobody assuming or being assigned to fulfil the trainer role, when the trainee is left to be his or her own trainer. Learning degenerated into 'picking things up' by observing in the role of spectator or member of an audience, or by going it alone.

What gets 'picked up' is a tangle of beliefs about interviewing (Shepherd, 1986a, b). Officers learn that 'interviewing' is distinct from 'interrogation'. The former is 'soft' questioning, which anyone and everyone can do (because all 'uniform' officers have to do this). The latter is 'hard' questioning, based on skills—hard won (in the world of CID) and hard to use—in overcoming the resistance of the 'guilty', to obtain that mark of personal and professional prowess 'a cough'. They come to learn that the 'guilty' (suspects and offenders) resist whilst the 'innocent' (victims, complainants, and witnesses) do not. Somehow, three types of conversational style—'befriending', 'businesslike' and 'authoritarian' (Irving, 1980)—fit into defining situations, talking to categories of people judged upon the basis of their 'personality', in encounters of differing levels of structure.

The whole tangle breaks down particularly when the officer is under time and other 'job' pressures, is unable to discriminate willingness to talk from ability to tell, and when witnesses, complainants and victims act out of character and resist. Intuition fails, disguised guesswork takes over. This pattern becomes well-established since trainees have more often than not gone it alone and survived.

Going it alone projects an officer into situations of unsystematic self-testing and self-diagnosis. An officer learns that if nothing 'went wrong' with an interview—the way the situation was defined, the decision-making and the judgements involved, the way things were managed, what was said and done and how it was said and done—then the interview was at least 'right'. Increasingly, going it alone becomes the dominant pattern for learning and rationalising action across the entire career span.

The effects of unsystematic 'on-the-job' training

Understandably, acting intuitively or 'playing it by ear' when 'experience' does not fit, creates long-term latent levels of stress and anxiety. It is always possible that using either of these two approaches to get it 'right' by seeking to keep on top in fact is construed as getting it 'wrong'. This creates an organisational culture in which feedback—a precarious process, once desperately sought—is now despairingly avoided. When, and if, it is forthcoming from peers its usual form is global, supportive and disposed to take the officer's 'part'. This contrasts with feedback from management. Managers, anxious and fearful of managers above them, are more disposed to punish than to praise (Smith and Gray, 1983), when officers fail to get things 'right' or to cope. Of the range of counselling interview available to management, there is an emphasis upon 'correct' interviews (to discipline 'incompetents'), rather than 'coach' interviews to help officers to develop competence, or 'consult' interviews to examine personal issues creating inappropriate performances (Hill, 1981). Hence, management style has been identified as stressful (Manolias, 1983).

Perceptions that stress is greater within the organisation than out on the streets (Manolias, 1983) necessarily affects an officer's occupational self-concept. The quality of police-police encounters affects the quality of police-public encounters. Inexorably, as an officer develops across the career span, as he or she grows older, becomes more senior in terms of rank, role and years of service, alienation increases, people are seen as the problem and are interviewed accordingly. The likelihood of burnout inexorably grows (Ianni and Reuss-Ianni, 1983; Russo, Engel and Hatting, 1983; Sparger and Giacopassi, 1983).

This pattern is not exclusive to the police service. It has been noted in other contact professions whose organisational cultures are also perceived as stressful. Their members were also exposed to a formal training system which ill-prepared them in the range of psychological knowledge and information processing and conversational skills to conduct anything but the most stereotyped of interviewing rituals, relying on role, psychological distance and deference to guide their own and other people's behaviour.

Their 'on-the-job' training was also characterised by a trainer with a multiple identity, often unskilled, unwilling, unprepared, untrained to train, unable to give anything but the most unhelpful feedback—unfocused, unrelated to the trainee's personal and professional development, unsupportive, or just left unsaid. They also were increasingly left to act upon intuition or disguised guesses. They also became more and more resistant to feedback. They also tend to react defensively when asked to account for their actions. They also perceive their managers as unready, unwilling and unable to counsel appropriately. For them also 'internal' conversations erode one's occupational self-concept, adding to the stress of applying tangles of intuition and guesswork to control 'external' conversations doing a 'job' with a "client" group from whom the professional becomes increasingly alienated (Cherniss, 1980; Sarason, 1986).

The links are clear and incontrovertible. Formal training has been woefully inadequate and condemned for this. Yet, the much respected 'on-the-job' training, which will always be the major medium for learning how to do, has left individuals to develop incoherently. In the absence of anybody to assume the responsibilities of an 'on-the-job' trainer, officers have had to train themselves—'picking things up' intuitively and making disguised guesses when intuition does not fit.

Incoherent development of interviewing skills creates all too many individuals at all stages of lateral and vertical progression within the culture who have no sense of coherence about what they are doing and how they are doing it or what to do and how to do it, when it comes to talking to each other and to members of the public. Yet such a sense of coherence is essential to well-being, the development of competence and the ability to cope with change—at the level of the organisation, the work group, and the individual (Antonovsky, 1979). Approaches to develop interviewing skills need to achieve such coherence.

Recent developments in interviewing training

Recent developments have focused upon *basic training* and *specialist training* to fulfil particular operational or administrative functions. In reviewing these developments the requirement for brevity has meant that mention cannot be made of every approach by every force or centralised training institution.

Basic interviewing

Before 1982 'interviewing' was literally thought about—being mainly the subject matter of notes, overhead projections, and one or two interviews observed by the rest of a course. This pattern was common but it was not universally incorporated into courses—whose size, apart from any other consideration such as training mentality, instructor expertise, and methodology—precluded any possibility of every student translating thought into action (and effect) (Phillips and Fraser, 1982). So recruits and managers were encouraged to think about it, as were police instructors and CID officers—but not too often and for not too long. Interestingly the vast majority of police officers, particularly street managers in their early, mid and late careers, were not included in the invitation to think.

The incorporation of Human Awareness Training (later termed Policing Skills) into the Metropolitan Police 20-week Initial Course in 1982 changed the pattern, albeit modestly so. Classes were too large, but at least more curriculum time was devoted to thinking and doing in the area of conversational skills and elementary investigative interviewing ("Purposive Encounters"). Class size still represented a barrier to fostering, maintaining and extending skills in every student over the entire period of the course.

In 1983 the 'Social Skills of Policing' package to be incorporated in Initial Training at Home Office Training Centres included an expansion of earlier material on "interviewing skills", though the content and the total amount of curriculum time was markedly less than that being covered at Hendon. These factors compounded the problem of class size and of instructors neither trained as interviewers nor trained to train others to interview.

Basic training for established officers—'catching-up' training—has been a focus of training effort in the Metropolitan Police since 1983. A Policing Skills Development Unit (later Team)—which has worked in parallel with both CID and management training staffs—designed a Policing Skills course for street managers (Cuthbertson *et al.*, 1983). Conducted in Divisional Training Units, by officers trained to interview and to pass on interviewing skills, the course contains an interviewing module.

Elsewhere across the country the pattern of 'catching up' has been uneven. Increasingly, forces are coming to terms with the necessity to train uniform officers in basic interviewing. This process was made all the more pressing by the introduction of the Police and Criminal Evidence Act 1984 and, increasingly, devolvement of crime investigation to uniform officers. Harder to understand is the still very uneven training of those considered to be specialists in operational interviewing.

Specialist operational interviewing

Traditionally CID officers have been viewed as the interviewing specialists. In its review of interviewing training the Heads of Detective Training Working Party (1983) came to the conclusion that:

"there was a great variation in the actual time spent on the subject, the type of instruction given and the use of films and video. It was our unanimous view that generally insufficient time and attention was being given to this all important subject and that there was a lack of any standard, co-ordinated approach to the matter."

The Working Party Report incorporated material on a range of topics culled from a range of sources. To achieve standardisation of training it recommended a series of overhead projections to be incorporated into CID courses to provide a standard coverage of essential topics. In contrast to this cognitive approach, however, two forces—the Metropolitan Police and Merseyside Police—made the strategic decision to develop a skills-based approach to interviewing.

The Metropolitan Police CID training staff, who had worked in parallel with the Policing Skills Development Team, introduced a module approach to training. The content is 'techniques' and 'strategies' based, being a synthesis of the original Human Awareness material and the source material which gave rise to the Heads of Detective Training Working Party Report.

Mindful of the possible final provisions of the (then) Police and Criminal Evidence Bill, Merseyside Police rejected a 'techniques' and 'strategies' approach, deciding to invest resources to research and design an entirely different approach (Shepherd, 1985, 1986a). Consistent with social skills training experience (Phillips and Fraser, 1982) maximum class size is eight. The first stage of development was an Interview Development course. This has been attended by the majority of the CID officers in the force, and is now being extended to uniform officers. The aim is for all officers to attend such a course once probationer training has been completed. At present the emphasis is upon attendance by uniform officers fulfilling specialist tasks upon divisions, including sexual offence interviewing.

No national standard policy exists concerning interviewing training on Sexual Offences courses. With notable exceptions, the courses again are cognitive in their approach to interviewing. They talk about the skills, with only a few students actually conducting an interview—with the rest looking on. Class sizes are not consistent with realistic skills training for all.

Alone as an appropriately conducted skills-based course, focusing on 'doing it', is the Negotiators' Course. Given that it is attended by officers within the police management structure the practical focus of this course contrasts the the training most have had to fulfil specialist administrative functions.

Specialist administrative interviewing

Course numbers have tended to preclude true skills development. With notable exceptions the standard management course pattern is still cognitive, in which students have limited opportunities to develop actual skills. Practicals tend to be rather narrowly focused—selection interviews, discipline interviews and the like. Counselling skills (de Board, 1983; Hill, 1981) are a rare feature within courses—though it is interesting that in some forces those assigned to instruct on management courses do get the opportunity to receive instruction in workplace counselling from contracted consultants.

The one-week residential course for Senior Officers in Merseyside (attended by officers from Chief Inspector to ACC) covers practical training in investigative interviewing and the range of management interviewing, including workplace counselling. In addition, Merseyside instructor courses for force training centre and divisional instructors (uniform and CID) covers the same interviewing range.

Some conclusions

It is clear that class size, related to availability of skilled trainers in sufficient numbers, has perpetuated a 'thinking about it' approach to interviewing training at the basic level and on specialist training courses. This is despite the fact that it has been known for years that the only way to learn to interview is to do it (Zweig, 1965; Phillips and Fraser, 1982).

The picture is of courses which are uneven in achieving the fundamental requirement to develop the necessary analytical and interpersonal skills to interview. Particular problems are experienced in facing up to the necessity to acquire levels of psychological knowledge consistent with being a contact profession.

The views of the Heads of Detective Training Working Party (1983) give an insight into the problems the police service has in facing up to the necessity to acquire levels of psychological knowledge consistent with being an occupation professing specialist knowledge of people:

"We feel it is not necessary or even desirous [sic] for detectives to be given in-depth psychological instruction in order for them to achieve a good knowledge of the available techniques."

These recent approaches are uneven in that they cannot achieve the sense of coherence essential to the development of professional development at the level of the individual. Courses are for officers just 'starting', 'catching-up' or to do specific jobs (in the absence of previous interviewing training of the basic or 'catching-up' kind). This creates conditions of information redundancy. The lack of an integrated perspective, one in which material from 'basic' courses need not be repeated in subsequent courses, means that the present approach to training is highly inefficient. Talking to officers for what might be for some the umpteenth time about 'basics', wastes that most precious of training resource—time; time which could be spent giving a student an opportunity to actually 'do it'.

Lastly it perpetuates the fundamental training weakness of the service. All of the approaches touched upon are located solely within the world of formal training. If the greater part of training occurs in the context of divisional and departmental day-to-day work then systematic training processes must be designed to enable officers to learn 'on-the-job'.

A coherent career perspective is urgently needed. One which ensures the progressive development of essential psychological knowledge, information processing skills, conversational skills, and the appropriate synthesis of these as an officer progresses laterally and vertically across his or her career span. An approach which equipped officers in terms of skills and appropriate educational technology to measure up to their responsibility to train others as well as train themselves in the 'real world' of the division and the department would achieve both organisational and personal objectives.

A career span perspective

Interviewing training across the career span implies a perspective which focuses upon the *individual* from induction to retirement. From a common starting point officers need to be given the wherewithal to follow a coherent path of lateral development (to fulfil the interviewing demands in different roles within a given rank) and vertical development (to fulfil the interviewing demands in different police management roles—including that of instructor). Three areas are involved: basic interviewing, interviewing development and specialist interviewing (Figure 2).

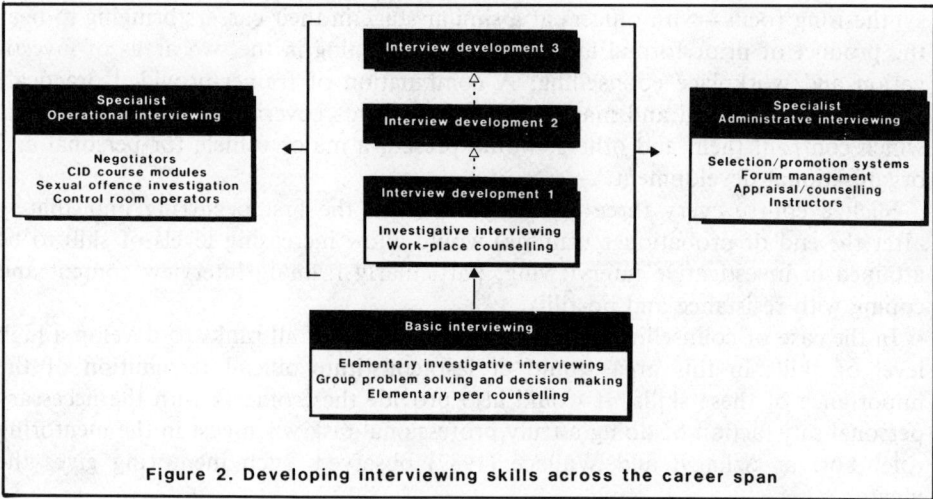

	Interview development 3	
Specialist Operational interviewing	Interview development 2	Specialist Administratve interviewing
Negotiators CID course modules Sexual offence investigation Control room operators	Interview development 1 Investigative interviewing Work-place counselling	Selection/promotion systems Forum management Appraisal/counselling Instructors

Basic interviewing

Elementary investigative interviewing
Group problem solving and decision making
Elementary peer counselling

Figure 2. Developing interviewing skills across the career span

Basic interviewing

Increasingly, as police officers are obliged to operate collaboratively with contact professions, within such contexts as child abuse (Shepherd, 1987a, b), their relative ignorance of psychology will become all the more apparent. Their personal and professional standing and the claim of the service to be a profession will become increasingly tenuous in the eyes of the public and other professions.

Police officers, as part of their basic grounding to carry out interviews, must acquire the range of knowledge of human beings and being human outlined in the earlier part of this chapter. Similarly, they must develop the necessary information processing skills to translate psychological knowledge and knowledge of conversational phenomena into, initially, skilled conversational (listening and looking) performances and, subsequently, skilled performance in three interviewing contexts:

a. Elementary investigative interviewing (content framing and conducting).
b. Group problem-solving and decision-making (Hanson, 1981; Leigh, 1983).
c. Peer counselling (Nelson-Jones, 1986; Priestley *et al.*, 1978).

Basic skills in these three contexts are essential to enable a trainee to measure up to the responsibilities of being a newly emergent street manager and to contribute to the consultative processes and practices contained within new approaches to police management.

The interviewing skills fostered in the basic training stage need to be maintained and extended across the entire career span. This is the case irrespective of an officer's rank or role. To achieve this interviewing development should match the career 'stage' of the officer's career. Schein (1978) has described the very different issues that an individual must confront and the different tasks to be fulfilled by an individual as he or she progresses through the stages of *full membership in early career, full membership, mid-career, mid-career crisis, late career in non-leadership role, late career in leadership role,* and *decline and disengagement.*

Almost wholly practical-based interview development courses could act as a synthesising focus—with officers at a similar stage in their careers bringing to bear the product of prior formal and 'on-the-job' training in the two areas of investigation and workplace counselling. A combination of trainer-provided practicals and practicals created and managed by the students covering the issues and tasks which confront them and others, would present a major vehicle for personal and organisational development.

Such a course every three to five years (with the first occurring immediately after the end of probationer training) would allow increasing levels of skill to be attained in investigative interviewing, particularly framing interview content and coping with resistance and hostility.

In the case of counselling skills, requiring officers of all ranks to develop a high level of skills in this area would at last constitute official recognition of the importance of these skills. It would also provide these officers with the necessary personal satisfaction of doing a truly professional task when cast in the mentoring role. For, as Szilagyi and Wallace (1987) observed, such mentoring gives the mentor:

"an opportunity to aquire some career direction and a way to develop a philosophy of management and self-confidence in managerial ability."

Specialist interviewing

As an officer progresses laterally and vertically the content of training to fulfil the tasks of particular operational and administrative roles could build upon knowledge and skills from both basic and interview development training. Figure 2 should be taken as illustrative of the lateral and vertical possibilities. For this reason it is not intended to cover each task area. Most are straightforward but three warrant some explanation.

Some readers might ask why training for control room operators. These officers exercise great discretion in their 'gatekeeping' and response co-ordination functions. However, Scott and Percy (1983) noted that many control rooms had become repositories of the unfit by dint of incapacity or inability:

"Departments have often assigned disabled or disciplined police officers to the sensitive tasks of answering calls or dispatching cars. Even persons assigned full-time to demand processing duties are frequently thrown into the breach with insufficient interpersonal communication skills and with no training in making crucial decisions in the pressure situations that frequently arise at police switchboards and dispatch consoles."

Although describing the American 'experience' the indications are that the same situation applies within the United Kingdom. These officers must be trained as forces are faced with increasing demands and diminishing resources to satisfy these, coming to rely more and more upon the interviewing skills of these officers—skills fundamental to the appropriate exercise of their discretionary decision making power.

Forum management skills are crucial to police managers who are tasked with participating in committee-type encounters with the public. These demand management skills of the facilitator kind. These challenge an officer's ability to listen actively to several people all at once and to assert himself or herself responsibly. They need the group interviewing skills to get a group to focus on a 'common' problem and a common process, to "protect" group members and to ensure equity of participation, whilst remaining neutral and building trust (Doyle and Straus, 1976). One needs to be trained in these skills.

Courses for instructors—of all ranks—to instruct, in force training centres, and on divisions, need to incorporate training to train officers in the analytical and interpersonal skills to fulfil investigative, problem solving, and counselling interviews, as well as managing forums. This again would build upon all of their own interviewing development up to the time of the instructor course.

All of the above may strike some readers as entirely 'pie in the sky'. It is entirely attainable, but would require the service to adopt a systematic approach to 'on-the-job' training.

The role of 'on-the-job' training: appropriate attitudes and appropriate technology

Formal training is well suited to passing on the requisite knowledge and skills within each of the points of progression shown in Figure 2. Furthermore, a fundamental theme is the fostering of mentoring and counselling skills from the very first stage of career development. At each stage of progression, whether within the context of interview development or training to be a manager or a designated instructor, counselling skills receive increasing emphasis.

True skills development will depend, however, on managers, peers and individual officers creating the conditions for systematic 'on the job' training. As with all human relations training conflicts of attitude are involved. Tellingly Maier (1952) observed that attitudes are always loaded with feelings, and the logic of feeling is different from the logic of thinking. None the less, a basic requirement is to change attitudes towards 'on the job' training. Many (perhaps most) of those who received no systematic 'on the job' training will need to be convinced why informal training needs to be systematic. With the appropriate attitude, particularly amongst police management, a career span perspective makes sense and the importance of 'on the job' training would *at last* take on the appearance of reality.

It is also essential to realise that 'on the job' training suffers from a similar limitation to formal training. When it comes to interviewing training both can only provide the student with *extrinsic* feedback—before or after the interviewing process—not *intrinsic* feedback—during the interviewing process. Yet interviewing is a stream of activity before the officer's ears and eyes, posing the officer with a stream of decision-making—multiple points at which the officer must make decisions. Neither the formal trainer nor the 'on the job' trainer can stop the stream, or create circumstances where the student could 'try again', finding out what might have happened if he or she had decided to say or do something else.

Yet one form of instructional technology exists to provide powerful intrinsic feedback—interactive video (Wooley, 1982).

The unique instructional properties of interactive video are not only suited to developing competence in the skills to frame interview content and conducting interviews. They are also perfectly suited to consolidate learning in respect of psychological knowledge, information processing and conversational skills. Interactive video can be used in any learning context: the officer training alone, with another officer or a group of officers, and with or without a trainer. Furthermore, it is a technology which is equally applicable to formal and 'on the job' training.

A career span perspective must accommodate officers already in the system. These officers would need to 'catch-up' in order to be incorporated into the lateral/vertical progression indicated in Figure 2. 'Catching-up' implies yet more resource—training of trainers to train small classes using dedicated interviewing 'suites' equipped with remote controlled video recording facilities. Furthermore, given the size of the problem it will take time. This constitutes yet another argument for interactive video technology—since those officers waiting to be trained *can* still develop skills ahead of any formal training eventually provided. Interactive video would allow skills to be fostered further, maintained and extended. It is understandable, therefore, why a major interactive video project is now underway to develop interviewing skills through the use of this technology and a 'library' of training programmes at sub-divisional level.

The implications of implementing a career span perspective

Adopting a career span perspective to interviewing development would have a number of implications. It would mean meeting the challenge of acquiring levels of psychological knowledge commensurate with other professions. It would mean acknowledging that a police officer really ought to have information processing skills commensurate with the complexity of the core task of policing.

It would mean being serious about 'on the job' training, that it is too important and too pervasive not to be as systematic as formal training. No longer can it be left to chance, to a variously competent and variously committed somebody or anybody, or disgracefully, leaving the officer to learn alone and to survive by virtue of intuition and disguised guesswork.

It would mean coming to terms with the fact that the formal training system needs resourcing to meet the demands of appropriate small group instruction. It would mean acknowledging that both the 'catching-up' problem and ensuring 'on the job' training really is training demand appropriate resourcing and a technology which allows officers to learn alone and with others.

This all means bidding farewell to the nil cost illusions concerning 'real' training 'on the job' and founded upon assumptions of simplicity and competence. The real cost for the service and the public has been too great and for too long.

14 Police training for handling domestic disputes

Peter Southgate and Florence Marden

Introduction

The problems faced by the police in responding to calls to domestic disputes* and violence are many and remain one of the continuing bugbears of day-to-day uniformed policing. This chapter sets out to consider some of these problems and to suggest how trainers in particular might be thinking about them. The chapter bases its discussion upon several sources: data from various Home Office research studies, in particular a recent observational study of police-public encounters which included just over one hundred disturbances, of which about a third were classed as domestic disputes (Southgate, 1986); other research and reports on the topic; and experience of the training and counselling of police officers by one of the co-authors. The last of these sources was supplemented by a series of interviews and questionnaires completed by thirteen experienced officers currently preparing to take on the training role; 20 such officers also contributed to the exercise by participating in small and large group sessions to explore the issues and feelings of the police in relation to domestic disputes and violence.

The chapter is not intended to be a comprehensive statement on the subject; a number of recent reports have reviewed the area and made proposals for change, many of which were backed up by a Home Office Circular issued in October 1986 which emphasised the need for the police to take the problem more seriously. Further studies are still in hand, including a review of the extensive literature on the subject (Smith, forthcoming), so that it would be premature to make any final judgements. But it is clear that there are many aspects to the problem and it can, therefore, be misleading to look at only one of these at a time. The four 'perspectives' which this chapter proposes that the police should consider are: (i) the safety and self-preservation of the officer; (ii) legal and procedural issues; (iii) organisational factors and; (iv) police-public relationships. These are not listed in any order of importance and neither is it suggested that, in practice, they can or should be separated for, in almost every case which police officers are called upon to handle, these various considerations come into play in some combination or other.

Training implications arise both directly and indirectly. The purpose of the chapter, though, is not to set out a training curriculum, but to suggest issues which those designing curricula should take account of. Also, training content must be a reflection of actual policing policy, practice and organisational arrangements, and there are important aspects of these still to be clarified. For these reasons it is not necessarily clear *who* should be trained, though the assumption is

---

* Through most of this chapter the term 'disputes' is used in a broad sense to encompass anything which involves a dispute in a domestic setting, whether or not this has escalated into actual violence. In doing this the intention is not to underplay the extent or seriousness of the violence which occurs in the context of such disputes. As mentioned later, the distinction between the two aspects is a crucial one with implications for both police practice and training.

made that training for the handling of disputes should, at a minimum, be part of probationer training.

(i) **Self preservation.** Handling domestic disputes is generally seen by police officers as an unpopular task and is often felt to be stressful, being associated with feelings such as anxiety, lack of control and unease (Dutton, 1981; Kroes, 1985; Stein, 1986). The interviews and group discussions conducted by one of the co-authors emphasised this as a problem for officers who have to deal with the more violent or emotional domestic disputes. Officers feel that, whatever they do, they cannot ever really solve the problems confronted in any meaningful way. Feelings of frustration may be aggravated by unrealistic public expectations as to what the police can do about the problems.

Particularly in the United States, a continuing theme in policing has been the belief that dispute handling may be one of the most—if not *the* most—physically hazardous task for an officer (Straus *et al.*, 1980). Police officers have always been concerned that, in intervening in disputes, they might find that violence is redirected against themselves or even provoked by their very presence. Recent American reports, however, throw some doubt upon this long-held belief: analysis of data from the FBI and from several independent studies (Garner and Clemmer, 1986) shows that, although officers are sometimes killed and injured at domestic disputes, the risk of this is considerably less than once supposed. The proportion of officer deaths which occur during such calls is less than one third of the number previously calculated, and the risk of death is certainly less than it is when dealing with robberies and burglaries. Past misperceptions arose from the apparently simple error of combining figures from domestic disturbances with those from other, more dangerous, disturbance calls, including bar and gang fights and general disturbances (short of actual riots) and incidents where someone was brandishing a gun. The evidence on assaults and injuries to officers is less reliable, and further analyses are proposed in order to take proper account of risk factors involved in various types of incident.

Given the much rarer use of firearms in this country it may be that the relevance of these findings is limited here. But it seems advisable to look more carefully before continuing in the belief that there is any more physical danger in domestic disputes than in many other types of incident. Certainly, very few of the small number of domestic disputes in the observational study of police-public encounters by Southgate (1986) involved any violence between the participants, let alone to the officer.

Some of the injuries sustained by officers may well stem from an escalation of disputes into violence, possibly as a result of inappropriate police responses. It is, therefore, important for training to look at how domestic *disputes* should be handled as opposed to actual *violence*. If they can be defused at this stage then they may not reach the point of becoming violent.

Another side to the theme of self-preservation is that officers will be concerned, in all their dealings with the public, to avoid things happening which lead to a complaint against them. Disputes are rarely clear-cut and it may be difficult to apply neat legal formulae, so that it is only too easy for the police to say or do the 'wrong' thing in the eyes of one party or the other. Faced with a situation of uncertainty the safest course of action may then seem to be to do nothing, but it is unlikely that this will often be an adequate course of action.

If the 'do nothing' option is excluded, then, from the officer's point of view, the way to minimise the trouble caused by domestic disputes is to be as competent as possible in dealing with them. In training terms this implies two main needs. First, factual information and understanding are needed about the nature and causes of domestic disputes, and about the proper role of the police—and other agencies—in responding to them. In this respect training must avoid superficial comments relating disputes to drink, sex and money; these may all be relevant but are not, of themselves, a proper explanation and can encourage stereotyped views if presented too briefly. Second, skills must be learned so that officers can more effectively handle and negotiate disputes and assaults, both in legal and in human relations terms. In addition, the availability of personal counselling for police officers might be considered to help officers cope with the pressures they face in these or other even more stressful situations.

(ii) **The legal and procedural** issues involved in domestic disputes are fundamental, and play a major part in determining how matters are handled by the police. The interviews and group sessions which one of us conducted with future police training officers suggested that training in the legal aspects of domestic disputes should have two main objectives. First, patrol officers need to know when they should be adopting a legalistic approach and, if necessary, arresting someone. Second, they need better information about the legal position of victims to pass on to them. It is no use, for example, telling someone that it is not a police matter and they should consult a solicitor if the solicitor then informs them that the civil law does not apply in their case and they should call the police.

Much has been written recently stressing the need for new approaches, involving not so much new law but rather new approaches to using existing legal provisions. The general theme of much recent argument has been the need for violence in the home to be treated more seriously as a criminal offence with all that implies as far as arrest and prosecution are concerned. Four recent reports worth noting here are: the Report of the Women's National Commission on "Violence Against Women" (1985); the London Strategic Policy Unit Briefing Paper on 'Police Response to Domestic Violence' (1986); the report of the Metropolitan Police Working Party on Domestic Violence (1986b); Edwards (1986) study of police processing of domestic assault cases. All these have commented in some detail on the legal issues arising in domestic violence cases. Government concern was registered by the issuing of Circular 69/1986 'Violence Against Women' to Chief Officers, attaching detailed comments on the various recommendations made by the Women's National Commission. The bulk of the Circular deals with the treatment of rape victims, but it also emphasises the need for concern about the victims of domestic violence and reminds the police of the powers of arrest for such offences now provided by the Police and Criminal Evidence Act 1984, and of its provisions for compelling spouses to give evidence in court. Also emphasised are the need to ensure that officers are in a position to help victims by advising them on how to contact victim support schemes and local authority departments such as housing and social services. The need for privacy is emphasised and the use of information leaflets for victims is recommended.

The demands of the WNC for improved police training are acknowledged in the Circular, though no detailed response is given. It is noted that much of the content, style and emphasis of police training is currently under review, and that

191

the recommendations of the WNC would be brought to the attention of those conducting reviews and of all chief constables. The Inspectorate of Constabulary are taking particular note of how forces respond to the recommendations of the Circular.

Reports such as those noted above are frequently critical of the way the police deal with disputes: officers are said to do little for the victim, ignore signs of physical assault, fail to attempt proper counselling or referral, and refuse to get involved in what they maintain is a civil, not a criminal, matter.

The more extreme critics might say that the police do nothing because they are the instruments of a sexist, male-dominated society which assumes that men are entitled to control women, using force if need be (Dobash and Dobash, 1979). Others might put it that such incidents get little police sympathy because they are seen as 'dross' or 'rubbish' and not in line with the officer's self image as a crime-fighter (Smith and Gray, 1985; Southgate, 1986). In conversation, police officers argue that they do very little because there is very little they can achieve, either within or outside the provisions of the law; they say they cannot use the criminal law unless there is evidence of physical assault. It is rare, of course, for there to be any witness other than the victim herself, and the common police belief is that she will probably withdraw her complaint later on even if she signs one at the time. Clear evidence on this is difficult to identify. For example, Edwards (1986) found a high rate of withdrawal while Wasoff (1982) and Faragher (1985) found a low one.

The Domestic Violence and Matrimonial Proceedings Act 1976 allows abused spouses to take out an injunction against their abusers, excluding them from the matrimonial home or prohibiting them from returning to it, or from molesting the applicant or a child living with them. Some injunctions also have a power of arrest attached so that, if they are violated, the police can arrest the respondent. The problem here is that often the officer on the scene is not sure whether there is an injunction in force or whether it has a power of arrest; when this kind of ambiguity exists the tendency is to do as little as possible. The Police and Criminal Evidence Act 1984 allows arrest where the officer has reasonable grounds for believing that ". . . arrest is necessary to prevent the relevant person. . . causing physical injury to himself or any other person" (S.24) or ". . . to protect a child or other vulnerable person from the relevant person" (S.25). PACE also makes spouses compellable witnesses where they have been assaulted or injured (S.80) so that the police could, in principle, pursue a case themselves against a man who assaults his wife.

However, until quite recently there was a general presumption that a 'treatment/counselling' approach was to be preferred to arrest. One of the best known accounts of such an approach and the training which went with it is contained in Bard (1970). This claimed benefits from training police officers in family crisis intervention skills, and subsequent studies have also shown that officers tend to overcome their initial resistance to such training, that disputants report greater satisfaction with trained officers, and that trained officers tend to refer more people to community agencies (Dutton, 1981; Pearce and Snortum, 1983; Buchanan, 1985). Unfortunately, though, it has never been very clear how far such activities can actually reduce repeated violence in the long term.

Pressure from the women's movement for a more aggressive police approach with more emphasis on treating domestic assaults as crimes led to the 'Minneapolis' experiment in the early 1980s (Sherman and Berk, 1984) which tried to randomly allocate disputes to one of three police responses: arrest of the man; sending him away for eight hours; or giving advice and counselling. The result appeared to be a clear success for the arrest approach: over a six-month period, repeat calls fell much more where this was used, and follow-up interviews with victims supported this view. Criticisms have been levelled at the methodology of the study and its generalisability has been questioned. A number of replications are currently underway in the United States to test these findings further, but the earlier findings have already been influential in determining the policies of police departments. Positive results have been reported from London, Ontario—a pioneer in this field—following the introduction of a policy whereby the onus for laying charges in domestic violence cases was passed to the police themselves (Jaffe and Thompson, 1985). In this country the Metropolitan Police initiative in pursuing a more active policy on reporting domestic assaults (introduced in the summer of 1987) seems to herald a trend in this direction in this country.

The London, Ontario scheme originally emphasised a counselling approach, though not by police officers themselves. A team of civilian counsellors was attached to the police department and put on call on an almost round-the-clock basis; although police officers still normally made the initial call they could rely on the counsellors for rapid follow-up and subsequent action. This, or even the use of specially trained police officer counsellors, may well be the best way of dealing with disputes, but the relative efficacy of different approaches is not clear. In any event, for counselling to work well may require the provision of quite comprehensive support services. The resource implications of this and the needs for inter-agency co-operation must be carefully considered.

Comparisons of counselling and arrest may be misleading because they are both probably appropriate solutions, but in different situations, distinguished by the presence or absence of violence. In considering arrest it is important not to blur the distinction between what is simply a verbal dispute and what is actual violence, especially as the first is normally a preliminary to the second. But there are important consequences for police procedure and training which need to be specified. The main procedural difference is that, whereas arrest may be the proper response to an act of violence, this is not likely to be so where the incident is merely at the verbal conflict stage (but see the provisions of PACE where a vulnerable person is at risk of future violence). The emphasis of recent times upon the need for arrest where there has been physical abuse might be counter-productive if it came to overshadow the need for other police responses in cases where the dispute is simply verbal.

Clearly, there is now wide recognition that domestic violence should be taken more seriously by the police, both in terms of concern for victims and in the reporting or arresting of offenders. One way to ensure that domestic calls are taken more seriously may be to emphasise to officers their law enforcement and order maintenance aspects and, thus, their centrality to the role of the police. Thus, if a basic task of policing is to investigate and prevent crime, then it is important to deal both with actual cases of *violence* in domestic settings and also with non-violent disputes, on the grounds that if the latter are not dealt with in good time they may well escalate into actual violence. Dispute handling can, in other words, be seen as a form of crime prevention for which the police officer has a very real and widely accepted responsibility. Disputes *not* involving any violence should also, of course, be recognised as a police concern where a public disturbance is being caused.

(iii) Organisational considerations, such as the provision of resources which can be called upon for help and advice are a third crucial factor. One basic distinction to be made before planning training is whether domestic disputes are to be dealt with using a 'specialist' or a 'generalist' model. A specialist approach would involve officers getting to grips themselves with whatever personal or social problems might be presented, apart from dealing with any breaches of the law. In particular, it would almost certainly involve giving effective counselling. A generalist model, on the other hand, would require the officer to concentrate on short-term legal and practical aspects and then to make proper referrals to specialist agencies—social, housing, legal, medical, statutory, voluntary—who could tackle the underlying or long-term difficulties. The two approaches are not totally mutually exclusive but, in allocating training resources, it is important to know which is to be emphasised.

Specialisation might work in large centres of population with a more or less constant flow of domestic calls; such places could possibly justify maintaining teams of police officers specialising in domestic crisis work. On the other hand, such teams might still not actually be able to cover all these calls at busy times. A more economical system might be one where specialist resources from outside the police service were available to police officers on an on-call basis. They could then refer disputants to this service or call it themselves as soon as the general nature of the problems became clear. Whichever model is used it seems inevitable that police officers will always have some involvement in domestic disputes and they must, therefore, be trained to an appropriate level. For the moment, it would seem that the primary need is for improved 'generalist' training, though bearing in mind the possibility of greater specialisation.

As things stand, are police officers aware of how to call upon specialist agencies? And do such agencies actually provide useful services? More emphasis on a multi-agency approach is now to be found in various areas of policing, and the views on domestic disputes which we heard from training officers reflected this awareness. Evidence from studies of policing (Southgate, 1986; Edwards, 1986) suggests that referral is not actually used as much as it could be. This may reflect either an unwillingness to admit that others can do any better job than the police, and/or an antipathy between the police and other agencies, especially social workers. A policy of closer liaison, along with better information for police officers in training about the work of various other agencies, might help to develop these relationships. The lessons of training will be put into action more readily if patrol officers have information at their fingertips to pass on to victims, either verbally or in the form of leaflets, cards or other written material. Such devices have been in use for some time in the United States and the recent circular (Home Office, 1986) recommends their use here.

Can the officer rely on useful support and advice from within his own organisation? As other chapters in this volume emphasise, training will achieve little unless the skills and attitudes it develops receive endorsement and reward from colleagues, supervisors and managers within the police organisation. There are a number of ways in which the organisation can help the officer on the beat to deal with domestic disputes. First, the officer needs to feel that there are resources he or she can call on if in difficulty, not simply in terms of physical protection but of advice about what to do. A further important support system is stress counselling, for dealing with complex human problems under often tense conditions can be a major source of stress for police officers (Manolias, 1983; Kroes, 1985).

Second, as far as possible—though this can be difficult in practice—deployments should be made in such a way that officers have the time to deal adequately with the problems they find. They should not always feel under pressure to get in and out of an incident as quickly as possible and on to the next call; if this in itself becomes the main priority then they may achieve nothing very constructive by their presence.

Third, a common problem is that patrol officers attending domestic disputes are often considerably younger than the disputants they are supposed to advise. Given the prevailing age profile of the police service there is rather limited scope for change here but, wherever possible, more mature officers should be sent to disputes. Younger officers do need to gain practical experience of this kind of work, but this should be in the company of more experienced ones.

Fourth, officers attending domestic disputes—and, indeed, many other calls—need the best available briefing before arriving. But it is clear that often the information they have is negligible. A large proportion of these calls are to addresses previously visited so that it should be perfectly possible for adequate records to be built up. It then becomes important that radio controllers have access to and make use of these records when they send patrols to a call.

Fifth, clearer messages may be needed about the priority and speed of response which a domestic dispute should receive. Our interviews suggested that constables may think in terms of rapid response to calls while supervisors favour a more delayed approach. More consistent policies and guidelines therefore seem called for. Directives about the general seriousness of domestic disputes are part of the answer (see Home Office, 1986). At the local level graded response schemes—now quite common—may be useful but, where there is a dispute call to an address not previously visited, it can often be very difficult to form an accurate judgement as to the seriousness of that call before an officer actually arrives there.

(iv) Relationships with disputants. Self-preservation, law and procedure and referrals must all be competently handled but, in order to achieve his or her objectives in these respects, the officer must be especially skilled in a fourth respect, namely the way he or she relates to disputants in human terms. This remains a priority whatever legal or procedural strategies are adopted, because the police will never be entirely free of the need to deal with domestic disputes. Whatever other resources are, or become, available, the way the police officer plays his part can affect the success of subsequent efforts by others, his immediate safety and job satisfaction and the quality of police-public relationships.

A full discussion of the methods and syllabuses of courses in interpersonal skills, social skills, or human awareness training is not the purpose of this chapter. But, as with other aspects of policing, such as dealing with ethnic minorities, motorists or youths, it is this training in basic human relations skills which lays the foundation for successful dealings with people in domestic crises. Some of the needed skills specifically mentioned by the officers we interviewed or implied by data from the observational study were:
—mediating in a non-judgemental way without taking sides
—dealing with people older than oneself
—achieving a correct balance between deference and authority
—showing sympathy for and understanding of the plight and feelings of the victim
—dealing with hostility from others and calming them

—coping with cultural differences
—mastery of verbal skills, including questioning and listening
—observing (eg for signs of child abuse)
—understanding non-verbal communication
—giving practical and legal advice in such a way that it can be accepted and understood by those in personal crisis—

A question sometimes raised is whether women officers have any particular role to play in the handling of domestic disputes. Since the Sex Discrimination Act 1975 brought full integration to the police service, of course, the role of women in the police has been officially regarded as no different from that of male officers. Previously, however, women had carried a major responsibility for tasks involving sexual and indecency offences and other matters concerning women and children as victims or offenders. Since integration there have been complaints from time to time that the previous specialist expertise of women officers has been lost. In practice, though, some women have still tended to work largely in these areas.

Apart from the idea that women officers might deal more sympathetically with women victims, it is also sometimes argued within policing that women may be better at dealing with situations of one-to-one conflict. The argument goes that, whereas a male officer's very presence might provoke or escalate violence, a woman—by force of necessity, perhaps, as she knows she has less brute strength to fall back on—is much better at 'talking down' aggressive people. There is no conclusive evidence to support this belief; it seems reasonable to suppose that many women do have or develop such skills (though so may many men). But any such advantage there may be, based on sex, will probably be outweighed by the disadvantages of youth: a young officer, however skilled, inevitably lacks the ability to present quite such a mature and reliable public face as would an older person. Particularly with older disputants, this can be something of a handicap. On this assumption, then, an older male officer could be inherently better equipped to deal with disputes than a young female officer.

In deploying officers to particular calls the scope for taking account of an individual's suitability—on grounds of their sex or any other attributes—for that task is fairly limited at any given time in any given sub-division. Training must, therefore, provide adequate preparation for all, and trainees should learn how to use their personal strengths to best advantage and how to compensate for their weaknesses. If, however, it was felt that women officers had any particular role in domestic disputes (which they might combine with responsibilities for rape victims, child victims and family issues generally) then specialist training might be implied.

Domestic disputes tend to fall between two stools: they require a sensitivity to human problems and behaviour on the one hand but, on the other hand, they may also require a quite authoritative approach by the police officer. This, in a sense, describes the task of the police as a whole, emphasising again that the skills needed to handle domestic disputes are not something unique or specialised, but simply those skills needed to be a good all-round police patrol officer who can deal well with the whole range of human relations problems encountered in police work.

Conclusions

If domestic disputes and violence are to be adequately handled by the police service then there is more at issue than simply the design of courses for patrol officers; change on a rather wider scale is implied, encompassing the adoption of revised legal and procedural standards (such as those within PACE), more emphasis in general upon the role of the police as a helping and referring agency for social problems, and a change in attitudes and priorities among police officers at all ranks. Training, though, clearly has a major part to play in implementing such change. The following areas in particular need attention.

Specialist or generalist? Once a clear view is established as to just what the role of police officers should be in handling domestic disputes and violence, training must convey an understanding of the general principles to be followed. Officers need to know whether they should be trying to solve as much of the problem as possible themselves, or whether their role is primarily to bring in other agencies as quickly as possible.

Law enforcement or social service? Training must help police officers to distinguish between calls when (a) a legalistic approach is called for, making an arrest if need be, (b) when practical help is the priority and (c) when longer term advice and counselling may the best solution. In each case it should then guide them as to who should best deal with the situation.

Reinforcement of training. The lessons of training must be reinforced on the job; by supervisors, by more experienced colleagues and by the reward system. If possible, measures of performance are needed which reflect not simply how much crime officers have dealt with, but how much crime they have helped to prevent. (The implications of this point do, of course, go much wider than the present topic of domestic dispute handling.)

Understanding the causes. If officers are to deal effectively with domestic disputes—in whatever manner—then they need an adequate understanding of the nature and causes of what they are dealing with. There is a danger at present that they take away from training too superficial a view of domestic problems and their causes (sex, drink . . . etc). More time and thought should go into studying and understanding the full complexity of these problems even though this, of itself, will not solve them.

Disputes as serious issues. Domestic disputes need to be presented to officers in training as complex and serious problems in order to counteract the tendency to see them as 'rubbish' work detracting from the police capacity to deal with 'real' policing issues. If more emphasis is put on making arrests in appropriate cases, then this in itself may make officers more inclined to realise that they are dealing with 'real' crimes in the case of violence, and *potentially* real crimes in the case of disputes.

Disputes or violence? Where violence has already taken place before the police arrive at a call then it should probably be treated as a case of assault. Verbal disputes may or may not escalate into physical violence, and it is important that an appropriate response is used by the attending police officer. More thorough training will help officers to judge situations better and make such crucial distinctions rather than avoiding them.

Training context. All training courses should be set in context, not presented in isolation from other training. It was evident from our observations and interviews that officers who deal helpfully and constructively with domestic disputes are likely to be those who also deal well with other human problems encountered in the course of patrol work. The skills needed for dispute handling need not, then, be presented as somehow unique or unrelated to those needed in other aspects of policing.

Human relations skills. Various types of knowledge and skill are needed by police officers to deal effectively with domestic disputes and violence. But, unless they have good ability in handling people in crisis situations of all kinds, then many of the possible strategies cannot be put into effect as well as they might be.

15 The tutor constable attachment, the management of encounters and the development of discretionary judgement

Steve Stradling and Keith Harper

"Experienced police officers will exercise any discretion they have as each situation demands. A probationary constable must be guided by any relevant force policies and by the advice and example of his tutor constable and supervisors." (Central Planning Unit Probationer's Student Lesson Notes.)

Despite its general regard as the 'jewel in the crown' of on-the-job police probationer training, little research or evaluation has been directed towards the Tutor Constable Attachment. An outcome evaluation of the Tutor Constable Attachment would concern itself with establishing the aims and objectives of the Attachment, operationalising these into quantifiable characteristics and gauging the extent to which the formal objectives of the exercise were being met. A comprehensive evaluation would, in addition, compare before and after measures to see how much 'value' had been added to the trainees by the training and seek to identify what changes had, as a matter of fact, been brought about by the Tutor Constable Attachment—whether intended or otherwise.

In this chapter we shall first examine the intentions of the Tutor Constable Attachment, and go on to outline some recent work on police officer's discretionary judgements (Stradling *et al.*, 1987), including findings that give indirect purchase on the effects of the Tutor Constable Attachment, especially on changes to the Individual Schemes (Hogarth, 1980) that inform the discretionary judgement of probationer constables, and conclude by arguing that the centrality of discretion to the daily work of street policing should be reflected in training arrangements in order to better prepare probationers for solo patrolling.

1. Aims and objectives of the Tutor Constable Attachment

There is little descriptive material on the development of the pairing, for a period of patrolling, of an inexperienced and an experienced bobby which, in recent times, has come to be referred to as the 'Tutor Constable Attachment'. In most provincial forces—the situation is somewhat different in the Metropolitan Police—new recruits typically commence their two-year probationary period with a brief Induction course, a 14-week Initial course at a District Training Centre, two weeks learning Local Procedures, initially at the Force Training School and then on divisions, followed by a 10-week period of patrolling on their assigned division under the tutelege of one or more Tutor Constables. They then go back to Force Training School for a further three weeks of classroom instruction before returning to divisions for operational deployment on reliefs. Tutor Constables are experienced officers, both male and female, who have been assigned to the task by divisional command and who have undergone Tutor Constable training at Force Training School.

The area now served by the large metropolitan force that we examined formerly supported four separate forces and these themselves represented amalgamations of several local forces. During the fifteen years prior to the reorganisation of 1974, periods of 'attachment' on the several forces concerned ranged from two days to eleven weeks. After inauguration of the single force, concern about training matters in general prompted a review of training practices in 1980 and the Tutor Constable Attachment was given some selective attention. The review found that periods of attachment and numbers of 'pairings' varied widely across divisions, and that selection of tutors was driven by a variety of criteria. The then Director of Training was moved to comment that descriptions of tutors, as recited by probationer constables, made ". . . horrific reading . . ."

The local force review concluded that the system was:

"very haphazard . . . and . . . that it was . . . a matter of chance as to whether the probationer was teamed up with a competent, interested Tutor or an incompetent disinterested one."

Following this review, three broad objectives were set for the attachment . . .

* to see an experienced police officer in action;
* to become involved, under guidance, in dealing with as many aspects of police work as possible; and
* to learn beat working and communicating with the public.

For the tutors themselves it was declared that each should possess sufficient experience and skill to develop the abilities of probationers in the six following areas:

1. Writing reports
2. Giving evidence
3. Communicating with the public
4. Interviewing and statement taking
5. Knowledge of law and procedure
6. Knowledge of the area and people where he operates

Recommendations also voiced a need for training to be offered for tutors and in October 1982 a residential 1-week course commenced at the Force Training School. Nationally, the situation was propelled by the Report of the Police Training Council Working Party on Probationer Training (Home Office, 1983b) whose recommendations represented the definitive authority in relation to the Tutor Constable Attachment, until the recent publication of the Police Training Council Stage II review (MacDonald et al., 1987). The pertinent recommendations may be summarised as follows:

1. The Tutor Constable Attachment should be retained and lengthened to 10 weeks.
2. During the Tutor Constable attachment the probationer should not be allowed to patrol alone.
3. Short visits to places of interest (eg courts, other agencies) should be permitted within the Tutor Constable attachment.
4. Chief officers should recognise the appointment of Tutor Constables by publishing their approval of the appointment in Force Orders.
5. Tutor Constables should be carefully selected (many constables who do not seek promotion might be suitable for this role).
6. Tutor Constables should undergo a special course of two weeks' training before taking up this role.

The response by the local force to these pronouncements represents its official current policy on arrangements for the Tutor Constable Attachment and includes the following:

* Tutor Constables are appointed by divisional commanders to perform duties . . . for ten weeks.
* Tutors should be officers of high calibre and possess the required personal qualities of integrity and commitment.
* The names of tutors are published in force orders.
* Constables appointed as tutors attend a course at Force Training School.
* Each probationer should have no more than two Tutor Constables—for five weeks each.
* Supervisors to ensure that probationers undertake both mobile and foot duties.
* Tutors to allow sufficient time at the end of a tour of duty to enable the probationer to properly complete any outstanding paperwork before returning to Training School.
* Tutors to discuss training needs with probationers.
* Tutors to liaise closely with other supervisors and write comments in the probationer's handbook.
* The specific *objectives* of the tutor constable attachment are that the probationer should:
  1. Become familiar with beat and patrol work in general
  2. Develop a good police/public relationship—talking to people.
  3. Be able to identify vulnerable lock up property.
  4. Recognise well-known active criminals.
  5. Be aware of the more prevalent offences in the area and how to deal with the offenders.
  6. Become proficient at traffic control.
  7. Develop the ability to interview and take statements.
  8. Have the ability to give evidence correctly.
  9. Become familiar with the correct use of the notebook.
  10. Develop skill in report writing.
  11. Investigate crime.
  12. Search prisoners and property.
  13. Conduct vehicle checks.
  14. Conduct accident reporting and action at the scene.
  15. Know how to deal with a variety of drunkenness offences.
  16. Know how to use the Local Intelligence Office.
  17. Have knowledge of court procedures.
  18. Have knowledge of support units.
  19. Develop proficiency in use of radio.

We believe the policy of this particular force to be generally typical of provincial forces, and its policy closely follows the recommendations of the Police Training Council Working Party save in just one regard—in relation to training for tutors: where the official recommendations favoured a two-week training course, here the training course extends for just one week.

Most programmes of training, of any kind, involve the development of that triumvirate, *knowledge, skills and attitudes*. In training for police work there is a lot of knowledge to be taken on board—principally learning the letters of the laws—and a range of technical and professional skills to be honed and practiced. The bulk of the specific objectives for attention listed above are what might be called 'technical' skills of police work (eg 3–19). Much on-the-job training consists of viewing and rehearsing the normal procedures of a job and, as most probationers will ruefully attest, much of their early training burden is practice at paperwork. However, we agree with the Inspector in our recent study (Stradling *et al.*, 1987) who wrote:

"All aspects of training should encourage the use of discretion".

Attitudes are developed by both formal and informal mechanisms during training, and it is commonly held that perhaps the single most important factor in the development of a good police officer is ensuring that he or she has 'the right attitude' towards the job. This attitudinal background will be often manifest in an officer's exercise of discretion. We believe that the development of technical skills must be complemented by the development of professional skills—and we would see such professional skills clearly displayed in the *quality* of an officer's *processes* of discretionary judgement.

2. The nature and nurture of discretion

"Successful policing depends upon the exercise of discretion in how the law is enforced. The good reputation of the police as a force depends upon the skill and judgement which policemen display in the particular circumstances of the cases and incidents which they are required to handle. Discretion is the art of suiting action to particular circumstances. It is the policeman's daily task." (Scarman, 1981, para 4.58).

In a recent study (Stradling *et al.*, 1987) which looked at the impact on the police of the Fixed Penalty Notice scheme and its effects on discretion, data from 65 inspectors and 78 traffic constables was collected on a range of questions concerning discretion. This data is germane in the current context as it gives some purchase on police officers' current views on the proper extent, limitation and development of discretion.

The Transport Act 1982 has the procedural effect of devolving—for a particular range of offences—complete discretion in the prosecution process to constable level. The decision to prosecute an offender for summary offences was previously the prerogative of superintendent rank, exercised in the 'marking up' of process. This authority was devolved to inspector rank by the force in question in January 1986. The effect of the FPN system is that the ultimate decision on prosecution now lies with the individual constable who issues the Fixed Penalty Notice. Previously police officers submitted 'process reports' through supervisors who made recommendations upon the matter and ultimately decided whether to prosecute or not. This situation still holds in those areas to which the FPN system does not apply, and is summarised in Figure 1. This formulation makes plain that, from the point of view of management, *a large amount of police work is invisible.*

It is a well-established principle that a constable enjoys a large degree of personal freedom of operation and discretion over whether or not to start the legal process by reporting an offender (eg Fisher and Oldham Corporation [1930] 2KB 364). The exercise of this discretion is bounded in a number of ways. On the one hand a decision to report an offender for a minor offence in respect of which there were many mitigating factors is likely to result in disfavour on the part of supervisors and could be made the subject of adverse comment by a court. On the other hand a decision to take no action under circumstances which clearly require action to be taken can amount to a 'neglect of duty' under the discipline

Figure 1. *The three stages of the enforcement process, at each of which discretionary judgement is exercised.*

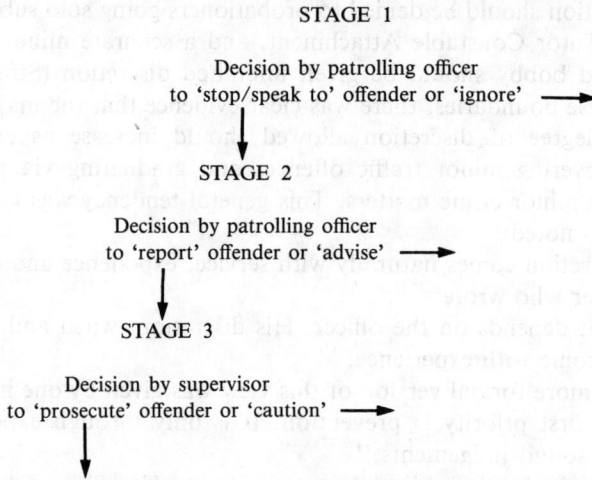

STAGE 1

Decision by patrolling officer
to 'stop/speak to' offender or 'ignore' ⟶

↓

STAGE 2

Decision by patrolling officer
to 'report' offender or 'advise' ⟶

↓

STAGE 3

Decision by supervisor
to 'prosecute' offender or 'caution' ⟶

↓

code and, in extreme circumstances, could constitute criminal behaviour—deliberate and culpable neglect by a public officer of any duty imposed on him by statute or common law can amount to a criminal offence (R V Dytham [1979] QB 722).

Recommendations covering what we are calling 'Stage 2 discretion' in, for example, the area of road traffic offences, are set out for the guidance and direction of officers in a number of places. For example, officers are given the licence to assess the intent behind an act:

> In deciding what action to take, a police officer is entitled to take into consideration whether or not the evidence suggests that an offence was committed deliberately rather than unintentionally. (Force Instruction Book, Section 23) . . .

and guidance as to what action to take when particular circumstances pertain. Thus, verbal advice is deemed appropriate where

> ". . . an offence appears to have been the result of a genuine mistake, a lapse of concentration or where it is trivial or due to some emergency' (ibid.),

whilst verbal advice would be inappropriate in the case of driving which is

> "deliberately anti-social, persistent and affects the safety of other road users" (ibid.).

Even where a decision in principle to prosecute has been taken at Stage 3, supervisors are enjoined to have regard both to the 'winability' of a case:

> "supervisors should determine whether a conviction is more likely than a dismissal" (ibid.)

and to the effective utilisation of resources . . .

> "proceedings should not be instituted where the effort is likely to be disproportionate to the result" (ibid.).

In addition, supervisors are expected to treat as special cases those offences

> "where there is local public interest or where there are grounds for local concern" (ibid.)

and, in such cases, to issue instruction to their officers as to what course of action to take, thereby (temporarily) removing the individual, Stage 2, discretion of the patrolling officer.

In our study, in response to the question "How much discretion do you think police officers should possess at different stages of their careers?", a minority held that discretion should be denied to probationers going solo subsequent to completing their Tutor Constable Attachment, and a separate minority believed that an experienced bobby should be given unlimited discretion (Stradling *et al.*, 1987). Within these boundaries, there was clear evidence that the majority of officers felt that the degree of discretion allowed should increase as experience increases, initially covering minor traffic offences and graduating via minor non-crime to encompass minor crime matters. This general tendency was typified by one traffic officer who noted:

"Discretion comes naturally with service, experience and common sense"
and another who wrote:

"A lot depends on the officer. His discretion, when and where to use it can only come with experience."

A slightly more formal version of this view was given by one inspector who noted:

"Our first priority is prevention. It is only through experience that we can make sound judgements."

A substantial minority of both inspectors and traffic officers felt that an experienced bobby should have unlimited discretion, perhaps believing with one traffic officer that

"Most police officers won't misuse discretion if bounded by . . . common sense attitudes"
and agreeing with an inspector who noted that

"The officer at the scene is the only person who can decide whether to use discretion, knowing the full facts, and facing the person responsible for the offence."

However, whilst recognising the primacy of the immediate circumstances and the devolution of decision-making to the man on the spot, some caveats were entered. One inspector succinctly drew attention to the complexity of the decision and its potential reverberations when noting . . .

"Discretion is a great power. It should be used 'with discretion'. The tact and diplomacy involved in ensuring that, whilst not necessarily reporting a person for an offence, the person has not 'got away with it' is clearly understood. The PR exercise is a good one and may allow the public to see the police in a more caring 'human' role."

Reservations about the quality of some decision-makers was expressed by a traffic officer who noted wryly:

"I have always considered that a PC using common sense will exercise the correct degree of discretion in any case. Trouble is that many people lack common sense."

This latter factor will contribute to the anxieties of supervisors about the quality of the 'invisible policing' taking place under their jurisdiction and suggests one reason for wanting to exert some control over enforcement practices. Inspectors and traffic officers were asked to rank a number of reasons for limiting or influencing the discretion of officers at different stages in their careers. They were agreed on the rankings for each level of experience, and differentiated clearly between what was considered appropriate for limiting the discretion of inexperienced and of experienced officers (Stradling *et al.*, 1987). The main reason for limiting the discretion of an experienced officer was to protect him against the consequences of making the wrong decision and this was more important, even for inspectors, than obtaining 'management information' concerning the officer's work rate.

In the case of probationary officers, it is of interest that our respondents did not consider the probationer "too inexperienced to make a balanced judgement" as he approaches the end of his training period (probationer at 22 months) whilst they did think this true of a probationer about to go solo after completing his or her Tutor Constable Attachment. And both groups consider the gaining of experience in enforcing the law as of primary importance for a probationer at this point. The emphasis here on 'practice at process' was counterpointed by the responses to the question "How is the skilful use of discretion acquired?" where both groups were asked to rank order a number of formal and informal on- and off-the-job training opportunities. The results are shown in Table 1. Here it is on-the-job training and experience that is unequivocally favoured over 'schooling' in promoting the acquisition of discretionary judgement. These findings are echoed in the view of one traffic officer who wrote . . .

"The best way to learn discretion is by practical experience and good example of others",

and such a view seems commonly held. The importance of supervisory advice was stressed by an inspector who commented:

"Most probationers are encouraged or forced to put lots of process in. This may lead to 'blanket' enforcement. Therefore it is important for supervisors to explain what discretion they can use."

Table 1. *"How is the skilful use of discretion acquired?"*
Rank order for Inspectors and Traffic Officers of the efficacy of on- and off-the-job training opportunities in developing the skilful use of discretion.

	Inspectors	Traffic Officers
The tutor constable attachment	1st	1st
On the job experience—working alone	2nd	2nd
Advice from supervisors	3rd	3rd
Divisional training	4th	4th
Informal conversations (eg 'canteen talk')	5th	6th
Force training school—Probationer training	6th	5th
Force training school—Refresher training	7th	7th
District Training Centre	8th	8th

Some officers held that, as one traffic officer put it,

"[discretion] is a skill that can't be taught at a training school"

and this view was reinforced by another who suggested:

". . . to be skilful in discretion one must already possess common sense."

Other comments focused on qualities already imbued or developed in the officer before joining the police service, for instance the inspector who wrote:

"An important element is an officer's social and educational background. Younger officers without previous work experience may tend to have no regard or sympathy to an offender's circumstances,"

or the Inspector who referred to

"An individual officer's general approach to life, his upbringing, the views of his parents and 'non-police' friends and relatives"

as likely influences on the *quality* of the judgement that a young officer might display.

We also asked whether police officers should or should not be encouraged to exercise greater discretion in their enforcement role. A little over a half of the respondents believed they should, somewhat under half held they should not. Despite, or perhaps because of, there being fewer of them, the latter—those opposed to any extension of discretion—were the more vocal in their views, often adopting a moral tone and expressing a concern for the maintenance of standards. Thus, one inspector noted that

". . . they already have sufficient discretion both by definition as police officers and via force policy. When considered against the above, the term 'greater discretion' can only be translated as 'abrogation of responsibility' ",

whilst another adduced public support claiming:

"We have gone far enough in recent years—I believe the majority of the public would support a sterner approach to offences."

Direct appeal to standards was made by the inspector who wrote:

"I feel that officers apply enough discretion as it is and this allied to recent constraints on prosecution applied by new enactments gives wrongdoers . . . a very fair crack of the whip. Certain standards should be maintained and members of the public should conform to these or risk prosecution."

In all of these last three examples, discretion is being interpreted as an (unduly lenient) *outcome* rather than as a *decision process*, and the potentially 'subversive' influence of training or advice in this regard was highlighted by one traffic officer who noted that

"Too much emphasis to a young officer in relation to discretion would make him give too much thought to 'letting off' offenders."

Those believing that officers should be encouraged to exercise greater discretion divided 60/40 as to whether or not further training would be necessary. One view from those in favour of training in discretion was that it would promote consistency of action. Thus one inspector wrote:

"I suggest at present no training is given to exercise discretion and to enable a more consistent standard initial training should be given."

Another view, also from an inspector, was that

"[discretion] is a facet of police work that is learnt the hard way by experience and by generally getting involved but wherever possible training should be given to assist in the decision-making process."

One traffic officer had a suggestion to make about a central factor in this decision process:

"I think that a lot of offenders (motorists in particular) are presently being reported where a caution would suffice. Training may be necessary with less experienced officers in order to differentiate the serious from the less seriously regarded offence."

Those who commented on their opinion that further training in discretion would *not* be necessary were generally of the view that discretion was untrainable, for example the two traffic officers who wrote:

"Discretion is an important part of policing the streets, but I don't know how you can teach discretion . . ."

and:

"I don't think it is something you can be told about in a classroom, it's a decision made in a split moment, not really one you can plan for."

Another view expressed, by a traffic officer, stressed the autonomy of the individual decision-maker—

"A police officer will exercise discretion as he sees fit according to his character and attitude to the public and to his own concept of the seriousness of the offence. I do not feel that any further training would be of benefit as the training officer may well have opposing ideas to the individual officer who in the end will formulate his own level of exercising discretion."

Of course training is, *inter alia*, a management tool for changing the repertoire of the work force. An increase in consistency of application could be seen as assisting in the management of discretionary practices—though a practice may, of course, be consistently poor—and there was support expressed by some officers for clearer guidelines. Thus one inspector wrote:

"Many officers are unsure of how far they can go; partly I find nobody has told them and partly each [supervisor] has his own limits on discretion. It needs to be clearly defined"

and a traffic officer pleaded that

"Guidelines should be laid down at training classes so that officers are aware what is required of them."

The seriousness of the consequences that can ensue from 'getting it wrong' were pointed up by the traffic officer who averred:

". . . it seems there are no guidelines other than personal opinion. This results in what is commonly termed 'the grey area'. To transgress into it too far may well lead to disciplinary offences."

Indeed, in the last analysis, it is the service's discipline code which sets the boundaries on selective enforcement practices by officers.

In summary, then, the officers we questioned saw 'discretion' as a fairly complex professional practice though one soundly based on 'common sense'. They believe it to be acquired through on-the-job training and experience—principally the Tutor Constable Attachment—and that its scope should be expanded as an officer's experience increases. The most important reason for placing a limit on its exercise is to protect the officer from the consequences of failure to exercise discretion properly. Officers were divided over whether, in general, there should be more of it, with a suggestion that these two camps were also divided as to whether the focus should properly be on the outcome ('undue leniency') or the process ('fittingness') of discretionary judgements. Different training implications would flow from these two views. On the first view the job of training would be to draw a clear line through the 'grey area' dividing it, so far as is possible, into black and white—the prescriptive view. On the second view training should be provided in how to handle complexity, reconcile sometimes competing demands and arrive at defensible, equitable adjudications—the 'Solomon' view. We align ourselves with this second view.

3. Discretionary enforcement: from policy to practice

Figure 1 gave a simple schematic representation of the three stages of the enforcement process, at each of which discretionary judgement is exercised. A patrolling police officer has, in practice, some freedom of action, first, over whether to intervene or to ignore an offence which comes to his attention (Stage 1); and rather more freedom of action over the proper sanction to apply, once he has intervened, across quite a broad range of offences (Stage 2). If he decides to report an offender for summons, then supervisory officers have some degree of choice over whether to support or rescind his recommendation (Stage 3).

In the light of our researches we have proposed a more detailed descriptive model of the factors which impinge upon the officer's decision making at Stage 2 (Stradling et al., 1987). These factors are summarised in Figure 2. The process has been broken into four broad phases, drawing on the work of Hogarth (1980) on the psychology of decision. The Decision Environment covers the encounter between officer and offender and, as reported in a number of studies (eg Dix and Layzell, 1983; Southgate, 1986; Stradling et al., 1987), a number of immediate, situational factors are operative here—for example, features of the offence (type, judged seriousness, etc.), features of the offender (principally his or her attitude during the encounter) and, in general, the circumstances (mitigating or otherwise) that pertained when the offence was committed.

Figure 2. *A model of the discretionary enforcement process.*

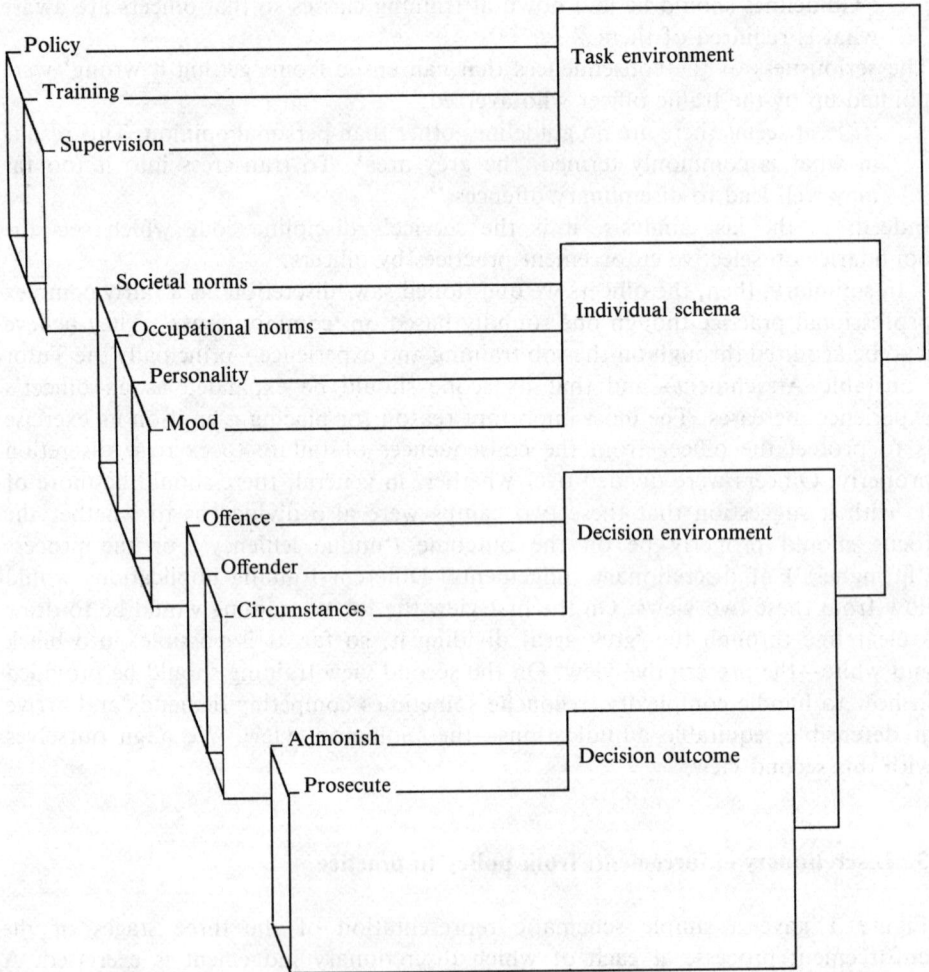

There are also a number of prior, background factors that may, or may seek to, have influence on the decision. We have divided these into two general classes, one individual and one organisational. We refer to the former as the Individual Schema that exists within the decision-maker which will be a complex combination of general social and moral influences upon the officer—his personal standards, criteria and values—listed as societal norms. In addition, there are the occupational norms of the police culture in general and of each officer's reference group within it in particular. For completeness we included personality and mood as well-known sources of variability in judgements.

While Individual Schemas *may* influence discretionary judgements, all those aspects we have listed under Task Environment are actively seeking to. Policy sets out to make plain in broad terms which Decision Outcome should eventuate when certain conditions are met (eg the transgression is 'trivial') and supervision and training are the mechanisms which seek to ensure that practice is in line with policy. Figure 2 makes plain that a considerable number of influences intervene between 'policy' and practice.

In this context, then, training and supervision are the two arms of management seeking to align practice with policy. How successful are they in this endeavour? As regards supervision, when we asked of inspectors whether they were able to monitor the day-to-day discretionary enforcement practices of their officers, exactly half said "Yes" but exactly half said "No" (Stradling *et al.*, 1987). This is an important result in the light of the central nature of discretionary judgements to much of police practice and the general expectation that any management will exert supervision and influence over crucial aspects of the work of its subordinates.

Almost half of those answering "No" cited pressure of work and/or lack of time as the main reason for their answer, nearly as many cited aspects of the general impracticability of the task of overseeing the work on the streets of all their relief, and a quarter (several officers gave more than one reason) spoke of the general inappropriateness of the mechanisms available to management to give them access to even the outcomes of all such occurrences. Some, for example, spoke of the low level of usage of the verbal advice book. Figure 1 identified three discretionary stages in the enforcement process—to intervene or not, to report or advise, to mark for prosecution or caution. For these inspectors, their only access to the discretionary enforcement decisions of their officers is to the outcomes of those Stage 2 decisions that led to paperwork being submitted. Recommendations for prosecution may then be approved or countermanded. For these managers much discretionary *practice* must be invisible.

The situation, however, is not very much better for those inspectors who felt they *were* able to monitor the day-to-day discretion of their officers. For many of the monitoring mechanisms they mentioned were indirect, involving sight of the paperwork that ensued from particular outcomes. Of the monitoring mechanisms, only "supervisory patrolling with PC" involves direct sight of the prevailing circumstances at the moment of decision, and it would not be surprising if officers acted somewhat differently when 'under inspection'. What such a mechanism does allow is fast feedback to officers on their handling of encounters, incidents and other tasks and an opportunity for supervision to expound on their own guidelines for discretionary—and other—practices.

Of those who indicated they were able to monitor discretion, three-quarters owned to taking *additional steps* in the case of probationary constables. About half of these inspectors cited "supervisory discussion with the PC" and about half "inspection of the probationer's handbook", but only one third indicated that they undertook "supervisory patrolling with the probationer" and a fifth delegated any "additional steps" in the case of probationers to their sergeants. Thus supervision generally has only indirect access to the 'moral calculus' (Stradling *et al.*, 1987) of discretionary decision-making by both experienced and probationary officers, even when they attempt to take extra steps with probationers. Reactive policing is, at least partly, a response to excessive workload and hence to the need to prioritise amongst tasks. Given that most police work on the streets is in reactive mode it is not surprising that much management of street policing should also be reactive. The discretionary judgements of police officers are generally only of concern to supervision when some transgression into what one of our respondents earlier called 'the grey area' results in a complaint coming to the supervisor's attention.

That leaves training as the main source for the translation of policy into practice. The purpose of selection and training is to produce officers whose Individual Schemas will lead them to act in the Decision Environment in ways which are consistent with policy. The Tutor Constable Attachment is one of the main mechanisms by which the police service seeks to achieve this effect—the direct oversight and development of probationer's practices is the responsibility of the Tutor Constable. But the Tutor Constable will also be instrumental in transmitting occupational norms to the probationer—that is, he or she is a source of both formal and informal guidelines, of both official policy and of the common interpretations placed upon official policy which inform standard practices. In the next section we will examine some preliminary evidence for the effects of early training—including the Tutor Constable Attachment—on probationers.

4. Differences on dimensions of discretion between probationers and Tutor Constables

As part of our larger study, an instrument was devised to study simulated discretionary judgements. The "Stop a Motorist" Discretion Instrument presents the respondent with the situation in which he or she has stopped a motorist for exceeding a speed limit. A list of 40 items is also presented, in which sets of additional circumstances are defined (eg "The motorist has a genuine urgent personal crisis which he is hurrying to attend to"; "The motorist is a commercial traveller who already has a record of minor traffic offences. If you report him he will probably lose his job"). The selection of items for inclusion was informed by the operational experience of the professional police officer among the authors (Keith Harper) and other officers, though we have no information on the objective frequency with which any of the circumstances occur. The respondent is asked to consider each item separately and to rate on a five-point scale how much influence each might have on his or her decision and in what direction that influence might be. The scale ranges from "Would influence A LOT *to prosecute*" (scored 1) to "Would influence A LOT *not to prosecute*".[5] This instrument was administered to 162 Tutor Constables and 128 probationer constables, amongst a sample of 559 officers which also included traffic officers and inspectors. The probationers were measured on completion of their Tutor Constable Attachment.

The 40 items gave a high degree of differentiation across circumstances in the effects they would produce, ranging from severity (eg "the motorist offers you

£25 to 'overlook the matter' ") to leniency (eg "the motorist is exceeding the speed limit by only 5 mph"). Probationers differed significantly from Tutor Constables on 19 of the 40 items (Stradling *et al.*, 1987). On 17 of these, probationers register a mean score which is *more severe/less lenient* than experienced officers. Compared to the occupational norm of their experienced colleagues there is a likelihood of probationers *over prosecuting* in each of these circumstances. Of course one corollary of this finding is that on 21 of the 40 items the responses of the probationers are in line with those of their experienced colleagues. But, on nearly half the items, probationers appeared somewhat more ready than Tutor Constables to reach for the book. We may ask of the data—are there particular *types* of situations which are more or less likely to call forth this tendency to over-prosecuting in probationers?

Thus, the next step in the analysis of the 'Stop a Motorist' data was to attempt to reduce the array of forty items to a smaller number of higher order constellations of items by factor analytic techniques which search for a number of independent 'dimensions' underlying the data set, looking for sets of items on which there is a strong tendency for officers' responses to co-vary. These factors may then be seen as some of the general categories which this sample of officers have available to them when classifying an encounter with a motorist whom they have stopped for exceeding a speed limit. The first six major factors extracted are included in the analysis reported here. They are summarised in Table 2. To the extent that the 'Stop a Motorist' scenario is typical of police-public encounters concerning minor malfeasances over which the officer on the spot may exercise his discretion as to the appropriate sanction, these factors may prove generalisable to other encounters.

Table 2. *Summary of the first six factors extracted from the 'Stop a Motorist' data using varimax rotation to orthogonal solution. The table reports high loading example items and suggested factor interpretation (from Stradling et al, 1987, Table 20). The six factors reported here account for 39% of the variance (n = 524). [Read 'm' as 'The motorist' throughout.]*

Loading	Example items
.73	m displays a marked 'anti-police' attitude
.64	local pop group in van, passengers loud and abusive
.61	m is belligerent and insulting to you personally

F1: LACK OF DEFERENCE. Actual or likely challenge to the legitimate authority of a police officer to stop a motorist.

.77	m is the wife of a work colleague
.73	m is a close relative
.69	m is a former school friend

F2: PERSONAL OBLIGATION. A sense of personal loyalty to family, friends and colleagues which officer is unwilling to compromise.

.75	m is the wife of your Chief Superintendent
.67	m is a senior officer, intimates he would be grateful if you 'considered this case appropriate for verbal advice'
.58	m is a local JP who is very embarrassed and most apologetic

F3: PROFESSIONAL OBLIGATION. A tension between due enforcement and organisational hierarchy.

Table 2.—*continued*

Loading	Example items
.72	m is physically handicapped
.63	m is an OAP, down at heel and driving an old but well cared for car
.59	HM Forces driver in an official Service vehicle

F4: PATRONAGE. From a position of personal power officer may extend privileges to others deemed to be outside the normal compass and deserving of special treatment.

| .80 | m is an 18 yr old youth riding a powerful motor bike |
| .78 | the vehicle is a large articulated HGV |

F5: DIFFICULT VEHICLES. Officer will be aware of a high likelihood of additional document or construction and use offences in such cases with the concomitant load of paperwork process.

| .72 | m is a petty thief, offers good information in return for a caution |
| .65 | m is the licensee of a pub used by CID, he has a reputation for good and reliable information about local thieves |

F6: TRADING FOR GAIN. Assigning priorities to possible courses of action, officer weighs the advances to 'real' police work—crime fighting—of trading a minor traffic misdemeanour.

Having identified a number of overarching factors which underlie the 'Stop a Motorist' data set, it is possible to use factor scores to summarise the areas of divergence between types of officers. Table 3 summarises these findings into three groups—matters on which probationers are likely to 'over-prosecute', matters on which inexperienced officers are 'in-line' with the likely practices of the Tutor Constables, and matters on which probationers are likely to 'under-prosecute'. All the probationers in this study were administered the 'Stop a Motorist' Discretion Instrument at the Force Training School immediately following the Tutor Constable Attachment. The disjunction between the sets of factors thus provides an index of the extent to which on- and off-the-job training has succeeded in producing a 'typical' officer by this stage in the training period and differentiates those areas where their discretionary judgement is 'in line' and where 'out of line' with force practice.

Table 3. *Summary of the main factors on which the probationers are more severe/less lenient than, no different to, and less severe/more lenient than Tutor Constables at the end of the Tutor Constable Attachment.*

Probationers more severe/less lenient ('over-prosecuting')	No difference ('in-line')	Probationers less severe/more lenient ('under-prosecuting')
F1 Lack of Deference	F2 Personal Obligation	F6 Trading for Gain
F5 Difficult Vehicles	F3 Professional Obligation	
	F4 Patronage	

A number of these hypothesised dimensions corroborate findings from the literature on police discretion, while others extend previous findings. Taken together they provide an update on the policeman's 'working personality', sketched by Skolnick in the USA in 1966. He regarded beat officers as having to adopt a certain 'persona' when they donned the uniform as a response to the elements of danger, authority, and the press for efficiency in the police milieu. Discussion with trainees at this point in their career makes plain that they have a general anxiety as to whether their shoulders will prove broad enough to support the uniform when they adopt the persona and embark on solo patrolling.

Over-prosecuting: threats to competence

"Establishing respect for police authority is [after self-protection] the second priority of the patrol officer involved in an encounter with citizens" wrote Lundman (1980) of the American situation, and the composition of the primary factor to emerge in this study, F1, indicates that it may well be the *first* priority in this country. Indeed, factor F1 may be viewed as constituted of actual or potential threats to that authority and its associated status and self-esteem.

Factor 1 grouped together both those who are likely to be exercised or incensed by being apprehended and those likely to be poorly disposed towards the police in general. The importance to an officer of maintaining respect for the authority that he represents is well documented, on both sides of the Atlantic (eg Wilson,1968; Bittner,1970; Skolnick,1975; Dix and Layzell,1983; Southgate,1986). The reason for this is likely to be partly the strong sense of occupational identity of the police (and see F2, F3 below), partly that the maintainance of public order requires coercive powers, but partly also that, psychologically, to abuse the police is to abuse the individual officer there present. Naturally, such attacks wound the pride and self-esteem of the individual—and a probationer is likely to be more vulnerable to such slings and arrows than an experienced bobby. As one of our respondents wrote, from the vantage point of 16 years' traffic experience:

"[The offender's] attitude towards me is irrelevant. I am totally uninsultable."
Such immunity usually takes some time to acquire.

In circumstances like this the offender is actually in a 'no-win' situation as the officer has the full panoply of the law at his disposal. The superior armoury of the officer is succinctly summarised by a British traffic officer quoted by Dix and Layzell (1983):

". . . if the member of the public got stroppy with me then I would get the better of them and book them."
The officer is exercising his discretion over the appropriate sanction to apply and the crucial datum is the judgement by the officer of the punishment necessary to deter this offender from continual commission of this offence. As one of our traffic officers succinctly put it:

"Would they benefit from a roadside rollicking?"
There was a general tendency among all officers in this sample towards prosecuting on the items in this factor—and probationers were more so inclined that the experienced officers. The results suggest, in line with previous studies, that motorists failing the 'attitude test' are likely to incline the officer towards prosecuting; but, in addition, our results show that probationers are particularly susceptible to a lack of deference from offenders. In all discretionary situations, the law is a resource upon which the officer may call to assist in the management of the 'micro-order' of a face-to-face encounter. In the absence of the kind of developed 'street skills' that experience provides, and given the anxieties that probationers commonly show at this stage in their training, it is not surprising that they seem more inclined than experienced officers to summon the letter of the law.

F5 is entitled 'Difficult Vehicles' as there is a strong likelihood of other, document, offences being revealed or, especially in the case of heavy goods vehicles, specialised, technical knowledge may be needed to fully assess 'Construction and Use' possibilities. Dix and Layzell suggested that there may be differences even among specialist traffic officers as to what types of offence receive attention:

". . . you can always pick and choose what you want to deal with. And you can sit still and let the stuff come past you until something of interest comes past—and go and stop it . . . trailers are my forte. If I see a trailer I normally stop it." (Traffic officer quoted by Dix and Layzell, 1983).

Again there was a general tendency among all officers in this sample towards prosecuting on the items in this factor—with probationers again more so inclined than the experienced officers. Heavy goods vehicle regulations are a notoriously complex area of traffic law and classes on this topic commonly draw a sigh of apprehension from probationers at Training School. In addition, paperwork—and its proper completion—is the bane of the trainee's early career. F1 and F5 may be seen, from the probationer's point of view, as constituting early and unwelcome challenges to his or her professional *and* technical competence.

'In-line': occupational solidarity

Skolnick (1975) is only one of many authors to attest to the high degree of occupational solidarity displayed by the police when he reported "Strong feelings of empathy and co-operation, indeed almost of 'clannishness' " within the police service. Factors F2 and F3 corroborate the importance of group loyalty, but add to previous research findings in an important way by clearly differentiating this complex of reciprocal obligations into two separate components such that an individual officer may score highly on one factor without scoring highly on the other. F2 tells of a sense of personal loyalty on the part of officers to friends, relatives and colleagues, whereas F3 firmly separates off from these the 'vertical', hierarchical sense of obligation to others 'on the side of' law enforcement.

Hahn (1971) suggested that "Police decisions often are based on popular concepts of morality rather than legalistic ones" and the ties that bind to family, friends and immediate colleagues (F2) are indeed powerful ones. In general, F2 and F3 group together, but also clearly demarcate two separate kinds of circumstance in which an officer would suffer a conflict of interests. There is a general tendency on the part of officers towards not prosecuting under the circumstances of F2 items, while all the component items of F3 generate genuine disagreement across all officers as to the proper course of action, with advocates of all three positions (prosecute, no influence, not prosecute). As a group, probationers do not differ statistically from experienced officers on F2 and F3. By this stage in their training their decision outcomes in this area are in line with force practice.

Factor 4 extends the notion of privileged treatment beyond hearth and workplace to general types of persons considered appropriate for special treatment. The two main items—physically handicapped driver and old age pensioner in a well cared for car—evoke the first half of the badge motto "Protect and Serve", being the closest amongst the set of 40 items to "the weak and defenceless", and, as one traffic officer put it:

"I would consider verbal advice in the case of OAPs or disabled people."

However the factor found here is more intricate than this, including types of persons who are patently not weak and defenceless—eg the armed forces. There was a general tendency towards 'not prosecuting' for the items of this factor which held across all groups of officers.

Under-prosecuting: the 'real work' of the police

Factor 6 was the only major factor on which probationers were out-of-line with their more experienced colleagues by virtue of tending further towards leniency. It is thus in the opposite direction to their much more common tendency remarked upon earlier towards greater severity. The factor clearly involves trading for gain, a straightforward exchange of non-enforcement for a potentially greater gain. Brown (1981) reports that the North American officer "will attempt, when he has the opportunity, to parlay a violation into an obligation". The information is the greater gain in so far as it pertains to the 'real work' of the police—fighting crime and locking up criminals. There was a general tendency among all officers in this sample away from prosecuting on the items in this factor—and probationers demonstrated this tendency significantly more strongly.

Policy and practice

This section has attempted to get some purchase on the effects of the Tutor Constable Attachment on the development of probationers' discretionary judgements as part of an endeavour to assess the effects of training in translating force policy into street practice. The analysis has identified areas where probationers' judgements are in-line and where out-of-line with those of experienced officers—Tutor Constables—at the end of the Tutor Constable Attachment. However, in the absence of any measure of the probationers pre-TCA, we are not free to attribute their current state wholly and solely to the effects of the Attachment, only to characterise their state at a point in a training programme of which the Tutor Constable Attachment was the most recent component. In the next section we shall review some other measures of probationers for which data was available before, as well as immediately after, the Tutor Constable Attachment.

5. Effects of the Tutor Constable Attachment on probationers' perceptions of police work

Recruits arrive at Training School with expectations of the type of work they are about to be involved in as police officers. We have some data, not previously reported, concerning these expectations and orientations. As the data was collected at Induction, again at the Local Procedure Course immediately prior to the Tutor Constable Attachment and once again at the Progress and Monitoring Course I immediately following the Tutor Constable Attachment, we are able to ask whether progress through training sees some change or development in these attitudes,and, particularly, whether the Tutor Constable Attachment makes any measurable impression on probationers in this regard.

One question asked of probationers at these three points was which of a range of occupations they perceived as being similar to that of a police officer. The results are shown in Table 4. It may be seen that at Induction the largest number of mentions was for "Public Relations Officer", followed by "Social worker" and "Armed Forces". However, it may also be seen that the proportions opting for these and, indeed, all the other alternatives, remain relatively constant as training progresses, with only small adjustments being made from occasion to occasion. Training in general—and the Tutor Constable Attachment in particular—seems to bring about little change in probationers' notions of what occupations are to be seen as similar to police work.

Table 4. *"Which of the following occupations do you consider to be most similar to that of a police officer—" Percentages of probationers mentioning each occupation at three stages in their training—Induction, prior to the Tutor Constable Attachment and immediately after the Tutor Constable Attachment.*

	at Induction	pre-TCA	post TCA
Public Relations Officer	28	34	33
Social Worker	19	24	18
Armed Forces	16	10	10
Security Guard	9	12	13
Lawyer	5	6	10
Fireman	10	6	3
Teacher	7	3	6
Civil Servant	3	4	5
Clergyman	1	1	2
n =	119	119	110

[A small number of 'other' responses are omitted from this Table.]

In Section 1 we noted that current policy in the force in question was that Tutor Constables should have sufficient skill and experience to develop the abilities of probationers in six particular areas. Probationers were asked to rank order these six abilities at each of the three points in their early training, and the results are presented in Table 5. Again we may see that the rank ordering remains almost invariant—the only amendment being that "writing reports" changes places with "Giving evidence" subsequent to the Tutor Constable Attachment.

Table 5. *Mean rank order amongst probationers of six "basic skills required of an efficient police officer", measured at three stages in their training—Induction, prior to the Tutor Constable Attachment and immediately after the Tutor Constable Attachment.*

	at Induction	pre-TCA	post TCA
Communicating with the public	1	1	1
Knowledge of law and procedures	2	2	2
Knowledge of local area and people	3	3	3
Interviewing and statement taking	4	4	4
Giving evidence	5	5	6
Writing reports	6	6	5
n =	119	119	110

In similar vein we also enquired after the 'implicit theory' of criminology recruits were holding at the three points in their training by asking whether they saw detection, conviction or punishment as the biggest deterrent to crime. The results are presented in Table 6 where, again, it may be seen that the attitudes

Table 6. *Percentages of probationers citing as optimal different deterrents to crime at three stages in their training—Induction, prior to the Tutor Constable Attachment and immediately after the Tutor Constable Attachment.*

The biggest deterrent to people committing crimes is . . .	at Induction	pre-TCA	post TCA
the likelihood of detection	47%	57%	54%
the severity of punishment	30%	29%	25%
the likelihood of conviction	22%	13%	21%
n =	116	119	110

held at Induction do not differ appreciably from those at the completion of the Tutor Constable Attachment with "likelihood of detection"—the police role—being the preferred alternative throughout.

These data suggest that recruits bring with them a set of orientations to police work and that the early part of their training—including the TCA—does little to change these perspectives. Differences between probationers at Induction are found in pretty much the same proportions at 7 months service. These attitudes and orientations are likely to form an integral part of each officer's Individual Schema which—as shown in Figure 2—informs their analysis and choice in the Decision Environment, their decision-making on the street.

6. Preparing probationers for solo patrolling

The recent Stage II Review of Probationer Training (MacDonald *et al.*, 1987), takes as its core position the view, first, that discretion is an essential component of police work . . .
  "the successful completion of policing tasks depends crucially on the quality of informed discretion exercised by the officers concerned";
secondly, that the judicious application of discretion is a professional skill . . .
  "this quality of discretion depends upon the confidence, coolness and depth of understanding which officers bring to bear in their diagnosis of problems calling for professional action";
and, thirdly, that this skill should be facilitated by appropriate organisational arrangements . . .
  "the professional accomplishment of this policing role requires an organisation that supports and expects effective, discretionary problem-solving by the uniformed constable".
While this view informs their recommendations for probationer training, none of their recommendations propose the direct training of discretionary judgement.

In this chapter we have seen, in Section 1 , that the current aims and objectives for the Tutor Constable Attachment in one provincial force stress the 'technical' skills of police work, subsuming professional skills—and discretion—under 'familiarity with beat and patrol work' and 'talking to people'. In Section 2 we noted the three stages of the discretionary enforcement process and the invisibility of the *processes* of discretionary judgement and outlined recent work on the views on discretion of a sample of operational officers. The Tutor Constable Attachment was viewed as the most important training opportunity for the development of discretion in probationers, but reservations were expressed about the trainability of discretion. In Section 3 we presented a model of the discretionary enforcement process which located a number of influences on judgement intervening between policy and practice. In particular, we suggested officers' Individual Schemas— comprised *inter alia* of both social and occupational norms—will affect the way they come to decisions. And we presented evidence that supervision has little purchase on daily discretionary practices. Section 4 looked at the development of some occupational norms and found that at the end of the Tutor Constable Attachment probationers were, as a group, 'in-line' with Tutors as regards occupational solidarity but were more affronted than Tutors by threats to their competence and a lack of deference from offenders. Section 5, however, showed that social norms—even occupationally relevant ones—were unaffected by early police training. One of the views that remained unchanged was that "Public Relations Officer" was the most similar occupation to police officer, another that "Communicating with the public" was the most important of the basic skills required of an efficient police officer.

The existence of recruits with quite different background orientations and hence different Individual Schemas highlights the problem facing police trainers— including Tutor Constables. Clearly further research is needed in a number of interrelated areas. What is the 'common sense' that officers attest to as the basis of discretion? How do officers effect a balance between offence seriousness, offender attitude and surrounding circumstances in the 'moral calculus' of discretion and the selection of the appropriate sanction? Can a typology of Individual Schemas within the police service be developed and do these 'types' have reliably consistent effects on the processes of discretionary judgement? How can probationer constables best be trained to improve the *quality* of their decision-making processes? How should Tutor Constables be trained to maximise their influence in this? And what organisational arrangements for the Tutor Constable Attachment would best facilitate this?

We believe the research techniques are available to address all of these questions and that answers to them will assist in the preparation of probationers for solo patrolling—for managing encounters and using their discretion judiciously—by enabling the development of operationally relevant methods for the training of discretionary judgement.

16 Evaluating training: the London Metropolitan Police's recruit training in human awareness/policing skills

Ray Bull and Peter Horncastle

Introduction

'Human Awareness Training' (HAT) comprises three related areas of training: interpersonal skills (said to embody conversational skills and the ability to manage encounters with others); self-awareness (self-knowledge and insight into one's effect on social situations); and community relations (embracing awareness of and knowledge about different cultures and sub-cultures). The training programme, designed by police officers with a background in the behavioural sciences, accounts for approximately a quarter of the 20-week Initial Training course for those recruited to the Metropolitan Police. Much of HAT is practical in its approach, and considerable use is made of such teaching techniques as role-play exercises and video feedback of students' performance.

While 'awareness' training for recruits is by no means a recent innovation for the Metropolitan Police, HAT (or 'Policing Skills Training' as it is now known) differs considerably from earlier recruit training programmes. In 1971 a social studies input to recruit training was authorised at Hendon. It was conducted by specially trained police instructors who had previously taught on other parts of the recruit course. Recruits received social studies-based training during the first two weeks of their course in an uninterrupted block of study periods.

This social studies input was soon judged by the Metropolitan Police to be ineffective, largely because it was considered too 'academic' and its content was incompatible with the law enforcement image which many of the recruits were believed to expect their training to reinforce. However, the social studies component of recruit training was not abandoned; it was in fact developed and improved during the period 1973–81. The content of the two-week block of social studies was spread throughout the syllabus and, in particular, the social studies inputs were related to appropriate practical police training subjects. The content of the social studies input to recruit training at this time drew on the disciplines of social and public administration, sociology and social psychology, with some limited coverage of communication concepts.

After this change in construction, the course became known as 'Integrated Police Studies' and its objective became that of training the constable on the street to become a competent manager of people and social situations. To achieve this recruits had to be well informed about the nature of the society they were going to police.

In March 1981, before the disturbances in Brixton and other parts of Britain, a working party was formed in the Metropolitan Police with a mandate to examine and report on all current methods of formal and informal training for recruits and probationers and to make recommendations for improvements in these areas. From the findings of the working party came recommendations to develop what became Human Awareness Training.

The first version of this training was implemented by the Metropolitan Police in April 1982. In June of the same year the independent evaluation described in this chapter began under the auspices of the Police Foundation and at the request of the Metropolitan Police.

Evaluation began not only after HAT had been designed but some months after it had been implemented. This research, therefore, has not been able to contribute to the design and implementation process; neither was a 'before and after' study feasible. However, such evaluations are rarely organised and conducted under ideal circumstances, and the authors hope that what follows overcomes the usual exigencies of carrying out field research on policing topics.

Social Science and police training: evaluations and interventions

The study was guided by previous evaluations of police training carried out in various countries. We reviewed the police training/behavioural science literature, visited foreign police forces, and undertook a questionnaire survey of the 42 forces in England and Wales (excluding the Metropolitan Police) together with a number of overseas forces in order to gather information about their recruit training.

The literature review covered a wide range of recruit training programmes and other interventions based on behavioural science theory applied to recruits. They include:

● community and race relations training;
● general 'awareness' and communication skills training; crisis intervention training;
● psychologists acting as 'in-house' mental health consultants to police departments;
● studies of recruits' attitudes;
● the search for a 'police personality'; and
● projects involving organisation reform and foot patrol programmes.

With one or two exceptions, the schemes reviewed have either not been evaluated or the evaluations which have been carried out are based on subjective assessments or on potentially misleading quantitative measures. While all evaluations, as the word implies, depend on a subjective judgement at some point about what objectives are being pursued, the success or otherwise of any scheme in terms of its stated objectives can only be gauged with some objectivity if these are carefully defined and progress towards them is measured with some precision. Many of the schemes described in the literature were evaluated with extremely small samples of officers from which sweeping generalisations about programme effects were made. Many used a single attitude questionnaire to evaluate an entire programme. Although the questionnaire is undoubtedly a useful research tool to both evaluators and psychologists alike, attitudes do not necessarily accurately predict behaviour and so an evaluator is wise to use a number of different approaches. Finally, very few of the schemes reviewed examined the extent to which positive training (or other) effects were maintained once the officers left the training programme. Operational police culture can have a powerful socialising effect, as can street work with the public. It is naive to assume that these effects will not interact with training outcomes.

Observation of training in police forces and the survey of a large number of forces allowed us to evaluate HAT in the light of current practice in police training. Seventy-four per cent of the UK forces and eighty-five per cent of the overseas forces surveyed returned questionnaires. In general, HAT compared favourably with social science-based training carried out in other police forces, both qualitatively and in terms of the time allocated to this type of training on the recruit syllabus. However, in some respects (eg the assessing of recruits' awareness) it was weaker than many of the overseas training programmes.

Pre-evaluation consultancy with HAT trainers

Preparation for the evaluation study involved extensive comparative study of police training methods and course content. During 1982–83 early versions of human awareness training were observed at the Hendon police training school and trainers and trainees were interviewed. As HAT was in a constant state of development, we were asked to advise Hendon of any improvements which in our professional judgement needed to be made in the course as it stood. The following suggestions were outlined in an interim report published in June 1983 (Bull and Horncastle, 1983).

1. There should be a substantial increase in the training concerned with the principles and processes governing and underlying human behaviour.
2. Substantial improvements to the 'community relations' component in HAT were essential; early coverage of this topic had been inadequate.
3. Assessment of recruits' HAT performance was too infrequent and informal; more rigorous and regular testing procedures were recommended.
4. The trainers themselves needed better training to cope with the exigencies of their roles.
5. Role playing, where it was used in HAT sessions, needed to be more realistic.

Subsequent changes in HAT training

Since the presentation of the interim report, there have been a number of developments in HAT in response to the report and supporting initiatives taken by those managing HAT. Foremost among these changes are:

- greater specificly about HAT aims and objectives;
- much more and varied assessment of recruits' HAT skills and knowledge;
- attempts to strengthen the community awareness component of the training;
- far better training of new human awareness trainers ; and
- a stronger focus on the use of discretion in policing.

Phase I of the Evaluation

Psychometric Questionnaires

The behavioural science literature on attitude and social skills training evaluation was reviewed along with that on police training to identify appropriate standardised, valid and reliable questionnaires which had been used in similar kinds of situations. Recruits completed these questionnaires in Week 1 and in Week 20 (ie at the end) of initial training, then twice again after six months and twelve months during their probationary period. The questionnaires used were as follows:

- a social-evaluative anxiety questionnaire (measures social avoidance and distress);
- a self-esteem questionnaire (measures perceived interpersonal threat; self-esteem; faith in people; and sensitivity to criticism); and
- an interpersonal relations questionnaire (measures need to establish satisfactory relationships; need to control them; and need for affection).

Groups of around 30 officers each answered the questionnaires. These question-naires were eventually supplemented by one specifically designed to assess the attitudes, beliefs and behavioural set which HAT aimed to inculcate. This instru-ment, which we called the recruit training questionnaire, was administered to groups of officers on the four testing occasions.

Because HAT started before the evaluation of it began, it was not possible to use non-HAT trained Metropolitan Police recruits as controls. However, if scores are obtained over time, each subject acts to some extent as his own control. If the training has a systematic effect, then scores over time should exhibit a significant and coherent pattern of change.

Background information was obtained from the final group of constables who were trained before the introduction of HAT (ie, they received the Integrated Police Studies course). One hundred and forty constables filled in an extensive attitude questionnaire to elicit views on their training in the light of their subsequent operational experience. A similar questionnaire was completed by over 100 proba-tioners approximately one year after they had received HAT.

Improving the social skills and street wisdom of constables is a somewhat vague goal which makes evaluation difficult to design: there is no obvious dependent variable. It was hypothesised that one of the most obvious improvements which HAT might produce would be a reduction in complaints against constables from members of the public. Thus, with the assistance of the Complaints Investigation Bureau at Scotland Yard, a comparison was made of the rate of complaints for HAT-trained officers and those who had received the earlier kind of recruit training. It was further hypothesised that the success or otherwise of recruit training might be most accurately assessed by sergeants supervising probationer constables. The views of supervising sergeants for 289 HAT probationers were, therefore, canvassed.

The social evaluative anxiety questionnaire

Police constables have to enter social situations which are often characterised by conflict between the participants or overt aggression. Constables may have to initiate interactions with members of the public in order to control or manipulate their behaviour, often against the other's will. To manage such social interaction, constables need to be able to control the anxiety which such situations engender, and to be able to put up with the negative evaluations made of them by those with whom they must interact. For obvious reasons constables must not avoid entering social situations, however unpleasant these situations may appear. The social-evaluative anxiety questionnaire can be used to measure:

- the tendency to be anxious in social situations;
- the tendency to avoid social situations; and
- the tendency to be afraid of being negatively evaluated by others.

With respect to the task of the constable, social anxiety, avoidance and fear of negative evaluation are prima facie undesirable characteristics and one of HAT's aims should be to minimise recruits' tendencies in these directions.

For one group, scores indicative of social anxiety and avoidance declined from an initial group mean of 3.97 to 1.64 after a year as a probationer (intervening means: week 20: 2.7; after six months: 2.28). Fear of negative evaluation scores were 8.9 (week 1), 8.33 (week 20), 7.04 (after six months), 6.52 (after twelve months).

For the other group completing this questionnaire, scores indicative of social anxiety and avoidance declined from an initial group mean of 2.91 to 0.83 after a year as a probationer (intervening means: week 20: 2.32; after six months: 1.36). Fear of negative evaluation scores for this group were 10.72 (week 1), 7.03 (week 20) 7.24 (after six months), 5.78 (after 12 months). Not only did these tendencies decline significantly during HAT but they continued to decline during probation. Changes during training were larger than after it. While it is not possible to identify precisely the cause of this effect from the evaluation, the utility of the questionnaire is established in this context and the effect in line with HAT objectives is powerful suggestive evidence.

The self-esteem questionnaire

In order to manage difficult social situations with authority, constables need to be relatively sure of themselves, of their own worth and their ability under pressure. They need to be relatively impervious to the kind of abuse and criticism which they may find directed at them by people they have to control. The self-esteem questionnaire taps people's underlying feelings of self-esteem or lack of it which affect the way social relations tend to be managed.

Results for this questionnaire did not display many systematic trends. Only when the data from three groups of officers were combined were there found to be any statistically significant changes. These were that "faith in people" and feelings of "interpersonal threat" decreased during but not after training.

There is no reason to suppose that this questionnaire is less appropriate than the social-evaluative anxiety questionnaire. A tentative interpretation is that while HAT taught officers how to cope, it did not strongly affect their underlying image of themselves as social beings. This may perhaps be entirely appropriate, as an occupational training which significantly altered personality could eventually run into ethical objections. Scores for officers varied considerably. Thus, not all recruits selected for training had high self-esteem.

The interpersonal relations questionnaire

This questionnaire was used to measure changes in how individuals tend to behave towards others and want others to behave towards them. Aspects which were specifically dealt with are the extent to which individuals want, and express, a need:
1. to set up and maintain relationships on the basis of interaction and association;
2. to set up and maintain relationships on the basis of controlling and having power over others; and

3. to set up and maintain relationships on the basis of affection.

There were few overall significant trends in the time series data. However, there was a gradual but systematic reduction over time in the extent to which officers said they wanted others in relationships to provide affection and the chance to engage in joint activity. Recruits seemed to become more self-sufficient over time, less dependent for their needs on relationships. This could obviously be a by-product of joining the police and not a side effect of HAT. There is no way of being more specific about this finding, although there is evidence to support the notion that socialisation into the police service tends to increase dependence on the occupational peer group and reduce the significance of other forms of relationships (Fielding, 1987; van Maanen, 1973).

The recruit training questionnaire (RTQ)

The questionnaire was sensitive enough to record some significantly different scores between the beginning and end of the evaluation period. However, these changes were often in the opposite direction to those predicted from HAT objectives. More recruits, for example, disagreed at the end of the course than at the beginning with the idea that social science concepts would be useful to them. Fewer trainees thought they would try to understand minority viewpoints, etc. by the end of training than at the beginning. Likewise, the importance attached to community relations decreased over training. At twelve months fewer officers disagreed with the proposition "Most racial prejudice comes from coloured people themselves". The welfare/social aspect of police work remained important to trainees but declined in importance for probationers once they began operational duties.

One or two beliefs and attitudes changed in appropriate ways. Notably, fairness and trustworthiness grew in importance as characteristics of 'the good police officer'. But overall basic attitudes and beliefs remained much the same and, given that the effect of training is being pitted against a lifetime of family and school experience, this is scarcely surprising. On balance it must be said, however, that such changes as were found by the RTQ were more in line with the expected peer group effect and institutional effect of the training experience than with the avowed intentions of the HAT component of the course. It may be that HAT and other elements of recruit/probationer experiences and training are antipathetic and that increasing efforts on any one element may have a negative effect on the others.

Other Types of Questionnaire

The probationer feedback questionnaire

The questionnaire was completed by 109 HAT-trained probationers with 30–100 weeks of service. While there was overall recognition of the need for and importance of HAT, 36% of the sample felt the training they had received (which was in the early days of HAT) was either inadequate or unsatisfactory for preparing them for their role as police officers. HAT was perceived as being of limited importance in aiding the probationers' interactive skills when compared with their experiences prior to joining the force and with subsequent experience as a probationer. Skills-based aspects of HAT were seen as being important aspects of a police officer's job, while knowledge-based aspects (eg an understanding of human behaviour) tended to be ranked lower.

Nearly half of the sample commented negatively upon their practical training. The most frequent criticism was that practicals lacked realism. "More practicals", "more community attachments" and "stress training" were areas in which probationers thought training might be improved.

A very clear majority of the sample felt that assessment would improve the efficiency of the training, with a majority agreeing that HAT tended to be taken lightheartedly by recruits partly because they knew that they would not be examined on it.

Although many comments were critical, these comments were retrospective and the content, approach and quality of HAT have been constantly refined in the months since the probationers in the study underwent their recruit training, particularly in the direction of the areas of concern described above.

The experienced officers' questionnaire

It was stated in the original evaluation proposal that the attitudes and opinions of constables who had *not* undergone HAT should also be examined. This exercise was carried out in order that the perceived strengths and weaknesses of the forerunner to HAT (Integrated Police Studies, or IPS) could be examined.

Overall, the experienced officers (n = 140) trained on the Integrated Police Studies course held less favourable views about their training than did the HAT-trained officers who responded to the probationer feedback questionnaire. It seems debatable whether difference in length of service alone could have caused this shift towards a more positive attitude. Less criticism of practicals was made by HAT-trained officers (who also seemed to attach a greater importance to "communicating well with others"). Experienced IPS-trained officers were divided in their opinion as to whether IPS training should be expanded, but given their many negative comments on IPS this is not surprising. They seemed receptive to many topics now covered by HAT which were not a major part of IPS, and many of the improvements they suggested for initial training have to some extent been incorporated into HAT. The constables reported a need for the conceptual/theoretical aspects of training to be integrated more with practical exercises, and indicated strongly that the IPS/HAT aspects of training should be formally and regularly assessed. This was the case even though they were not enthusiastic about the community relations training they had received.

The data gathered from the experienced officers suggested, as did the data from HAT-trained probationers, that once out of Initial Training the officers undergo experiences which push them to police in ways not in line with the apparent aims of their Initial Training. This conflict between the formally expressed and the informally perceived nature of the policing task is a recurring problem for police trainers, supervisors and managers.

Complaints and Supervisors' Assessments

How the public respond to probationers and how their supervisors evaluate them are two crude but vital indicators of the success of initial training.

Complaints data

We considered that data concerning complaints made by the public about police officers could act as an index of the effectiveness of their training. With the assistance of the Complaints Investigation Bureau at Scotland Yard a comparison of any complaints made against 380 IPS-trained (pre-HAT) and 700 HAT-trained (post-HAT) officers was carried out.

Data on police complaints often reveal a relationship between frequency of complaints and length of service. Consequently, the two samples needed to be matched in terms of length of service. The data collected for each sample consisted of complaint code(s), outcome and date of incident. No reference was made to the name or warrant number of any officers. These figures were then collated for both samples according to the outcome of each complaint, noting complaints which occurred in the first eighteen months of service and complaints which occurred thereafter. It was found that the HAT-trained officers received 17% fewer complaints per officer, per month of service compared to the IPS-trained officers. (This difference was found not to be due to the IPS officers having, on average, 12 months longer police service.) Statistical tests showed that the difference would have occurred by chance in only eight out of 100 occasions. Thus the 17% reduction in the rate of complaints was not likely to have been a chance finding, but seems to have been a result of the training, as this was the major factor consistently differentiating the two groups of subjects. While tying this reduction to HAT alone is problematic, HAT, which emphasises the discretionary role of the police officer, at least cannot be said to increase the probability of officers so trained incurring complaints.

Supervisors' questionnaire

The questionnaire was distributed to the supervising officers of 298 probationers; 89% returned completed questionnaires.

Results indicated no consistent areas of perceived weakness in probationers' competence. However, taking specific skills which HAT was intended to develop, supervisors' rankings of satisfaction indicated that certain parts of the course may have been working better than others. The following skills were not ranked quite so favourably as were others:

● questioning members of the public and assisting them to recall information;
● racial awareness; and
● ability to defuse troublesome situations.

These are arguably among the most difficult skills to acquire and current developments in HAT are addressing these issues. Nevertheless, the supervising sergeants rated 40% of probationers as "average" or less in terms of their effectiveness in questioning members of the public in order to gain information, and 42% as only "sometimes" or "infrequently" demonstrating a good overall ability in helping others to recall events and details. Other areas of interpersonal skill were rated more highly. The sergeants indicated that only 53% had demonstrated an appreciation that the behaviour or attitude of an individual may be affected by that individual's cultural background, and 37% showed "good" or "excellent" understanding of the relevance to police work of the viewpoints, customs and traditions of local minority groups. However, since there was a small, yet significant relationship between the amount of probationers' policing experience with members of the public from various ethnic groups and the quality of their ratings, lack of experience of multi-ethnic policing may account for some of the lower ratings. Just over one third of the probationers' ability, on arrival, to defuse potentially troublesome situations was rated as average or below, whereas other aspects or interpersonal control were rated more highly.

Concluding Remarks Regarding Phase I

The data gathered from the various areas of phase I of the evaluation supported the constructive criticisms we made of the training in our Interim Report. The community relations/racial awareness aspects of the training needed to be improved and it is hoped that the modifications which have since been made to this area of training will be substantial enough. If the planned formal assessment of HAT turns out to be competently conducted, then this should readily help determine if trainees' community relations and racial awareness have been sufficiently affected by the training.

With regard to the practical component of the training, there is evidence that this aspect is a vast improvement over that which preceded it. The aspect of the training to which these sessions most strongly relate, ie "interpersonal skills", is clearly the best, and even though we consider this to be among the best in the world, more extensive training of the instructors can only serve to make it even better.

The much more extensive training to be received by the trainers should also help them to include more in training on the principles and processes underlying human behaviour. When this is done, the apparent gap between understanding/ concepts/notions on the one hand, and skill/practice on the other will, hopefully, be bridged so that trainees will no longer be under the illusion that the very wide range of interpersonal skills required of a police officer can be effectively and appropriately exhibited without an enhanced understanding of human behaviour.

From the data gathered during the period 1982-84, we felt that of the three components of HAT, "interpersonal skills" was clearly the best; the component described as "self-awareness" was of a reasonable standard; and that described as "community relations" was at that time rather poor. However, should an evaluation merely compare that which is being evaluated with some ideal? Or should it focus on a comparison with what is replaced? If the latter (and we feel this is the more appropriate perspective), then there can be little doubt that HAT is a substantial improvement over that which preceded it. We have seen very little evidence that police recruit training in the rest of Britain even approximates the Metropolitan Police's Human Awareness Training.

It was our recommendation that the Metropolitan Police's initial recruit training programme in human awareness is a worthwhile achievement of considerable substance and promise. However, we were concerned by whether the desirable achievements of the initial training were to some extent being dissipated by post-initial training experiences. Since the force's initial recruit training in HAT appeared likely to be operating with considerable efficiency, it seemed appropriate to determine the extent to which the effects of this training are being manifested in constables' policing behaviour.

Phase II of the Evaluation

Partly in the light of the information presented in our final report, the Metropolitan Police agreed to fund a second phase of the evaluation. This second phase, (1985–87) examines the extent to which officers are putting HAT skills into practice on the street.

Psychometric Questionnaires

The psychometric questionnaires used in phase I are being employed in phase II. In addition, a Self-Monitoring Scale is being completed by probationers, as is a revised version of the Recruit Training Questionnaire (called the District Training Questionnaire) which, among other things, has a greater focus on the use of discretion. Probationers complete these questionnaires at the very end of their Initial Training (ie at week 20) and then again at weeks 40, 60 and 86 approximately.

Observation of Officers on Patrol

The major component of phase II of the evaluation involves the behavioural observation of HAT-trained officers whilst on patrol. Officers who have between 18 and 36 months service are observed whilst going about their normal policing duties on the street. The Metropolitan Police selected eight of its stations as being representative of policing in London, and in each of these stations in turn our observational evaluation is taking place.

Organisation

Great effort has been put into organising this part of our work. In each station our initial meeting has been with the chief superintendent or a superintendent. At this meeting the aims of the evaluation are spelt out (ie to see to what extent the HAT aims and objectives are being manifested in patrol policing, and to determine whether today's policing puts requirements on constables which the training may not fully address). Our next meeting in each station is with the remainder of the senior management team. Again, the evaluation is described and questions answered (this sometimes consumes a fair amount of time). At approximately this stage the evaluation is also explained to representatives of the Police Federation. In each station our next meeting is with the relief inspectors and sergeants. Only after all these meetings have been held and all concerned are satisfied, do we approach constables who have the relevant length of service (ie those who received HAT after most of our 1983 recommendations had been implemented). Each constable is seen separately by the three observers (ie the second author plus two Metropolitan Police constables who have degrees in Psychology and who spent a year devising the HAT assessment procedures requested by us in phase I). The evaluation is explained to each constable. They are informed that all data/information gathered by the observers will be treated in confidence and that they have the right to refuse to participate. To date only one constable out of several dozen has refused to have one or more of his 8-hour tours of duty observed.

Schedule construction

The schedule which we constructed to make the observations of each police officer-citizen encounter is based upon (i) the aims and objectives of the training, (ii) the published literature (sparse though it is) on studies of police patrol behaviour, (iii) the outcomes of phase I of our evaluation, (iv) the contribution of the two constables (mentioned above) who have been seconded for 9 months to the evaluation, and (v) the outcome of a pilot study conducted at another police station.

The schedule contains 89 data scales, half of which are concerned with demographic information (eg location of encounter, each of which must last for at least 30 seconds and be with no more than two citizens). The remaining scales focus on the behaviour of the police officer and of the citizen at the beginning, middle and end of each encounter (up to the point of arrest, where relevant). These scales are concerned with the interpersonal style, listening skills, confidence, demeanour, manner, etc. of the participants. Each observer carries with him a small portable tape-recorder and this is used to aid his 'paper and pencil' coding of each encounter at the end of the shift.

On some occasions two observers are going out on patrol with one constable. This is for two reasons. One is to gather data on the reliability of our behavioural observations, and the other is to conduct interviews with the constable and with the encountered member of the public (separately) once an encounter has finished. The questionnaires used for these interviews are concerned not only with the respondent's views on the behaviour objectively recorded (but not disclosed) by the observers, but also with matters which may be important in police-citizen encounters which are not easy to observe and record objectively (ie inner feelings).

Interpretation of the observational data

Given that the observational schedule and the interview questionnaire were based largely (but not exclusively) on the aims and objectives of the training we should be in a position to determine to what extent they are being met in practice. Clearly such information should contribute to the continuing development of Human Awareness/Policing Skills Training. However, in addition, we should be able to offer data-based comment on the possible ways in which the requirements of today's policing in London are not squarely addressed by the training.

Furthermore, by relating the interview data to the observational data we should be in a position to determine the extent to which police officers' perception and awareness of their own behaviour, and of the public's, are in line with the observers' independent judgements of that behaviour. Again, this type of information will contribute to the training's development.

Overall conclusion

We trust that this chapter has revealed ways in which those outside of police forces can make a meaningful contribution to police training. In our opinion such contributions are, in Britain, not as common nor as substantive as they should be. For 'academics' and police forces to work together is not a worry-free experience. However, the benefits to society may well justify the effort.

17 Conclusions

Peter Southgate

Emerging from the preceding chapters are a number of themes, of which four are particularly important in considering the future of training. First, there is the question of what police training should be like—its content, style and methods. Second, there are organisational and contextual questions to consider. Third, the role and career of trainers is of central importance. Finally, the need for evaluation of training is a vital issue.

Content, style and method

Without a doubt the most consistent theme in this book has been the need for a more open and questioning approach to the learning process. The term 'learning process' is used here because that is what 'training' is now taken to be describing, rather than a system in which teachers stand up in front of classes of pupils and present information to them. Instead, there is now an emphasis upon 'student-centred' rather than 'teacher-centred' learning; that is to say, in general terms, that learning content and activities should be geared to the needs of the learner rather than being determined primarily by how the teacher finds it convenient to proceed. There is an emphasis upon a 'facilitative' (informal and helping) rather than a 'didactic' (formal instruction) style of presentation; the role of the teacher is to enable the learner to learn, so that the teacher's skill lies in knowing how best to provide the appropriate learning experience at the most appropriate moment for the individual learner. This means using a range of educational experiences, including practical demonstrations, reading, projects, visits, discussions, role play, reflective learning based on self-diagnostic questionnaires and experiential group methods with feedback. Even traditional lecture methods may sometimes be appropriate if that is judged to be the best way to help particular learners to learn about a particular thing at a particular time.

In order to use such methods to best advantage the learner must be encouraged to adopt an exploratory, experiential and questioning approach, not simply to expect to be 'spoon fed' or told what he or she must learn. The earlier 'systems' approach to learning may have had some attractive features, but a weakness lay in its tendency towards setting pre-determined learning objectives. Although trying to provide full and thorough coverage of the syllabus and having the advantage of relatively easily testable learning goals, the systems approach unintentionally tended to discourage creative learning. There is clearly an interplay here between the learner and the learning environment; an unsuitable environment will not encourage the learner to question and explore, while without enquiring learners a stimulating environment will be difficult to maintain. But, from a practical point of view, it is the environment which will need to be changed first.

A further basic aspect of the approach to training advocated in these pages and elsewhere concerns its content as opposed to its style. What is now being empha-

230

sised is the need to provide more effectively for the learning of practical policing skills. These are now understood to involve not simply technical, legal and procedural skills and the use of the 'correct' methods of enforcing the law (ie 'by the book') but the performance of them with 'discretion' and with sensitivity to the human relations and social issues involved. Past attempts to reform probationer training have involved the insertion of an element of 'social studies', first as a discrete block of lessons and, later, as a set of lessons to be slotted into the timetable at strategic points during the course. What is different about current approaches is that it is now recognised that social studies or social skills are not something which can or should be separated out in such ways. The point is that they should be completely integrated with the more traditional legal and technical material which is to be learnt, so that trainees learn how to perform these tasks while, at the same time, taking account of the personal and social dynamics which are in play. Thus, for example, race relations, body language or active listening may be interesting fields of academic study, but they are of no value or interest to the police officer as someone with a practical job to do unless they are given a context. Previously, it was not that these subjects were totally ignored, but they were dealt with in a relatively superficial and academic manner, and the officer himself was left to make the connection with the technical and legal procedures. Now, the agenda for trainers is to help trainees learn about all facets of practical situations at the same time.

The message here is, in fact, twofold: first, there is the recognition that policing must be taught at a primarily practical level. Second, it is clear that there should be a reconsideration of what practical policing skills actually consist of. Thus, policing is now seen as primarily a job of talking, negotiation, persuasion, mediation, etc. If this task is done well then the police officer will be able to perform other more directly instrumental tasks, but practical policing is not to be defined simply in terms of those tasks themselves.

Particular attention has been given, in this book and elsewhere, to the needs of probationer training, simply because that is where so much of the tone is set for the remainder of a recruit's career, and where those officers are trained who will have the most direct contact with members of the public. As John Shaw and Mike Plumridge have reminded us though, most of the same principles can be seen to apply to training for more senior officers. The tone of the working environment can be strongly set by senior officers, and the influence which they have upon their staff can be as crucial a factor as Probationer Training itself in the ultimate impact on police-public relationships. The nature of the instrumental tasks may be different for senior and junior officers but, once again, it is the ability to talk and negotiate which determines how well their job gets done. On the face of it there seems less of a problem in experimenting with new training methods and content with senior officers, because they are fewer in number and are generally more accustomed to expressing themselves in seminars and meetings. On the other hand, few of them have previously been exposed to the methods of self-development and experiential learning, and they have spent many years being conditioned by and learning to work within a fairly rigid, hierarchical system. In some ways, therefore, they may find it even more difficult to adapt to new approaches.

The principles outlined above are hardly new or innovative ones within educational theory and in training for other occupations where contact with people and their problems forms a major component of the work. More open and experimental approaches to learning have been in use for many years now in schools, and management training has built up a body of relevant experience. Surprisingly, though, developments such as facilitative learning and the inclusion of social skills training within the curriculum have been quite recent developments in training even for some of those professions, such as medicine, where it is now taken for granted that they are fundamental. As several of the contributors here have shown, there is still a considerable way to go in putting such approaches into full-scale practice in police training establishments. But it is important for police trainers to bear in mind that the experience of other occupations is there and is available to the police service in developing its own training.

There may be some with reservations as to how far we should go in building such principles into the police training system. In institutions such as District Training Centres where trainees pass through in large numbers it will be no easy task to provide individually tailored learning. In the interests of administrative convenience it might be much easier for everyone in such establishments if life were pre-planned, packaged and well ordered with little demand made for the use of individual initiative. Also, it can be argued that, in the interests of fair and equitable delivery of law and order services, police officers must all go through identical, standardised courses and that they should not, therefore, be encouraged to pursue individual learning programmes and develop their own interests. But the experiences of the last decade in this country suggest that there must be changes, and the police service is now actively pursuing them. This may, indeed, involve some risk and some administrative inconvenience, but the benefits should compensate for this. The task for those implementing new training systems is to avoid throwing the baby out with the bathwater and to ensure that worthwhile features of existing training are retained, along with newer innovations, and that the system maintains enough basic stability while becoming at the same time more adaptive. But this must still involve long-term change in the nature of the organisation, rather than being simply a one-off exercise. All recruits to the police will need to learn certain basic skills. But recent developments have brought into question both what those basic skills are and what are the best ways of learning them.

Organisational context

The overall aim of the 'new approaches' to training which have been illustrated and discussed in this book can, perhaps, best be summed up as being to produce "the reflective practitioner". This term, developed by Schon (1983) in a book of that title, and referred to by a number of the authors here, describes professionals who think and reflect about what they do, and who see their work as a learning experience from which they can develop new and improved ways of acting in future circumstances. This may seem no more than a formalised statement of something which any good professional has always done, but the very act of setting out such a statement can, of itself, be a valuable exercise which helps to clarify for trainees the approach which is expected of them in learning how to do their job well. In formally espousing such an approach to the learning of the police task one is making a statement about rather more than a learning syllabus; one is expressing principles which reflect the ethos of a whole organisation. This opens up a much wider question about the nature and function of the police.

Although this is not one which this book aims to discuss in detail or, certainly, to resolve, it cannot be evaded. For, in looking at what the goals of training should be, one is asking what the goals of the police service are and, if training does not aim to produce police officers who will pursue the goals of the service, then it is failing in its basic task. At the end of the day, then, the goals of training have to be the same goals as those of the service. The need for this correspondence is implied in most of the book, but it comes out especially clearly in what Tony Butler has to say about training needs from the perspective of the divisional commander. The significance of this point will be discussed further in considering the need for the evaluation of training.

As several of the writers here note, training cannot be isolated from the broader question of how the police organisation should respond to the demands made on it by the public, and what its values and priorities should be. A basic requirement of any good training must be that it reflects and encourages acceptance of the values and practices of the organisation in which trainees are being prepared to work. Thus, several of the authors have recognised the logical extension of this principle by writing not simply about training as a self-contained activity, but about organisational development and change, and about training as just one medium through which such change may be brought about. They imply that what should really be first on the agenda is organisational change, and that training needs will be more readily defined once it is clear what the overall objectives are. By the same token, the manager in the police organisation has potentially greater scope than does the training officer to influence the values and priorities of officers at the grass roots.

As already noted, there is a call for a more questioning approach to learning, and for a movement away from traditional 'didactic' styles of teaching. Without such a change in training style, it is argued, there will be less chance of encouraging more thoughtful and less authoritarian approaches to the job and to the public. If probationers are not adequately prepared to deal with the complexities and uncertainties of life which will confront them, then they may fall back on to stereotypes of human character and behaviour; these may see them through up to a point, but can then let them down severely and with undesirable effects upon relationships with the public. It is inevitable that the police task will always involve a certain amount of conflict, but it is also now generally accepted that the service should strive to minimise that conflict and should not be an organisation which is authoritarian, unbending and overbearing in its dealings, particularly with those who are law abiding.

The other side of this coin is that a non-authoritarian (rather than authoritative, which is what police officers often *do* need to be) police officer, who constantly questions what he and his colleagues and superiors are doing, will not fit easily into an organisation which is still largely authoritarian and hierarchical in style. Unless there is a correspondence between the values and practices taught in training schools and those which are practiced and advocated in real-life policing, then the oft-mentioned problem will persist of the new recruit arriving at his first station to be told to "forget all you learned at training school, this is real life". If the values of training school and divisional policing continue to diverge then little progress will be made. Trainers can set the tone but most of an officer's career is spent doing the job, and it is life on the division which maintains—or destroys—that tone. From this proposition flow various points, but perhaps the most important concerns the need for a closer relationship between training officers and operational policing. Also, in relation to setting the right tone and examples, it should be noted that there are still few instances of higher management teams 'learning together' and so helping to develop a climate throughout the organisation in which reflective learning focuses upon the activities of that organisation.

The preceding discussion has been concerned with the organisational context in terms of values and priorities. A further issue is that of what priority the police service gives training in terms of time and money. A common complaint of recent years has been that it has been difficult to maintain even basic training provision, let alone new and innovative approaches, because of the need to respond to the flow of demands for training to cope with other priorities, particularly PACE and public order training. As Mike Plumridge notes, forces often now find themselves in the position of wanting to develop new management approaches or other policing innovations, but unable to meet the costs of training their officers to do so. There are no easy solutions to such constraints. One partial solution can be to make much more use of outside help, through consultancies; this eases the demand for police manpower, but is still not a cheap solution. The service could get a lot more than it does from a cross-fertilisation of ideas and experience with other occupations and organisations; a lot of this could be free in money terms, but it is still time consuming.

The training role and career

Good police officers do not automatically make good trainers, but it is unlikely that a person will be a good trainer unless he or she *is* a good operational officer as well. The role of trainer, though, is a very demanding and time-consuming one to perform well. It might, in some respects, be desirable to combine it with a practical policing role, but it is unlikely that a person would be able to adequately meet the demands of both at the same time. Thus, the present system is that individuals are seconded as full-time training officers for a certain period of their careers, mostly for two to three years. What is not clear is whether this is the most suitable period and, if not, then how long this period should be. If the involvement in training is not long enough then trainers will not be able to develop their skills as trainers to best advantage. Two or three years seems a very short period of time when considering how much time and expense goes into the preparation of the trainer him or herself. The problem is, though, that when the secondment period becomes much longer than this, very real dangers arise of the officer becoming out of touch with the world of day-to-day policing which is supposed to form his subject matter. Similar dilemmas exist, of course, for occupational training in many other fields. To some extent the problem is dealt with in the police service by moving officers in and out of training, with operational postings interspersed, but it is difficult to know just what the ideal balance is.

There are also concerns that officers will miss out in the promotion stakes by remaining in the 'backwater' of training. Some feel that they are judged for promotions on the basis of their work in operational policing and that any achievements in the training field somehow do not count for this purpose. This may or may not actually be true, but the concern certainly exists. A career structure within training with its own formally recognised hierarchy of posts would solve the problem in one sense but, on the other hand, it would increase the danger of officers spending too long in the training function and getting out of touch. Clearly, what is needed is for trainers to be chosen on their merits as practical police officers and also on their potential abilities as trainers. This potential must then be maximised through good quality preparation for the training role. But, once into the training world, the officer must keep constantly in touch with the world of operational policing. He may do this through his own initiative, but this can be hard to find time for, so that it may be necessary to have some more formalised system by which trainers return at regular intervals to operational policing.

As Les Poole has noted, future probationer training will involve much more interlinking of theory and practice, by interspersing periods of police duty with formal training. One way to maintain this link may well be to integrate the Tutor Constable more firmly into the system. Steve Stradling, Nigel Fielding, Eric Shepherd and others in this book have pointed to a potentially greater role for the Tutor Constable, and the Stage II Review team had a considerable amount to say on this. What is needed is for a link to be made between street experience and the classroom, in such a way that the probationer can understand each in terms of the other. Particularly in the early stages, there needs to be someone to help him make that connection, and the Tutor Constable is the obvious person to do this. At the moment, though, TCs are not routinely used in this way, but operate simply on the street experience side of the equation. The probationer could simply draw upon his street experiences by reporting back on them to a Centre-based trainer but, if the TC could share those street experiences with him and then also help to *interpret* them with trainers and other probationers in the classroom, there could be much greater continuity and more effective learning.

At present, TC schemes can be very ad hoc affairs and are, at worst, more a case of the blind leading the blind than of the experienced officer easing the new recruit into the world of street policing. This is because of the relative youth and lack of experience of so many police constables, because of shortages of suitable officers to perform this role over the required periods of time, and because of the limited preparation of those nominated as TCs. There has been repeated criticism in recent years of the 'sitting by Nellie' system of learning on the job in policing; ie, learning the job by watching 'old hands' doing it, on the assumption that they know the best way to do it and actually put that into practice. Even someone who seems experienced at a task has not necessarily learnt the best way to do it. Or, even if they have, that way may now be outdated, or they may not be able to pass their own skills on to others effectively. The demand, therefore, is now for Tutor Constables to be much more formally prepared 'Nellies' and much more skilled, both in practical policing and in passing on to probationers what they need to know. It is vital to get this right because, however good classroom learning can be made, most of the good it does could be dissipated if the probationer is then sent out to divisions into an unstructured and undirected working environment. Understandably, in order to get through, he will then fall back on incomplete learning and possibly stereotyped attitudes and responses which he has picked up so far.

Any such 'upgrading' of the Tutor Constable role clearly raises important resource questions: there may be a genuine lack of suitable (and willing) candidates for the role; there will be problems in scheduling the use of their time, so as to allow for street work, street work with their probationer, and for work in training establishments. One-to-one training is an expensive affair in any context, and it is important to establish effective methods of preparing officers as Tutor Constables and then using them to best advantage.

One further resource point concerns the use of civilian tutors. In principle, they should be able to play just as important a part in the police service as civilian evaluators or management consultants. But some unfortunate experiences have been reported in the past in using 'outside speakers', especially for community relations courses, where some have been of dubious quality as presenters and some have been seen as arguing political points or taking an anti-police stance. Even where the content has been less emotive there have been problems with trying out new training methods, and the police service is now rather wary of making similar mistakes. The central function of probationer training must be to help recruits learn practical policing skills, and this is probably not something which non-police trainers could do at all well. There may be exceptions, but the link with policing must always be made and, whether at probationer or management training level, the need is for learning to have a proper *context*. This does not mean that new learning always has to fit in to what exists but that, in exploring new ideas and methods, it must take the existing environment and previous experiences of the learners as a significant reference point. It seems unsound, then, to propose that anyone should take on the training role unless he or she has an awareness of and sensitivity towards the nature of practical policing.

On the other side of the coin, however, there is an important point of principle which argues in favour of the greater involvement of non-police trainers. The general tendency now developing in police training circles is towards greater openness, exploratory learning and interdisciplinary endeavour. This parallels the attempts in practical policing to develop much better inter-agency links in coping with crime prevention and social problems. One way to help sustain the philosophy of policing as a co-operative and overlapping enterprise is to involve non-police agencies and individuals in training, so that this too becomes an area of inter-agency co-operation. Two approaches may be possible. First, there may be scope for actually sharing some training courses between the police and trainees in other occupations. Second, those in other occupations which involve public contact under often difficult conditions could share their experiences with the police without this necessarily being presented as 'teaching' the police what they ought to be doing.

Clearly, the Tutor Constable is one very crucial 'key role' in the police organisation as far as training is concerned. Others which are mentioned in this book are the Divisional Commander and the Community Liaison Officer. It would involve straying too far into questions of police organisation to give a detailed consideration of what these or other roles do or should involve. The point here is to emphasise that, in taking a broad definition of 'training', one must look to the contribution made by those other than trainers and then, in turn, to the training needs of those people. This follows on from what was said earlier about organisational context: on a broad definition *all* those officers with whom the probationary constable comes into contact are, in a quite real sense, responsible for the way that probationer learns how to perform the job. This responsibility needs to be formally recognised in defining training needs for all ranks and specialisms.

One final point worth noting about the role and career of trainers is that, as in most spheres of life, some individuals have particular 'charisma'—more power to pursuade, inspire and influence others. It is clear from some of what has been written here that this has helped develop new thinking in police training at certain times and places. Such personal influence is something which it would be difficult, and probably undesirable, to legislate for, though its potential value should be recognised. What can be done, though, is to take every opportunity to attract into training those people who do seem to have particular aptitudes and flair for this type of work. If they can help maintain a creative and stimulating environment for both trainers and trainees then other like-minded individuals will continue to come forward. Quite a lot is now known about the 'profiles' of such individuals and more strenuous efforts are needed to identify, develop and encourage them to make a contribution as trainers.

Evaluation

At the 'bottom line' of any useful discussion of training, whether for the police or any other organisation, comes the difficult question of how to judge the effectiveness of that training. Such evaluation is essential for two reasons: first, the resources going into training are so great that they cannot be used haphazardly; there needs to be allowance for experimentation, but this must be controlled and measured experimentation rather than a hit-and-miss affair. Second, the potential impact of training upon the quality of policing—and, therefore, upon the public— is such that this cannot be left to chance; we must know what it is rather than simply make assumptions about it. Basic questions to be asked about training are, then: What is actually being delivered? Does it have the desired impact upon those being trained? Does it have a lasting impact, both upon those people *and* upon the public they deal with? It would have been most satisfying if this book could have provided the answers to these questions, especially the last one, but they are extremely difficult to answer.

The apparently relatively simple question of what training is being delivered is, in reality, a complicated one, for the range of training involved is considerable. Experience suggests that the provision of training can be remarkably variable, so that it cannot simply be assumed that because certain 'standard' elements are stipulated that they are necessarily being provided everywhere they should be. Even if a subject appears on the timetable one cannot judge from that what is being provided under the heading concerned. What is all important is that the material is being presented in the appropriate style and manner; its quality as well as its quantity. Particularly as the new styles of teaching and learning proposed in this book are developed, it will be more than simply a matter of asking whether a subject is on the timetable. Thus, the social skills of policing will not simply be a subject in its own right on the timetable, but will be an underlying theme at numerous points: in learning about traffic stops, domestic disputes or juvenile offenders, and so on.

Responsibility for ensuring uniform and adequate standards of provision lies partly with the Inspectorate but, on a more detailed level, with the Central Planning and Training Unit. The CPTU (and others) also need to consider the second basic question posed above about the impact of training. As new and more creative ideas are incorporated into both national and local training provision it becomes vital to see that appropriate learning is taking place. With the movement towards a more open and questioning approach in place of systems-based learning with its neatly defined 'objectives', this becomes a more complex task than simply 'validation'. It requires quite fundamental thought about what the trainee should be getting out of a particular course or learning experience in terms of new knowledge, skills and attitudes. Difficult though this task of evaluation is it is one which should be done, and it is not a one-off exercise. It is now recognised that the training system cannot be static but should be constantly changing and adapting, so that it will be important to repeatedly examine its impact. This is an exceptionally difficult thing to do, given the nature of the subject matter and the methods needed to deliver it.

The central point of much of what has been said in these chapters is that recruits will only become properly sensitised to many of the issues arising in policing if they can stop expecting to have clear-cut answers presented to them and start asking questions instead. A corollary of this is the need for more facilitative approaches to learning. The problem this raises for evaluation is that it is less easy to test the acquisition of understanding than the acquisition of clearly specified items of information. In the long term, some sort of balance will probably develop so that training is partly 'traditional' and partly 'progressive' in its approach but, in the transitional period, the task is exceptionally difficult for trainers and others who need to evaluate the impact of training. There are good reasons why police training should be a relatively standardised product, but this should not mean inflexibility and discouragement of new thinking. A constant danger is that standardisation brings with it standardised forms of testing and that these, in turn, lead to questions which compartmentalise the information to be learned. Thus, a 'good' score becomes one where the person tested correctly answers 'yes' or 'no' to a series of short questions, regardless of whether they understand what their answers mean. This is an extreme example, but the point is that such an approach to the testing of learning becomes even more inappropriate in a period of change and movement towards a learning climate where critical questioning plays a much larger part.

The question of the long term impact of training upon police officers and their relations with the public is the most difficult of all to address. To establish any direct relationship between current training inputs and the outputs of policing on the street at future times is a daunting, if not impossible task, because of the large number of other influences—known and unknown—which will intervene and confound any such observed relationship. Apart from such confounding influences, evaluation is difficult because the real test of learning is far away from the classroom and out on the street, where the recruit is removed from trainers or senior officers who would wish to judge his performance. The person who *could* be in touch with his work, though, is the Tutor Constable; once more it seems clear that there is a key role for the TC in providing feedback from the street to the classroom.

The true test of training effectiveness is not even the performance of the individual officer, but the impact which that performance has upon such broad and nebulous things as law and order and police-public relations. To establish any meaningful relationship between training inputs (at individual or group level) and these broadly defined outputs is a mammoth task. The whole shift in the approach to training with which this book is largely concerned did, of course, come about because there appeared to be such a mismatch between what was happening in the classroom and on the streets. Training was not the sole area of deficiency which Lord Scarman identified in his report on the inner city riots; but it was certainly one area in which he—and many others—saw a need for change if new attitudes, approaches and priorities were to be developed. By implication, then, an important long-term test of the efficacy of new forms of training will be the extent to which public tranquillity returns to inner-city streets and the extent to which other indicators of good police-public relations show a positive turn. Ray Bull and Peter Horncastle's current attempt to compare—through observation and other means—the street experiences and behaviour of patrol officers with different training backgrounds is a bold attempt to face some of these problems of evaluation and test the link between the classroom and the street. Its findings could have significant implications for future training developments, and they will be awaited with great interest.

Returning to the point raised earlier about training as part of organisational change, one should also take a rather broader, though methodologically less ambitious, approach to the matter of long-term training impact. This would involve simply taking an overall programme of organisation change as the input variable and then relating this to equally broad output measures of organisational performance on the other side of the equation. This would not address questions about the impact of particular elements of training courses, but it would show whether or not the broad emphasis of policing, training included, was going in the right direction. In thinking about evaluation in these terms, there is one final basic point to bear in mind which follows on from what was said about the need for training to reflect the needs and values of the organisation as a whole. This is simply that the desired outputs of training should have already been defined by the organisation; for the objectives of training and the objectives of the organisation should, logically, be one and the same as far as basic principles are concerned.

As the contents of this book demonstrate, there are now a considerable number of non-police researchers and academics active in the field of police training and development. Ray Bull and Peter Horncastle have also noted this fact in concluding their chapter and it is, perhaps, worth further brief mention. Those who study and write about any organisation from the outside—whether as management consultants, academic researchers with special access to the organisation, or simply as external critics—are almost bound to come up with findings or recommendations from time to time which are inconvenient or embarrassing to that organisation. They may contradict policies which the organisation is strongly committed to continuing with, and they may provoke public and media demands that things be done in different ways. It is to the credit of the police service, therefore, that it has opened up to outside scrutiny one of its most important activities and one where it was, in some respects, open to criticism. The cynic might suggest that the service had little choice in the matter; but, whatever the precipitating reasons for the self-induced scrutiny which police training has been undergoing, the evidence which volumes such as this provide is that very real progress is being made, and that this progress is not simply being forced upon the police by 'outsiders' but is something which they themselves are becoming increasingly involved in advancing.

There has certainly been cooperation between police trainers and those from academic disciplines, and what is notable is the enthusiasm with which police officers have involved themselves in such disciplines as education, psychology and sociology. Many more than at present need to do so, however, if new approaches are to spread through all police training establishments. One way to encourage this could be to stress the need for continuing monitoring and evaluation of training; if training officers have a responsibility for monitoring and evaluation of what their work achieves then they will be increasingly motivated both to call upon outside advice and help and to learn and practise the necessary skills themselves. This would not only lead to a better quality of research, but would also encourage the continuing dialogue about training which will be so essential to sustain its vigour.

Conclusions

The burden of the case presented in this book is that training should change its character and reflect a different set of priorities. Because the policing task does involve so much dealing with people it is the skills of doing this which should receive priority over the learning of factual information about law and procedure, at least at the early stages of probationer training. Even now, despite efforts to achieve more integration of the different types of lesson, the danger is that social skills (or human skills, or policing skills) ends up as something which gets fitted in to the spaces left around the more traditional technical and legal subjects. Not only does this mean that such skills are being given second place, but it means that they are *seen* by probationers (and supervisors) as being secondary. The priorities which probationers come to have as a result of their early months in the service are conditioned by a variety of influences, of which formal training is one of the most important. But it is vital that this training should suggest a clear set of priorities and that these are priorities which reflect the working practices of the service itself.

Even the most enthusiastic trainers do not claim that training alone—or training in human relations and nothing else—is the answer to better policing and better police-public relations. The case for training as *the* solution can only be made if it is redefined as that whole process by which officers learn the skills, knowledge and attitudes they use in their job. From this perspective we need, then, to think of training not simply as something which takes place in training establishments, but as a programme of development which helps individuals, groups and the organisation as a whole to learn how to learn and how to take a proactive, creative and adaptive stance towards the environment in which they have to work.

References

ABELSON, P. H. and HAMMOND, A. L. (1977). *The Electronics Revolution*. Oxford: Basil Blackwell.

ADLAM, R. (1986). 'Developing excellence'. *Police*, 2, 4, 307–317.

AINSWORTH, P. and PEASE, K. (1987). *Police Work*. London: British Psychological Society/ Methuen.

AJZEN, I. and FISHBEIN, M. (1980). *Understanding Attitudes and Predicting Social Behaviour*. New Jersey: Prentice-Hall.

ANTONOVSKY, A. (1979). *Health, Stress, and Coping*. San Francisco: Jossey-Bass.

ARCHER, M. S. (1984). *The Social Origins of Educational Systems*. London: Sage.

ARGYRIS, C. and SCHON, D. (1974). *Theory in Practice: increasing professional effectiveness*. London: Temple-Smith.

ARGYRIS, C. and SCHON, D. (1979). *Organisational Learning: a theory of action perspective*. Reading, Mass: Addison-Wesley.

ASHWORTH, P. (1979). *Social Interaction and Consciousness*. New York: John Wiley.

AUSUBEL, D. P. (1968). *Educational Psychology: a cognitive view*. New York: Holt, Reinhart and Winston.

BACK, K. and BACK, K. (1982). *Assertiveness at Work*. New York: McGraw-Hill.

BANTON, M. (1984). 'But what do we mean by "racism"?' *Police*, 17, 4, 44–46.

BARD, M. (1970). *Training Police as Specialists in Family Crisis Intervention*. Washington DC: US Department of Justice.

BATTEN, E. R. and BATTEN, M. (1965). *The Human Factor in Community Work*. London: Oxford University Press.

BECKER, H. S. et al. (1961). *Boys in White*. Chicago: University of Chicago Press.

BECKHARD, R. (1969). *Organisation Development: Strategies and Models*. Reading, Mass: Addison-Wesley.

BECKHARD, R. and HARRIS, R. T. (1977). *Organisational Transitions: managing complex change*. Reading, Mass: Addison-Wesley.

BEER, M. and HUSE, E. F. (1977). 'Concepts and management applications'. In: Hackman, J. R. and Shuttle, J. L. (Eds.). *Improving Life at Work*. Santa Monica, California: Goodyear Publishing.

BENNETT, R. (1984). 'Becoming blue: a longitudinal study of police recruit occupational socialisation'. *Journal of Police Science and Administration*, 12, 1, 47–58.

BENNIS, W. G. (1966). *Changing Organisations*. New York: McGraw-Hill.

BERGER, P. and LUCKMANN, T. (1967). *The Social Construction of Reality*. Harmondsworth: Penguin.

BITTNER, E. (1970). *The Function of the Police in Modern Society*. Washington DC: US Government Printing Office.

BLACKMORE, J. (1978). 'Are police allowed to have problems of their own?' *Police*, 1, 3, 47-55.

BLANCHARD, K. and JOHNSON, S. (1982) *The One Minute Manager*. London: Fontana Books.

BLIGH, D. (Ed.) (1986) *Teach Thinking by Discussion*. Guildford: SRHE and NFER-Nelson.

de BOARD, R. (1983). *Counselling People at Work*. Aldershot: Gower.

BOYDELL, T. and PEDLER, M. (1981). *Management Self-Development: Concepts and Practices*. Aldershot: Gower.

BRACCO, S. (1984). *Integrated Planning in a Poor Country: UNESCO's work in gaming/simulation*. Paper given at ISAGA Conference, Elsinore, Denmark.

BRADFORD, S. and COHEN, A. (1984). *Managing for Excellence: the guide to developing high performance in contemporary organisations*. New York: John Wiley.

BRADLEY, D., WALKER, N. and WILKIE, R. (1986). *Managing the Police: law, organisation and democracy*. London: Wheatsheaf Books.

BRITISH BROADCASTING CORPORATION. (1987). *File on 4*. Transmitted 31st March.

BROWN, C. (1984). *Black and White in Britain: the third PSI Survey*. London: Heinemann.

BROWN, L. (1983). 'The future face of police training'. *Police Journal*, 56, 2, 121-127.

BROWN, L. and WILLIS, A. (1985). 'Authoritarianism in British police recruits: importation, socialization or myth? *Journal of Occupational Psychology*, 58, 97-108.

BROWN, M. K. (1981). *Working the Street: police discretion and the dilemmas of reform*. New York: Russell Sage Foundation.

BRUNER, J. S. (1963). 'Needed: a theory of instruction'. *Educational Leadership*, 20, 523-532.

BRUNER, J. S. (1979). 'The control of human behaviour.' In: *On Knowing: essays for the left hand*. Cambridge, Mass: Harvard University Press.

BUCHANAN, D. R. (1985). 'Attitudes of police recruits towards domestic disturbances: an evaluation of family crisis intervention training'. *Journal of Criminal Justice*, 13, 561-572.

BULL, R. (1986). 'An evaluation of police recruit training in human awareness'. In: Yuille, J. C. (Ed.). *Police Selection and Training*. Dordrecht: Martinus Nijhoff.

BULL, R. and HORNCASTLE, P. (1983). *An Evaluation of the Metropolitan Police Recruit Training in Human Awareness*. Interim Report. London: Police Foundation.

BULL, R. and HORNCASTLE, P. (1986). *Metropolitan Police Recruit Training: an independent evaluation*. London: Police Foundation.

BUTLER, A. J. P. (1982). *An Examination of the Influence of Training and Work Experience on the Attitudes and Perceptions of Police Constables*. Paper given at the International Conference on Psychology and Law, University College, Swansea.

BUTLER, A. J. P. (1984). *Police Management*. Aldershot: Gower.

BUTLER, A. J. P. (1986). 'The limits of police community relations training'. In: Yuille, J. C. (Ed.) *Police Selection and Training*. Dordrecht: Martinus Nijhoff.

BUTLER, A. J. P. (1987). 'Strictly confidential'. *Police Review*, 20, 580-581.

BUTLER, A. J. P. and COCHRANE, R. (1977). 'An examination of some elements of the personality of police officers and their implications'. *Journal of Police Science and Administration*, 5, 4, 441-50.

BUTLER, A. J. P. and SKITT, B. H. (1974). *In-Service Training: a new approach*. Police Federation Occasional Paper No 3. London: Police Federation.

BUTLER, A. J. P. and THARME, K. (1981). *An Examination of the Effectiveness of Community Relations Training*. West Midlands Police.

CENTRAL PLANNING AND TRAINING UNIT. *Communication Course*.

CENTRE FOR THE STUDY OF COMMUNITY AND RACE RELATIONS. (1985). *Results of CRR Training Initiative Survey and Results of Replies to National CRR Training Initiatives Survey*. (Unpublished).

CHATTERTON, M. (1987). 'The misuse of sergeants'. *Policing*, 3, 2, 106-116.

CHERNISS, C. (1980). *Professional Burnout in Human Service Organisations*. New York: Praeger.

COFFEY, J. (1987). 'Race training in the USA'. In: Shaw, J. W., Nordlie, P. G. and Shapiro, R. M. (Eds.). *Strategies for Improving Race Relations: the Anglo-American experience*. Manchester: Manchester University Press.

COLMAN, A. and GORMAN, L. (1982). 'Conservatism, dogmatism and authoritarianism in British police officers'. *Sociology*, 16, 1, 1-11.

COOK, P. (1977). 'Empirical survey of police officers'. *Police Review*, 85, 1042, 1078, 1114, 1140.

COOPER, C. L. (1986). 'Job distress: recent research and the emerging role of the clinical occupational psychologist'. *Bulletin of the British Psychological Society*, 39, 325-331.

COOPER, C. L. and SMITH, M. J. (1983). *Job Stress and Blue Collar Work*. Chichester: Wiley.

CRUSE, D. and RUBIN, J. (1973). *Determinants of Police Behaviour*. Washington DC: US Department of Justice.

CUTHBERTSON, G., WARD, R., BULTITUDE, G., SCAMMELL, L. and JOHNSON, G. (1983). *Policing Skills Development Course*. London: Metropolitan Police.

DAS, P. K. (1987). 'State-mandated training in police community relations: an evaluation'. *Police Journal*, 60, 3, 232-48.

DAVIES, I. K. (1971). *The Management of Learning*. New York: McGraw-Hill.

DENKERS, F. (1986). 'The panacea of training and selection'. In: Yuille, J. C. (Ed.). *Police Selection and Training*. Dordrecht: Martinus Nijhoff.

DEWEY, J. (1913). *Interest and Effort in Education*. Boston: Houghton Mifflin.

DIX, M. C. and LAYZELL, A. D. (1983). *Road Users and the Police*. London: Croom Helm.

DOBASH, R. and DOBASH, R. P. (1985). *Violence Against Wives*. London: Open Books.

DOWNIE, R. and TELFER, E. (1969). *Respect for Persons*. London: George Allen and Unwin.

DOYLE, M. and STRAUS, D. (1976). *How to Make Meetings Work*. New York: Jove.

DOYLE, P. and TINDAL, C. R. (1987). 'Developing human resources'. In: Pfeiffer, J. W. and Goodstein, L. (Eds.). *Developing Human Resources*. California: University Associates.

DUMMETT, A. (1973). *Portrait of English Racism*. Harmondsworth: Penguin.

DUTTON, D. G. (1981). 'Training police officers to intervene in domestic violence'. In: Stuart, R. B. (Ed.). *Violent Behaviour: social learning approaches to prediction, management and treatment*. New York: Brunner/Mazel.

EDUCATION 2000. (1983). *A Consultative Document on Hypotheses for Education in AD 2000*. Cambridge: Cambridge University Press.

EDWARDS, S. S. M. (1986). *The Role of Police Discretion in Domestic Violence in London*. Polytechnic of Central London.

ELLIOTT, J. (1985). 'Educational action-research'. In: Nisbet, J. and Nisbet, S. (Eds.). *World Year Book of Education, 1985—Research, Policy and Practice*. London: Kogan Page.

ELLIOTT, P. (1972). *The Sociology of the Professions*. London: Macmillan.

FARAGHER, T. (1985). 'The police response to violence against women in the home'. In: Pahl, J. (Ed.). *Private Violence and Public Policy*. London: Routledge and Kegan Paul.

FARBER, B. (1983). *Stress and Burnout in the Human Service Professions*. New York: Pitman.

FEAGIN, J. and FEAGIN, C. (1978). *Discrimination American Style: institutional racism and sexism*. Englewood Cliffs, New Jersey: Prentice-Hall.

FELL, R. D., RICHARD, W. C. and WALLACE, W. L. (1975). 'Psychological job stress and the police officer'. *Journal of Police Science and Administration*, 8, 2, 139–144.

FIELDING, N. G. (1984). 'Police socialisation and police competence'. *British Journal of Sociology*, 35, 4, 568–90.

FIELDING, N. G. (1987a). 'Evaluating the role of training in police socialisation: a UK example'. *Journal of Community Psychology*, 14, 319–330.

FIELDING, N. G. (1987b). 'Police culture and police practice'. In: Irving, B. and Weatheritt, M. (Eds.). *Contemporary Police Research*. Farnborough: Croom Helm.

FIELDING, N. G. (Forthcoming). *Joining Forces*.

FISHER, R. (1980). *Small Group Decision Making*. New York: McGraw-Hill.

FORRESTER, T. (Ed.). (1980). *The Microelectronics Revolution*. Oxford: Basil Blackwell.

FRANKLIN, R. V., et al. (1984). *Review of Sergeants' Duties and Training Needs*. London: Metropolitan Police.

FRENCH, W. L. and BELL, C. H. (1978). *Organisation Development*. Englewood Cliffs, New Jersey: Prentice-Hall.

FURTHER EDUCATION UNIT. (1987). *Assessing Experiential Learning*. London: Longman.

GAGNE, R. (1977). *The Conditions of Learning*. New York: Holt, Reinhart and Winston.

GAGNE, R. (1985). *The Conditions of Learning and Theory of Instruction*. New York: CBS College Publishing.

GARNER, J. and CLEMMER, E. (1986). *Danger to Police in Domestic Disturbances: a new look*. Washington DC: US Department of Justice.

GARRATT, R. (1987). *The Learning Organisation: the need for directors who think*. London: Fontana.

GIBRAN, K. (1980). *The Prophet*. London: Heinemann.

GOLDSMITH, W. and CLUTTERBUCK, D. (1984). *The Winning Streak*. Harmondsworth: Penguin.

GOLDSTEIN, H. (1979). 'Improving policing: a problem-orientated approach'. *Crime and Delinquency*, 25, 236–258.

GOODALE, J. (1982). *The Fine Art of Interviewing*. Englewood Cliffs, New Jersey: Prentice-Hall.

GREINER, L. E. (1967). 'Patterns of organisational change.' *Harvard Business Review*. 45, 3, 119–130.

HACKMAN, J. R. and SHUTTLE, J. L. (1977). *Improving Life at Work*. Santa Monica, California: Goodyear Publishing.

HAHN, H. (1971). 'A profile of urban police.' *Law and contemporary problems*, 36, 449–466.

HAMBLIN, A. C. (1974). *Evaluation and Control of Training*. New York: McGraw-Hill.

HANSON, P. (1981). *Learning Through Groups*. San Diego: University Associates.

HARGIE, O., SAUNDERS, C. and DICKSON, D. (1981). *Social Skills in Inter-Personal Communication*. London: Croom Helm.

HARRIS, R. (1973). *The Police Academy: an inside view*. New York: Wiley.

HARRISON, R. (1972). 'Understanding your organisation's character.' *Harvard Business Review*, (May—June) 119–128.

HARRISON, R. (1987). *Organisation Culture and Quality of Service*. London: Association for Management Education and Development.

HAUTALUOMA, J. E. and GAVIN, J. F. (1975). 'Effects of organisational diagnosis and intervention on blue-collar 'blues''. In: French, W. L. and Bell, C. H. (Eds.). *Organisation Development*. Englewood Cliffs, New Jersey: Prentice-Hall.

HEADS OF DETECTIVES TRAINING WORKING PARTY. (1983). *Interviewing Techniques and Skills*.

HENDERSON, W. (Ed.). (1985). *Teaching Academic Subjects to Adults: continuing education in practice*. Department of Extramural Studies, University of Birmingham.

HERZBERG, F. (1966). *Work and the Nature of Man*. New York: World Publishing Company.

HILL, N. (1981). *Counselling at the Workplace*. New York: McGraw-Hill.

HIND, D. W. G. (1986). 'The process of interpersonal skills training'. *Bulletin of Educational Development and Research*, Winter, 1986–87, 27–31.

HINRICHS, J. R. (1976). 'Personnel training'. In: Dunnette, M. (Ed.). *Handbook of Industrial and Organisational Psychology*. Chicago: Rand McNally.

HOGARTH, R. M. (1980). *Judgement and Choice: the psychology of decision*. Chichester: John Wiley.

HOLDAWAY, S. (1984). *Inside the British Police*. Oxford: Basil Blackwell.

HOLMES, T. H. and RAHE, R. H. (1967). 'Social re-adjustment rating scale.' *Journal of Psychosomatic Research*, 2, 213–218.

HOME OFFICE (1983a). *Manpower Effectiveness and Efficiency in the Police Service*. Circular 114/83. London: Home Office.

HOME OFFICE (1983b). *Police Probationer Training*. Report of the Police Training Council Working Party on Police Probationer Training. London: Home Office.

HOME OFFICE (1983c). *Community and Race Relations Training for the Police*. Report of the Police Training Council Working Party. London: Home Office.

HOME OFFICE (1983d). *The Training of Probationary Constables. Initial Course: student's lesson notes*. London: HMSO.

HOME OFFICE (1986). *Violence Against Women*. Circular 69/1986 London: Home Office.

HOME OFFICE (1987). *Report of Her Majesty's Chief Inspector of Constabulary for the year 1986*. London: HMSO.

HONEY, P. and MUNFORD, A. (1983). *The Manual of Learning Styles*. Surrey, England: Peter Honey Publications.

HOPE, R. O. (1987). 'The Defense Equal Opportunity Management Institute'. In: Shaw, J. W., Nordlie, P. G., and Shapiro, R. M. (Eds.). *Strategies for Improving Race Relations: the Anglo-American experience*. Manchester: Manchester University Press.

HOPSON, B. and ADAMS, B. (1976). 'Towards an understanding of transition: defining some boundaries of transition dynamics'. In: Adams, J., Hayes, J. and Hopson, B. (Eds.). *Transition: understanding and managing personal change*. London: Martin Robertson.

HOUSE, E. R. (1974). *The Politics of Educational Innovation*. Berkeley, California: McCutchen.

HOVLAND, C. I., JANIS, I. L. and KELLY, H. H. (1953). *Communication and Persuasion*. New Haven, Connecticut: Yale University Press.

HUDSON, L. (1978). *Human Beings*. St. Albans: Triad Paladin.

HUNT, R. (1987). 'Coping with racism: institutional change in police departments'. In: Shaw, J. W., Nordlie, P. G., and Shapiro, R. M. (Eds.). *Strategies for Improving Race Relations: the Anglo-American experience*. Manchester: Manchester University Press.

IANNI, F. A. J. and REUSS-IANNI, E. (1983). ' "Take this job and shove it!" A comparison of organisational stress and burnout among teachers and police'. In: Farber, B. (Ed.). *Stress and Burnout in the Human Service Professions*. New York: Pitman.

IRVING, B. (1980). *Police Interrogation: a case study of current practice*. Royal Commission on Criminal Procedure, Research Study No. 2. London: HMSO.

JAFFE, P. and THOMPSON, J. (1985). *Family Consultant Service with the London Police Force*. Report to the Solicitor General of Canada.

JAMIESON, I. and LIGHTFOOT, M. (1982). *Schools and Industry*. London: Methuen.

JELINEK, M., SMIRCICH, L. and HIRSCH, P. (1983). 'Introduction: a code of many colours'. *Administrative Science Quarterly*, 28, 331–338.

JONES, F. and HARRIS, M. W. (1971). 'The development of interracial awareness in groups'. In: Blank, L., Gottsegen, G. B. and Gottsegen, M. G. (Eds.). *Confrontation: encounters in self and interpersonal awareness*. New York: Macmillan.

JONES, S. (1986). 'Police and public perceptions of the police role: moving towards a reappraisal of police professionalism'. In: Yuille, J. C. (Ed.). *Police Selection and Training*. Dordrecht: Martinus Nijhoff.

JONES, S. and JOSS, R. (1985). 'Surviving training'. *Policing*, 1, 4, 206–225.

JONES, S. and JOSS, R. (1986). *Training for effective professional practice: an analysis of the mismatch between provision and need*. Centre for the Study of Community and Race Relations, Brunel University.

JONES, S. and LEVI, M. (1983). 'The police and the majority: the neglect of the obvious?' *Police Journal*, 56, 4, 351–363.

JOSS, R. (1986). *The Viability of Training-Led Change in the British Police Service*. Paper given at the IAAP Conference, Jerusalem.

KAKABADSE, A. (1984). 'The police: a management development survey'. *Journal of Industrial and Commercial Training*, 5, 1–48.

KANT, I. (1964). *Groundwork of the Metaphysics of Morals*. (Translated by H. Paton). London: Harper and Row.

KATZ, D. and KAHN, R. L. (1966). *The Social Psychology of Organisations*. New York: John Wiley.

KATZ, J. (1978). *White Awareness: a handbook for anti-racism*. Norman, Oklahoma: University of Oklahoma Press.

KELLY, G. A. (1963). *Theory of Personality: the psychology of personal constructs*. London: W. W. Norton.

KELMAN, H. (1961). 'Processes of opinion change'. *Public Opinion Quarterly*, 25, 4, 57–78.

KINGET, G. (1975). *On Being Human: a systematic view*. New York: Harcourt, Brace Javanovich.

KIRKHAM, R. (1979). *Signal Zero*. New York: Ballantine.

KLEMP, G. O. (1977). *Three Factors of Success in the World of Work: implications for curriculum in Higher Education*. Paper for the 32nd International Conference on Higher Education, American Association for Higher Education.

KNOWLES, M. S. (1983). 'Releasing the energy of others: making things happen'. *Journal of Management Development*, 2, 2, 26–35.

KOGAN, M. (1978). *The Politics of Educational Change*. London: Fontana.

KOLB, D. A., RUBIN, I. M. and McINTYRE, (Eds.) (1978). *Organisational Psychology*. Englewood Cliffs, New Jersey: Prentice-Hall.

KROES, W. H. (1985). *Society's Victims—the Police: an analysis of job stress in policing*. Springfield, Illinois: Charles C. Thomas.

KUYKENDALL, J. and ROBERG, R. R. (1982). 'Mapping police organisational change: from a mechanistic to an organic model'. *Criminology*, 20, 2, 241–256.

LEIGH, A. (1983). *Decisions, Decisions!* London: Institute of Personnel Management.

LINDSAY, P. R. (1984). 'Development needs analysis'. *Training and Development,* (October) 10–12.

LIPPITT, G. (1981). *Management Development as the Key to Organisational Renewal*. Speaker's papers. First World Congress on Management Development, London. Bedford: Cranfield Institute of Technology.

LIPSKY, M. (1980). *Street-Level Bureaucracy: dilemmas of the individual in public service*. New York: Russell Sage.

LONDON STRATEGIC POLICY UNIT. (1986). *Police Response to Domestic Violence*. Police Monitoring and Research Group Briefing Paper No. 1. London: LSPU.

LONDON STRATEGIC POLICY UNIT. (1987). *Racism Awareness Training—a critique*. London: LSPU.

LUBANS, V. A. (1982). *Validation study. New York City Police Department Police Officer Recruit Training—Law Curriculum*. New York City Police Foundation.

LUBANS, V. A. and EDGAR, J. M. (1979). *Policing by Objectives: a handbook for improving police management*. Hartford, Connecticut: Social Development Corporation.

LUNDMAN, R. J. (1980). 'Police conduct.' In: Lundman, R. J. (Ed.). *Police Behaviour: a sociological perspective*. London: Oxford University Press.

MACDONALD, B., ARGENT, M., ELLIOTT, J., MAY N. H., MILLER, P. J. G., NAYLOR, J. T., and NORRIS, N. F. J. (1987). *Police Probationer Training: the final report of the Stage II Review*. London: HMSO.

MACLAREN-ROSS, J. (1973). 'Behavioural objectives: a critical review'. *Instructional Science*, 2, 1–52.

McCLELLAND, D. C. (1973). 'Testing for competence rather than for "intelligence"'. *American Psychologist*, 28, 1–14.

McCLELLAND, D. C. and WINTER, D. G. (1969). *Motivating Economic Achievement*. New York: Free Press.

McIVER, J. and PARKS, R. (1983). 'Evaluating police performance: identification of effective and ineffective police actions'. In: Bennett, R. (Ed.). *Police at Work: policy issues and analysis*. Beverly Hills, California: Sage.

MAIER, N. (1952). *Principles of Human Relations*. New York: John Wiley.

MALES, S. (1983). *Police Management on Division and sub-Division*. Home Office Police Research Services Unit. London: Home Office.

MANAGEMENT REVIEW TEAM, (1987). *Interim Report on Sergeants Training*. Central Planning and Training Unit.

MANNING, P. K. (1975). 'Deviance and dogma'. *British Journal of Criminology*, 15, 48–67.

MANOLIAS, M. (1983). *A Preliminary Study of Stress in the police service*. Conclusions and recommendations as submitted to the Association of Chief Police Officers Working Party on Police Stress. London: Home Office.

MARGERISON, C. (1984). 'Where is management education and development going?—some key questions.' In: Kakabadse, A. A. and Mukhi, S. (Eds.). *The Future of Management Education*. Aldershot: Gower.

MARK, R. (1979). *In the Office of Constable*. Glasgow: William Collins.

MASLOW, A. H. (1954). *Motivation and Personality*. New York: Harper and Row.

MASON, G. (1987). 'Sussex Chief attacks Home Office for manpower "snub"!' *Police Review*, 31 July, 1513.

MENZIES, I. (1970). *The Functioning of Social Systems as a Defence against Anxiety*. London: The Tavistock Institute.

MEREDITH, N. (1984). 'Police brutality and stress.' *Psychology Today*, (May), 21–26.

METROPOLITAN POLICE (1985). *The Principles of Policing and Guidance for Professional Behaviour*. London: Metropolitan Police.

METROPOLITAN POLICE (1986a). *Area Policing Skills Facilitators Manual. Part Three: Interpersonal skills*. London: Metropolitan Police.

METROPOLITAN POLICE (1986b). *Report of the Working Party into Domestic Violence*. London: Metropolitan Police.

METROPOLITAN POLICE, (1987). *Instruction Book for the Guidance of the Metropolitan Police Force*. London: Metropolitan Police.

MORRIS, J. (1972). 'Three aspects of the person in social life'. In: Ruddock, R. (Ed.). *Six Approaches to the Person*. London: Routledge and Kegan Paul.

MUMFORD, A. (1980). *Making Experience Pay: management success through effective learning*. New York: McGraw-Hill.

NACRO RACE ISSUES ADVISORY COMMITTEE. (1986). *Black People and the Criminal Justice System*. London: NACRO.

NELSON-JONES, R. (1986). *Human Relationship Skills: training and self-help*. Eastbourne: Cassel.

NELSON-JONES, Z. P. and SMITH, W. (1970). 'The law enforcement profession: an incident of high suicide'. *Omega*, 1, 4, 293–299.

NEWSOME, A. (1985). *Employee Assistance in the USA: a contribution to the management of organisational and personal change*. Report to the Bloomsbury Health Authority.

NEIDERHOFFER, A. (1967). *Behind the Shield*. New York: Doubleday Anchor Books.

NIJKERK, K. J. (1986). 'The development of training and the need for in-service training'. In: Yuille, J. C. (Ed.). *Police Selection and Training*. Dordrecht: Martinus Nijhoff.

NORDLIE, P. G. (1987). 'The evolution of race relations training in the US Army'. In: Shaw, J. W., Nordlie, P. G. and Shapiro, R. M. (Eds.). *Strategies for Improving Race Relations: the Anglo-American experience*. Manchester: Manchester University Press.

NUTLEY, P. (1987). *Riot, Rhetoric and Reality: an enquiry into factors in police organisations which affect the dissemination and implementation of police policy*. Manchester: University of Manchester Institute of Science and Technology.

PANZARELLA, R. (1984). 'Management versus policing by objectives'. *Police Journal*, 57, 5, 110–128.

PATTEN, T. H. (1971). *Manpower Planning and the Development of Human Resources*. New York: John Wiley.

PEARCE, J. B. and SNORTUM, J. R. (1983). 'Police effectiveness in handling disturbance calls'. *Criminal Justice and Behaviour*, 10, 71–92.

PEPPARD, N. (1980). 'Towards effective race relations training'. *New Community*, 8, 1, 99–106.

PEPPARD, N. (1983). 'Race relations training: the state of the art'. *New Community*, 11, 1 and 2, 150–59.

PETERS, R. (1966). *Ethics and Education*. London: George Allen and Unwin.

PETERS, T. J. and WATERMAN, R. H. (1982). *In Search of Excellence*. New York: Harper and Row.

PETTIGREW, T. F. (1981). 'The mental health impact'. In: Bowser, B. P. and Hunt, R. G. (Eds.). *The Impact of Racism on White Americans* Beverly Hills, California: Sage.

PHILLIPS, K. and FRASER, T. (1982). *The Management of Interpersonal Skills Training*. Aldershot: Gower.

PHILLIPS, S. V. (1986). 'Community liaison specialists—a British perspective.' In: Yuille, J. C. (Ed.). *Police Selection and Training*. Dordrecht: Martinus Nijhoff.

PHILLIPS, S. V. and COCHRANE, R. (1985a). *The Role, Function and Training of Police Community Liaison Officers—Final Report*. Birmingham: University of Birmingham.

PHILLIPS, S. V. and COCHRANE, R. (1985b). 'Community liaison—a specialist role?' *Home Office Research Bulletin*, 19, 30–32.

PHILLIPS, S. V. and COCHRANE, R. (1987). *The National Course for Newly Appointed Community Liaison Officers—an Evaluation*. Birmingham: University of Birmingham.

PLUMRIDGE, M. D. (1983). *A Study of Police Management and Command Roles*. The Police Staff College.

PLUMRIDGE, M. D. (1985). 'Dilemmas of police management and organisation'. In: Thackrah, R. (Ed.). *Contemporary policing*. London: Sphere Books.

PLUMRIDGE, M. D. (1985). *Probationer Training—an Organisation Culture Perspective*. Paper given at the BPS Symposium on Psychological Aspects of Policing Today, London.

PLUMRIDGE, M. D. (1987). *Personal Communication*.

POLICE TRAINING COUNCIL (1985). *Police Training Strategy*. London: Home Office.

POOLE, L. (1986). *Development Skills in Police Training. Central Planning Unit—The Way Ahead*. Paper given at the IAAP Conference, Jerusalem.

POOLE, L. (1986). 'The contribution of psychology to the development of police training in Britain'. In: Yuille, J. C. (Ed.). *Police Selection and Training*. Dordrecht: Martinus Nijhoff.

PRIESTLEY, P., McGUIRE, J., FLEGG, D., HEMSLEY, V. and WELHAM, D. (1978). *Social Skills and Personal Problem Solving: a handbook of methods*. London: Tavistock.

PUNCH, M. (1979). *Policing the Inner-City*. London: Macmillan.

PUNCH, M. (1979). 'The secret social service'. In: Holdaway, S. (Ed.). *The British Police*. London: Edward Arnold.

PYE, L. (1979). Letter to the editor of *Psychohistory Review*, 8, 3, 50–53.

REINER, R. (1985). *The Politics of the Police*. Brighton: Wheatsheaf Books.

REUSS-IANNI, E. and IANNI, F. A. J. (1983). 'Street cops and management cops: the two cultures of policing'. In: Punch, M. (Ed.). *Control in the Police Organisation*. Cambridge, Mass: MIT Press.

ROGERS, C. (1967). *On Becoming a Person: a therapist's view of psychotherapy*. London: Constable.

ROGERS, C. (1983). *Freedom to Learn for the '80s*. Columbus, Ohio: Charles E. Merrill.

ROTELLA, R. J. (1984). 'The psychology of performance under stress.' *FBI Law Enforcement Bulletin*. (June) 1–11.

ROWBOTTOM, R. and BILLIS, D. (1977). 'The stratification of work and organisational design'. *Human Relations*, 30, 1, 53–76.

ROYAL, R. and SCHUTT, S. (1976). *The Gentle Art of Interviewing and Interrogation*. Englewood Cliffs, New Jersey: Prentice-Hall.

RUNYAN, W. M. (1984). *Life Histories and Psychobiography: explorations in theory and method*. London: Oxford University Press.

RUSSELL, H. and BEIGEL, A. (1982). *Understanding Human Behaviour for Effective Police Work*. New York: Basic Books.

RUSSELL, L. (1972). *The ABC of Interviewing*. London: Pitman.

RUSSO, P. A., ENGEL, A. S. and HATTING, S. H. (1983). 'Police and occupational stress: an empirical investigation.' In: Bennett, R. (Ed.). *Police at Work: policy issues and analysis*. Beverly Hills, California: Sage.

SARASON, S. (1986). *Caring and Compassion in Clinical Practice*. San Francisco: Jossey-Bass.

SAVITZ, L. (1982). 'An officer requires assistance'. In: Johnston, N. and Savitz, L. (Eds.). *Legal Process and Corrections*. New York: John Wiley.

SCARMAN. (1981). *The Brixton Disorders 10–12 April 1981: Report of an Inquiry by the Rt. Hon. the Lord Scarman, OBE*. Cmnd 8427. London: HMSO.

SCHEIN, E. (1978). *Career Dynamics: matching individual and organisational needs*. Reading, Massachusetts: Addison-Wesley.

SCHEIN, E. (1985). *Organisational Culture and Leadership: a dynamic view*. San Francisco: Jossey-Bass.

SCHON, D. (1972). *Beyond the Stable State: public and private learning in a changing society*. London: Temple-Smith.

SCHON, D. (1983). *The Reflective Practitioner: how professionals think in action*. London: Temple Smith.

SCHUMACHER, E. F. (1973). *Small is Beautiful*. London: Blond and Briggs.

SCHWEITZER, D. and GINSBURG, G. (1966). 'Factors of communicator credibility'. In: Backman, C. W. and Secord, P. F. (Eds.). *Problems in Social Psychology*. New York: McGraw-Hill.

SCOTT, E. and PERCY, S. (1983). 'Gatekeeping police services: police operators and dispatchers'. In: Bennett, R. (Ed.). *Police at Work: policy issues and analysis*. Beverly Hills, California: Sage.

SELYE, H. (1975). *The Stress of Life*. New York: McGraw-Hill.

SHAW, J. W. (1987). 'Planning and implementing race relations seminars: the Holly Royde experience'. In: Shaw, J. W., Nordlie, P G. and Shapiro, R. M. (Eds.). *Strategies for Improving Race Relations: the Anglo-American experience*. Manchester: Manchester University Press.

SHEPHERD, E. (1982). 'Coping with the first person singular'. In: Shepherd, E. and Watson, J. (Eds.). *Personal Meanings*. New York: John Wiley.

SHEPHERD, E. (1984). 'Values into practice: the implementation and implications of human awareness training'. *Police Journal*, 57, 286–300.

SHEPHERD, E. (1985). 'Interviewing development: facing up to reality'. In: Yuille, J. C. (Ed.). *Police Selection and Training*. Dordrecht: Martinus Nijhoff.

SHEPHERD, E. (1985). *Being Professional: problems with the bottom line*. Paper presented at BPS symposium on Psychological Perspectives on Policing Today, London.

SHEPHERD, E. (1986a). 'Interviewing development: facing up to reality'. *Police Journal*, 59, 35–44.

SHEPHERD, E. (1986b). 'The conversational core of policing'. *Policing*, 2, 294–303.

SHEPHERD, E. (1987a). *Telling Experiences: conversations with child victims*. Paper presented at the British Psychological Society Conference, University of Sussex.

SHEPHERD, E. (1987b). 'Getting a child to tell'. *Police Review*, 95, 1080–81.

SHERMAN, L. W. and BERK,. R. A. (1984). 'The specific deterrent effect of arrest for domestic assault.' *American Sociological Review*, 49, 261–272.

SHIPLEY, P. and ORLANS, V. (1983). *A Survey of Stress Management and Prevention Facilities in a Sample of UK Organisations*. Stress Research and Control Centre, Department of Occupational Psychology, Birkbeck College, London.

SILVERZWEIG, S. and ALLEN, R. (1976). 'Changing corporate culture'. *Sloane Management Review*, 17, 33–49.

SIVANANDAN, A. (1985). 'RAT and the degradation of the black struggle'. *Race and Class*, 36, 1–33.

SKOLNICK, J. H. (1975). *Justice Without Trial*. 2nd ed. New York: John Wiley.

SKOLNICK, J. H. (1986). Police: the new professionals. *New Society*. 77, 9–11.

SMITH, D. J. and GRAY, J. (1983). *Police and People in London*. London: Policy Studies Institute.

SMITH, L. J. F. (forthcoming). *Domestic Violence: a critical review of the literature*. Home Office Research Study. London: HMSO.

SMITH, P. B. (1987). 'Group process methods of intervention in race relations'. In: Shaw, J. W., Nordlie, P. G. and Shapiro, R. M. (Eds.). *Strategies for Improving Race Relations: the Anglo-American experience*. Manchester: Manchester University Press.

SOUTHGATE, P. (1982). *Police Probationer Training in Race Relations*. Research and Planning Unit Paper 8. London: Home Office.

SOUTHGATE, P. (1984). *Racism Awareness Training for the Police*. Research and Planning Unit Paper 29. London: Home Office.

SOUTHGATE, P. and EKBLOM, P. (1984). *Contacts Between Police and Public: findings from the British Crime Survey*. Home Office Research Study 77. London: HMSO.

SOUTHGATE, P. (1986). *Police-Public Encounters*. Home Office Research Study 90. London: HMSO.

SPARGER, J. and GIACOPASSI, D. (1983). 'Copping out: why police leave the service'. In: Bennett, R. (Ed.). *Police at Work: policy issues and analysis*. Beverly Hills, California: Sage.

SPENCER, L. M. (1979). *Soft Skill Competencies*. Boston, Mass: McBer.

STAMMERS, R. and PATRICK, J. (1975). *The Psychology of Learning*. London: Methuen.

STAMP, G. (1980). 'Levels and types of managerial capability'. *Journal of Management Studies*, 3, 277-297.

STEIN, F. M. (1986). 'Helping young policemen cope with stress and manage conflict situations'. In: Yuille, J. C. (Ed.). *Police Selection and Training: the role of psychology*. Dordrecht, Holland: Martinus Nijhoff.

STEVENS, P. and WILLIS, C. (1979). *Race, Crime and Arrests*. Home Office Research Study No. 58. London: HMSO.

STRADLING, S. G., ROBERTS, R., HARPER, K. and QUINN, F. M. (1987). *Force Training Implications of the Transport Act 1982 with Special Reference to the Exercise of Discretion*. University of Salford.

STRAUS, M. A., GELLES, R. J. and STEINMETZ, S. K. (1980). *Behind Closed Doors: violence in the American family*. New York: Anchor Books.

SYKES, R. E. and CLARK, J. P. (1975). 'A theory of deference exchange in police-citizen encounters'. *American Journal of Sociology*, 81, 584-600.

SZILAGYI, A. and WALLACE, M. (1987). *Organisational Behaviour and Performance*. Glenview Illinois: Scott, Foresman.

THOMAS, L. F. and HARRI-AUGSTEIN, E. S. (1985). *Self Organised Learning: foundations of a conversational science for psychology*. London: Routledge and Kegan Paul.

THOMAS, L. F. and HARRI-AUGSTEIN, E. S. (1987). 'Learning to learn: the personal construction and exchange of learning.' In: Howe, M. J. A. (Ed.). *Adult Learning: psychological research and applications*. New York: John Wiley.

TORBE, M. (1986). 'Language across the curriculum: policies and practice'. In: Barnes, D., Britton, J. and Torbe, M. (Eds.). *Language, the Learner and the School*. Third edition. Harmondsworth: Penguin.

TUCKMAN, B. W. (1965). 'Developmental sequences in small groups.' *Psychological Bulletin*, 63, 384-399.

VAN MAANEN, J. (1973). 'Observations on the making of policemen.' *Human Organisation*, 32, 407-418.

VAN MAANEN, J. (1975). 'Police socialisation: a longitudinal examination of job attitudes in an urban police department.' *Administration Science Quarterly*, 20, 207-208.

VAN MAANEN, J. (1976). 'Breaking in: socialisation to work.' In: Dubin, R. (Ed.). *Handbook of Work, Organisation and Society*. Chicago: Rand-McNally.

WALTON, R. E. (1974). 'Improving the quality of work life.' In: Hackman, J. R. and Shuttle, J. L. (1977). *Improving Life at Work*. Santa Monica, California: Goodyear Publishing.

WASOFF, F. (1982). 'Legal protection from wifebeating: the processing of domestic assaults by Scottish Prosecutors and Criminal Courts'. *International Journal of the Sociology of Law*, 10, 187-204.

WELLS, R. (1982). *Training the Police for the People*. Paper given at the 15th Cropwood Conference on the Future of Policing.

WILSON, J. Q. (1968). *Varieties of Police Behaviour*. Cambridge, Massachusetts: Harvard University Press.

WOMEN'S NATIONAL COMMISSION (1985). *Violence against Women: report of an ad hoc working group*. London: Cabinet Office.

WOOLEY, R. (1982). 'Training applications: making interactive video technology work efficiently'. In: de Bloois, M. (Ed.). *Videodisc/Microcomputer Courseware Design*. Englewood Cliffs, New Jersey: Educational Technology Publications.

ZILLER, R. (1973). *The Social Self*. Oxford: Pergamon.

ZWEIG, R. (1965). *The Quest for Fellowship*. London: Heinemann.

Other books from the Home Office Research and Planning Unit published by HMSO:

Designing out Crime. (eds R. V. G. Clarke and P. Mayhew) 1980.

Policing Today. (eds K. Heal, R. Tarling and J. Burrows) 1985.

Managing Criminal Justice: a collection of papers. (ed D. Moxon) 1985.

Situational Crime Prevention: from theory into practice. (eds K. Heal and G. Laycock) 1986.

Communities and Crime Reduction. (eds T. Hope and M. Shaw) 1988.

Much of the research conducted or commissioned by the Research and Planning Unit is published by HMSO in the series "Home Office Research Studies". The latest of these are:

No. 99. Directing Patrol Work: A study of uniformed policing. (J. Burrows and H. Lewis) 1988.

No. 98. Triable-Either-Way Cases: Crown Court or Magistrates' Court? (D. Riley and J. Vennard) 1988.

No. 97. The Tape-recording of Police Interviews with Suspects: a second report. (C. Willis, J. MacLeod and P. Naish) 1988.

No. 96. Schools, Disruptive Behaviour and Delinquency: a review of research. (J. Graham) 1988.

No. 95. Economic Aspects of the Illicit Drug Market and Drug Enforcement Policies in the United Kingdom. (A. Wagstaff and A. Maynard) 1988.

Subject Index

Author Index

Hautaluoma, J. E. 106
Heads of Detectives Training WP 183. 184
Henderson, W. 42
Herzberg, F. 77
Hill, N. 179, 181, 183
Hind, D. W. G. 75, 78
Hinrichs, J. R. 39
Hirsch, P. 177
Hogarth, R. M. 199, 208
Holdaway, S. 63
Holmes, T. H. 133
Home Office 8–10, 54, 59, 63, 85, 91, 115, 123, 125, 189, 191, 194, 195, 200
Honey, P. 104
Hope, R. O. 35
Hopson, B. 171
Horncastle, P. 21, 47, 76, 221, 239
House, E. R. 13
Hovland, C. I. 30
Hudson, L. 172
Hunt, R. 25, 37
Huse, E. F. 106

Ianni, F. A. J. 181
Irving, B. 180

Jaffe, P. 193
Jamieson, I. 18
Janis, I. L. 30
Jelinek, M. 177
Johnson, S. 116
Jones, F. 29
Jones, S. 13, 40, 41, 43, 46, 47
Joss, R. 13, 40, 41, 43, 45, 46, 47

Kahn, R. L. 27
Kakabadse, A. 40, 43
Kant, I. 175
Katz, D. 27
Katz, J. 14
Kelly, G. A. 114
Kelly, H. H. 30
Kelman, H. 36
Kinget, G. 172
Kirkham, R. 62
Klemp, G. O. 75, 151, 159, 161–2, 164
Knowles, M. S. 118
Kogan, M. 13
Kroes, W. H. 190, 194
Kuykendall, J. 114

Layzell, A. D. 208, 213, 214
Leigh, A. 185
Levi, M. 40, 41
Lightfoot, M. 18
Lindsay, P. R. 39
Lippitt, G. 119
Lipsky, M. 21
London Strategic Policy Unit 15, 191
Lubans, V. A. 94, 123
Luckmann, T. 171
Lundman, R. J. 213

MacClelland, D. C. 165

Macdonald, B. 3, 20–1, 40, 47, 79, 90, 148, 200, 217
Maier, N. 187
Maine, A. 106
Males, S. 115, 118
Management Review Team (CPTU) 80
Manning, P. K. 71
Manolias, M. 115, 138, 181, 194
Margerison, C. 118
Maslow, A. H. 77
Menzies, I. 136
Meredith, N. 136
Metropolitan Police 76, 170, 174, 175, 191
Morris, J. 171
Mumford, A. 104, 120

NACRO Race Issues Advisory Committee 54
Neiderhoffer, A. 70
Nelson-Jones, R. 185
Nelson-Jones, Z. P. 135
Newman, Sir K. 146
Newsome, A. 145
Nijkerk, K. J. 40
Nordlie, P. G. 37
Nutley, P. 115

Orlans, V. 134

Pain, B. 125
Panzarella, R. 115
Patten, T. H. 27
Pearce, J. B. 192
Pedler, M. 124
Peppard, N. 10, 57
Percy, S. 186
Peters, R. 175
Peters, T. J. 75, 98, 116
Pettigrew, T. F. 37
Phillips, K. 182, 183, 184
Phillips, S. V. 39, 41, 48, 50
Plumridge, M. D. 44, 46, 115, 118, 120, 231, 234
Police Training Council 74
Poole, L. 44, 76, 77, 235
Priestley, P. 185
Punch, M. 61, 69
Pye, L. 155

Rahe, R. H. 133
Reiner, R. 127
Reuss-Ianni, E. 181
Richard, W. C. 135
Roberg, R. R. 114
Rogers, C. 122
Rotella, R. J. 143
Rowbottom, R. 40
Royal, R. 180
Rubin, J. 71
Runyan, W. M. 155
Russell, H. 172
Russell, L. 170
Russo, A. P. 181

Sarason, S. 181
Savitz, L. 62

255

Printed in the UK for
Her Majesty's Stationery Office
Dd289422 5/88 C15 G443 10170